EVALUATING ENVIRONMENT IN INTERNATIONAL DEVELOPMENT

This book provides novel and in-depth perspectives on evaluating environment and sustainability issues in developing countries.

Evaluating Environment in International Development focuses on the approaches and experiences of leading international organizations, not-for-profits, and multilateral and bilateral aid agencies to illustrate how systematic evaluation is an essential tool for providing evidence for decision-makers. Moving beyond projects and programmes, it explores normative work on the environment as well as environmental consequences of economic and social development efforts. This new edition reflects on the 2030 Agenda for Sustainable Development and Sustainable Development Goals and considers how they have influenced efforts in a wide range of countries and what the implications are for evaluation. It also explores ways in which Big Data and geospatial approaches might be utilized.

Significantly updated throughout to reflect recent developments in climate change research, and on the implications of the 2020 pandemic, this volume will be of great interest to students and scholars of environmental studies, development studies, international relations, sustainable development and evaluation, as well as practitioners in international organizations and development and environmental NGOs.

Juha I. Uitto is a leading thinker and practitioner in environmental evaluation. Since 2014, he has been director of the Independent Evaluation Office of the Global Environment Facility (GEF). Prior to coming to his current position, he worked for more than two decades on evaluation and research on environment and development, most recently in the UNDP Independent Evaluation Office.

"This updated edition builds on the key message put forward by its editor, Juha I. Uitto: 'Evaluation must up its game.' This makes the book a great contribution to long-term and current events thinking on evaluation, environment and development."

—***Jean-Marc Coicaud***, *Rutgers School of Law, State University of New Jersey, USA*

"This second edition addresses the challenges of identifying the intended and unintended consequences of development interventions on the environment, particularly those driven by the search of growth. It calls for a truly systemic view of the interaction between natural and human systems. It provides innovative interpretative frameworks and examples of evaluations that contribute to environmentally sound sustainable development. A must-read as countries redouble efforts to recover from the COVID-19 crisis with the aim of building forward better."

—***Oscar A. Garcia***, *Director, Independent Evaluation Office, United Nations Development Programme (UNDP)*

"For thinkers and practitioners alike, this volume brings together state-of-the-art thinking in evaluation related to environment, while combining it with real-world experiences and lessons on the ground. The scholarship and wisdom of this volume is illustrated by the range of topics it covers in environmental evaluation that cover, for instance, the challenges of examining trans-boundary problems on the one hand and precisely defined disaster risk reduction on the other. I recommend this collection highly."

—***Jyotsna Puri***, *Director of the Environment, Climate, Gender and Social Inclusion Division, at the International Fund for Agricultural Development (IFAD)*

EVALUATING ENVIRONMENT IN INTERNATIONAL DEVELOPMENT

Second Edition

Edited by Juha I. Uitto

Routledge
Taylor & Francis Group
LONDON AND NEW YORK

earthscan
from Routledge

Second edition published 2021
by Routledge
2 Park Square, Milton Park, Abingdon, Oxon, OX14 4RN

and by Routledge
605 Third Avenue, New York, NY 10158

Routledge is an imprint of the Taylor & Francis Group, an informa business

First edition published by Routledge 2014

British Library Cataloguing-in-Publication Data
A catalogue record for this book is available from the British Library

Library of Congress Cataloging-in-Publication Data
Names: Uitto, Juha I., editor.
Title: Evaluating environment in international development / edited by Juha I. Uitto.
Description: 2. | Milton Park, Abingdon, Oxon; New York, NY: Routledge, 2021. | Includes bibliographical references and index.
Identifiers: LCCN 2020044247 (print) | LCCN 2020044248 (ebook)
Subjects: LCSH: Sustainable development. | Sustainable development–International cooperation. | Climatic changes. | Climatic changes–International cooperation.
Classification: LCC HC79.E5 E849 2021 (print) | LCC HC79.E5 (ebook) | DDC 338.9/27–dc23
LC record available at https://lccn.loc.gov/2020044247
LC ebook record available at https://lccn.loc.gov/2020044248

ISBN: 978-0-367-55709-6 (hbk)
ISBN: 978-0-367-55711-9 (pbk)
ISBN: 978-1-003-09482-1 (ebk)

Typeset in Bembo
by SPi Global, India

CONTENTS

FIGURES

TABLES

FOREWORD

To understand and appreciate the importance of this book, I will offer readers my perspective on two things: (1) the significant contributions to evaluation found herein and (2) the global context within which those contributions occur. Let me begin with the global context.

The first edition of the book came out in 2014 before the Sustainable Development Goals (SDGs) had been adopted but when it was clear that the Millennium Development Goals (2000–2015) would not be met. We are now a third of the way through the SDG commitments (2015–2030) in which the trajectory towards attainment of those goals is dismal. Nowhere is this trend towards failure starker than on climate. As I write this in June 2020, global temperatures in May were the warmest on record: 0.63°C warmer than the 1981–2020 average for May; warmer by 0.05°C than May 2016, the previous warmest May; and warmer by 0.09°C than May 2017, the third warmest May. Earth's carbon dioxide levels hit record high, despite a coronavirus-related emissions drop. There is more carbon dioxide in the air now than at any time in 3 million years. The Scripps Institution of Oceanography and the National Oceanic and Atmospheric Administration (NOAA) reported that the amount of CO_2 in the air in May 2020 hit an average of slightly greater than 417 parts per million (ppm). This is the highest monthly average value ever recorded and is up from 414.7 ppm in May of 2019.

Such specific data are usually avoided in a book because they will be out-of-date by the time of publication and subsequently whenever readers come to the book. I have included these data as an invitation to readers to update the trendlines to provide an immediate and timely context for the critical importance of evaluating environment in international development–and, in so doing, affirm that we are in the midst of a deepening global emergency.

Global emergency

Each year the *Oxford Dictionary* editors select a word of the year. The word for 2019 was "climate emergency."

> Climate emergency is defined as "a situation in which urgent action is required to reduce or halt climate change and avoid potentially irreversible environmental damage resulting from it."
>
> This year, heightened public awareness of climate science and the myriad implications for communities around the world has generated enormous discussion of what the UN Secretary-General has called 'the defining issue of our time'....
>
> Usage of the phrase *climate emergency* increased steeply over the course of 2019, and by September it was more than 100 times as common as it had been the previous year....
>
> This data is significant because it indicates a growing shift in people's language choice in 2019, a conscious intensification that challenges accepted language use to reframe discussion of 'the defining issue of our time' with a new gravity and greater immediacy.
>
> (Oxford Languages, 2019)

The Intergovernmental Panel on Climate Change has warned that 2030 is likely to be a point of no return on climate change. But the global emergency involves more than climate, as this books makes clear.

Beyond climate

In mid-June, coronavirus infections worldwide exceeded 9.1 million with nearly one-half million deaths. Worldwide economic depression looms from the pandemic. The global pandemic has given rise to another new word, *infodemic*, meaning an overwhelming amount of information about a problem including wide and rapid spread of misinformation. Also part of the global context as this is being written are worldwide protests against racism and injustice sparked by the murder in May, 2020, of George Floyd, an unarmed African-American man killed by a white police officer in Minneapolis. These global patterns are deeply interconnected: the growing climate emergency, the global pandemic, the exacerbating worldwide infodemic, and protests in cities around the world against systemic and structural injustices.

Beyond just evaluating environment: a nexus perspective

I have provided this context to emphasize and highlight the significant perspective offered in this book. This book is about much more than evaluating environment. It is about environment at the *nexus* of humanity's future. Evaluating *sustainability* includes ecosystem health, more just and equitable societies, and evidence-based decision-making. The sustainability framework offered here integrates social, economic, and environmental goals and criteria. This holistic approach requires upgrading and enhancing environmental evaluation, but not as an isolated function. The fundamental framework offered here is one of *nexus*:

- the nexus of social, economic, and environmental interventions.
- the nexus of environment and development.
- the nexus of development and sustainability.
- the nexus of human and natural systems.
- the nexus of environmental degradation and poverty.
- the nexus of evidence and decision-making.
- the nexus of local and global initiatives;
- the nexus of projects, programmes, and larger-scale initiatives;
- the nexus of multi-stakeholder governance; and
- the nexus of evaluation and action.

In essence, this second updated edition of the book, *Evaluating Environment in International Development*, demonstrates that a sustainable environment is at the centre of humanity's future. Everything is ultimately connected to the environment. The book, then, is about evaluating those interconnections not environment as a stand-alone, isolated, or siloed focus.

Juha I. Uitto, the book's editor, as director of the Independent Evaluation Office of the GEF, and Rob van den Berg, president of the International Development Evaluation Association (IDEAS) in 2019, gave voice and leadership to this perspective in crafting with others a *Declaration on Evaluation for Transformational Change* adopted by participants at the 2019 IDEAS conference in Prague. One of the ten items in that Declaration asserts:

> **Focus on sustainability**. In all our evaluations, we commit to evaluating for social, environmental and economic sustainability and transformation, including by assessing contextual factors and systemic changes. We commit to assessing and highlighting, in all evaluations, unintended negative social, economic and environmental effects.

That is the perspective of this book. It is a breakthrough perspective for evaluation going forward in the context of interconnected global emergencies of climate, pandemic, infodemic, economic turbulence, and massive inequalities and injustices. Evaluating environmental sustainability is the thread that can intersect with, illuminate, and connect these global challenges and guide humanity's responses. Time is of the essence. The point of no return looms large.

Michael Quinn Patton

Author of *Blue Marble Evaluation: Premises and Principles*

PREFACE

Most of the time change is incremental and it is difficult to detect while one lives through it. Therefore, it is heartening to note that there has actually been quite much progress in the international environmental domain since the first edition of *Evaluating Environment in International Development* came out in 2014. The following year, the United Nations member States agreed to the 2030 Agenda for Sustainable Development, which promises to transform the world for people, planet, and prosperity. The Sustainable Development Goals (SDGs) linked to the Agenda have been subscribed to by 193 countries all around the world. The SDGs stand on three equally important pillars: the social, economic, and environmental.

In that same year, another UN initiative, the Sendai Framework for Disaster Risk Reduction 2015–2030 was created. In 2016, the Paris Agreement was signed by the parties to the UN Framework Convention on Climate Change, promising to keep global warming well below 2°C above pre-industrial levels, while pursuing efforts to limit the temperature increase to 1.5°C above pre-industrial levels, recognizing that this would significantly reduce the risks and impacts of climate change. There has been unprecedented support to these international agreements aimed at keeping the world safe from increasing environmental and climate-related hazards. It is unlikely, however, that most of these goals and the associated targets will be reached in time, so there is a growing need for adapting to climate change. Recognizing this need, another major international initiative was launched, the Global Commission on Adaptation.

Not all developments have been positive either. At the end of 2019, a novel coronavirus spilled over to humans in China and quickly spread across populations creating a global pandemic of magnitude not experienced by recent generations. The pandemic has its root causes in human–nature interactions. The continued expansion of human activities—and abuse—deeper into the natural domains puts us in closer touch with non-human animals that increases the risk of spill-over of pathogens to humans. It is clear already at the time of this writing that the corona virus epidemic is going to lead to a worldwide recession and will further jeopardize the achievement of many if not most of the SDGs.

Evaluation has emerged as a field that has a lot to offer as humankind searches for sustainable solutions to deal with pressing global problems, such as those represented by climate change, ecosystem degradation, deforestation, unmanaged urbanization and expansion of agriculture, and indeed pandemics. The field of evaluation itself is evolving rapidly—and it must continue to evolve in order for evaluation to remain relevant to the increasingly complex world where human and natural systems intertwine in a myriad ways. The Second Edition of the book has been significantly updated to reflect all of these developments in the international development and environment arena, as well as the evaluation profession. A few chapters have been dropped. Most chapters have been significantly updated and three entirely new ones have been added.

One of the chapters, however, remains the same as in the first edition. Its author, Prof. Michael Stocking passed away in the spring of 2018 after a brief illness. Michael was primarily a researcher and a development practitioner, rather than an evaluator. But as he would often remind me, the distinction is quite meaningless, as evaluation must be based on solid research and good development research has practical implications on the ground. Michael's research was good and it was influential in informing natural resources management on the ground in Africa and other developing regions of the world. His work also lives on through his many dedicated students. I had the pleasure of knowing Michael and working with him on many occasions over a quarter century, and enjoying every moment of it.

I sincerely hope that this collection of essays will contribute to the discipline and practice of evaluation and, more so, to the discourse at the nexus of environment and development. It is my conviction that evaluation can make an important contribution by providing evidence-based lessons for more environmentally sustainable and socially just world. To achieve this, evaluation itself must shed its focus on individual projects and embrace a more holistic approach encompassing both human and natural systems.

Juha I. Uitto

CONTRIBUTORS

Anupam Anand is an Evaluation Officer at the GEF Independent Evaluation Office (IEO). He has more than 15 years of combined experience in international development and academia. Anupam holds a PhD in geographical sciences from the University of Maryland. He has published more than 20 peer-reviewed articles on remote sensing, ecology, and environmental policy.

Geeta Batra is Chief Evaluation Officer and Deputy Director at GEF IEO. Prior to joining the GEF, she worked for many years at the Independent Evaluation Group (IEG) of the World Bank Group and the International Finance Corporation (IFC). She has a PhD in economics and strong academic and professional background in international economics, econometrics, and development.

Heather Bryant is an Evaluation Advisor and Chief of the Capacity Development Section at the UNDP Independent Evaluation Office. She has 20 years' experience in results-based planning, programming, monitoring, and evaluation, with a special interest in gender equality, social inclusion, and human rights.

Carlo Carugi is Senior Evaluation Officer at the GEF since 2009. He arrived there after 20 years of experience in environment and development, 16 of which were spent in the developing countries. All along his career Carlo has conducted a variety of evaluations. Among Carlo's interests is the integration of the socioeconomic with the environmental in evaluation.

Sulan Chen is Programme Advisor for the GEF Small Grants Programme (SGP) where she leads the global policy development of SGP's international waters and chemicals and waste portfolio development, and country programmes in Asia, Europe and CIS countries. She holds a PhD from the University of Maryland at College Park and has received her undergraduate degree from Nankai University, China.

Rob Craig has a Master's degree in Environment and Development and is an expert in biodiversity conservation, with a focus on Africa. He has worked extensively as a Consultant, Programme Director and Technical Adviser with a range of organizations and has made important contributions to evaluation in this sector.

Alan Fox is Chief of Section for Corporate Evaluation at the Independent Evaluation Office of UNDP. Since 2009 he has been a lead evaluator for UNDP, managing thematic evaluations, especially on sustainable development and resilience-related programming. Mr. Fox came to UNDP after 25 years' of local and national government service, including Associate Assistant Administrator for Water at the US EPA.

Ronal Gainza serves in the Secretariat of the Partnership for Action on Green Economy (PAGE), where he works closely with five UN agencies (UNEP, UNDP, ILO, UNITAR, and UNIDO) on creating an enabling macroeconomic environment that supports the transition to an inclusive green economy in partner countries. He has over 15 years of work experience in the sustainability field and holds a PhD in Environmental Economics and Climate Policy from the Swiss Federal Institute of Technology in Lausanne, Switzerland (2011).

Jeneen R. Garcia is an Evaluation Officer at the GEF IEO where she has led evaluations assessing the impacts of GEF support and developed frameworks for assessing impact in complex adaptive systems. Her previous work in her native Philippines was in the fields of multi-stakeholder watershed governance. Jeneen obtained a Joint European MSc in Water and Coastal Management and a Bachelor's degree in Environmental Science.

Roberto La Rovere, senior Evaluation Advisor, has interests in evaluation and R4D. He worked at three CGIAR centres in West and East Africa, Syria, and Mexico. After this he worked extensively at the Independent Evaluation Office (IEO) of UNDP, and the Green Climate Fund. His research background led him to a hundred publications, a third peer reviewed. He has a Ph.D. in NRM economics, M.Sc. in Development Economics, and B.Sc. in agriculture, from Bologna, Kent, and Wageningen. He has also been consultant in evaluation for IFAD and FAO.

Simon Lobach is a PhD candidate in environmental history at the Graduate Institute for International and Development Studies in Geneva, Switzerland. His research focuses on the traditional populations of the Guiana Shield in the context of resource exploitation and deforestation. Prior to this, Simon has worked as a consultant in the UN system for several years.

Segbedzi Norgbey is currently Chief Executive Officer of the Sustainable Development Group International Ltd., a group of very seasoned international development professionals and academics who provide consulting services in Environment and Development Evaluation. Dr Norgbey is the recent past head of the Evaluation

Office in the United Nations Environment Program. Dr Norgbey holds a PhD in Resource and Environmental Management from Michigan State University.

Andy Rowe is a former President of the Canadian Evaluation Society and a Fellow of the Society. He has a PhD from the London School of Economics, is a member of the Technical Evaluation Reference Group of the Climate Adaptation Fund, and publishes and consults on evaluation of sustainability and climate.

Michael Spilsbury joined UNEP in 2005 and has performed various roles in the Evaluation Office, serving as its Director since 2013. Prior to joining UNEP, he worked as an international research scientist for the Centre for International Forestry Research (CIFOR) based in Bogor, Indonesia. He holds a Doctorate in forest ecology and a Master of Science in forest management both from Oxford University and Bachelor of Science in biology from York University.

Michael Stocking was Emeritus Professor of Natural Resources Development, School of International Development, University of East Anglia, UK. He also served on the Scientific and Technical Advisory Panel (STAP) of the GEF, as Vice-Chair and later Adviser to the Chair. He worked with the Overseas Development Group and advised many agencies, such as FAO, UN University, UNDP, and the Swiss Science Foundation.

David Todd, PhD, is a Social Anthropologist with many decades of work in international development, particularly in evaluation. After working in the DFID Evaluation Office, he became Senior Evaluator in the GEF, with a particular focus on impact. He has conducted many consultancies for a broad range of UN, bilateral, and multilateral bodies.

Hazel Todd has an M.Sc. in Disaster Management from Cranfield University in the UK. She has conducted many international consultancies and was Deputy Director of the Barbados Department of Emergency Management. She is an Emergency Planning Officer in the UK and an elected Member of the Institute of Civil Protection and Emergency Management.

Juha I. Uitto is Director of the GEF Independent Evaluation Office (IEO). He has been a full-time evaluator with the GEF and UNDP for more than two decades, focusing on evaluations at the nexus of environment and development. He spent the 1990s as research and training programme manager at the United Nations University. His PhD is in Social and Economic Geography. He has held visiting positions at Kyoto University in Japan and Rutgers, the State University of New Jersey.

Vijayalakshmi Vadivelu is a Senior Evaluation Advisor with the UNDP Independent Evaluation Office. She has 25 years of experience in international development policy, evaluation, and research. She has led and managed evaluations of development and crisis-related programmes at the global and country levels. She was a visiting professor at the Division of Global Affairs, Rutgers University,

New Jersey. Before joining UNDP, she researched on decentralization issues and gender in development at the Institute for Social and Economic Change, Bangalore, India.

Rob D. van den Berg is Visiting Professor at King's College, London, as well as an Honorary Associate of the Institute of Development Studies in Brighton. He serves as Chair of the Advisory Group on Evaluation and Learning of the Climate Investment Funds and is a member of the Advisory Council of Wilton Park in the UK.

Christine Wörlen is a geographer, environmental scientist, and economist and founder of Arepo Consult. She searches for what works with respect to transforming our energy system. Observing national and international initiatives for overcoming inertia in this process inspired her for the Theory of No Change.

Aaron E. Zazueta is an evaluator with over 30 years of experience. He has led multiple evaluations on international waters, biodiversity, cleaner industrial production, and climate change in Latin America, Asia, Eastern Europe and Africa for the World Bank, the GEF, the Green Climate Fund (GCF), several UN agencies, bilateral organizations, and private foundations.

PART I

Introduction and conceptual background

1

EVALUATING ENVIRONMENT IN INTERNATIONAL DEVELOPMENT

An introduction

Juha I. Uitto

Introduction

The year 2020 was defined by a pandemic that started in China sometime in late 2019. The pandemic, dubbed COVID-19, quickly spread across the world, sparing no continent and virtually no country. By mid-2020, some 8 million people around the globe had been infected. The fatality rates for the pandemic were not as dramatic as in the case of earlier zoonotic viruses, such as Ebola, which kills about half of those infected and up to 90% of the victims in some areas. SARS, the severe acute respiratory syndrome, closely related to the 2020 pandemic—COVID-19 is caused by a virus called SARS-CoV-2—also had a fatality rate of 14–15%,[1] but its spread was contained and it infected less than 10,000 people. COVID-19, in contrast, had by mid-2020 killed some half a million people worldwide—about a quarter of them in the United States—due to its rapid spread.

At the face of it, the pandemic has been seen primarily as a health crisis, leading to severe economic and societal disruptions. The World Bank estimates that COVID-19 may push an additional 71–100 million people into extreme poverty.[2] Most of these people will be in countries that already struggle with poverty: almost a half in South Asia and a third in Sub-Saharan Africa.

Fundamentally, however, COVID-19 is an environmental crisis. It has provided a very concrete example of how human health and ecosystem health are closely intertwined—and how human systems are dependent on natural systems.

Zoonotic viruses, like SARS-CoV-2 originate in animals and spill over to humans. The frequency of such spill-overs and subsequent epidemics has increased in the past couple of decades because of how we interact with the natural environment (Vidal 2020; Quammen 2012). It is a direct function of increased contact humans have with other animals, both wild and domesticated. COVID-19 may have started at a wet market in the city of Wuhan in China where many kinds of live animals were for sale—for food or for traditional Chinese medicine (TCM)—kept and slaughtered in crowded and unhygienic conditions. The likely origins of the virus are in bats but there may have been an intermediary host (perhaps pangolin, which is used for TCM). It is also possible that a farmer collecting bat guano for fertiliser was directly infected. Irrespective of the transmission mechanism, which we may never determine with certainty, the root causes of the pandemic—as well as those before it and those yet to come—are known. In fact, such a pandemic was widely predicted by scientists before it happened (Osterholm and Olshaker, 2020).

The root causes lie in the fact that human impact has been constantly expanding deeper into the natural world, as we make more space to accommodate and feed the increasing number of people and seek raw materials for continued economic growth. Cities and suburbs, transport networks, agriculture, logging and mining all penetrate deeper into hitherto undisturbed ecosystems thus bringing people into closer contact with new species—and their pathogens. At the same time, ecological balance is disturbed. As large predators (like wolves or big cats) are killed off, the animals that benefit are those that thrive alongside humans: rats, bats, racoons and the like. They are also the ones whose viruses are most susceptible to jump over to humans. In Africa, hunting bush meat for human nutrition includes primate species whose genome is very similar to that of humans, making spill-over all that easier.

It is obvious that in order to prevent future pandemics, we need a better way of interacting with the natural environment. This is not true only for pandemics, although it is a concrete matter that has finally caught the attention of policymakers and the wider populace as well. Healthy ecosystems and biodiversity are essential for the well-being of humankind in a myriad ways providing ecosystem services from clean air and water to climate regulation and protection against floods and storms. Yet, anthropogenic climate change caused by the burning of fossil fuels for energy and transportation, deforestation and cattle ranching, and the destruction of natural habitats pose constantly increasing threats to global sustainability. There are indications that these unsustainable developments already threaten the very drivers of these developments: wanton drive for economic growth, the continued increase in human numbers and wealth. Global excess mortality caused by air pollution has been estimated at 8.8 million people annually (Lelieveld et al. 2020).

The pandemic has also brought to the forefront drastic inequalities in societies all over the world that pose hindrances to sustainable development. An analysis of CDC (Centres for Disease Control) data in the United States found that the crude death rates from COVID-19 for Blacks was twice that for whites, and that for Hispanics/Latinos about the same as for whites. However, given that these populations have much younger age structures than whites, a huge gap emerges: the age-adjusted death rate for Black people was 3.6 times and for Hispanic/Latino people 2.5 times for whites (Ford, Reber and Reeves 2020). The factors behind these differences reflect endemic and entrenched inequalities that have left especially Black residents impoverished, with fewer jobs, and in poor health (Eldeib et al. 2020). Many minority people also work in occupations, such as services and transport, which do not allow for distance work. In Singapore, which saw a rapid rise in infections following a highly successful curtailment, 90% of the infections were among migrant workers. In Mexico, despite rapid measures taken by the government, people in the informal sector, including street vendors many of whom are women, were not able to stop working and thus suffered disproportionately from the pandemic. These examples reveal the close relationship between economic, social, environmental and political issues that determine the outcome of what on the surface is simply a health crisis.

The potential of evaluation

Evaluation as a discipline and practice has the potential to contribute to finding solutions to these problems. However, to do so—for it to continue to be relevant—evaluation must up its game. Evaluation must change to become part of the solution, rather than part of the problem (Patton 2020). Evaluation has the specific role of bringing forth knowledge and understanding of what works, under what circumstances and for whom based on past experiences. At a basic level, this is looking at past programmes and projects: What strategies worked, where and why? What helped interventions adjust successfully to changing conditions—including sudden crises—so that they could continue supporting the people on the ground?

Traditionally, evaluation looks at the past to inform future. This has become an increasingly challenging endeavour as global situations change and as past development efforts—especially the most 'successful' ones—are the ones that have got us into this situation. Identifying and replicating what is often called 'best practices' thus no longer makes sense (if it ever did). Such thinking is based on the notion of continuous improvement, defined as progress, inherent in Western thinking since Enlightenment, irrespective of political ideology (Mishra 2017: 39). The imperative of growth—both economic and population—epitomises this (Uitto 2020). Such linear thinking is no longer possible. Environmental destruction and climate change have introduced uncertainty and unknown discontinuities into the global system.

On the social side, the prevalent development model has resulted in huge inequalities that in themselves threaten stability and sustainability. Evaluation as a discipline and practice has a longer history dealing with social issues. Therefore, they tend to be better covered than environmental matters. For instance, the United Nations Evaluation Group (UNEG) has provided guidance on integrating gender and human rights in evaluations, as well as evaluating institutional gender mainstreaming, which are widely applied in the UN system (UNEG 2014, 2018). Such guidance on the environmental side is still under preparation.

Furthermore, what has proved challenging is operating in the coupled human and natural systems (CHANS), which requires a broad understanding of both. This limitation holds true for evaluation, as well as programming more generally, and stems from both the complexities involved as well as the different cultures that prevail in social and natural sciences (Rowe 2019a)

If evaluation is to learn from the past, it must start looking more broadly beyond assessing whether individual interventions have achieved their stated goals and instead analyse how such interventions—as well as broader policies and strategies—contribute to or hamper sustainability. Evaluation must shed its project mentality.

It is imperative for evaluation to look systematically for unintended consequences of any intervention, including notably the consequences on the natural environment. It is safe to assume that all interventions irrespective of their focus will have an impact on the environment.

At a higher level, evaluation must be able to provide evidence of how actions in the development domain affect the environment and vice versa. We must be able to demonstrate the close interlinkages between social and economic development and the environment in light of evidence from the real world. In this task evaluators must base their work on scientific knowledge as well as analysis of concrete examples from the field. This is not an approach that comes easily to all evaluators who have been used to looking at discrete interventions in isolation through their internal logic. Instead, we now need to place these interventions in the broader landscape and analyse how they interact with the larger natural and human systems. We need to be on the lookout for unanticipated results and unintended consequences, not just those foreseen in the project or programme's own theory of change.

This second updated edition of the book, *Evaluating Environment in International Development*, sheds light on how evaluation can contribute to environmentally sound sustainable development in the international cooperation context. It focuses on approaches and experiences from the field with leading international organisations, non-profits and multilateral and bilateral aid agencies. Understanding context is important, as programmes work differently in varying situations through different change mechanisms (Pawson and Tilley 1997). To fully achieve these objectives, evaluation must move beyond assessing individual interventions in isolation and contribute to the understanding of how environmental concerns can be incorporated into development efforts in the national, regional and global contexts.

The book will familiarise readers with approaches, challenges, choices and tools that focus on environmental results in international development. It provides novel and in-depth perspectives on evaluating environment and sustainable development mostly in the global South. Moving beyond projects and programmes, it also considers aspects such as evaluating normative environmental work. It makes a strong case for considering the wider environmental and sustainability consequences of development efforts, including both intended and unintended impacts as well as trade-offs between them. The book emphasises praxis and brings together leading international thinkers and practitioners who have decades of experience working in the field. The book offers both conceptualisations and practical examples based on lessons from the field regarding evaluation and environment.

Sustainable development and the environment

In 2015, world leaders adopted the 2030 Agenda for Sustainable Development and the attendant Sustainable Development Goals (SDGs) under the auspices of the United Nations (UN). To date, 193 countries have signed on to the agenda, which is intended as a universal set of principles to move humanity towards a sustainable future. The 2030 Agenda[3] preamble starts with the following:

> This Agenda is a plan of action for people, planet and prosperity. It also seeks to strengthen universal peace in larger freedom. We recognise that eradicating poverty in all its forms and dimensions, including extreme poverty, is the greatest global challenge and an indispensable requirement for sustainable development.

The three Ps—people, planet and prosperity—reflect the interlinkages between human and natural systems. The 17 SDGs are all construed as standing on three pillars: social, economic and environmental. While each of the SDGs approaches development from its unique entry point, the three pillars or dimensions are present in every goal in different ways. The achievement of all of the goals depends on every one of the three pillars to remain solid. In fact, it has been suggested convincingly that a better analogy than a stool resting on three legs, would be a cake with three layers (Rockström and Sukhdev 2016). The bottom layer of the cake consists of the biosphere goals on which the social and economic layers rest.[4] If the bottom layer collapses, the layers upon it will by necessity collapse too.

In practice, however, the attention that the pillars—or layers—have received is far from equal. Most attention has gone to the economic goals and unabated growth in gross domestic product (GDP) remains the main focus of most governments and the predominant way in which development is measured. Some progress has been made in the social domains and discussions about distribution of the proceeds of the economic growth, as well as gender equality, have made headway in some fora, albeit tentatively. The environmental dimension for its part is almost entirely relegated to a subservient role (Reid et al. 2017). Deforestation and destruction of ecosystems continue unabated, as does loss of biological diversity (Caballos. Ehrlich and Dirzo 2017). When the environment is mentioned, it is usually only with reference to climate change, while other important aspects—biodiversity loss, overfishing of oceans, persistent organic pollutants, air pollution and others—are forgotten.

The Intergovernmental Panel on Climate Change has issued dire warnings that we are moving fast towards irreversible and severe consequences for both the planet and people in terms of disturbances to weather patterns and sea-level rise lest we limit anthropogenic global warming to less than 2°C as compared to pre-industrial levels (IPCC 2018). The Paris Agreement that went into effect in 2016 with 195 signatories under the UN Framework Convention on Climate Change (UNFCCC) has the stated aim to do just that. However, there is meagre chance that this will materialise under the current regime. The Paris Agreement is based on voluntary, intended nationally determined contributions, which even if fully implemented would not add up to sufficient reductions in greenhouse gas emission reductions to reach the goal. Marred by a free-rider problem, the agreement is unlikely to reach even the nationally determined commitments (Nordhaus 2020).

In addition to setting insufficiently ambitious goals for emission reduction and not following through with them, countries continue to promote practices that are directly harmful to the climate and the environment. It is estimated that the G20 countries have provided at least US$77 billion in public subsidies to oil, gas and coal projects annually since the establishment of the Paris Agreement (Oil Change International and Friends of the Earth 2020).

The consequences of climate change are already being felt and bear a true and measurable cost to society. They are not limited to poor countries, as clearly demonstrated by the wildfires caused by extended drought in Australia in 2019 and California the year after. While it is impossible to attribute any specific hurricane or typhoon to climate change, scientists are able to calculate likelihoods of such storms happening and linking these likelihoods to trends in global climate. In 2020, two strong tropical storms—Arthur and Bertha—formed in the Atlantic already before the season officially started in June. The massive Cyclone Amphan slammed into India in the Bay of Bengal causing heavy damage in May 2020, also un-seasonally early.

Sea-level rise that is caused by melting icecaps at the poles and thermal expansion of seawater with warming temperatures will inundate low-lying islands and coasts. Small island developing states (SIDS), such as the Marshall Islands and the Maldives, bear the brunt of the onslaught of the sea, risking disappearance under the waves. Sadly, the SIDS are among those countries least responsible for climate change (Uitto, Kohlitz and Todd 2017). Sea-level rise also threatens major urban conglomerations from Miami and New York to Tokyo and Shanghai. These cities are also the drivers of the global economy so damage done to them will be felt across the world in terms of significant economic disruptions. The reinsurance giant Swiss Re estimates that claims due to natural disasters in 2017 amounted to US$144 billion.[5] With advancing climate impacts, such claims will only increase.

As it becomes increasingly evident that efforts to mitigate climate change will not be sufficient, attention has turned to adaptation and to increasing societal resilience to impacts of changing climate. The Global Commission on Adaptation, a high-level body bringing together public and private interests, released its landmark report in 2019 (Global Commission on Adaptation 2019).

More broadly, it has been argued that the achievement of the SDGs in general is threatened by the pandemic (Naidoo and Fisher 2020). The 2030 Agenda, alongside other ambitious global accords like the Paris Agreement and the Sendai Plan of Action for Disaster Reduction, were adopted by countries at the height of globalisation when both economic growth and international cooperation were seen with significant optimism. All of this started to change already before COVID-19 but the pandemic has certainly made things more dire. Governments will have urgent priorities to rebuild their national economies after the immediate shock.

Evaluation can play a more important role than ever in feeding in lessons from development efforts and helping to ensure building back better, with sustainability principles, benefiting both the people and the planet.

Valuing natural capital

The lack of attention to the environmental dimensions reflects broadly societal values. As we only measure changes to the GDP and make decisions based on it, financial and economic capital get the lion's share of appreciation. Social capital receives attention to the extent that it gets measured in quantitative ways. Natural capital, despite the fact that it provides almost all raw materials for economic growth (from timber to minerals to medicines) as well as a variety of essential ecosystem services, usually does not get valued at all. Its depreciation is only seen as an externality. We focus on economic capital and less on social capital. Natural capital is just simply ignored.

Over the past years, environmental economics has emerged as an important field of inquiry (Heal 2007). Much of it is based on economic valuation of ecosystem services. In standard economics, most environmental factors are considered to be externalities, and as such do not feature in economic calculations. This is a root cause of much environmental destruction. Companies and governments do not factor in the costs of pollution into their cost–benefit analyses, largely because pollution's effects are not seen as directly bearing on individual operations. The costs are often long term and shared by many actors and the society as a whole—a classic case of the tragedy of the commons (Hardin 1968). Climate change provides an extreme example of this, as the emission of greenhouse gases from energy generation, transportation, industry and agriculture will result in widespread and devastatingly costly impacts on regional and global scales—the brunt of which will be disproportionately borne by the poorer countries and the poor people, rather than the polluters themselves.

In recent years, there have been some signs of hope, as companies are sometimes moving faster than governments to curb the environmental damage their operations are causing. Partly this is because their leaders realise the risks associated with climate change and other environmental (and social) disturbances to their business models. Partly it is because of genuine concern for the environment. The private sector is huge and spans a vast range of different types of companies. It has been calculated that three agricultural commodities—palm oil, soya beans and beef—account for almost 80% of tropical deforestation (Brack et al. 2016). Markets of these daily commodities are dominated by a handful of multinational firms, some of which have taken sustainability at heart. At the same time, they depend on thousands of smallholders for their supply chains and are not able to control their environmental practices.

There are also specific challenges to environmental economics stemming from uncertainties. Pindyck (2007: 47–48) has identified three factors that are crucial to policy design and evaluation:

1. Environmental cost and benefit functions tend to be highly non-linear (i.e. the likely damage from environmental pollution may increase exponentially, and there is uncertainty about the existence and/or position of a 'tipping point', which has policy implications and emphasises the importance of the 'precautionary principle');
2. Environmental policies usually involve important irreversibilities that often interact with uncertainty in complex manners; and

3. Environmental problems tend to involve very long time horizons, which exacerbate the uncertainties inherent to policy costs and benefits.

Conservation of biological diversity often relies on the proper valuation of ecosystem services (Braat and de Groot 2012). For example, adding the value of different products and services from a forest, including that of the forest as a carbon sink offsetting climate change, may make it more economical to leave it standing than to clear cut it for timber or new agricultural land. The concept of payments for ecosystem services has emerged to signify that the beneficiaries of ecosystem services (be it clean water or recreational uses) pay others for adopting resource use models that preserve the ecosystem (Ruijs, Dellink and Bromley 2008).

However, there are limits to how one can—and whether one should—put a monetary value on everything. From a practical point of view, how do you calculate the value of, say, a rhinoceros horn? Is it the price it gets on the black market in Hong Kong or Bangkok? If so, shouldn't there then be a legal market that would reduce the price and to make rhinoceros' horns more abundant on the market? At the same time, incentive and disincentive structures should be built to make trade in rhinoceros horns less lucrative. That way, poaching and illegal trade could be regulated and, perhaps, rhinoceros populations stabilised at a sustainable level.

Nadeau (2008) provides a penetrating critique of environmental economics based on the fact that the sub-discipline is grounded in mainstream economic theory, which itself is based on assumptions that do not stand up to any scientific scrutiny. Environmental economists assume that the relative price of an environmental good, service or amenity reveals its 'real marginal values'. Environmental economists then use cost–benefit analyses to place a value on environmental externalities—or environmental goods and services that are 'external' to market system. The problem is that the damage done to the natural environment cannot be valued in simple monetary terms in comparison with the direct economic benefit arising from the damaging activity. Therefore, environmental economists employ methods to estimate the 'use-value' of the environmental resources. The results are often absurd. Citing a number of studies, Nadeau shows results that suggest that, based on survey results regarding household willingness to pay to preserve or use natural resources, the marginal cost of air pollution is just US$26 per year or that preserving the species of bald eagle (which apart from its ecosystem value holds high symbolic value to Americans) is indeed only US$11 per year.

There is an argument that the valuation of ecosystems and species should consider other aspects, including, in the example above, the aesthetic value of rhinoceroses and their niche in the ecosystem. There is an intrinsic value to species diversity, which goes beyond its instrumental value to humans (Washington et al. 2017). Relying only on economic valuation of species and ecosystems risks undervaluing this intrinsic, existence value. Furthermore, calculating the current economic value will not take into account the precautionary principle, that is, the possible and unknown key role of a species or ecosystem, the loss of which may trigger unexpected, even irreversible consequences.

Still, in a world that seems largely unmoved by the loss of unique species or ecosystems, and where many people are willing—or indeed compelled due to poverty and deprivation—trade environmental amenities to immediate economic benefits, the economic value of natural capital cannot be ignored. When there are many competing priorities for a limited amount of money—and in the post-pandemic world these demands are even more severe—it is important for environmental evaluators to be able to back their claims about the importance of environmental conservation, ecosystem services and tackling climate change with concrete dollar figures. The Independent Evaluation Office (IEO) of the Global Environment Facility (GEF), for instance, has pioneered methodologies for calculating the value for money of investments into biodiversity conservation, sustainable forest management and land degradation (GEF IEO 2018, 2019). These studies demonstrate that GEF projects have had global net positive impacts on both forest cover and vegetation productivity with measurable positive economic valuations in terms of carbon sequestrations and soil retention.

Evidence also supports the conclusion that political, social and economic inequalities tend to translate into environmental damage, and that addressing disparities in power and wealth is a necessary, although not sufficient, precondition for sustainability. Boyce advances two hypotheses regarding this case: (i) environmental harm is not randomly distributed across the population, but instead reflects the distribution of wealth and power, and (ii) the total magnitude of environmental harm depends on the extent of inequality (Boyce 2008: 274–275). Citing a number of empirical studies in the United States and at international levels, Boyce is able to find strong evidence that inequality is bad for the environment. He concludes that 'rectifying the market failures and governance failures that lead to environmental harm requires repairing the disparities of wealth and power that enable these failures' (ibid: 284). Along the same lines, COVID-19 has shown how even the impact of a pandemic is not randomly distributed. In the United States, a highly disproportionate share of the infected persons and fatalities has been among African Americans.

All of this shows how environmental, social and economic sustainability are intertwined in complex ways. Business as usual, simply pursuing economic growth at any cost will have detrimental outcomes for all three. Instead of eternal growth as an objective, we should aim for a steady-state economy that will operate within the natural limits (Hickel 2018; Czech 2020). We need to focus on creating an economy that is regenerative, where resources are reused and recycled, and redistributive, so that those still living in poverty can be lifted out of their situation, while we ensure that we do not overshoot the ecological boundaries of the planet (Raworth 2017).

There are a number of efforts to develop measurements to value the non-monetary (or at least not directly monetised) aspects of life. The suggestion of expanding measurement of human well-being beyond GDP has gained strength. One of the earliest and most successful efforts has been the Human Development Index launched by the United Nations Development Programme (UNDP) in 1990, which defined human development as a 'process of enlarging people's choices' (UNDP 1990). It further elaborated that the most critical and wide-ranging choices are to live a long and healthy life, to be educated and to have access to resources needed for a decent standard of living. UNDP later introduced the concept of sustainable human development in order to integrate environmental concerns into human development measurements (UNDP 1992). Another innovative concept is the Gross National Happiness that the small Himalayan Kingdom of Bhutan uses to measure its development (Centre for Bhutan Studies and GNH Research 2016). As reported by the Guardian newspaper in May 2020, the majority of Britons would like quality of life indicators to take priority over economic indicators.

Evaluating the environment beyond projects

Evaluation suffers from the same lack of attention to the environmental foundations of sustainable development. Evaluation as a profession and practice has its roots firmly in social sciences, either through social inquiry into the determinants of social outcomes (notably in the fields of education and health) or through econometric impact evaluation using experimental and quasi-experimental designs to determine correlations between policy and programmatic actions and outcomes. Both approaches have tended to be narrowly focused on the direct outcomes of a well-defined intervention. While the former may often use a variety of methods, including participatory approaches, the latter tend towards a mechanistic exploration of correlations in specific situations (Donaldson, Christie and Mark 2009). In recent years, there has been a trend in evaluation theory towards acknowledging the importance of taking account of complex systems (Bamberger, Vaessen and Raimondo 2015). Networks such as the UN Evaluation Group[6] have also developed solid approaches to evaluating social aspects, such as human rights and gender, in all interventions irrespective of the field in which they take place. Such approaches focusing on the environmental effects are missing.

The close interlinkages between environment and development pose specific challenges to the evaluation community. Some of these pertain to particular characteristics of environmental issues, as well as the programmes and projects designed to address them. Birnbaum and Mickwitz (2009: 3–4) categorise them as follows:

1. Differing and frequently long time horizons;
2. Disparities in scaling;
3. Data quality and credibility issues; and
4. The problem of research designs for assessing attribution in environmental policies and programmes.

The different time horizons for observing changes in natural and social systems and the often short policy and programme cycles are challenging for evaluating environmental programmes. Similarly, the spatial scales of environmental problems (e.g. pollution or climate change often do not match the scales of political jurisdictions, migratory species move across national boundaries), which makes evaluation at appropriate scales challenging. To address these issues, Rowe (2012) has proposed a two-system evaluand approach that takes into account the different temporal and spatial frames of the human and natural systems.

As for issues pertaining to data availability and research designs, environmental programmes are often not amenable to be evaluated using experimental designs. Still, evaluation rigour can be significantly enhanced by formulating complex theories of change (e.g. by including causal hypotheses with explicit assumptions or by making observations regarding baselines and key indicators) (Vaessen and Todd 2008; Ferraro 2009). Focusing specifically on evaluation of environmental conservation programmes, a Foundations of Success team makes a case for rigorous design alternatives using qualitative, non-experimental approaches (Margoluis et al. 2009). They emphasise the context in the conservation situation, purpose of the evaluation, programme structure and circumstances, resources and capacity in selecting the most appropriate design option.

Climate change poses additional challenges to evaluation—notably a greater focus on risk, uncertainty and complexity. It also implies shifts in the objects of evaluation (e.g. new metrics and more emphasis on the policy dimensions of rich countries' engagement with poor countries) and a judicious evaluation of governance arrangements (Picciotto 2009).

Efforts to mitigate climate change and to adapt to its impacts are closely related to economic development, particularly in developing countries. Evaluating climate change-related initiatives requires different approaches (van den Berg and Feinstein 2009). Evaluation can help keep an eye on the big picture, both in development and environment, and consider relevance, effectiveness, impact and long-term sustainability.

For the above reasons, evaluating at the nexus of environment and development is challenging, as it requires operating comfortably in the coupled human and natural systems. Few individual evaluators have competencies in both and, as noted above, the cultures and methodologies of social and natural sciences also differ considerably making collaboration hard (Rowe 2019a). Most evaluators have their background in social sciences, based either in social inquiry or in quantitative economics favouring experimental and quasi-experimental research designs.

On the other side of the divide, a lot of research is carried out that relates to the effectiveness of strategies and efforts towards environmental conservation, climate change mitigation and adaptation, energy transitions, management of harmful chemicals and so forth. Most often, this is not framed in terms of evaluation, which in itself reflects the divide in language used. Similar needs have been recognised by natural scientists. Bennett et al. (2016) identify four types of barriers to mainstreaming social sciences into conservation science: ideological, institutional, knowledge and capacity. They call for more inclusive and integrative conservation science that will enable more ecologically effective and socially just conservation.

Apart from the particular challenges of evaluating environmental programmes and projects, there is a strong argument for moving beyond evaluating only individual interventions. Environmental concerns, which should feature in all national development strategies to render them sustainable, must be evaluated. First of all, there is a need to move beyond focusing on development cooperation projects into a broader vision of sustainable development (with and without development cooperation).

The implication to be drawn from both the evaluation and environmental research traditions is that evaluating at the nexus will most often require collaboration and multidisciplinary teams using multiple mixed methods (Uitto 2019; Patton 2020)

Picciotto (2007) has argued that the main unit of account for evaluation should shift from the project level to the country level, making development evaluation a country-based and country-owned process instead of a donor imposition. The country focus is also built into the evaluation of the SDGs (Uitto 2016). The downside of this approach is that aggregating all county-level results will not add up to a global picture. This is particularly true given the fact that the SDGs have lent themselves to a menu of options from which countries can choose to prioritise some over others.

In the climate change arena, the nationally determined contributions are similarly not readily rolled up to a global level in a meaningful way. Evaluation must also address the issue that though many individual interventions seem to succeed in reaching their objectives, there is little to show by way of solving the broader national- or global-level problems.

Another powerful option to using the country as the unit of analysis is evaluating portfolios of interventions addressing related problems (Patton 2020: 115–116). This approach has been taken by many agencies (such as the World Bank, UNDP, Climate Investment Funds and the GEF) that have portfolios of similar projects or programmes implemented either globally or regionally. Such portfolio-level evaluations can be particularly useful for extracting lessons for future programming strategies.

When it comes to approaches and methods, it is time for evaluators to put aside battles about 'gold standards' and the superiority of certain types of methods. Evaluating at the nexus of environment and development requires a broad range of methods that capture the complex interlinkages between natural and human systems. This mixed methods approach should be based on the selection of those most suited to answer specific evaluation questions. Too often, it seems, it is vice versa: the methods choice is determined by the preferences and abilities of the evaluator, and it in turn determines what kinds of questions are asked. Context matters in evaluations and there is a huge variety of situations that demand a variety of approaches. Patton (2020: 101–103) has called for eclecticism—a *bricolage* methods principle—in choosing among a wide range of tools, both quantitative and qualitative, to answer the right questions. In environmental evaluation, such methods include geospatial tools, which can be used in combination with other more traditionally utilised approaches, including household surveys and participatory approaches (Lech et al. 2018; Sidman, Fuhrig and Batra 2020; Runfola et al. 2020).

Themes

This book is organised into two sections. The first section consists of chapters that address conceptual issues related to evaluating international cooperation around environment and development. Following this introduction, in Chapter 2, Rob van den Berg traces the historical shift in development cooperation towards a sustainable development perspective that considers global public goods at its centre. The chapter emphasises the need to consider risk when evaluating sustainability. Climate change has added new elements of unpredictability that pose the need to turn sustainability into an adaptation issue to be considered when evaluating how to best address global public goods. The chapter places the discussion in the context of the 2030 Agenda and the SDGs as well as the Paris Climate Agreement, tracking the new thinking on sustainable development and how this relates to managing and evaluating global public goods.

In Chapter 3, Andy Rowe discusses the poverty–environment nexus, analysing factors such as connectivity and scale, differing worldviews and a weak intellectual infrastructure for evaluating natural resource interventions. He considers how evaluation needs to adapt to enable it to contribute to sustainable development for which the urgent deployment of the full phalanx of evaluation methods and capacities is needed. The chapter reflects the changing landscape following the adoption of the SDGs and experiences in the field applying the principles and approaches for sustainability-ready evaluation.

In Chapter 4, Hazel and David Todd explore the increasingly damaging effects of climate change on the global environment and observe that it is the poor, who are most severely challenged by it. Weather-related events are increasing in frequency and severity, and in regions such as Asia-Pacific and the Caribbean disaster risk is outpacing resilience, posing severe limitations on poverty reduction. They observe that many international interventions attempt to address the overlaps between climate change adaptation and disaster risk reduction within a poverty reduction framework. Evaluation among international agencies has struggled to assess the progress and results of these efforts, given their exceptional complexity. While theory-based evaluation approaches have proved useful, they have often failed to find a suitable level of theory, which can provide clear findings and actionable lessons and recommendations. The chapter recommends an approach in which different levels of theory, from project through to the global environment, can be 'nested' within each other, so that each addresses a specific aspect, while contributing towards evaluation of higher levels of social and environmental change.

The second section of the book focuses on approaches and challenges to evaluating environment in development programmes bringing together cases from actual evaluations in the field. In Chapter 5, Anupam Anand and Geeta Batra suggest that remote sensing and geospatial methods are useful, innovative tools for measuring environmental impact. They provide reliable and cost-effective baseline information, help detect changes over time and track progress towards the achievement of environmental and other development targets. Given scarce resources and time constraints, remote sensing and geospatial data and tools are valuable in complementing other qualitative and quantitative evaluation methods. Using data on interventions implemented by the GEF, they present the application of geospatial approaches in addressing relevance, efficiency and effectiveness of interventions on forest cover, habitat quality and carbon sequestration.

Impact evaluation has gained importance as a way of analysing whether programmes and projects make a change in people's lives. However, the use of impact evaluations in international cooperation around environment and development is challenging, because such programmes are seldom amenable to counterfactual analysis that forms the basis of experimental evaluations. A rare exception from a large-scale programme is the impact evaluation of the GEF's support to the South China Sea, the object of Aaron Zazueta and Jeneen Garcia's chapter (Chapter 6). The evaluation sought to assess the progress towards impact in this large and complex setting by establishing causal linkages between the programme's interventions and the changes observed in the field, and by identifying GEF interventions' specific contributions in relation to other actors and confounding factors. The chapter looks at the extent to which the assumptions of the GEF-supported interventions and the evaluation's theory of change have remained valid over the ten years since the evaluation took place. Taking a longer time perspective, the chapter reflects on how contextual developments in the South China Sea have affected the long-term objectives and outcomes of the interventions under evaluation.

In Chapter 7, David Todd and Rob Craig present an approach to gauge progress towards impacts in environmental programmes utilising a theory of change methodological approach. This field-based Review of Outcomes to Impacts (ROtI) takes into account the lengthy time span of environmental change and the complexity of impact pathways, which complicate evaluation of environmental programmes. The approach has benefited from practical application in the GEF impact evaluation programme. The revised chapter introduces the application of the ROtI methodology in the climate change arena, beyond the original focus on biodiversity and natural resources management, drawing upon a concrete example from Jamaica.

In evaluating climate change mitigation interventions, many questions revolve around the impacts on the emissions themselves (e.g. Did the intervention actually produce emission reductions? Who can claim credit for the reductions?), even though the interventions themselves are often systematic, and the impact of specific intervention aspects on greenhouse gas emissions is hard to identify and attribute. Assessing various aspects' relative contributions requires a clear understanding of the reasons why (and in what context) more sustainable technologies are used and what hampered the use of the technologies prior to the intervention. In Chapter 8, Christine Wörlen develops a programme theory for climate mitigation interventions that does not rely on outcome-based positive contributions to poorly tangible intermediate project objectives, but on an assessment of the situation in which a market for sustainable energy products or services does not exist. By representing a full programme theory for market development, the 'theory of no change' is able to assess whether or not an intervention contributed to a more favourable framework for the market for a sustainable energy technology. It can be transferred with small modifications to other types of behaviour or systems change. The framework is able to integrate the context of a project into the assessment and can help optimise the match between interventions, barriers and change (or the lack thereof).

Not all international cooperation takes place through projects and programmes in the field. An important field of work pertains to developing global governance frameworks and to influencing international and national policy-making processes. Evaluation of such normative work has received even less attention than the evaluation of projects and programmes. In Chapter 9, Segbedzi Norgbey and Michael Spilsbury argue that there are no major differences between methods to evaluate normative work in the environment and methods to evaluate operational activities. Their ideas are informed by the evaluation work conducted in the UN Environment Programme (UNEP), a major actor in global environmental governance.

In Chapter 10, Carlo Carugi and Heather Bryant discuss the opportunities and challenges of conducting joint evaluations in the SDG era. The integrated nature of the SDGs calls for greater synergy, harmonisation and complementarity in development work, which is increasingly being reflected in evaluation. While the SDGs have brought the social, the economic and the environmental closer to each other in discourse, development practice and evaluation are often carried out with a focus on the human or the natural system, rather than both, which does not bode well for sustainability. Carugi and Bryant argue that one way to address the integrated nature of the SDGs is through joint evaluation where diverse institutions bring together their corporate skills, data, technical knowledge, expertise and experience to the assessment of the social, economic and environmental dimensions of development initiatives. The chapter describes how, despite challenges, joint evaluations offer significant advantages that can lead to important institutional and strategic changes with a view to strengthening development results in both the human and environmental spheres.

In Chapter 11, Michael Stocking examines the theoretical and practical issues faced by evaluators in Africa. After reflecting on the scope and approach of the Evaluation of UNDP Contribution to Environmental Management for Poverty Reduction and challenges of evaluating such a complex, cross-cutting topic, he highlights the evaluation's overall findings and what they mean for organisations attempting to integrate poverty and environment in their programming.

Launched in 1991, the GEF Small Grants Programme (SGP) helps developing countries to protect the global environment and contribute to sustainable development through mostly community-based small projects. Since its inception, SGP has funded some 24,000 small projects in over 120 countries. In Chapter 12, Sulan Chen and Juha Uitto highlight issues related to the relationship between global environmental objectives and national and local development results within the context of SGP. The authors question the assumptions behind evaluating the programme on the grounds of aggregating its direct environmental impacts—whether with regard to protecting fragile ecosystems or promoting development that reduces greenhouse gas emissions—from thousands of small projects to the global level. Instead, they argue for taking a broader approach to defining SGP results to include national-level effects on policy and institutional development and on advocacy and inclusiveness.

An important element of sustainable development and the transition to a green economy is knowing how to assess the implicit trade-offs among economic growth, environmental sustainability and social equity. Efforts merely perceived as 'green economy' may not deliver other promised social and economic outcomes. In Chapter 13, Ronal Gainza and Simon Lobach demonstrate how evaluation requires a thorough understanding of the outcomes and measurement framework that helps to assess the magnitudes of such trade-offs. Using four case studies, their chapter presents a framework for such measurements and provides examples from Latin America and the Caribbean of how the framework may be used in international and national decision-making.

A significant amount of the world's freshwater resources is located underground. The urgency of better aquifer management is widely recognised, especially as more regions become acutely water stressed. Efforts have been underway over the last two decades to focus greater attention on the wise management of aquifers, and to forge greater cooperation among nations sharing transboundary aquifer resources. The GEF has been an important funding source for this work, sponsoring projects focused on improved aquifer management. These projects aim to better understand the boundaries, volume, extraction rates and pollution risks to aquifers, and forge agreements among nations to better manage their shared resources. In Chapter 14, Alan Fox draws important lessons from the evaluations of GEF-sponsored aquifer projects, emphasising the challenges to better stewardship of these vital resources. While some progress has been made in groundwater modelling and mapping, in the development of methodologies for aquifer protection and replenishment, and the establishment of a few cross-border institutional frameworks, the overall picture is negative. There remain wide gaps in understanding about groundwater systems, and effective governance and institutional frameworks are scarce.

Natural disasters have a disproportionate impact on the poor because the risks and human costs are strongly associated with poverty. The SDGs and the Sendai Framework for Disaster Risk Reduction have provided a renewed impetus by recognising disaster risk as one of the key constraints in reducing economic loss, sustaining development gains and reducing poverty. The extent to which international agreements resulted in national policies that promote integrated approaches to development, to reduce disaster risk and enable climate change adaptation is evolving. In the area of climate-related disasters including slow-onset disasters, disaster risk reduction and climate change adaptation have similar goals, which calls for more coordinated programming at the national level. There has been increasing financing for climate change adaptation through various funding mechanisms further strengthened by Paris Agreement in 2016, while there remain resource challenges for similar goals in the area of slow-onset disasters. This highlights the importance of combined efforts in the area of adaptation and climate-related disaster risk reduction efforts, specifically integrating such efforts as part of key development strategies rather than as stand-alone efforts. Facilitating humanitarian and development nexus to enable linkages between disaster response and long-term development has been on the agenda of the national and international agencies for over a decade. Drawing on evaluations of the UNDP, in Chapter 15, Vijayalakshmi Vadivelu revisits the disaster risk reduction efforts at the national level and at UNDP since the adoption of the SDGs and Sendai Framework. The chapter examines the extent to which disaster management and adaptation and their intersecting dimensions are integrated into development efforts.

In Chapter 16, Roberto La Rovere outlines the approach to the evaluation of climate change, environment and natural resource management in the context of the Consultative Group on International Agricultural Research (CGIAR). Evaluating the impact of research activities poses specific challenges that differ from evaluating development programmes or normative work. Given the nature of the work of the CGIAR system, it is important to take a systematic and common approach to evaluation that covers the network's various dimensions—including its environmental, social and economic dimensions. Over the last decade the relative importance, urgency and share of the CGIAR investments in climate change research in agriculture has grown dramatically, together with the gearing up of the Research Programme on Climate Change, Agriculture and Food Security (CCAFS) and its various evaluations.

Conclusion

Environment and development are intrinsically interlinked. Even in the post-industrial societies in the global North, economic development rests on a healthy natural resource base. This relationship is even more pronounced in poorer communities and among poor people who eke out a living from agriculture, fisheries, forestry and extractive industries—people whose livelihoods depend directly on ecosystem health. We also know that gender considerations are at the centre of sustainable development. Women form the majority of small farmers in developing countries responsible for cultivating land and feeding their families. Indigenous peoples in many parts of the world often live close to the nature. Their worldviews also often reflect a holistic perspective that sees humankind as part of the natural world (Rowe 2019b).

There is an environment–poverty nexus that is often neglected in development endeavours that aim for economic growth and/or poverty reduction. Too often activities that aim for economic development end up destroying the very environmental and natural resource base on which the people and, ultimately, the economy depend.

More than three decades ago, the World Commission on Sustainable Development[7] introduced the concept of sustainable development to our vocabulary, calling for making 'development sustainable to ensure that it meets the needs of the present without compromising the ability of future generations to meet their own needs' (United Nations 1987). Their work clearly recognised the linkages between environment and development and the importance of preserving the natural resources that sustain the Earth and its people. Still today, no country has fully adopted these principles. On the contrary, destruction of the natural environment and rampant pollution continue unabated. Many people in both the global North and South believe that there is a necessary trade-off between economic progress and preserving natural resources, despite evidence to the contrary—especially when taking a long-term view. The COVID-19 pandemic has provided a brutal warning of what hardships ignoring the natural environment inevitably brings.

The environment is a global public good that gets short shrift as the world pursues economic growth, as in the short term it is seen as an externality. Natural capital is routinely ignored in economic calculations. There is a tendency that development projects ignore the environment, whereas environmental projects operate in isolation and, consequently, fail to instigate larger, meaningful change that broadly benefits people. There is a need to be better able to demonstrate the economic value of the environment and natural resources, while not losing sight of the intrinsic value of nature that cannot be measured in monetary terms. Such valuations must also take into account the non-linearity and uncertainty associated with environmental change and unknown tipping points.

Evaluation must contribute to a better understanding of how environment and development interact and to identifying win–win solutions and approaches to the problems. Evaluation must also consider the big picture, the larger impacts that all of our projects, programmes, strategies and policies aim to contribute to. Although providing accountability for results and resources used at the level of individual interventions continues to be needed, it is important to ensure that these interventions effectively contribute to the overall goal of a more sustainable and just future. Evaluation should not be seen as a control function, but as an essential tool among others to improving the design and implementation of development efforts.

To remain relevant in the increasingly complex and interconnected world, it is absolutely essential for evaluation as a profession and as a practice to engage in the discourse at the nexus of human and natural systems. That is where we as a community can contribute, with our practical knowledge anchored in research, to a transformation towards a more sustainable development path. As evaluators, we must play a role in ensuring that, after a crisis such as the COVID-19 pandemic, we build back better towards a society that is environmentally more sustainable and socially, economically and politically more just.

It is my hope that the chapters in this collection will make a useful and interesting contribution to how to better utilise evaluation for achieving development that is more sustainable for people, the planet and prosperity.

Notes

1 https://www.cidrap.umn.edu/news-perspective/2003/05/estimates-sars-death-rates-revised-upward.
2 https://www.worldbank.org/en/topic/poverty/brief/projected-poverty-impacts-of-COVID-19 (accessed on 20 June 2020).
3 https://sustainabledevelopment.un.org/post2015/transformingourworld.
4 Biosphere goals: 6 – clean water and sanitation, 13 – climate action, 14 – life below water, 15 – life on land; Society goals: 1 – no poverty, 2 – zero hunger, 3 – good health and well-being, 4 – quality education, 5 – gender equality, 7 – affordable and clean energy, 11 – sustainable cities and communities, 16 – peace, justice and strong institutions; Economy goals: 8 – decent work and economic growth, 9 – industry, innovation and infrastructure, 10 – reduced inequalities, 12 – responsible consumption and production. Note: Goal 17 – global partnerships is cross-cutting to all.
5 https://www.swissre.com/media/news-releases/2018/nr20180410_sigma_global_insured_loses_highest_ever.html (accessed on 17 January 2021).
6 http://unevaluation.org/.
7 The so-called Brundtland Commission, named after its chair, the former Norwegian prime minister Gro Harlem Brundtland.

References

Bamberger, M., J. Vaessen and E. Raimondo, *Dealing with Complexity in Development Evaluation: A Practical Approach*. Thousand Oaks, CA, Sage, 2015.

Bennett, N.J., R. Roth, S.C. Klain, et al., 'Mainstreaming the social sciences in conservation', *Conservation Biology*, 31(1): 55–66, 2016.

Birnbaum, M. and P. Mickwitz, eds., Environmental Program and Policy Evaluation: Addressing Methodological Challenges, *New Directions for Evaluation*, 122, San Francisco, Jossey-Bass and the American Evaluation Association, 2009.

Boyce, J.K., 'Is inequality bad for the environment?' *Research in Social Problems and Public Policy*, 15: 267–288, 2008.

Braat, L.C. and R. de Groot, 'The ecosystem services agenda: Bridging the worlds of natural science and economics, conservation and development, and public and private policy', *Ecosystem Services*, 1: 4–15, 2012.

Brack, D., A. Glover and L. Wellesley, *Agricultural Commodity Supply Chains: Trade, Consumption and Deforestation*. Research Paper. London, Chatham House, 2016.

Caballos, G., P.R. Ehrlich and R. Dirzo, '*Biological annihilation via the ongoing sixth mass extinction signaled by vertebrate population losses and declines*', *Proceedings of the National Academy of Sciences*, 2017 (www.pnas.org/cgi/doi/10.1073/pnas.1704949114)

Centre for Bhutan Studies and GNH Research, A Compass towards a Just and Harmonious Society: *2015 GNH Survey Report*, Thimpu, Centre for Bhutan Studies and GNH Research, 2016 (http://www.grossnationalhappiness.com/wp-content/uploads/2017/01/Final-GNH-Report-jp-21.3.17-ilovepdf-compressed.pdf)

Czech, B., 'Five myths about economic growth', In: B. Czech, ed., *Best of the Daly News: Selected Essays from the Leading Blog in Steady State Economics, 2010–2018*, 38–40, Arlington, VA, Steady State Press, 2020.

Donaldson, S.I., C.A. Christie and M.M. Mark, eds., *What Counts as Credible Evidence in Applied Research and Evaluation Practice?*, Thousand Oaks, CA, Sage, 2009.

Eldeib, D., A. Gallardo, A. Johnson, A. Waldman, N. Martin, T. Buford and T. Briscoe, '*The first 100: COVID-19 took black lives first. It didn't have to*', ProPublica Illinois, 2020 (https://features.propublica.org/chicago-first-deaths/covid-coronavirus-took-black-lives-first/)

Ford, T., S. Reber and R.V. Reeves, '*Race Gaps in COVID-19 Deaths are Even Bigger than They Appear*', Washington, DC, Brookings Institution, 2020. (https://www.brookings.edu/blog/up-front/2020/06/16/race-gaps-in-covid-19-deaths-are-even-bigger-than-they-appear/)

Global Commission on Adaptation, *Adapt Now: A Global Call for Leadership on Climate Resilience*, Rotterdam and Washington, DC, Global Center on Adaptation and World Resources Institute, 2019.

Ferraro, P.J., 'Counterfactual thinking and impact evaluation in environmental policy', In: M. Birnbaum and P. Mickwitz, eds., *Environmental Program and Policy Evaluation: Addressing Methodological Challenges, New Directions for Evaluation*, 122, 75–84, San Francisco, Jossey-Bass and the American Evaluation Association, 2009.

GEF IEO, *Value for Money Analysis for GEF Land Degradation Projects*, Washington, DC, Independent Evaluation Office, Global Environment Facility, 2018. (https://www.gefieo.org/evaluations/value-money-analysis-gef-land-degradation-projects-2016)

GEF IEO, *Value for Money Analysis of GEF Interventions in Support of Sustainable Forest Management*, Washington, DC, Independent Evaluation Office, Global Environment Facility, 2019. (https://www.gefieo.org/evaluations/value-money-analysis-gef-land-degradation-projects-2016)

Hardin, G., 'The tragedy of the commons', *Science*, 162 (3859): 1243–1248, 1968.

Heal, G. 'A celebration of environmental and resource economics', *Review of Environmental Economics and Policy*, 1 (1): 7–25, 2007.

Hickel, J., *'Why growth can't be green', Foreign Policy, 12* September 2018. (https://foreign-policy.com/2018/09/12/whygrowth-cant-be-green/)

Lech, M., J.I. Uitto, S. Harten, G. Batra and A. Anand, 'Improving international development evaluation through geospatial data and analysis', *International Journal of Geospatial and Environmental Research*, 5 (2), Art. 3., 2018. (https://dc.uwm.edu/ijger/vol5/iss2/3/)

Lelieveld, J., A. Pozzer, U. Pöschl, M. Fnais, A. Haines and T. Műnzel, 'Loss of life expectancy from air pollution compared to other risk factors: A worldwide perspective', *Cardiovascular Research*, Mar 3, 2020, doi: 10.1093/cvr/cvaa02. (https://pubmed.ncbi.nlm.nih.gov/32123898/)

Margoluis, R., C. Stem, N. Salafsky and M. Brown, 'Design alternatives for evaluating the impact of conservation projects', In: M. Birnbaum and P. Mickwitz, eds., *Environmental Program and Policy Evaluation: Addressing Methodological Challenges, New Directions for Evaluation*, 122, 85–96, San Francisco, Jossey-Bass and the American Evaluation Association, 2009.

Mishra, P., *Age of Anger: A History of the Present*, New York, Farrar, Straus and Giroux, 2017.

Nadeau, R., 'Brother, can you spare me a planet? Mainstream economics and the environmental crisis', *Scientific American*, 19 March 2008. (https://www.scientificamerican.com/article/brother-can-you-spare-me-a-planet/?print=true)

Naidoo, R. and B. Fisher, 'Reset sustainable development goals for a pandemic world', *Nature*, 583, 198–201, 2020. (https://www.nature.com/articles/d41586-020-01999-x)

Nordhaus, W., 'The climate club: How to fix a failing global effort', *Foreign Affairs*, 10–17 May/June 2020.

Oil Change International and Friends of the Earth United States, *Still Digging: G20 Governments Continue to Finance the Climate Crisis*, Washington, DC, 2020. (http://priceofoil.org/content/uploads/2020/05/G20-Still-Digging.pdf)

Osterholm, M.T. and M. Olshaker, 'Chronicle of a pandemic foretold: Learning from the COVID-19 failure—before the next outbreak arrives', *Foreign Affairs*, 10–25 July/August 2020.

Patton, M.Q., *Blue Marble Evaluation: Premises and Principles*, New York, The Guilford Press, 2020.

Pawson, R. and N. Tilley, *Realist Evaluation*, Thousand Oaks, CA, Sage, 1997.

Picciotto, R., 'The new environment for development evaluation', *American Journal of Evaluation*, 28 (4): 509–521, 2007.

Picciotto, R., 'Evaluating climate change and development', In: R.D. Van Den Berg and O. Feinstein, eds. *Evaluating Climate Change and Development*, 19–45, World Bank Series on Development, Volume 8, New Brunswick, NJ, and London, Transaction Publishers, 2009.

Pindyck, R.S., 'Uncertainty in environmental economics', *Review of Environmental Economics and Policy*, 1 (1): 45–65, 2007.

Quammen, D., *Spillover: Animal Infections and the Next Human Pandemic*, New York: W.W. Norton, 2012.

Raworth, K., *Doughnut Economics: Seven Ways to Think Like a 21st-Century Economist*, New York, Random House Business, 2017.

Reid, A.J., J.L. Brooks, L. Dolgova, B. Laurich, B.G. Sullivan, P. Szekeres, S.L.R. Wood, J.R. Bennett and S.J. Cooke, 'Post-2015 Sustainable development goals still neglecting their environmental roots in the Anthropocene', *Environmental Science and Policy*, 77: 179–184, 2017.

Rockström, J. and P. Sukhdev, 'Present new way of viewing the sustainable development goals and how they are all linked to food', *Stockholm Resilience Centre*. 2016 (http://www.stockholmresilience.org/research/research-news/2016-06-14-how-food-connects-all-the-sdgs.html)

Rowe, A., 'Evaluation of natural resource interventions', *American Journal of Evaluation* 33 (3): 382–392, 2012.

Rowe, A., 'Sustainability-ready evaluation: A call to action', In: G. Julnes, ed., *Evaluating Sustainability: Support for Managing Processes in the Public Interest. New Directions for Evaluation*, 162, 29–48, San Francisco, Josey-Bass, 2019a.

Rowe, A., 'Evaluation for the anthropocene: Introduction', *Evaluation Matters—He Take To Te Aromatawai*, 5, 145–150, 2019b. (https://www.nzcer.org.nz/system/files/journals/evaluation-maters/downloads/ EM2019_144.pdf)

Ruijs, A., R.B. Dellink and D.W. Bromley, 'Economics of poverty, environment and natural-resource use: Introduction, In: R.B. Dellink and A. Ruijs, eds., *Economics of Poverty, Environment and Natural-resource Use*, 3–15, Dordrecht, Springer, 2008.

Runfola, D., G. Batra, A. Anand, A. Way and S. Goodman, 'Exploring the socioeconomic co-benefits of Global Environment Facility projects in Uganda using a quasi-experimental geospatial interpolation (QGI) approach', *Sustainability*, 12 (8), 3225, 2020. (doi:10.3390/su12083225)

Sidman, G., S. Fuhrig and G. Batra, 'The use of remote sensing analysis for evaluating the impact of development projects in the Yellow Sea large marine ecosystem', *Sustainability*, 12 (9), 2628, 2020. (doi:10.3390/su12093628)

Uitto, J.I., 'The environment-poverty nexus in evaluation: Implications for the Sustainable Development Goals', *Global Policy*, 7 (3): 441–447, 2016. (https://www.globalpolicyjournal.com/articles/climate-change-energy-and-sustainability/environment-poverty-nexus-evaluation-implications-)

Uitto, J.I., 'Sustainable development evaluation: Understanding the nexus of natural and human systems', In: G. Julnes, ed., *Evaluating Sustainability: Evaluative Support for Managing Processes in the Public Interest. New Directions for Evaluation*, 162, 49–67, San Francisco, Josey-Bass, 2019.

Uitto, J.I., '*The pandemic and the global environment: Which way next?*', *Global Policy*, May 2020. (https://www.globalpolicyjournal.com/articles/climate-change-energy-and-sustainability/pandemic-and-global-environment-which-way-next)

Uitto, J.I., J. Kohlitz and D. Todd, 'Evaluating sustainable development in SIDS: Lessons from the Pacific and the Caribbean', In: R.D. van den Berg, I. Naidoo and S.D. Tamondong, eds., *Evaluation for the 2030 Agenda: Providing evidence on progress and sustainability*, 119–133, Exeter, UK, International Development Evaluation Association, 2017.

United Nations, *Our Common Future*, Report of the World Commission on Environment and Development, New York, 1987.

United Nations Development Programme (UNDP), *Concept and Measurement of Human Development*, New York and Oxford: Oxford University Press, 1990.

UNDP, *Global Dimensions of Human Development*, New York and Oxford: Oxford University Press, 1992.

UNEG, *Integrating human rights and gender equality in evaluations*, UNEG Guidance Documents, United Nations Evaluation Group, 2014. (http://unevaluation.org/document/detail/1616)

UNEG, *Guidance on evaluating institutional gender mainstreaming*, UNEG Guidance Documents, United Nations Evaluation Group, 2018. (http://unevaluation.org/document/detail/1616)

Vaessen, J. and D. Todd, 'Methodological challenges of evaluating the impact of the global environment facility's biodiversity program', *Evaluation and Program Planning*, 31: 231–240, 2008.

Van Den Berg, R.D. and O. Feinstein, eds., *Evaluating Climate Change and Development*, World Bank Series on Development, Volume 8, New Brunswick, NJ, and London, Transaction Publishers, 2009.

Vidal, J., 'Destroyed habitat creates the perfect conditions for coronavirus to emerge', *Scientific American*, 18 March 2020. (https://www.scientificamerican.com/article/dest royed-habitat-creates-the-perfect-conditions-forcoronavirus-toemerge/?fbclid=IwAR3Vw3lKf-N6chSiH7Tq7lvOYo yHoQUpnGfIKdUMKQt7roNwRieHbbd9dfaA)

Washington, H., B. Taylor, H. Kopnina, P. Cryer, and J.J. Piccolo, 'Why ecocentrism is the key pathway to sustainability', *The Ecological Citizen*, 1: 35–41, 2017.

2

A GLOBAL PUBLIC GOODS PERSPECTIVE ON ENVIRONMENT AND POVERTY

Rob D. van den Berg

Redefining international cooperation

In international cooperation it seemed for a while that a perspective of public goods and costs became dominant. Partly, this was due to redefining international cooperation in changing circumstances: a world in which North and South and East and West are no longer the clear categories they were during the Cold War. Partly, it was due to the prevailing dominance of an economic vision of the world, rather than a sociocultural, religious or ethnic one. We live in a world in which many problems and challenges demonstrate the limits of a neoclassical economic world-view, and this is increasingly recognized. A new perspective on international cooperation is of prime importance; given the limits of natural resources on our planet, it increasingly needs to be a sustainable development perspective.

This has not always been the case. The first major effort in international cooperation, development aid, started after the Second World War, even before many countries achieved independence. Aid was couched in terms of historical obligation, mutual benefits and ethical norms and standards. The rich, developed countries felt castigated for their history of colonialism, imperialism and unbridled capitalism and were urged to help and support the newly independent developing countries to develop their economies, improve their institutions, ensure health and prosperity for their citizens and to fight absolute and relative poverty.

However much feelings of guilt and responsibility legitimized international support, the early conceptualization of aid was economic and politic in nature. Two competing paradigms influenced early international cooperation: one of economic development and mutual benefit, the other of self-reliance and socialist or social-democratic economic and social arrangements. The economist paradigm was prevalent in the West and the socialist paradigm in the East. The South, the developing world, was the arena in which the fight between the two paradigms would turn warm or hot from time to time. The link between the development of poor nations and the Cold War between capitalism and communism was evident at the time, as reflected, for example, in one of the famous tracts on economic development: W.W. Rostow's (1960) *The Stages of Economic Growth: A Non-Communist Manifesto*.

For the developed world to spend funds on international cooperation was thus an ethical obligation, an economic investment and a geopolitical move. Policy papers often mentioned both economic and national interests – public goods did not play a substantive role. One could argue that the concept of public goods was developed in parallel with development cooperation: the economist Paul Samuelson (1954) is often credited with the first discussion of public goods. As is typical of new concepts, they were at first more or less ignored in mainstream discussions. When Rostow presented his vision of economic development in 1960, public goods did not come into the argument. He presented economic development as a series of technical steps that countries had to go through in order to achieve the economic heaven of a "mature" economy which would offer "mass-consumption" to its citizens. Aid could help remove obstacles on the way to this state of bliss.

However, economic and geopolitical motives were gradually accompanied by new motives and new modalities. Humanitarian crises (e.g. the Bihar famine of 1966 in India) led to proposals for humanitarian aid to help and support countries that went through natural or man-made disasters and whose populations needed food, shelter and emergency care. The 1983–1985 famine in Ethiopia led to increased international recognition for the need to provide aid and assistance. Humanitarian aid is mostly funded on ethical arguments and appeals to humanity's better nature to help and care for those in need. Other arguments have also supported humanitarian aid (e.g. security considerations, where a natural or man-made disaster may destabilize a region or a country). Economic reasons have also been put forward: focusing on the need to quickly rebuild an economy to ensure that more permanent solutions can be found for resolving humanitarian crises. Nonetheless, ethical and normative arguments tend to form the core of the justification of humanitarian aid.

The United Nations (UN) has been involved in a third line of international cooperation, one that predates its birth. In fact, the specialized agencies that predate the UN have been instrumental in their respective fields to formulate and reach agreement on international norms and standards, such as on meteorology, postal arrangements, food and many other issues. This *normative* work of the UN became more dominant over time. The UN remains the first and foremost institution in the world in which the global community can reach agreement on issues of common interest. Arguments for normative work have often been couched in terms of the necessity to reach agreement on how states should interact and how international conventions should be implemented.

Thus, the UN's three major domains of work (normative, humanitarian and development) are often addressed in terms of ethical behaviour and mutually beneficial agreements on common standards and approaches. However, when the Cold War ended, the inextricably intertwined geopolitical and economic self-interest arguments that supported the funding of international cooperation fell largely away. The concept of public goods, as introduced by Samuelson (1954), could provide a new rationale for international cooperation. Dr. Inge Kaul, then Director of Development Studies for the United Nations Development Programme (UNDP), made a significant contribution in this direction, formulating the need for action from a global public goods perspective.

In the decade up to 2015, global public goods increasingly became central to discussions on the role of public finance for global problems. Several bilateral donors were redefining their aid programmes from a public goods perspective. In international efforts to address environmental problems, the public goods nature of these efforts has always been taken more or less as granted. What was new is that the UN and other international actors were increasingly framing their activities in terms of public goods. The challenge is to see whether a common framework for analysis, action and evaluation can be derived to address environmental issues on the one hand and development and poverty reduction on the other.

With the adoption of the Sustainable Development Goals (SDGs) in Agenda 2030 and the Paris Agreement on Climate Change[1] in 2015, an integrated, holistic agenda was presented with the aim of "transforming our world." The UN resolution which proclaims this lofty goal mentions public goods in one paragraph, number 41, as an important objective of public financing, without any further definition or explanation.[2] The Sustainable Development Report 2019, published by an independent group of experts and providing detailed information and data on progress towards the SDGs, does not contain the term "public good" anywhere in the document and it may seem the concept has left the arena of international development and has been retired to a bygone age (Sachs et al. 2019).

Yet at the same time we see an emerging paradigm fight in economics where public goods and related concepts (such as public value) are becoming increasingly important. Kate Raworth's efforts to integrate sustainability perspectives in economic theory are peppered with public good aims throughout the new paradigm she proposes (Raworth 2017). The value of public sector investments and efforts is central to the work of Mariana Mazzucato, who focuses on the role of the public sector in innovation (Mazzucato 2019 – see especially chapter 8 "Undervaluing the public sector"). Both institutional economics and evolutionary economics tend to include public good perspectives, so even while the term has receded into the background in recent years, it is good to define what we mean by public goods and what role they play in tackling and solving the global crises we face. The larger challenge we face is to integrate a public good perspective into sustainable development approaches that will ensure that environmental services for future generations (e.g. clean air, water and healthy food) simultaneously alleviate poverty, in line with the SDGs and the Paris climate agreement of 2015.

Defining public goods

At first sight, it may seem that there is a strong connection between the relatively new arguments regarding public goods and public value and the normative functions of the UN. One could argue that it is a public good to have internationally accepted norms and standards on many issues, because without them communication, trade, travel and many other interactions between nations and peoples would become difficult and likely much more dangerous. However, to say that global public goods are identified by the norms and standards of the UN does not solve the problem. How are these norms and standards identified? When are these norms and standards really needed, and when should the global community leave things to markets or to bi- and multilateral actions among states? When can the global community hold differing opinions and when should it agree? Thus, defining public goods through global norms and standards leads to a discussion of the public goods status of norms and standards – which returns to the question of what public goods are.

In general, public goods tend to be defined by what they are *not*: anything that markets fail to effectively and efficiently produce. Leaving public goods to markets thus leads to market failure and to negative externalities – in other words – to *public bads* (Feinstein 2019: 21). In economics, this "negative" definition is most clear; most often public goods are defined by what they are not, as *non-rival* and *non-excludable*. Non-rival means that whatever you take of a resource does not significantly reduce others' ability to take the resource (e.g. the quantity of air that you breathe does not significantly diminish the quantity of air that can be breathed by others). Non-excludable means that access to the product cannot be limited to a group of people (e.g. paying customers). Air again serves as an example: one cannot sell air to a customer if air is otherwise freely available. The example of air can be expanded to illustrate the ongoing debate about public goods and the role of governments and markets. With the advent of air-conditioners, cool air has become something that can be sold, for example, to companies that want to ensure that their employees are working in productive conditions or to citizens who prefer to sleep in a cool bedroom during the summer. What once was completely non-rival and non-excludable becomes marketable if the quality of it can be influenced in a closed space. In open space, it affects markets in a reverse way: housing in areas of high pollution is generally cheaper than housing in areas with clean air.

For positive definitions of what constitute public goods, one would need to examine other sciences and political debates: there, public goods may be identified as issues that should be dealt with by the government, by the public or through shared cultural and societal norms. Certainly the latter seems directly connected to the UN's normative work. A positive identification of public goods could define them as at least anything that the UN provides norms and standards on, but we have noted that this may turn into a tautology, as these norms and standards may have been identified from a public goods perspective in the first place. Furthermore, such a definition would clash with the economist's perspective on public goods, as economists could argue that some of the normative work of the UN could be better left to markets and market forces – and poverty alleviation could be one of them.

Addressing poverty is perceived in the UN as both a normative and a development issue. UNDP, which is arguably the anti-poverty programme of the UN, is seen as a development agency rather than a normative one. Development issues tend to be argued in economic terms, even if social and normative issues play an important role. Thus, the starting point for action on public goods issues tends to be to focus on market failure.

Public action on public goods

Market failures often manifest themselves through externalities – external costs (or public bads) that are created by the market and that are additional and external to the product that was produced for and bought on the market. Meeting these costs, or preventing them, is a public good, because they will not be met privately (i.e. through the market). In general, governments have three ways to address market failures and ensure public goods. They can use their judicial powers to criminalize behaviours that lead to external costs (e.g. environmental pollution); they can use their regulatory powers to change behaviours to such an extent that external costs no longer appear (e.g. promote sorted collection of household waste); and they can use their taxation powers to recover costs and shift externalities back into the market (e.g. taxing pollution or greenhouse gas emissions). Some argue that public goods and bads are the foundation of taxation and public spending. It could also be argued that perceiving both poverty and environmental degradation as market failures provides an economic justification to address both through normative measures and through public spending.

Just as Rostow (1960), through his theory of the stages of economic growth, provided a technical perspective on how to develop countries and end poverty, another influential publication threw light on the role of governments and the public sector: John Kenneth Galbraith's 1973 publication of *Economics and the Public Purpose* led to a discussion in economics and politics on whether markets should be curtailed in order to serve the public purpose or whether markets should be improved to solve problems in society. Over time, the neoclassical perspective gained ascendancy, which led to the perception of market regulation and taxation as distortions that prevent markets from becoming fully efficient.

The 2008 financial crisis demonstrated to many that governments need to regulate markets. However, many Republicans in the United States continue to claim that it was actually government interference with the markets that caused the subprime lending crisis, signalling that the debate is far from over.

One lesson to be learned from a historical perspective on public goods is that though the concept may be timeless, the actual application is not. There is a dynamic in what constitutes a public good or cost. For example, before streetlights were introduced, the public good of a well-lighted street at night did not exist. When streetlights became more ubiquitous, their costs became evident on municipalities and transport authorities' budgets. Public costs regarding the environment started to soar to previously unseen heights when population pressure and use of natural resources reached levels that brought the limits of environmental services in sight.

Ending poverty: a global public good?

Whether public funding should be made available to alleviate poverty is an issue that has been vociferously debated. Neoclassical economists tend to take the position that government should create an environment in which the poor can fend for themselves. Support to the poor has failed – and will always fail – they claim. This was most aptly phrased by Ronald Reagan in his 1988 state of the union address: "the Federal Government declared war on poverty, and poverty won."[3] In this perspective, direct aid will actually make it more difficult for the poor to escape poverty. Many (if not most) other political perspectives on the government's role disagree with this perspective and perceive poverty as an issue where government should play an important role, both to help people out of poverty and to prevent people from spiralling down into poverty. However, if on a national-level poverty is not unanimously seen as a public issue, what can the public goods perspective contribute to the idea of helping other countries to alleviate poverty? Would the concept of global public goods be helpful to support aid for poverty reduction?

The international discussion of global public goods was actively promoted and supported by UNDP through the groundbreaking work of Dr. Inge Kaul. Together with colleagues and researchers, she was the first to propose a definition of global public goods as goods whose benefits extend to all countries, people and generations (Kaul, Grunberg and Stern 1999). Together with Ronald Mendoza she developed a perspective on how global (as opposed to local or regional) goods should be supported through public funding: "local public goods should be provided locally, national public goods at the level of the central government, and global public goods at the international level" (Kaul amd Mendoza 1999: 91). This division of labour seems reasonable, but it also seems to marginalize poverty as a global issue. Poverty itself is, after all, localized and thus seems to be largely the domain of national governments.

Although Inge Kaul does not mention poverty as the most obvious global public good, she does include the eradication of poverty from a human rights perspective, and thus identifies poverty as a global bad that the global community needs to address. Also, indirect linkages to global issues could be explored: migration caused by poverty can create havoc in other countries. Political movements aimed at reducing poverty may become revolutionary or may lead to violent action and destabilize countries and regions. States may descend into chaos and may lead to considerable economic loss (e.g. pirates from Somalia were a regional problem for international shipping, with a global impact, from circa 2000 to 2015). To prevent this from happening, a public goods perspective may justify regional and even global action.

The gist of this is that no universal agreement exists as to whether poverty is a public issue and whether poverty alleviation should be funded from public means. An underlying reason for the lack of agreement is whether poverty is globally significant. Some perceive poverty as a local problem for which local (market-oriented) solutions may be found. However, poverty can be perceived of as globally significant, and thus the eradication of poverty can be seen as a global public good. This could be argued from human rights, normative and ethical perspectives. It could also be argued from an economic perspective, as Paul Collier (2007, 2010) has done in both *The Bottom Billion* and in *Plundered Planet*. Collier approaches both poverty and the environment from a utilitarian perspective and sees it as the imperative of an economist to strive for the greatest good for the greatest number of people. Furthermore, he approaches poverty and the environment from a market failure perspective, which requires government intervention, including international intervention to support countries to break out of what he has termed "traps."

For the environment, Collier focuses on the tragedy of the commons. Collier and Kaul recognize global environmental public goods as expressing the tragedy of the global commons. However, the environmental community uses a slightly different definition of global public goods. A global environmental benefit, as defined by Global Environment Facility (GEF), is a good that has *global significance*. In other words, it can be very local in nature, but if it has global significance it can be termed a global good. There are good reasons for this perspective. Many unique species have global significance: if they are lost, they are not just lost to the area where they live, but they are also lost to the world.

Furthermore, the multilateral environmental agreements for which the GEF is a financial mechanism have identified the division of labour regarding funding of global goods that are localized in countries. In principle, countries should fund local issues, even if they have global significance, but only up to the level that they can afford given their level of development. They should be supported by the international community for additional efforts that are needed to safeguard the global good. Furthermore, given the developed world's historic responsibility for creating environmental problems (demonstrated most clearly through the history of greenhouse gas emissions, which for a long time were dominated by industrialized countries), developed countries should make available the requisite additional and incremental funding needed to safeguard global goods.

Ensuring environmental services: a global public good

The environment provides a range of services: clean air and water, soil for crops to grow on and weather that supports the agriculture and stability in housing and infrastructure. These environmental services have been conceptualized in the so-called ecosystem approach and have been formulated most consistently in the Millennium Ecosystem Assessment (2005). In mainstream economic theory, these environmental services are recognized as externalities (costs and benefits that are public rather than private in nature).[4] Of these externalities, the benefits usually do not pose a problem – the costs are of increasing concern, as climate change discussions are demonstrating.

Many economists tend to speak of external costs in terms of market failures, and Nicholas Stern, a former Chief Economist of the World Bank, has done so most dramatically. In the *Stern Review on the Economics of Climate Change*, a report to the

UK government on the costs of climate change, both on mitigating it and adapting to its consequences, he noted that climate change is a result of "the greatest market failure the world has seen." His conclusion was that "those who damage others by emitting greenhouse gases generally do not pay."[5] There is controversy over whether Stern and his team correctly calculated the damages and the costs of preventing them, but the point he raised concerning market failure was not disputed.[6]

The global public good nature of environmental issues is perhaps most persuasively illustrated through the ozone layer. This stratospheric layer in the atmosphere absorbs approximately 97–99% of the sun's ultraviolet light, which would otherwise cause severe genetic damage. It thus provides a service to all life on earth: protection against a possible annihilating force. In 1985, it was discovered that the ozone layer showed a decrease in density of 4% per decade and was exhibiting growing holes in the polar regions. Further analysis uncovered that chlorofluorocarbons were the main cause for the reduction of ozone. These chemicals were introduced in the 1920s and 1930s and had been mainly used in air conditioning and refrigerators. Along with other chemicals that were later identified, they became known as ozone-depleting substances.

Research established that these substances – and these substances only – were responsible for the gradual destruction of the ozone layer. When they were introduced to industrial production, their destructive consequences were unknown. Given the ozone layer's crucial role in protecting life on earth from harmful rays, international action started immediately: in the year of discovery the Vienna Convention for the Protection of the Ozone Layer was designed. It entered into force in 1988, when a sufficient number of countries ratified the convention. It has been ratified by 196 states. Action against the production and consumption of ozone-depleting substances was initiated through the Montreal Protocol, which was opened for signature in 1987 and was ratified by a sufficient number of countries in 1989 to become active. To date it has been signed by 197 countries and is often considered the most effective international agreement. Research and evaluations have shown the Montreal Protocol on track to rescue the ozone layer, which should be restored to its former full strength by 2050.

It was clear that in this case only one option was open to the international community: forbid the production and use of ozone-depleting substances. The ozone layer cannot be privatized and regulated to ensure that market forces would keep it healthy. It benefits all life on earth equally. Environmental problems can be seen on two dimensions: one dimension ranges from uncontested public goods to private and marketable ones (i.e. from the ozone layer through climate change to biodiversity loss, pollution issues, marketable commodities such as organic food and areas of outstanding natural beauty), and a second dimension from global to local (e.g. from the ozone layer through climate change to biodiversity loss, to pollution, land degradation and local instances of environmental degradation). How these environmental problems are linked to development and poverty is thus also reflected in a wide range of different relationships.

Linkages between poverty and the environment

In general, the linkages between poverty and the environment can be seen as a specific case of the general linkages between development and the environment. The concept of sustainable development aims to integrate environmental issues into development notions. As defined by the Brundtland Commission in 1987, sustainable development is "development that meets the needs of the present without compromising the ability of future generations to meet their own needs." The report of the Commission, *Our Common Future* (UN World Commission on Environment and Development 1987), emphasized the needs of the poor and proposed that poverty alleviation (as well as gender equity and wealth distribution) is a crucial strategy for environmental conservation. Recognition of the links among environment, development and poverty can be found in Agenda 21 of the 1992 United Nations Conference on Environment and Development, as well as in the texts of the conventions on climate change and biodiversity that were initiated at the Conference.

However, merely recognizing that linkages exist does not identify easy ways forward. The Brundtland Commission focused on population, food security, loss of biodiversity, energy, industry and human settlements and concluded that all of these were connected and "cannot be treated in isolation one from another" (UN World Commission on Environment and Development 1987: 27). However, action in the real world is by necessity often unconnected, as well-focused interventions tend to be much more effective than comprehensive, holistic programmes. It is thus no surprise that since 1992 (when actions to prevent climate change and loss of biodiversity began to take shape), many evaluations have highlighted the successes of isolated rather than holistic actions. For example, after a decade of activities to promote protected areas in order to provide wild species a refuge of at least 10% of the earth's surface (as agreed on in the Convention on Biological Diversity), critics increasingly voiced concerns that environmentalists aimed to achieve this by focusing on conservation only; banning humanity, and especially poor local communities and indigenous people, from protected areas. The goal of reaching 10% of the earth's surface as protected areas has been achieved; however, many protected areas in the world have not yet solved the puzzle of how local people can help maintain the area and benefit through higher incomes and better livelihood opportunities. Yet a strong involvement of local communities and indigenous people is now conceptually integrated into more recent perspectives on how protected areas should be managed.

In development policies and interventions, the linkages among the social, economic and environmental domains were mainly recognized through lip service. For example, although most countries and donors started policies and programmes on renewable energy (e.g. by promoting solar, wind and other forms of clean energy), their other policies and programmes often did not take into account how "regular" development investments would undermine gains made in the environmentally oriented programmes. In international discussions, recipient countries often voiced concerns that developed countries had depleted their own natural resources in order to achieve development and poverty reduction, and that developing countries had no choice but to go the same route – unless they could receive access to the latest technology, free of charge, or, as was stated at the 1992 Earth Summit, on "concessional terms."

One can conclude that though the linkages between the environment and poverty have been long recognized, the international community has been unable to sufficiently mainstream environmental issues into development and poverty alleviation policies and programmes. International organizations' evaluation units have published briefing documents that confirm this conclusion from many independent evaluations of these organizations. The first briefing document focuses on mainstreaming efforts to stop biodiversity loss (ECG 2010). It provides evaluative evidence that although efforts and interventions to sustain biodiversity are working and have had impacts, they do not yet reach the scale that would change overall trends. It states that development banks and United Nations institutions have not sufficiently integrated biodiversity issues into their development and poverty reduction strategies. The second briefing note (ECG 2011) pointed to a lack of integrating a climate change perspective into the support that development banks had given to the traditional energy sector in developing countries.

The concept of sustainable development with three foundational pillars – societal, economic and environmental – has received much recognition in speeches and statements, but not in implementation. UNDP, the main UN programme active on poverty reduction, and the GEF, the main global fund active on environmental protection, provide interesting examples in this regard. Both recognize the linkages between poverty and the environment in principle. However, both encountered difficulties to translate words into action. UNDP's evaluation of the poverty–environment nexus concluded that there is "substantial recognition" in UNDP of the linkages, but that "cooperation across sectors" has not materialized (UNDP 2010). Similarly, the GEF has focused on the achievements of global environmental benefits without paying too much attention to development or poverty at first. The evaluation of the role of local benefits in achieving global environmental benefits noted that GEF-funded projects tended to focus on the global benefits in the expectation that other funders (e.g. governments, other donors) would take care of the local benefits. Lack of coordination and integration then led to interventions that were less effective on both local and global benefits (GEF EO 2006: 7). Both evaluations led the way in putting the linkage between development, poverty reduction and the environment back on the organizations' agendas. What general lessons can be learned from these evaluations on linkages between environment and poverty? An important issue to explore is the geographical scope of the public nature of alleviating poverty and ensuring environmental services, from local to national, to regional and global.

Local, national, regional and global public goods

Much of the discourse on public goods, the role of governments and the efficiency of markets considers what should happen within one country.[7] However, many market externalities are of a transboundary nature. For example, greenhouse gases transcend political boundaries and will influence the global climate, not a local microclimate. Similarly, benefits from local reductions in greenhouse gas emissions will accrue globally. The globalization of the world, and especially its economy, is of course a thoroughly discussed phenomenon and opinions differ wildly on whether or not it is beneficial. However, the transboundary costs of markets are a fact, and many local actions have global consequences, just as global action has local consequences. The linkage between environment and poverty in terms of public goods can be seen to range from global environmental issues to local poverty issues: global issues such as climate change can have its worst impact on the poor, who barely have the resources to adapt to changed circumstances, whereas local actions that deplete scarce resources may have global implications. A wide range of possible linkages between nations, regions, local and national issues can also be discerned.

The lack of mainstreaming noted in the previous section has also affected how geographical scale was addressed. This has been uncovered most clearly in GEF policies and interventions. Recognizing that developing nations did not have the financial resources to adopt alternative or modern technologies, the Earth Summit mandated that GEF provide funding for "agreed incremental costs" – the additional costs associated with transforming a project with local or national benefits into a project with global environmental benefits. The oft-used example is an investment in a power plant. A country considers whether to invest US$750 million in a new coal power plant or $800 million in a geothermal plant. The $50 million difference is the incremental costs that the country would incur to change its plans and adopt the more expensive alternative. This alternative, which would emit considerably lower greenhouse gases, would have huge global environmental benefits in terms of climate change mitigation and substantial local and regional benefits in terms of lower pollution, transportation and infrastructure costs (and as noted earlier, these apparently localized benefits can also extend to the global scale in terms of regional stability and prosperity).

Furthermore, the United Nations Framework Convention on Climate Change also recognizes the differentiated responsibilities of groups of countries. This refers to developed countries' history of greenhouse gas emissions. This historic responsibility for starting the build-up of CO_2 in the atmosphere also calls for support from developed to developing countries in order to enable them to adopt more environmentally friendly technologies.

This focus on incremental cost funding led to GEF treating local and global benefits separately. Because incremental costs are related to global benefits, local benefits tended to be left to others. Depending on the project, these others could be local governments, executing agencies or consultancy firms. GEF wanted to be sure that the global benefits were generated, and even in projects where local benefits were recognized as an essential means to achieve global benefits, the focus in management and reporting tended to be on the global issues, as noted in the major evaluation undertaken by the GEF Evaluation Office: *The Role of Local Benefits in Global Environmental Programs* (GEF EO 2006). The evaluation started from the perspective that local benefits included "outcomes that, directly or indirectly, have positive impacts upon people and ecosystems within or adjacent to project areas and that provide gains, present and future, in the livelihoods of communities and to the integrity of ecosystems." It noted that GEF partners recognized the importance of these benefits in principle, but tended to leave them to co-funders and national and local authorities and organizations so that the GEF partners could concentrate on achieving the global benefits. One can see the repeat in a different form (noted in the evaluation's section on mainstreaming) of the lack of a holistic approach and the focus on a more pragmatic ambition to get something done which would more directly achieve global benefits. As a consequence, trade-offs between local and global benefits were often not incorporated into project design and management, which led to lower achievements on both local and global benefits.

From trade-offs to win–win options

The *Role of Local Benefits* noted that many GEF projects were approached from a firm belief in win–win options and that often trade-offs between poverty/local development and the environment had to be negotiated – but projects did not accommodate these trade-offs, because they were supposed to support win–win solutions. The study found that there are winners and losers in almost all interventions and that solutions promoting sustainable environmental trends had to be negotiated in the majority of cases. This would involve compromises – in which some lower *local* benefits would achieve some higher *global* benefits (or alternatively, some lower *global* benefits would ensure higher *local* benefits) – that would sustain these benefits. Interventions that aimed for higher global benefits at the detriment of lower local benefits tended to be unsustainable over the long term. In contrast, interventions that accepted lower global benefits but achieved higher local benefits tended to ensure their sustainability.

This can perhaps best be illustrated with findings from the support of the GEF for protected areas (see GEF EO 2006: 61–63). The majority of protected areas are located in rural and isolated areas with low levels of development and high marginalization and often have a higher incidence of indigenous peoples. The resources from protected areas often provide a safety net for the poor, and the poor (and more specifically the indigenous communities) often have the knowledge about natural resource access and use in the protected area concerned. This understanding of the linkage between poverty issues and conservation is pertinent to the design and implementation of support for protected areas. Socio-economic studies have repeatedly demonstrated that the poor bear most of the direct local costs of access restrictions stemming from newly created protected areas (or areas where protections were increased). However, *The Role of Local Benefits* (GEF EO 2006) found that in 27 GEF projects supporting protected areas, the poor and poverty issues were not addressed consistently and were not effectively incorporated.

One strategy to ensure higher incomes for local communities was to focus on opportunities for ecotourism. Theoretically, this would create tourism income and provide local communities with a strong incentive to maintain an ecosystem that would attract ecotourists – if there is no biodiversity hot spot to observe, ecotourism will fail. However, *The Role of Local Benefits* (GEF EO 2006) found that ecotourism tended to fail in countries that lacked a generalized tourism infrastructure, where entering the country was bureaucratic and costly, and where hotels, roads and transportation did not encourage tourists to visit the country. In these countries, ecotourism also raised insufficient interest from the potential clientele in developed and neighbouring countries. But even in countries where ecotourism was successful, it often did not lead to increased income for local or indigenous communities, as it turned out to be difficult to involve them in income-generating tourist activities. One often noted problem was the lack of language capacities, which entailed a reliance on interpreters to ensure communication between local guides and tourists.

Most importantly, when the anticipated win–win solution of higher income and better management of the protected area did not materialize, many projects did not include mechanisms to negotiate a trade-off (e.g. such trade-offs could have included direct compensation to local communities for reduced natural resource use). As a result, short-term achievements in global environmental benefits were undermined in the long term because impoverished communities returned to increased natural resource use to survive.

However, the negative spiral of increased natural resource use observed in many poor and overpopulated areas can increase the possibility for win–win solutions. Increasingly, communities are reaching the limits of their local natural resources. In Samoa, for example, fishing was becoming less rewarding because destructive fishing techniques (which also destroyed the habitat in which fish stock could restore) have resulted in fewer adult fish and fewer varieties as well. Through the GEF Small Grants Programme, local communities were supported in preserving the coral reefs. A community would adopt a specific area of the reef as a marine protected area. This area would then regenerate and start producing ample fish again, leading to fish migrating to neighbouring areas that were open for fishing. The catches sold well at the local market, leading to interest from other communities – and in time adoption of similar restrictions. In a relatively short time, sustainability, catches and income increased. When the GEF Evaluation Office evaluated the GEF support in Samoa in 2007, 50 communities had adopted these new practices (GEF EO 2008a: 5). This kind of win–win intervention is increasingly becoming possible as local environments become further degraded and stop providing essential eco-services to local communities. Where such eco-services are of global significance, there is a strong positive linkage between local and global benefits and between global and local public goods. This interconnectedness has been incorporated in the Sustainable Development Goals and should thus be taken up in evaluations that are done from the perspective of the SDGs.

Conclusions for evaluators

How can evaluators help identify the linkages between poverty and the environment in a way that will bring forward pragmatic solutions to local and global problems? Evaluators can conclude that the fragmented, often isolated and pragmatically focused nature of international organizations' and national governments' strategies, policies and interventions calls for a broader contextualization, which has been reinforced through the call for such a broader contextualization in the SDGs. Environmental evaluations need to take social and economic contexts into account in order to ensure that they achieve better understanding of the sustainability of environmental gains. Evaluations of social and economic programmes need to better include the environmental context and identify how eco-services are supporting (or undermining) achievements in social and economic development. This is particularly important for the situation of the poor, of gender issues and of the position and role of indigenous people.

Further, within these contexts environmental evaluators need to pay attention to local and national public goods that would support rather than deplete environmental goods. Social and economic evaluators need to identify environmental issues of global significance. This may involve a geographic scope (from local to national to regional to global), and/or a time scope (from an immediate significance to a time horizon of decades).

These call for further strengthening two directions in evaluation. First, evaluations need to look beyond the narrow context of the intervention, programme or policy being evaluated. Second, both the time horizon and the geographical scope of evaluations need to be enlarged. No new evaluation criteria are needed – what is called for is a shift in how some of these criteria are placed in a logframe, theory of change or logic of interventions perspective. Evaluation criteria such as relevance, efficiency and effectiveness describe relationships: relationships between inputs and outputs (efficiency), between outputs and outcomes (effectiveness) and between outcomes and longer term impact (relevance; see Figure 2.1). Elsewhere I have argued for a shift of some of these criteria to later stages in the theory of change (van den Berg 2011), and I present an overview of the positioning of these criteria

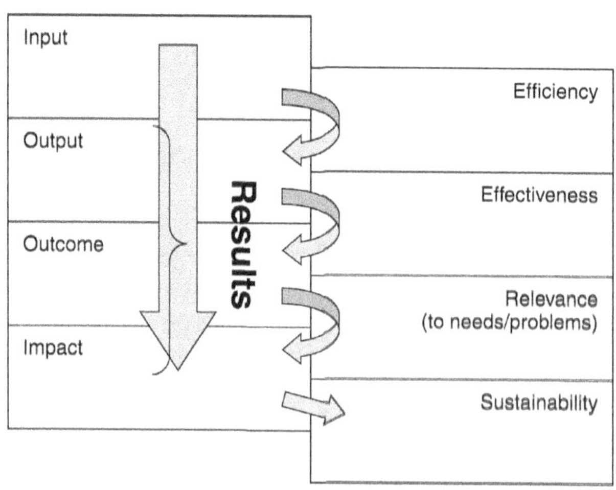

FIGURE 2.1 Evaluation Criteria

as they make most sense in the current challenges that we face. Furthermore, I relate these proposals to the revised version of the evaluation criteria as published by the OECD in December 2019 (OECD/DAC 2019). These issues are further explored in the following sections.

From ex ante to ex post "relevance"

Relevance was defined in the 2002 version of the Organisation for Economic Co-operation and Development (OECD) Development Assistance Committee (DAC) glossary of evaluation terms as "the extent to which the objectives of a development intervention are consistent with beneficiaries" requirements, country needs, global priorities and partners' and donors' policies (OECD/DAC 2002: 32). As I have argued elsewhere,[8] this is a retrospective ex ante assessment, because it focuses on the objectives of the intervention rather than the outcomes or the impact. My plea was to shift the relevance criterion to an ex post analysis. I also noted that this was in line with a growing share of evaluation practice (van den Berg 2011). The revised OECD criterion on relevance recognizes an ex post perspective and is thus a move in the right direction (OECD 2019: 7).

This move towards judging ex post relevance is especially important in cases where contextual factors are paramount and where the aim is for longer term impact. For example,[9] a single mother in a remote village in Western Africa received training to make soap bars that she could then sell at the local market so that she earns sufficient money to take care of herself and her child. She also received a small loan to get started. Five years later, an evaluator comes to the village. The evaluator concludes that the intervention was relevant, because it addressed the woman's livelihood. The evaluator also concludes that the intervention was effective, because the woman succeeded in making and selling soap bars. On impact, she notes that the woman now is independent and can take care of herself, whereas a comparable woman in a neighbouring village who did not receive the training has become dependent on her family.

In a relatively stable environment, this may be sufficient. In a more dynamic environment, it may not. For example, assume that the country is going through a process of transformation, that a new middle class is emerging and that recently the first supermarket opened its doors in the village. Suddenly, the simple bars of soap that our heroine offers on the local market are not that attractive anymore. She may have the advantage of regular customers, and she may be able to offer cheaper soaps than the more glamorous brands in the supermarket. However, in the end she will not be able to compete against cheap, mass-produced bars of soap – her livelihood is in danger. An evaluator returning to the village after 10 years may conclude that the intervention was not so relevant after all as the solution to the woman's livelihood turned out to be temporary.

Furthermore, the value of money may change as well. Ravi Kanbur (2001) called attention to the purchasing power of money and the potentially dramatic consequences for the poor. If they have a slight increase in earnings, but food and essentials become more expensive, they may have an increased income but be unable to buy sufficient food. If the emergence of a new middle class sees a parallel increase in inflation, our soap-making woman may continue to sell in her niche of the market but she may find buying essentials for her family increasingly problematic – her income will not rise in accordance with the prices of other goods.

If these contextual factors are taken into account, our evaluator may conclude that the project was very effective, but that its impact is in danger of disappearing, not so much because the intervention did not work, but because the intervention is no longer as relevant. With the benefit of the hindsight, the evaluator may conclude that it would have been more relevant to teach the woman how to become a successful entrepreneur, rather than a producer of soap bars.

Consider a poverty-focused intervention that takes the environment into account.[10] In Kenya, a smallholder farmer and his wife manage to feed their family but lack the necessary monies to send their children to school. Agricultural researchers arrive at their farm and provide a diagnosis: their farm is biodiversity poor and will probably not be productive in the long run. They offer recommendations on how to make the farm more sustainable by introducing more variety and improved farming practices. The researchers have a proposal: they will provide – free of charge – new varieties of plants and fruit trees and will advise on farming practices such as intercropping and water catchments, provided that the husband and wife test these new varieties and practices on the farm. They agree, and in just a few years, they manage to improve both the quantity and the quality of their crops. Some plants worked out and some did not. Some practices were beneficial; others did not work out as expected. In three years, they manage to treble their income and are now able to send their children to school.

Five years later, an evaluator arrives and finds that the intervention was very relevant in its objectives, because the poverty was alleviated through increased income that was based on improving farm practices. Further, the environment was served as well: biodiversity at the farm level was increased and the farm is more sustainable, less susceptible to diseases and crop failure. Both economically and environmentally, the farm had become sustainable. The evaluator leaves satisfied, observing a tangible win–win situation in which poverty was significantly reduced and the environment was improved.

However, if the evaluator took the broader context into account, the picture would perhaps not be so rosy. The variety of mango introduced on the farm was very successful: easy to grow, better tasting and more resistant to drought. This has not escaped the attention of some entrepreneurial farmers. Several farmers with larger farms have introduced the same variety on a larger scale. After a while, the new mangoes are not only coming from our farmer husband/wife team, but also from the larger farms. These larger farms may aim for larger markets and distribute their mangoes to nearby cities. But some of their mangoes will compete with the mangoes of the husband/wife team, may thus reduce their income and may stop them trying to compete – and thus reduce biodiversity on their farm as well. The larger farms may eventually start exporting their mangoes to Europe (provided they can demonstrate that the mangos are disease free). If so, many smallholders may be bought out of their farms to create new, large-scale farms. Ultimately, the success of the larger farms may lead to uprooting of smallholders for an uncertain life in the city or as farm hands, more mono-cropping in the region and may ultimately reduce overall biodiversity.

These possible developments may undermine the very positive early assessment of the intervention. In themselves, they do not need to be bad. For example, exports may provide much-needed foreign exchange that will support the country's economic development, or reductions in biodiversity in areas that are better suited to monoculture farming and investments may be offset by gains in biodiversity in other areas. Increasing economic activities in cities may provide former smallholders with new opportunities for increased incomes and longer-term security. However, it is clear that the original intervention of providing some well-intentioned advice to smallholders could not take all of this into account at the start.

If the linkage between poverty and the environment is taken seriously, and if an intervention aims to address both through win–win solutions – or a reasonable trade-off that is agreed with stakeholders – relevance needs to become an ex post criterion in addition to an ex ante criterion. Evaluators should look at outcomes and impacts and assess whether the outcomes are relevant to the impacts that are meant to be achieved or whether that relevance is endangered through contextual factors or a dynamic in the social, economic or environmental domains.

The revised OECD criteria also take contextual factors into account in a new criterion: coherence, which focuses on "the compatibility of the intervention with other interventions in a country, sector or institution" (OECD 2019: 8). While this is certainly important and needs to be included in evaluations, this does not cover the developments that I just sketched: supermarkets reaching remote villages and offering competing products to local production, or a new variety of fruit being taken over by agro-industries and out-competing smallholder production. The focus of the DAC is very much on coherence of interventions, and while the strategies of a supermarket chain and an agro-industry could be described as "intervention" or at least "interventionist," they are not part of efforts of a society or economy to "harmonise" and "co-ordinate" efforts, but rather of competition on markets and market development. A full ex post assessment of relevance will take these into account, whereas an assessment of coherence may or may not capture it.

From impact as relationship to impact as final goal

The Development Assistance Committee glossary of key terms in evaluation and results-based management defined impacts as "positive and negative, primary and secondary long-term effects produced by a development intervention, directly or indirectly, intended or unintended" (OECD/DAC 2002). This is not defined as a relationship, but as a kind of final state or a snapshot of effects a long time after the intervention terminated. However, in much of the current debate on aid effectiveness, "impact" is used to denote a scientific proof of a *causal* relationship between input, output and outcomes. This is evaluated in so-called impact evaluations, which seek to assess the changes brought about by an intervention (the impacts) by comparing the observed result with a "counterfactual" (the result likely to have been observed without the intervention). If the counterfactual is carefully specified and empirically grounded, then the difference between results observed and the counterfactual can reasonably be attributed to the intervention itself, and not to extraneous factors. Ideally, this counterfactual should be built into the design of the project and observed during its implementation. This kind of evaluation and what it studies could be referred to as "direct impact" evaluations.

If evaluations need to address the complex interrelationships between poverty and the environment over a longer period after the project has ended, they will need to focus on the broad processes of change in which the intervention was one of many factors. These evaluations tend to focus on contribution analysis rather than counterfactual analysis and are ideally undertaken several years after the intervention has stopped in order to assess whether the processes of change that the intervention started have been replicated, scaled up or have catalysed trends in society or the economy. Provided that the intervention's contributions can be demonstrated, these evaluations tend to provide crucial information on the intervention's relevance, that is, if they really lead to longer-term processes of change or trends that are solving the problems. The focus of these evaluations could be referred to as "final or ultimate impact."

In my speech to the International Development Evaluation Association in 2010 (van den Berg 2011), I proposed to make a clear distinction between "direct" and "final" impact issues, because both practices bring us benefits and the relevance of interventions for solving problems in society, the economy and the environment needs to be found at the final or ultimate impact level. We need to be able to refer to "impact" at the highest level in our results chain, also because this conforms to ordinary usage of the term (e.g. in public debates about whether "aid had any impact on Africa"). It would help us take into account the time horizon that is necessary for a sustainable interaction between the social, economic and environmental domains.

The revised OECD criteria follow my argumentation to a large extent, by focusing on "The extent to which the intervention has generated or is expected to generate significant positive or negative, intended or unintended, higher-level effects" (OECD: 11). The OECD does not see the need for a recognition of direct impact, as I argued, as they note that "valid attribution is embedded in all criteria". While I applaud this perspective, it is a battle with the impact evaluation community that is not yet won.

From sustainability to adaptability

As an evaluation criterion, sustainability can be a frustrating concept. DAC defined it as "the continuation of benefits from a development intervention after major development assistance has been completed. The probability of continued long-term benefits. The resilience to risk of the net benefit flows over time" (OECD/

DAC 2002: 8). This definition includes two approaches that would allow us to say a bit more about sustainability: assessing the probability that benefits would continue and assessing the risks to continued benefits. The revised OECD criterion on sustainability strengthens this perspective and places this within a systems perspective as an improved and transformed balance between "financial, economic, social, environmental and institutional capacities of the systems needed to sustain net benefits over time" (OECD 2019: 12). While I applaud the direction this takes, I continue to argue that we need to explore this further in terms of probabilities and risks.

A thoughtful example of a well-developed approach to the probability of sustainability can be found in the Swedish International Development Cooperation Agency (SIDA) evaluation manual *Looking Back, Moving Forward*. The manual describes factors that may influence sustainability and presents key questions that could be asked to ascertain whether the benefits of the intervention under evaluation have the "potential" to be sustained in future (SIDA 2004: 35–37). Key questions include a focus on whether the intervention is in line with local priorities, culture and social conditions; whether there is institutional and financial continuity; and whether the intervention is compatible with a sustained use of natural resources. It points out that each evaluation of sustainability of an intervention would have its own set of questions, specific to the context of the intervention.

GEF follows the risk approach to sustainability. In its guidelines for terminal evaluations of GEF-funded projects, it identifies five areas of risk that need to be explored: financial risks, socio-political risks, risks to the institutional framework and governance risks and last – but not least – environmental risks (GEF EO 2008b). In principle, these risks should cover long-term developments in all three pillars of sustainable development. This risk approach can help us identify what is of local or global significance, where a public good perspective is needed to reduce risks and what can be done to ensure longer-term sustainability.

However, climate change is making it increasingly difficult to correctly identify environmental risks. Concurrently with the ongoing assault of climate change (leading to, among other things, higher temperatures, greater variability in weather and more extreme events), predictability has become elusive. Reduced local predictability leads to higher levels of risk, as temperatures fluctuate more than before, water availability becomes more seasonable and extreme weather events become more severe and frequent. These risks need to be taken into account and have led to calls for climate change adaptation.

The best current approaches to climate change adaptation, both in specific interventions focused on adaptation itself and in regular mainstream development or in poverty alleviation strategies, are risk-based and aim to reduce the risks to society and economies from climate change. This risk reduction is very similar to the risk approach to sustainability assessments. My contention is that this kind of risk approach is appropriate for sustainable development, including a public goods approach to poverty and the environment.

It also recognizes the unpredictability of the future. Achieving a sustainable balance among civil society, the economy and the environment will require constant adaptation to the three pillars' specific requirements. Adaptation calls for adaptive management, and in the final analysis, for adaptive evaluation: one that recognizes the sudden shifts in the different domains and uses those as a basis to formulate sustainability issues, rather than relying on the goals and perspectives that existed at the outset of a strategy or intervention, whether it targeted poverty or the environment. Finally, when we turn sustainability into an adaptation issue, we are able to take the public goods perspective into account when looking at what can be solved by markets and private initiatives versus a perspective in which governments and international organizations are essential to ensuring a sustainable future.

Notes

1 Paris Agreement under the United Nations Framework Convention on Climate Change, drafted in December 2015 in Paris and signed on 22 April 2016 in New York, USA.
2 United Nations General Assembly, Resolution adopted by the General Assembly on 25 September 2015, A/Res/70/1.
3 State of the Union address, 1988, available at http://janda.org/politxts/State%20of%20 Union%20Addresses/1981-1988%20Reagan/rwr88.html.
4 This section is based on van den Berg (2011).
5 Interview with Nicholas Stern in *The Guardian*, Thursday, 29 November 2007, available at guardian.co.uk.
6 And when confronted with criticism of his calculations, Stern corrected them – upwards. See D. Adam, 'I underestimated the threat, says Stern', *The Guardian* (London), 18 April 2008, https://www.theguardian.com/environment/2008/apr/18/climatechange.carbonemissions, accessed 13 August 2020.
7 This section is adapted from van den Berg (2011).
8 Speech to the IDEAS conference in Amman, Jordan, in April 2011. Speech available at https://player.vimeo.com/video/22901848.
9 This example is derived from a rural development IFAD project I visited in 2001.
10 This example is derived from a 2007 visit to Kenya to a UNEP-implemented GEF-funded project.

References

Collier, P., *The bottom billion: Why the poorest countries are failing and what can be done about it*, Oxford, Oxford University Press, 2007.

Collier, P., *The plundered planet: Why we must – and how we can – manage nature for global prosperity*, Oxford, Oxford University Press, 2010.

Evaluation Cooperation Group (ECG), *Ensuring biodiversity in a sustainable future*: Lessons from evaluations', Briefing note, 2010.

ECG, *Overcoming barriers to energy efficiency: New evidence from independent evaluation*', Briefing note, Evaluation Cooperation Group, 2011.

Feinstein, O., *Dynamic evaluation for transformational change, in: van den Berg, R.D., Magro, C., Salinas Mulder, S., Evaluation for transformational change: Opportunities and challenges for the sustainable development goals*, Exeter, IDEAS, 2019, 17–32.

Galbraith, K.J., *Economics and the public purpose*, New York, Houghton Mifflin, 1973.

Global Environment Facility (GEF) Evaluation Office (EO), *The role of local benefits in global environmental programs*, Washington, DC, 2006.

GEF EO, *GEF country portfolio evaluation: Samoa (1992–2007)*, Washington, DC, Global Environment Facility Evaluation Office, 2008a.
GEF EO, '*Guidelines for GEF agencies in conducting terminal evaluations*', Washington, DC, Global Environment Facility Evaluation Office, 2008b.
Kanbur, R., 'Economic policy, distribution and poverty: The nature of disagreements', *World Development*, 29(6): 1083–1094, 2001.
Kaul, I., I. Grunberg and M.A. Stern, eds., *Global public goods: International cooperation in the 21st century*, New York, Oxford University Press, 1999.
Kaul, I. and R. U. Mendoza, 'Advancing the concept of public goods', in: *Global public goods: International cooperation in the 21st century*, New York, Oxford University Press, 1999.
Mazzucato, M., The Value of Everything. *Making and taking in the global economy*. S.l., Penguin ed., 2019.
Millennium Ecosystems Assessment, *Ecosystems and human well-being: Synthesis*, Washington, DC, Island Press, 2005.
Organisation for Economic Co-operation and Development (OECD)/Development Assistance Committee (DAC), '*Glossary of key terms in evaluation and results based management*', Paris, 2002.
OECD/DAC Network on Development Evaluation, *Better Criteria for Better Evaluation: Revised Evaluation Criteria, Definitions and Principles for Use*, Paris, OECD, 2019.
Raworth, K., *Doughnut Economics: Seven ways to think like a 21st-century economist*, London, Random House, 2017
Rostow, W.W., *The stages of economic growth: A non-Communist manifesto*, Cambridge, Cambridge University Press, 1960.
Sachs, J., Schmidt-Traub, G., Kroll, C., Lafortune, G., Fuller, G., *Sustainable development Report 2019*. New York, Bertelsmann Stiftung and Sustainable Development Solutions Network (SDSN), 2019.
Samuelson, P.A., 'The pure theory of public expenditure', *Review of Economics and Statistics*, 36(4): 387–389, 1954.
SIDA, *Looking back moving forward: SIDA evaluation manual*, Stockholm, Swedish International Development Cooperation Agency, 2004.
UNDP, 'Evaluation of UNDP contribution to environmental management for poverty reduction: The Poverty-Environment Nexus', New York, United Nations Development Programme Evaluation Office, 2010.
UN World Commission on Environment and Development, *Our Common Future*, Oxford, Oxford University Press, 1987.
van den Berg, R.D., 'Evaluation in the context of global public goods', *Evaluation*, 17: 405–415, 2011.

3

EVALUATION AT THE NEXUS

Evaluating sustainable development in the 2020s

Andy Rowe

Sustainability-ready evaluation

In the earlier chapter, sustainable development was described as a mode of development in which present needs are met without compromising future generations' ability to meet their own needs (World Commission on Environment and Development 1987). Sustainable development depends on recognising and incorporating into development strategies the connectivity and mutual interdependence of natural, economic, political and cultural systems. There is tension in balancing contributions from – and returns to – human and natural systems. However, when appropriately balanced, these positions form the nexus where there is the possibility that the needs of the present can be met without compromising the future of either human or natural systems. Unfortunately, human and natural system interests too often stand opposed to each other (or outright ignore each other), a situation that is detrimental to programming and evaluation. There also seems to be an opportunistic approach to incorporating sustainability into evaluation where climate and sustainability are recognised as central issues, but this is translated into arguments why a sector or population segment that is strongly affected requires additional priority and resources. In fact the interventions are likely to face diminishing resources and pressures to address public policy goals (Williams 2019) as well as the necessity of adapting their approaches to reduce the environmental footprint.

I posit that evaluation of sustainability and of natural resource interventions necessarily occurs where human and natural systems connect, which I have characterised as a two-system evaluand (Rowe 2012) and which Juha Uitto terms the nexus (United Nations Development Programme - Evaluation 2010). The call *All Hands on Deck – Everyone to the Nexus* adopts Uitto's approach pointing to the nexus where both human and natural systems are present, which, for sustainable development is everywhere. Mainstreaming sustainability means that all interventions are nexus interventions, and thus all evaluations are potentially addressing a two-system evaluand. Learning and adapting from practice is an important feature of evaluation, and especially for development evaluation, meaning that evaluation will learn from efforts to mainstream sustainability at the nexus and evaluation capacity will move towards the visions of CHANS (Ostrom 1990; Liu 2007) and Sustainability Science (Clark and Dickson 2003; Kates 2011) to more fully understand and evaluate sustainability.

Theory of Change for sustainability-ready evaluation

While evaluation has been very slow to recognise and respond to extinction it has begun to do so largely, I suggest, because the messages from the broader context are reaching evaluators and raising questions of the relevance of the field, as well as providing new opportunities. This is the core of the underlying mechanisms in the Theory of Change[2] for sustainability-ready evaluation – evaluation will be open to everyone and incorporate sustainability. Members of the constituent elements in the field of evaluation – commissioners, practitioners, researchers and evaluation organisations, stakeholder and beneficiary groups – are daily receiving the message of the urgency for humans to adapt, reduce our footprint and transform our relationship to the natural system. This also expands present opportunities for evaluation. This barrage of messaging and recognition of reality will bring evaluation to nexus, much more than evaluation writing, conceptual development or conference presentations, and is the *initiating mechanism of change* bringing evaluation to sustainability. Moreover, the urgency of the task and the fact that evaluation is predominantly a practice-based undertaking means that rapid and practical change is needed to effectively mainstream evaluation. That means that in addition to external (to evaluation) messages and knowledge precipitating and demanding change, evaluation practice and reflection from practice is the key *operational mechanism of change* that will bring the field to effectively mainstream sustainability and start to usefully contribute to slowing the pace of extinction through learning and improving interventions that focus on both systems by operating at the nexus and beyond that towards CHANS (Basurto 2009).

Between the *initiating* mechanisms for mainstreaming sustainability provided by external messages and the *operational* mechanism of practice-based experimentation and learning lies the capacities of evaluation practice and of practitioners and the capacities of the essential co-generators of the knowledges required for sustainability-ready evaluation coming from other sciences. A recent stocktaking by the Canadian Evaluation Society (CES) of the readiness of evaluation to mainstream sustainability and address the nexus reveals a significant gap in our practice and intellectual resources. Thus between the two key mechanisms of change towards sustainability mainstreaming where external forces and knowledge are the *initiating* mechanism generating pressure to mainstream sustainability, and the *operational* mechanism of evaluation practice and learning in commissioning and executing evaluations at the nexus lies the question whether we can do it – can evaluation as a field actually mainstream sustainability?

I have argued elsewhere that the challenges in evaluating at the nexus are not technical, but political and socially determined by the worldviews of evaluation, programmes and organisations (Rowe 2019). Sufficient technical capacities and use-encouraging approaches to evaluate at the nexus can be found in existing evaluation, social science and biophysical science and evaluations of interventions applying biophysical sciences. This is illustrated by the use of mixed methods for evaluating at the nexus (Garcia and Zazueta 2015) experimental designs to evaluate natural system matters such as conservation (Ferraro 2006; Mascia 2017), Systematic Reviews for natural resources and conservation (Pullin and Stewart 2006) and efforts to link conservation monitoring and assessment to evaluation (Mascia et al. 2014). And the testimonies of Canadian evaluators who work internationally collected as part of the CES Stocktaking suggest that development evaluation could be point of more consistently addressing both human and natural systems in evaluation.

And very importantly evaluation is awakening to Indigenous approaches to evaluative thinking and assessment that are already at nexus and often realise CHANS (Bowman-Farrell 2018; Gilio-Whitaker 2019).

There can be little doubt that the external evidence from reports such as produced by the Intergovernmental Panel on Climate Change (IPCC) and the International Resource Panel (IRP) and the obvious reality of increasing frequency and intensity of storms, drought, terrestrial and marine temperature rise, flooding and other climatic events and their obvious impacts for development contributed to moving from the Millennium Development Goals (MDGs) to the Sustainable Development Goals (SDGs). As did sustainability-linked convenings such as the Conference of the Parties (COPs), reality from UN member states, pressures and evidence mobilisation from NGOs and Indigenous organisations and other contributors. However as is frequently the case the early celebration of the SDGs reflected relief that the various mandates of UN organisations were "reauthorised" and structured in such a way as to enable continued siloed approaches through a large number of individual SDGs that need not be connected, and without requirement to connect to natural system SDGs (Reid et al. 2017). This has changed and discourse and practices are now much closer to or already at the nexus (GEF Scientific and Technical Advisory Panel 2018). While this is affirming of the *influencing mechanism* in the ToC for sustainability-ready evaluation, it raises the matter of the feasibility of the *operational mechanism of change*. And here emerging practice also confirms that addressing this is a political rather than a technical challenge. As the influencing mechanism gains strength – as organisations, programmes and evaluation functions recognise and incorporate sustainability – they are finding that the necessary capacities and intellectual infrastructure do indeed already exist though not just in evaluation. A mix of methods and sciences will enable evaluation to function reasonably well at the nexus. One important observation from the CES stocktaking is that nexus evaluation requires teams that include relevant knowledge of each system and capacities to work together (Field 2019).

Is evaluation ready for sustainability?

To understand how it can address sustainability as one of three thematic principles for evaluation in its Strategic Plan, the CES undertook a stocktaking of the readiness of evaluation in Canada to mainstream sustainability – the operational mechanism of change.[3] The underlying premise of the stocktaking is that evaluation has strong capacity and activity for the human system, and that for nexus capacity and actions are needed for both systems. Thus the focus was on nexus and evaluation of natural systems. The stocktaking was conducted by four leading Canadian evaluation firms[4] and is indicative rather than definitive. However it should be noted that the CES is the oldest of national evaluation associations, that evaluation is a systematic aspect of governance at the federal level in Canada with the National Evaluation Policy and evaluation units in every department, that CES likely has the highest per capital membership of any evaluation association and that it has actively supported the development of evaluation globally such as through being the organisational home to the International Organization for Cooperation in Evolution (IOCE). Considering the strength of evaluation in Canada the sustainability stocktaking might be indicative of evaluation in general. The CES stocktaking covered federal evaluations, philanthropic/non-governmental/First Nations evaluations, Canada-based international evaluators and the intellectual infrastructure.

These results of the CES sustainability stocktaking are consistent with observations included in the first version of this chapter (Rowe 2014) and reinforce the observation that evaluation only rarely considers the natural system or sustainability in practice and in writing and training.

Some implications of ignoring sustainability and the natural system

One of the few evaluation publications addressing sustainability was the recent issue of New Directions in Evaluation published by the American Evaluation Association (Julnes, 2019). Using the illustration of an infrastructure project I illustrated how evaluation systematically ignores the natural system, and that, as a result, evaluation has a systematic positive bias, with the effect of reinforcing existing silos that separate the human and natural systems and that are very intervention-centric unconnected to the wider human (Chelimsky, 2012) or as the CES stocktaking demonstrates to the natural world. I further argued that any knowledge undertaking that systematically favours organisations that commission the inquiry through excluding considerations that would reflect less positively on the intervention (thereby creating positive bias and reinforcing silos) cannot be regarded as credible. Moreover continuing to ignore sustainability and natural systems at a time when these are obviously central to everyone everywhere does not auger well for evaluation being regarded as relevant. And things that are not relevant or credible generally have short shelf lives. This means that while evaluation does not itself have the necessary intellectual infrastructure to work at the nexus, it can do so by engaging other relevant knowledges, and has strong incentives to do this since to not do it threatens sustainability of the

TABLE 3.1 Observations from CES Sustainability-Ready Stocktaking

Federal Evaluations in Canada (2018): - *Sustainability and natural resource impacts are largely ignored in Canadian federal evaluations* - Sustainability is not addressed in a systematic or standardised way in federal evaluations in Canada. - Little guidance on how to evaluate sustainability. - Departments that are expected to contribute to environmental sustainability mostly do not consider natural system impacts. - Only Global Affairs Canada addresses sustainability as a cross cutting issue in programming and evaluations.	Intellectual infrastructure – North America 2017–19 - *Sustainability and natural resources do not have a presence in the North American evaluation intellectual infrastructure* - Only 4% of the articles in the four leading North American evaluation journals addressed natural resources or sustainability. - Roughly the same proportion of conference sessions (workshops, presentations and plenaries) addressed natural resources or sustainability. - Evaluation has little presence in schools of natural resources; natural resources and sustainability do not have a presence in evaluation programmes or departments in North America.
Philanthropic, NGO and First Nation evaluation - *Evaluations largely single system, emerging Indigenous evaluation focuses on nexus* - Conservation is primary focus for ENGOs, a few approach nexus, some apply evaluation or econometric methods to assess conservation impacts. - Philanthropic organisations with natural system portfolios evaluate within the programmatic area (e.g. conservation, climate, fisheries, protected areas), where the focus was human (e.g. fish harvesters) the focus is human system. - Emerging field of Indigenous evaluation is grounded in values that acknowledge and honour the interconnectedness of human and natural systems and there are nexus examples (e.g. in Canada, the Indigenous Circle of Experts and Indigenous Guardian programmes).	Canada-based international evaluators working in nexus interventions – 10 of 60 invited evaluators participated - *Employ mix of methods, choice influenced by institutional setting* - Participants from varied backgrounds (engineering, political science, economics, biology, and project management) work with international organisations in private and non-profit sectors. - Some projects directly related to environmental programming (e.g. clean energy, promotion of sustainability), others focused on the ecological footprint of programming. - Use a mix of methods: Non-profit sector places a strong emphasis on participatory methods, understanding local context and constraints, the private sector respondents identified the need for better and more in-depth analysis of big data.

evaluation field itself. This fails to recognise that absolute limits are being reached. To illustrate, recent work by the International Resources Panel (www.resourcepanel.org) has demonstrated that the planet does not have the material resources (such as aggregate and land for food production) to meet urban populations forecasted for 2050 with continued population increases and rates of urbanisation (Swilling, 2018).

This suggests that development evaluation that mainstreams sustainability would expect interventions to address and achieve concrete reductions in urban migration and assess their performance against these expectations.

This brings us to a further question – why are we like this? Why is our interest and capacity so impoverished for evaluating at the nexus, for including natural systems in evaluation? And based on that, the final question for this chapter is what do we have to do going forward to evaluate at the nexus which based on current accepted and emerging knowledge including Covid-19, considers what are the most important underlying elements of evaluation that need to change.

Key elements of evaluation at the nexus

Evaluation must change immediately and systematically to be able to work at the nexus and contribute to slowing extinction. The two top priorities are:

1. Value the natural system
2. Attend to critically important characteristics of the natural system and evaluation: connectivity, scales, and evaluation use

These are briefly described here. Value is used in the more general sense of merit, worth, value and significance and is the most fundamental change that faces evaluation in addressing sustainability. Addressing these in evaluation practice and thought will have challenges. Two important initiatives are underway to provide the necessary framing and guidance, Blue Marble Evaluation[5] and Footprint Evaluation.[6]

Value the natural system

Evaluation is not unique in according zero value to the natural system, this is endemic in considerable human decision making, especially those with European origins, and traceable to already held positions articulated in the Christian bible and is captured by the concept of dominion (Rowe 2018: pp. 28,40). Neoclassical economics firmly embraces dominion (Nadeau 2007). It is of course not universal, Indigenous concepts of stewardship differ totally and can be expressed as regarding the world as single system comprised of "humans and our non-human relatives"[7] with humans having stewardship responsibilities as one has towards relatives, instead of extraction privileges conveyed through ownership or access rights.

Industrialised nations began to value some elements of the natural system from self-interest when the connection between the natural and human systems was indisputably recognised as potentially harming humans such as the effect of pollution or pesticides (Carson 1962). This is the basis of the broad environmental regulatory framework around air and water, chemicals, and other contaminants.

Value is multi-dimensional: Economic, social, cultural, spiritual, traditional and above all political

Control or access to the natural system is at the core of much political struggle (The EU-UN Partnership on Land, Natural Resources and Conflict Prevention 2020), whether diamonds, fossil fuels, water, land and trees; the political dimension is also where differing positions on economic, social, traditional and cultural dimension are asserted.

At its core the economic dimension rests on access to essential aspects of the natural system through ownership or rights, and on the division of returns along the value chain. The prevailing position is that the economic should not be fettered, pursuit of the economic benefits benefit society broadly and economic growth is the priority thereby enabling improving social benefits. The extinction crisis clearly demonstrates the shortcomings of that argument.

- Some elements of the natural system have high status for their ascribed cultural attributes: certain reef species are harvested for important ceremonies and celebrations, rhino horn and elephant tusks, shark fins and seal penises are ascribed high values for perceived attributes such as aphrodisiacs. The value of ground rhinoceros horn in eastern medicinal markets is higher than world prices for gold, diamonds or cocaine (Menda 2011). Also the relative indifference of many tribal cultures to wild and wild-interbred-with-hatchery salmon reflecting stewardship responsibilities for all non-human relatives, compared to the adamant preference for wild salmon by (largely European origin) recreational anglers.
- Spiritual values are another important dimension. Allen Putney (Putney 2008) provides a useful description of the spiritual values of landscapes. Bears provide a good example of conflicting spiritual and cultural values: some male human populations value bear gall bladders highly as an aphrodisiac, some North American tribal and aboriginal nations consider bears to have great spiritual significance. And some people enjoy killing bears and pay significant amounts for access and assistance while others are dedicated to protecting them as important members of ecosystems and invest in their protection.[8]
- Traditional values are very important. Gilio-Whitaker (2019) has solidly demonstrated the environmental justice issue that the forced separation of North American Indigenous people from traditional lands has directly and measurably impaired physical and mental health.

Concepts and methods for valuing elements of the natural system are available with a solid underlying knowledge base and direct relationships from the one system to the other, for example with toxic materials in landfills near or on which children play or work extracting materials. The connection between exposure to the toxic materials of human populations and human health can be determined without much difficulty and connects directly to health knowledge of the likelihood of adverse health outcomes. Interactions that harm humans are accorded priority and can be investigated using the solid knowledge base.

Emerging threats such as current and recent pandemics also arise from the connections between human and natural systems where the connections are being intensified with deeper and deeper exploitation of the natural system by humans. These connections are less well known and are currently challenging to consider in an evaluation of say, road and settlement expansion enabling satisfaction of human preferences for traditional foods or improved access to wildmeat for subsistence. However evaluation using theory-based evaluation approaches can incorporate risks such as these into assessments of interventions that involved expanded penetration into landscapes and thereby correct the positive bias and silo-reinforcing contributions of evaluation.

When the causal and harmful pathways move in the opposite direction, efforts to assess effects have a weak knowledge base and operate in a contested political and cultural environment. For example, the impact of deforestation on climate through lost sequestration is now being incorporated into evaluations. However forest sciences are now able to provide a defensible but hard to grasp understanding of forests as systems involving importantly trees and fungi as well as other resident flora and fauna (Wohlleben 2016). The recent discovery of the largest organism on earth and its role in nutrition and communications in a hardwood forest is fascinating and instructive (Casselman 2007). As is understanding that trees function as sustainability-focused mutual assistance collectives. These contributions reflect a growing knowledge in the science of forests (and other natural domains) that shows interspecies connectivity and the collective interdependence of a forest as an ecosystem rather than as a collection of trees that can be individually cut without regard to the whole. It is illustrative of the scope that an evaluation involving forests (such as for roads or settlements or to create plantation agriculture) requires assessing the range of adverse impacts from cutting and the counterfactual benefit of preserving natural functioning forests from the perspective of carbon sequestration, water quality and flow management, cooling, integrated forest-farm smallholder production and so on. Such nature-based approaches to mitigating extinction are essential and reduce the need for generally less systematically effective human engineered solutions (Raymond 2017). And perhaps surprisingly what is catastrophic for one system can be beneficial for the other; human efforts to reduce the spread of Covid-19 have directly, promptly and strongly contributed to the environment (Uitto 2020).

To address sustainability evaluation must value natural systems from these different perspectives even if we cannot place a monetary value on them. This is akin to a list of non-monetised prioritised benefits in a cost–benefit analysis. This will prove messy and problematic to those seeking a single metric, such as return on investment that they can use to compare across different interventions. It will necessarily involve a struggle with extractive interests including those within the evaluation expanded economic extraction. However, not including the messy natural system values means that evaluation itself will continue to be a source of bias favouring the human system and extractive interests, reinforcing silos and advancing extinction.

Attend to core technical differences

There are critically important differences between natural and human systems that evaluation must embrace, requiring adaptation in commissioning and methods. Three of these are essential for evaluating sustainability:

- Evaluating sustainability requires recognition of the different temporal and spatial scales in natural and human systems, and in the units of account.
- Evaluating sustainability requires recognition of the connectivity within and between the two systems as well as the connectivity of interventions to public interest goals for the two systems.
- Incorporating sustainability in evaluation will be a radical change requiring enhanced attention by the evaluation to promote use.

Scales and units of account

There is not a lot of variation in human *temporal scales* which are importantly set by our relevant lifespans, electoral and programme and policy cycles. Evaluation is undertaken within human scales (e.g. under the National Evaluation Policy in Canada all programmes and policies must be evaluated at least once every five years). While human temporal scales can be complicated they are largely known and less wide ranging than found in the natural system where temporal scales range from centuries (e.g. trees, sea turtles, Greenland shark) to what seems to us as a few moments (e.g. Mayfly live for five minutes to one day, Cicada one day). To put this in perspective evaluation clearly recognises the importance of life stages of humans (e.g. infants, adolescents, adults and elders) but generally applies a binary temporal frame to the natural system (not yet ready or ready for harvest). Reproductive frequency is important in both systems, for example top masting bamboo reproduce every hundred years or so, important to both humans and animals such as giant panda whereas some insects flutter by at a pace closer to the blink of a human eye. Both masting bamboo and small short-lived insects are essential for the ecosystems within which they exist. Evaluation at the nexus needs to accommodate temporal scales that are relevant and sufficient for the species involved.

Spatial scales also differ. Human system structures and constructs, such as ownership or management and control conventions (e.g. fisheries management areas), spatially define human systems. In contrast, the spatial logic of natural systems is an ecosystem or connected ecosystems. Thus, for example, the natural range of a wolf crosses many different human-contrived natural resource management areas and structures, communities and often cultures. Sometimes, management structures are at odds with each other, such as protecting wolves and their habitat, on one hand, and managing grasslands leased to ranchers for cattle grazing, on the other. A significant portion of marine life is mobile and crosses regulatory and national boundaries, and with changing climatic conditions is now on the move (e.g. many fish stocks are moving towards the Poles due to ocean warming). Air and water might be regulated within human regulatory boundaries but their movements are not affected by these boundaries. In these and almost all ways the spatial boundaries of the human and natural system differ. It is akin to a multi-site evaluation where the specificities of each site need to be incorporated into the advance thinking about and commissioning, design, implementation and analysis (King and Lawrenz 2011).

Units of account. Humans are but one of a huge number of species. To understand the human system we consider one species with important traits (e.g. race, gender). Evaluation in the natural system at the nexus has multiple often highly connected species. Full consideration of natural system units of account likely exceeds current evaluation and social and natural sciences and is something that evaluation will need to "learn its way to" as we gain capacity to work closer to CHANS. However evaluating sustainability now requires us to start by mapping the affected and contributing units of account (species) and incorporate these into the evaluation as best we can. To briefly illustrate, reintroduction of wolves into northwestern US landscapes has had direct ecosystem side effects and has affected most fauna and considerable flora in multiple ecosystems.

Connect to natural and broader human systems

The problem of siloed or partitioned[9] programmes has been well documented and is widely accepted as problematic. Consider a fisheries development programme to improve food security and livelihoods designed without regard to sustainable levels, places and methods of extraction, or to the connectivity of the targeted populations to other marine life. The main development issues for fisheries in both industrialised and developing nations have been who gets access and who captures most from the value chain.

With partitioned governance we often lose the connectivity that binds and coordinates efforts in pursuit of large goals such as poverty reduction, biodiversity and ultimately sustainable development. To an ecologist, this sounds like a loss of landscape connectivity creating fragmented populations and resulting in an overall reduction in ecosystem function. Even if all the contributors to sustainable development are successful, including communities, individuals, different levels of government, multilateral agencies and non-governmental organisations, there is no assurance that such efforts will result in development that is sustainable. Partitions fragment the public policy agenda and constrain pursuit of the larger and more important goals (Rowe 2013).

Fragmentation presents a challenge for evaluation of sustainable development because programming tends to focus either one of the systems. Understandably, programme managers will resist efforts by evaluators to pursue the connections from the partitioned intervention they are evaluating to the other system. It is not uncommon for evaluators themselves to adopt a view that interventions should be evaluated against their intended and stated goals, with due regard for unintended effects; indeed, it is a near-official position enshrined in the programme evaluation standards adopted by many professional evaluation organisations (Yarbourough, Shulha, Hopkins and Caruthers 2011). But if sustainable development is to encompass both the natural and human systems per the Brundtland definition, then evaluation of sustainable development initiatives must always have an eye on both of the systems involved, that is, on both poverty reduction and environment. And where interventions ignore important connections to the other system or in their own system, it falls to the sustainable development evaluator to assess the implications for both human and natural system populations. This is an important way that evaluation can contribute to improving sustainable development interventions. Theories of change are the essential vehicle for articulating connectivity. Every evaluation should begin with an open exercise to develop a Theory of Change that is not bound by the formal limits of the reach of the programme and its accountability and maps and incorporates all that the intervention draws upon from both systems and all that it effects in both systems (Rowe 2018: 26–29).

Emphasise use

Far better an approximate answer to the right question, which is often vague, than the exact answer to the wrong question, which can always be made precise (Tukey 1962).

The importance of use and influence in evaluation has received considerable research attention and is the subject of a copious amount of evaluation writing (Henry and Mark 2003; Patton 2008; Johnson et al. 2009). Sustainable development, involving both natural and human systems, adds an additional element. This is because each system has a distinct knowledge domain – social sciences for human systems and natural and physical sciences for natural systems.

Often, the two applied knowledge domains are unfamiliar with and suspicious of each other's methods and practices. Managers from the natural sciences often find some social science methods in the evaluator's portfolio troubling. Likewise, social scientists are often frustrated by the unwillingness of natural scientists to address attribution and the extended and expensive natural science primary data collection methods. Inevitably, evaluation of sustainable development at the nexus will bring social and natural sciences together. For evaluation, these different knowledge domains mean there are likely to be differences deciding which questions are salient and agreeing on standards for legitimate and credible knowledge. The importance of multiple knowledge domains should be understood in the context that agreement on salience, legitimacy and credibility is a critical factor that affects prospects for the uses of science knowledge (Clark, Mitchell and Cash 2006).

Fortunately, there is solid practice and theory knowledge on collaborative decision making (Field 2019) and on use-inspired science research that aligns very well with the evaluation literature on use and influence. The key to both is focus on the knowledge process, not the knowledge product (evaluation report). Engaging decision makers and stakeholders in the evaluation process greatly enhances prospects that the evaluation will be more salient, legitimate and credible, thereby promoting use (Rowe and Lee 2013).

Use and influence are the vehicles by which evaluation contributes to improving interventions such as sustainable development. Engaging decision makers and stakeholders as well as other relevant sciences in the evaluation is how we can achieve use and influence. It also facilitates progress on the tricky attribution issue to achieve comparisons or other approaches to identifying the incremental contribution of the intervention.

Summary

Evaluation is finally starting to recognise that humans and our goals for human development, rights and security rest on our extraction from the natural system. Indeed sentient humans everywhere are increasingly aware of and concerned about the looming threat of extinction. Evaluators are sentient but have until recently ignored the natural system. This has created a systematic positive and silo reinforcing bias in evaluation and risks rendering evaluation irrelevant for the major issues of the day – extinction and the climate crisis.

As evaluation recognises and addresses its responsibilities to contribute to forestalling extinction it will need to mainstream sustainability meaning that all evaluation will need to start from the nexus with connected human and natural systems. This requires an evaluation capacity and functions that are ready for sustainability. Clearly, as described with the stocktaking of the CES, evaluation is not sustainability-ready. The pathway to evaluation that is sustainability-ready requires that all evaluation undertakings value the natural system and immediately recognise and address important differences between human and natural systems, scale, units of account and connectivity. The knowledge and methods exist in evaluation, social and biophysical sciences, the challenge is therefore not technical but political. It is political because the origins of evaluation and the social sciences on which evaluation rests are in the values and structures that are strongly founded on a claim that humans have dominion over all other things and that all value rests upon human effort. This claim of dominion extends to other, that is, non-European, humans and underpins colonialism and racism.

Mainstreaming sustainability will prove challenging and for evaluation to progress it will have to elevate the importance of pursuit of use.

The premise of this chapter is that evaluation has an important role in assisting sustainable development efforts get closer to a sustainable and productive nexus where we can make gains in poverty reduction and improve the environment in the present, thereby contributing to a sustainable and better future.

Notes

1 The importance of language and messaging is described in an article by Kate Yoder describing an inquiry by SPARK Neuro into responses to the terms "global warming" and "climate change" (Yoder 2019).

2 In the sense articulated by Carol Weiss as the mechanisms that mediate between the delivery (and receipt) of the programme and the emergence of the outcomes of interest. The operative mechanism of change isn't the programme activities per se but the response that the activities generate (Weiss 1998).

3 The work was undertaken by the CES Sustainability Working Group and included valuable material and metrics for greening organisations and conferences led by Andrealisa Belzer https://docs.google.com/document/d/1hp9Gks1Idd8h_9mmHQdLDbf3ftnB_8D9JWwR1DTJzNM/edit#heading=h.lim26mvuuo6g and implementation of this for the 2021 conference https://c2020.evaluationcanada.ca/about-the-conference/sustainability/.

4 Baastel www.baastel.com, Goss Gilroy www.ggi.ca, Prairie Research Associates www.pra.ca, Universalia www.universalia.com.

5 See bluemarbleeval.org.

6 Footprint evaluation was initiated by Patricia Rogers, Jane Davidson, Dugan Fraser and the author to provide guidance materials and capacity building to assist evaluators in mainstreaming sustainability in all evaluations. https://www.betterevaluation.org/en/themes/footprint_evaluation

7 I acknowledge and value the assistance of Nicky Bowman and others in learning of this valuable framing. Nicky uses the concept *all things Creator made are our relatives*.

8 It is instructive that the Coast Funds (https://coastfunds.ca/) created from an endowment as part of the Great Bear Rainforest and addressing economic development of First Nations in the Great Bear Rainforest and in Haida Gwaii have two evaluation functions: for donors and managers a traditional accountability function and a second function developed by and for First Nations that uses storytelling, songs and other traditional community processes.

9 I use the term *partitioned* to describe functionally separated but logically connected units, and suggest that it results in *fragmented* public policy agendas. Silos infer an impenetrable separation, whereas the reality is that many programmes or interventions are located within the same policy agenda but are partitioned into smaller units that are designed to better fit contemporary performance and accountability structures. Thus, whereas organisational charts and logic models provide the appearance of a linked approach to the broader policy goal, the organisational reality is that the units are partitioned and their connectivity to each other and the larger goal is impaired.

References

Basurto, X. and Ostrom, E. (2009). Beyond the tragedy of the commons. *Economia delle fonti di energia e dell' ambiente*, 52, 35–60.

Bowman-Farrell, N. R. (2018). Looking backward but moving forward: Honoring the sacred and asserting the soverign in indigenous evaluation. *American Journal of Evaluation*, 39, 1–26.

Carson, R. (1962). *Silent spring*. Houghton Mifflin, Boston, New York.

Casselman, A. (2007). Strange but true: The largest organism on earth Is a fungus. *Scientific American*.

Chelimsky, E. (2012). Public-interest values and program sustainability: Some implications for evaluation practice. *American Journal of Evaluation*, 35, 527–542.

Clark, W. C. and Dickson, N. M. (2003). Sustainability science: The emerging research program. *PNAS*, 8059–8061.

Clark, W. C., Mitchell, R. B. and Cash, D. W. (2006). Evaluating the influence of global environmental assessments. In R. B. Mitchell, W. C. Clark, D. W. Cash and N. M. Dickson (eds.), *Global environmental assessments* (pp. 1–28). Cambridge: MIT Press.

Ferraro, P. and Pattanayak, S. K. (2006). Money for nothing? A call for empirical evaluation of biodiversity conservation investments. *PLoS Biology*, 482–488.

Field, P. (2019). Evaluation for the anthropocene: Consensus building. *Evaluation Matters—He Take Tō Te Aromatawai*, 165–172.

Garcia, J. R. and Zazueta, A. (2015). Going beyond mixed methods to mixed approaches. *IDS Bulletin*, 30–43.

GEF Scientific and Technical Advisory Panel. (2018). *Integration: To solve complex environmental problems*. Washington, DC: GEF.

Geoghegan, T., D'Errico, S., Garcia Acuña, M., El-Saddik, K., Lucks, D., Ocampo, A. and Piergallini, I. (2019). *Evaluating sustainable development: How the 2030 Agenda can help*. London: iied.

Gilio-Whitaker, D. (2019). *As Long as Grass Grows*. Beacon Press, Boston.

Henry, G. and Mark, M. (2003). Beyond use: Understanding evaluation's influence on attitudes and actions. *American Journal of Evaluation*, 24, 293–314.

Johnson, K., Greenseid, L. O., Toal, S.A., King, J.A., Lawrenz, F. and Volkov, B. (2009). Research on evaluation use: A review of the empirical literature from 1986 to 2005. *American Journal of Evaluation*, 377–410.

Kates, R.W. (2011). What kind of a science is sustainability science? *PNAS*, 108, 19449–19450.

King, J. J. and Lawrenz, F. (2011). Multisite evaluation practice: Lessons and reflections from four cases. *New Directions in Evaluation*, 129, 59–71.

Liu, J. D. (2007). Coupled human and natural systems. *Ambio*, 36, 639–649.

Mascia, M. B., Pailler, S., Thieme, M. L., Rowe, A., Bottrill, M. C., Danielsen, F., … Burgess, N. D. (2014). Commonalities and complementarities among approaches to conservation monitoring and evaluation. *Biological Conservation*, 169, 258–267.

Mascia, M. F. (2017). A novel framework for analyzing conservation impacts: Evaluation, theory, and marine protected areas. *Annals of the New York Academy of Sciences*, 1399, 93–115.

Menda, J. (2011, October 26). Rhino horns worth more than gold, leads to a wave of thefts in Europe. *Huffington Post*. Retrieved 12 September 2013.

Nadeau, R. (2007, December 13). *Environmental and ecological economics*. Retrieved June 26 2020, from The Encyclopedia of Earth: https://editors.eol.org/eoearth/wiki/Environmental_and_ecological_economics

Ostrom, E. (1990). *Governing the commons: The evolution of institutions for collective action (Political Economy of Institutions and Decisions)*. Cambridge: Cambridge University Press.

Patton, M.Q. (2008). *Utilization-focused evaluation*. Los Angeles: Sage.

Pullin, A. S. and Stewart, G. B. (2006). Guidelines for systematic review in conservation and environmental management. *Conservation Biology*, 20(6), 1647–1656.

Putney, A. (2008). *Sacred dimensions: Undertanding the cultural and spiritual values of protected areas*. Gland, Switzerland: International Union for Concerned Scientists.

Raymond, C. B. (2017). *An impact evaluation framework to support planning and evaluation of nature-based solutions projects*. Report prepared by the EKLIPSE Expert Working Group on Nature-based Solutions to Promote Climate Resilience in Urban Areas. Wallingford, United Kingdom: Centre for Ecology & Hydrology. Retrieved from Nature-Based Solutions.

Reid, A. J., Brooks, J. L., Dolgova, L., Laurich, B., Sullivan, B. G., Szekeres, P., . . . Cooke, S. J. (2017). Post-2015 sustainable development goals still neglecting their environmental roots in the Anthropocene. *Environmental Science & Policy*, 179–184.

Rowe, A. (2012). Evaluation of natural resource interventions. *American Journal of Evaluation*, 33, 384–394.

Rowe, A. (2014). Evaluation at the Nexus: Principles for evaluating sustainable development interventions. In J. Uitto, Ed., *Evaluating environment in international development* (pp. 45–61). New York: Routledge.

Rowe, A. (2018). Ecological thinking as a route to sustainability in evaluation. In R. Hopson and F. Cram, eds., *Tackling Wicked Problems in Complex Ecologies: The Role of Evaluation*, Stanford: Stanford University Press.

Rowe, A. (2019). Sustainability-ready evaluation: A call to action. In G. Julnes, ed., *Evaluating Sustainability: Evaluative Support for Managing Processes in the Public Interest. New Directions for Evaluation*, 162, 29–48.

Rowe, A. and Lee, K. (2013, April 15). *Linking knowledge with action*. Retrieved August 5 2013, from David and Luckile Packard Foundation: http://www.packard.org/2013/04/science-subprogram-shares-new-materials-about-strategy

Swilling, M. H. (2018). *The weight of cities: Resource requirements of future urbanization*. Nairobi, Kenya: UN Environment – International Resources Panel.

The EU-UN Partnership on Land, Natural Resources and Conflict Prevention. (2020, April 14). *The EU-UN partnership on land, natural resources and conflict prevention*. Retrieved 2020, from https://www.un.org/en/land-natural-resources-conflict/

Tukey, J. (1962). *Journal of the Annals of Mathematical Statistics*, 33(1): 1-67.

Uitto, J.I. (2016). The environment-poverty nexus in evaluation: Implications for the sustainable development goals. *Global Affairs*, Global Policy.

Uitto, J. I. (2020). *Coping with the post-pandemic commute*. Retrieved from Medium.com: https://medium.com/@JuhaUitto/coping-with-the-post-pandemic-commute-dee7eec46faa

United Nations Development Programme – Evaluation. (2010). *Evaluation of UNDP contribution to environmental management for poverty reduction: The poverty-environment nexus*. New York: UNDP.

Weiss, C. H. (1998). *Evaluation*. Upper Saddle River, NJ: Prentice Hall.

Williams, R. (2019). Evaluation in a dangerous time: Reflections on 4 years in a central policy agency in the Government of Nova Scotia. *Evaluation Matters—He Take Tō Te Aromatawai*, 5, 41–62.

Wohlleben, P. (2016). *The hidden life of trees: What they feel, how they communicate – Discoveries from a secret world*. Greystone Books, Vancouver.

World Commission on Environment and Development. (1987). *Our common future*. Oxford: Oxford University Press.

Yarbourough, D., Shulha, L., Hopkins, R. and Caruthers, F. (2011). *The program evaluation standards: A guide for evaluators and evaluation users*. Thousand Oaks: Sage.

Yoder, K. (2019, April 29). *Why your brain doesn't register the words 'climate change'*. Retrieved from Grist: https://grist.org/article/why-your-brain-doesnt-register-the-words-climate-change

4

POVERTY, CLIMATE CHANGE AND DISASTER RISK REDUCTION

Too complex to evaluate?

Hazel Todd and David Todd

Climate change and poverty

This chapter explores the increasingly damaging effects of climate change on the global environment and observes that it is the poor, who are most severely challenged by this trend. "Weather-related events" are increasing in frequency and severity under Climate Change and in regions such as Asia-Pacific and the Caribbean disaster risk is outpacing resilience, posing severe limitations on poverty reduction. Many international interventions attempt to address the overlaps between climate change adaptation (CCA) and disaster risk reduction within a poverty reduction framework. Evaluation among international agencies has struggled to assess the progress and results of these efforts, given their exceptional complexity. While theory-based evaluation approaches have proved useful, they have often failed to find a suitable level of theory, which can provide clear findings and actionable lessons and recommendations. This chapter recommends an approach in which different levels of theory, from project through to the global environment, can be "nested" within each other, so that each addresses a specific aspect, while contributing towards evaluation of higher levels of social and environmental change.

Background

In the last two decades, substantial progress has been reported in addressing global poverty. This progress was catalysed by the Millennium Development Goals (MDGs), which were adopted by leaders of some 189 countries at the United Nations Millennium Summit in 2000.

> By 2011, all developing regions, with the exception of sub-Saharan Africa, had achieved the target of halving the number of people living in extreme poverty.

> The most populous countries in the world – China and India – played a major role in the worldwide reduction of poverty. The remarkable progress in China led to reduction in extreme poverty in Eastern Asia from 61 percent to 4 percent between 1990 and 2015. Southern Asia's progress has also been impressive, with a decline from 52 to 17 percent within the same time period, but with accelerated reduction since 2008.[1]
>
> According to the most recent estimates, in 2013, 10.7 percent of the world's population lived at or below $1.90 a day. That's down from 35 percent in 1990 and 44 percent in 1981. This means that ending extreme poverty is within our reach. In April 2013, the World Bank set a new goal to end extreme poverty in a generation. The new target is to have no more than 3 percent of the world's population living on just $1.90 a day by 2030.[2]

The MDGs were superseded by the Sustainable Development Goals (SDGs), which were adopted by all United Nations Member States in 2015. At the heart of the 2030 Agenda for Sustainable Development are 17 SDGs, which are an urgent call for action by all countries – developed and developing – in a global partnership. These recognise that ending poverty and other deprivations depends on implementation of strategies that improve health and education, reduce inequality, and spur economic growth – while tackling climate change and working to preserve oceans and forests.

Climate change was to some extent embedded in the MDGs, through MDG 7: "It is critical that the natural resources base and ecosystems are managed sustainably." This focus was made more explicit and operational under the SDGs, with SDG 13 requiring countries to "Take urgent action to combat climate change and its impact." Annual reporting on progress towards the goal is provided on the SDG website.[3] However, this has largely focused on countries meeting process steps, such as communicating on Nationally Determined Contributions and on fund flows, rather than on progress towards the target of sustainable management. There is also some reporting on disasters and their potential relationship to climate change. However, this tends to be of a generic nature and does not permit exploration of the empirical interconnections between these phenomena, or between them and poverty. For example, it is reported that,[4] "during the period 1998–2017, direct economic losses from disasters were estimated at almost $3 trillion. Climate-related and geophysical disasters claimed an estimated 1.3 million lives".

While there has been substantial progress globally with regard to poverty reduction (although with variable performance across regions), achievements with regard to climate change mitigation have been challenged by the apparently weak commitment of some major polluting countries to sign up to, still less meet, targets necessary to reduce greenhouse gas emissions. Although substantial and increasing funds have become available for adaptation efforts, the effects of these have been hampered by inadequate implementation capacity at country level and relatively slow release of committed resources by funding bodies.

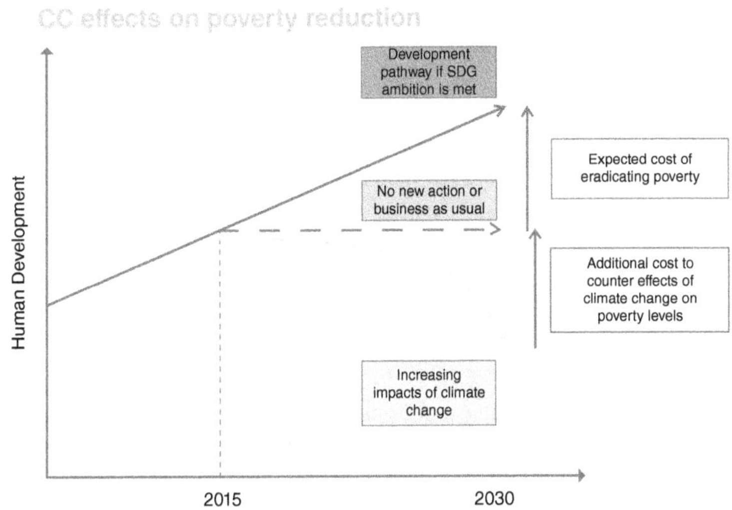

FIGURE 4.1 Potential Effects of Climate Change on Poverty Reduction

In the light of these complex phenomena and interactions between them at all levels, from global to local, a critical emerging question is: Will climate change be a "killer blow" for poverty reduction? It is evident that, if mitigation measures are not effective, climate change will have major damaging effects on the global environment. These will be cumulative and probably irreversible. At national level, environmental damage will affect all aspects of society. The poor will be most severely impacted, since they are often directly dependent on natural resources for livelihood or live in the most fragile locations. Attempts to strengthen resilience through adaptation measures will have varying levels of effectiveness and are likely to be geographically dispersed, with many communities unsupported; while major challenges will be posed for the sustainability of adaptation gains, since these will often require continuing resource support, which will overstretch the resources of countries and international partners.

Given these factors, there is high potential for the progress, which has been made against poverty to be reduced or even reversed. If poverty reduction continues in a "business as usual" mode, the impacts of climate change are highly likely to increase, with particularly strong effects on the poor. The costs of delivering intended development pathways will substantially increase. This is illustrated in Figure 4.1.

Poverty–climate interactions

Climate effects, although ubiquitous and continuous, are most directly experienced through "weather-related events", such as hurricanes, tropical storms and typhoons.

In urban areas, low-income communities are most affected by these events, because of such factors as inappropriate location (for example through susceptibility to such forces as flooding and strong winds, poor drainage, sloping land), fragile housing quality and poor roads. In such areas houses and small-scale businesses are frequently damaged or destroyed, roads are washed away and schools and clinics closed down as extreme events strike. When this occurs, the poor have no income reserves and low access to credit to enable them to renovate or rebuild their homes and/or to recommence small-scale income generation activities.

In contrast, although affected by adverse events, non-poor households have more resilient houses, better access to services, insurance coverage and credit worthiness to recover. This being so, weather-related events increase inequalities in urban areas, including through effects on housing, income, education, employment and health-care; and often have disproportionate effects on women and children.

Poverty effects of weather-related events in rural areas are often even more severe than in urban centres. Overall, rural housing stock is often less robust than that of urban areas and is prone to severe damage or destruction, while possessions, animals and crops are all likely to be lost. Increased rural poverty promotes migration to urban areas, which weakens rural communities and economies, as well as contributing to urban inequality and challenging the provision of infrastructure and services in these areas.

Whether in urban or rural locations, two types of settlement are particularly affected by extreme weather events:

- Coastal communities, which are subject to sea surges, winds and heavy rain on often inadequately drained surfaces.
- Hillside/mountain communities, built on unstable land are subject to landslides and flash floods (which often cause fatalities), road collapse and resultant inaccessibility, which may last for some time. Such areas often cannot be reached by vehicles bringing rehabilitation equipment and supplies for some time and are also cut off from markets to obtain necessary supplies or sell products to restore their income.

Responding to climate change

Climate change mitigation activities are intended to protect the global environment by slowing down or eliminating negative climate change effects. While environmental benefits gained from reduced GHG emissions are often envisaged at the macro level and in the long term, interventions have been targeted at all levels, ranging from global agreements and funds, through national policies and strategies to local level activities.

Although climate change mitigation efforts may reduce aggregate climate change effects (assuming they are at a consistently high level and well-targeted), disasters will continue to occur, so disaster risk reduction must play a critical role, particularly for the poor.

Disaster risk reduction

Disaster risk reduction and the SDGs

Disaster risk reduction (DRR) must take account of the shifting risks associated with climate change and ensure that its measures do not accidentally increase vulnerability towards them. For example, hazard analysis has traditionally been based on historical data. This approach is no longer sufficient, since hazard characteristics are worsening as a result of climate change.

The principle of disaster resilience is central to the SDGs of the 2030 Agenda. As indicated under Goal 1, during the period 1998–2017, direct economic losses from disasters were estimated at almost $3 trillion. Climate-related and geophysical disasters claimed an estimated 1.3 million lives. The Sustainable Development Goals are to be achieved through a comprehensive global framework of six separate but interrelated agreements, one of which is The Sendai Framework for Disaster Risk Reduction 2015–2030.

The Sendai Framework for disaster risk reduction 2015–2030

The stated outcome of the Sendai Framework is: "The substantial reduction of disaster risk and losses in lives, livelihoods and health and in the economic, physical, social, cultural and environmental assets of persons, businesses, communities and countries". A major Goal contributing to attainment of this outcome is as follows:

> Prevent new and reduce existing disaster risk through the implementation of integrated and inclusive economic, structural, legal, social, health, cultural, educational, environmental, technological, political and institutional measures that prevent and reduce hazard exposure and vulnerability to disaster, increase preparedness for response and recovery, and thus strengthen resilience.

The Sendai Framework lists climate change as "one of the drivers of disaster risk" Accordingly, in order to reduce disaster risk, it will be necessary to reduce the effects of climate change. While mitigation will play a critical long-term role in this process, for many communities around the world and particularly in the Asia-Pacific region adaptation measures will be essential in the short to medium term.

Climate change and disaster risk reduction across regions

The first section of this chapter has outlined the interconnections between climate change and poverty to date and how these may be expected to evolve in future. The connections are complex and operate at various social and economic levels. The poor are particularly vulnerable to climate change effects. Many of these effects are experienced as disasters; although others are long-term changes adversely affecting livelihoods of the poor over time, through such trends as increasing land aridity or salinity, which reduces the crop yields of marginal farmers on poor quality or vulnerable land. (These are sometimes brought into the disaster arena as "slow onset disasters".) This section takes a brief look at some interactions between climate change and disasters in different regions and sub-regions and shows that, although each has its specific characteristics and may be affected by specific types of weather-related events, there are also common factors emerging across them.

Disasters in the Asia-Pacific region

Recent events such as floods across South Asia and typhoons in East Asia continued a series of catastrophes in the region, which is one of the most vulnerable in the world to natural disasters. According to the Asia-Pacific Disaster Report 2017, disaster risk is outpacing resilience in the region. It estimates that an average national disaster in the region leads to a 0.13 increase in the country's Gini coefficient.[5] Figure 4.2 illustrates some of the major events in the region in the last 50 years. Although earthquakes have had a major destructive impact, weather-related events, such as cyclones, typhoons and floods have also played a major part in reducing the economic and social potential of the region. Some estimates of the possible cost and numbers affected by such events are shown in Table 4.1.[6]

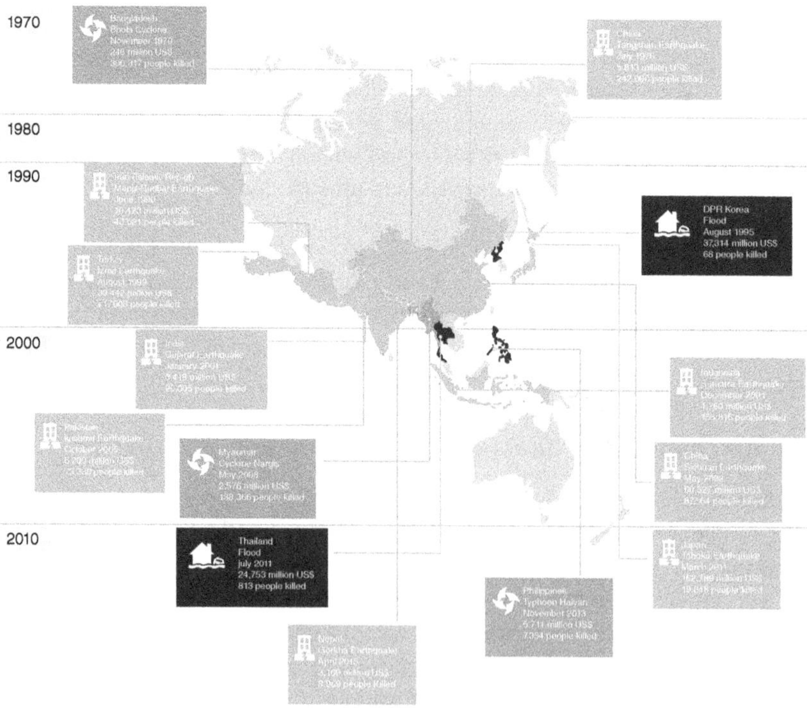

FIGURE 4.2 Some Major Disasters in Asia-Pacific 1970–2016[7]

TABLE 4.1 Some Estimated Impacts of Disasters in the Region

Disaster impacts in Asia and the Pacific, 2016

	Lives lost	*People affected*	*Cost of estimated damage ($ million current)*
Floods	**3,250**	**13,787,307**	**35,846**
Storms	**880**	**6,345,793**	**11,409**
Droughts	**–**	**13,381,000**	**3,000**
Extreme Temperature	336	158,100	1,727
Earthquakes	198	613,022	24,407
Other	323	240,480	835
Total	4,987	34,523,702	77,223

The Asia-Pacific Disaster Report (2017) suggests that in future the region could account for 40% of global economic losses resulting from disasters. Average annual GDP losses may be 4% for its Small Island Developing States and 2.5% for its Least Developed Countries.

Climate change has magnified the risk of disasters and increased their costs. As the climate system has warmed, the number of weather-related hazards globally has tripled, while the number of people living in flood-prone areas and cyclone-exposed coastlines has doubled – and these trends will increase. The impact of climate change will be felt particularly through periodic weather events such as monsoon rainfall and El Niño – as well as through heat waves, sandstorms, floods, cyclones and droughts.

South Asia

In South Asia, weather-related disasters present a major challenge, which is exacerbated both by climate change and by rapid population growth. "The entire population is vulnerable to change in climate and extreme events because of the low level of institutional capabilities, economic vulnerability, and great dependence on climate sensitive resources."[8] A broad range of DRR activities may substantially overlap with CCA measures, including "those related to hydrometeorological events such as drought-proofing, flood protection, cyclone warning and shelters, malaria eradication, resistant agriculture, mangrove conservation, saline embankment, and alternative livelihood development".[9]

As with the East Asia and Pacific region discussed in Section "Disasters in the Asia-Pacific region" above, losses incurred from weather-related events are devastating: between 2005 and 2014, disasters were calculated to be responsible for 1.2 million deaths in southwestern and southern Asia, accounting for over 20% of all global deaths and led to economic losses of some $80 billion in 2005 value.[10]

In the region, although climate change and disasters are clearly interlinked and overlapping, the institutional structures, legislative provisions and national and regional policies dealing with them have largely developed as independent strands. The implication of this trend has been well explored by Mall et al.[11] Their analysis shows that that there is a lack of coordination and awareness among the nodal agencies, which critically limits their proper functioning. In most cases, stand-alone adaptation and disaster reduction policies were found to exist and DRR including climate change adaptation policies seemed extremely challenging due to the involvement of multiple institutions within similar kinds of projects. In certain cases, duplication or even triplication in the execution of similar projects was identified, which often hindered the pace of effective execution in terms of both economy and benefit to the people. A lack of coordination also implies an excessive budgetary burden in executing similar types of projects and plans by different institutions and agencies.[12]

The Caribbean region

The Caribbean Development Bank (CBD) plays a major role in advising and supporting its Borrowing Member Countries (BMCs) in their efforts to combat poverty. Disasters, often in the form of weather-related events, are increasing in intensity and frequency in the region and often challenge these efforts. There are no agreed estimates of the economic impact of climate change on Caribbean countries[13] in a "no adaptation scenario". Such estimates are difficult because of rapid changes in global climate change projections as well as because of the limited climate model projections at suitable spatial scales available for the Caribbean, and the limited inventory of the Region's environmental resources and assets. Various studies have estimated annual impact at anywhere between 5% and 30% of GDP. Even taken at the low end of this range, the impact of climate change on CDB's BMCs is expected to be devastating to their long-term growth and development.[14]

As far back as 1998, CDB implemented a Natural Disaster Management Strategy and Operational Guidelines (NDMSOG), under which some 11.37% of the Bank's total lending and technical assistance was expended in the period up to 2008. This was replaced by an updated Disaster Management Strategy and Operational Guidelines (DiMSOG) in 2009. The DiMSOG is intended to support and inform the following areas of CDB intervention[15]:

a) Proactive assistance to BMCs to reduce risk through institutional strengthening, knowledge management, risk reduction measures and enhanced community resilience
b) Post-disaster response
c) Mainstreaming Disaster Risk Management into CDB's grants and loans
d) Effective collaboration by CDB with regional and national DRM partners.

The CDB Climate Resilience Strategy[16] was approved in 2012. It seeks to develop and operationalise a robust environmental sustainability risk framework that explicitly considers climate resilience in CDB's operations and assists BMCs and regional institutions to mobilise financing, and design and implement policies, strategies and investment programmes to address climate resilience and deliver on their sustainable development objectives. It notes that Disaster Risk Reduction is a priority for the Bank and is acknowledged as a critical short-term response to climate change adaptation. The Bank will continue to provide assistance for post disaster rehabilitation and for mitigation interventions (under its DiMSOG); but will place greater emphasis on identifying/developing innovative risk transfer instruments and initiatives and building community resilience. Under the CRS, CDB intends to support BMCs to design and mainstream climate risk management strategies in regional, national and sectoral policies.

Although funding under the DiMSOG has intended to support countries to develop disaster risk reduction approaches, take up of funds for this purpose has been slight. To a limited extent, post disaster-response funding has incorporated an element of "building back better", which may contribute to future DRR, but overall, countries have proved reluctant to borrow money to reduce disaster risks. Furthermore, in most of the countries concerned, active approaches to DRR are not strongly incorporated in national policies and strategies, so there is little impetus to borrow money in this area.

To some extent, the growing fundability of climate resilience and adaptation interventions appears to offer potential support to effective disaster resilience programmes. Many CDB activities funded under climate resilience are expected to raise the resilience and preparedness of countries for disasters, thereby reducing the need for separate disaster-specific funding. However, an evaluation by the Bank's Independent Evaluation Office (IEO) found no evidence that the theoretical connections between the two strategies have yet been systematically realised. Projects in one area rarely specify the effects they will produce in the other, so that overall benefits are not maximised and the potential for duplication remains. Given the increasing intention to mainstream DRM, including on infrastructure projects, the use of Climate Risk Assessment as an input into project design will be an essential aspect of "building back better", although the cost implications of responding to such assessments will need to be monitored. Such Assessment is one potential method to specify the overlap between climate and disaster related effects of investments.[17]

The IEO evaluation of the DiMSOG developed (retrospectively) a theory of change to help analyse the extent to which the strategy (in association with CCA approaches) has assisted Borrowing Member Countries to move towards poverty reduction. This is presented as Figure 4.3.

Overview of climate change adaptation and disaster risk reduction

As shown by a brief overview of these issues in three regions, the overlaps between disaster risk reduction and climate change adaptation have not been well recognised or incorporated into international, regional and national approaches to either of the two phenomena. Attempts to address both issues simultaneously are also rare. This partly reflects a "silo" approach emanating from the different institutional and funding streams through which climate change and disasters are addressed. The silo approach is ineffective since there are substantial issues, which could be more effectively addressed through collaboration, as shown in Figure 4.4.

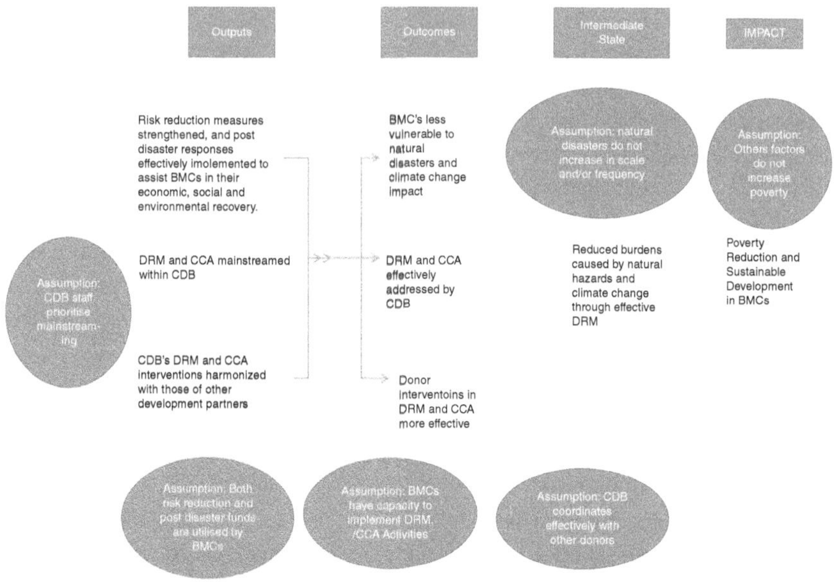

FIGURE 4.3 Initial Theory of Change for DiMSOG

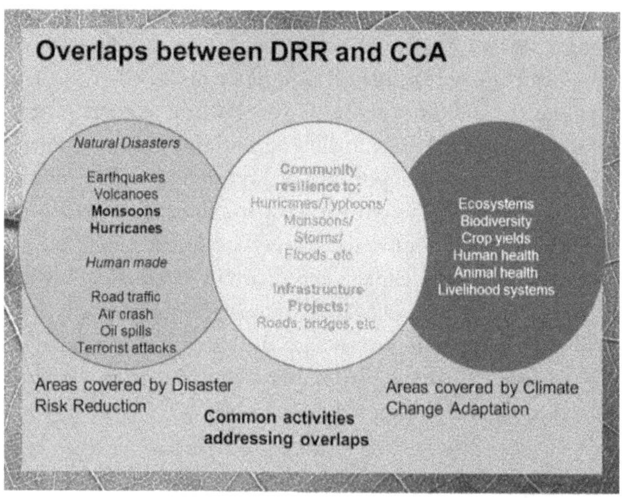

FIGURE 4.4 Overlaps Between Disaster Risk Reduction and Climate Change Adaptation

In terms of national and international development funding, common types of intervention, which call for effective collaboration between planners and implementers in the fields of CCA and DRR, include:

- Improved design, construction and maintenance of roads and bridges
- Housing standards and quality

- Quality of buildings and systems for continuous service provision: especially schools and clinics
- Design resilience of electricity, water supply, drainage and communications systems.

In terms of poverty reduction, it can be seen that most activities, which are currently addressed within approaches to DRR or CCA would previously have been funded as poverty-focused development interventions.

Evaluation challenges of interventions in overlapping areas

The evaluation repertoire

It has been demonstrated above that poverty, climate change and disaster risks are inextricably bound in complex and dynamic ways. These linkages operate at all institutional levels:

- global development and environment institutions
- regional environment and development institutions
- national policies and institutions
- governments, NGOs, CBOs, traditional institutions
- communities.

International development and environment support are provided by numerous agencies, many of which focus largely on one of the three elements – poverty, climate or disasters. Evaluation follows funding and largely targets individual elements rather than their interconnections. Most evaluations commissioned by international or national agencies draw on a set of relatively standard methods, which are combined differently according to the type and level of intervention, as shown in Table 4.2.

TABLE 4.2 Common Types and Methods of Evaluation at Various Levels of Intervention

Level	*Types of Evaluation*	*Predominant Methods*
Global/Cross-cutting	Overall Performance	Meta analysis, statistical analysis, big data, secondary data, case studies
Sectoral/Cross-cutting	Thematic Programme	Meta analysis,statistical analysis, secondary data, big data, field missions, case studies
Annual Cross-cutting	Annual Performance Report	Meta analysis, statistical analysis, secondary data
Country Portfolios	Country Office Country Portfolio	Field missions, case studies, document review, surveys, secondary data

Evaluation among international agencies

Can evaluation adequately address the increasing complexity posed by climate change and disasters?

The common types and methods of evaluation presented in Table 4.2 are conventionally framed under the umbrella of the "DAC Criteria" of relevance, efficiency, effectiveness and sustainability. A fifth DAC criterion, impact, is often left out of Terms of Reference for evaluations in view of its perceived complexity and long duration; or else it is intended to be addressed under sustainability, with which it is assumed to be related. The DAC criteria are in the process of review by the OECD.

While the DAC Criteria have played an important role in bringing a level of consistency across evaluations in the context of international development, they have not been found ideal for interventions targeting complex, multi-layered changes with a medium to long time-span: which characteristics include most interventions targeting poverty reduction, climate change mitigation and adaptation and disaster risk reduction.

In the extremely challenging global development context, those commissioning evaluations are increasingly focused on the urgent need to learn lessons, which can be applied to future interventions; rather than dwelling too much on accountability issues, which have traditionally been central to evaluations conducted within the framework of the DAC criteria. Since even the largest development interventions are in themselves a small contribution to the challenges facing the global environment and the societies, which depend upon it, the most important evaluation lessons for future interventions revolve around the issues of sustainability and impact. Given that an activity has been evaluated as (more or less) relevant, efficient and effective how will its approaches and results be sustained over time and scaled up to a more significant level?

The answer to this fundamental question is often the weakest link in completed evaluations for all levels of intervention. Indeed, it is common for evaluations to simply state that it is "too early" to make any assessment on these dimensions or to give speculative scenarios based on largely unsupported assertions of increased government resources and commitment. Intrinsic to this weakness is the possibility and temptation to treat each of the DAC criteria as an isolated box for evidence and interpretation, without considering the inter-relationships between them and, more specifically, the contribution the activity under evaluation is likely to make in the future. This critical gap in analysis often rests on the failure to answer a simple question during the evaluation inception phase, namely, how was this intervention intended to generate a lasting and scalable contribution to the issue it addresses? In fact, in many (possibly most) original project documents presented to evaluators, this is not at all clear.

The nearest most project document sets get to such a consideration provided by a Logical Framework document, which could potentially provide key inputs to understanding how the activity is expected to "work" in the long run. Unfortunately, over time Log Frames became primarily a progress tracking tool, focused almost entirely on what could be counted with inadequate attention to where these "deliverables" were leading. Most of the essential information on how the intervention might contribute to intended long-term change was "parked" in a peripheral column of assumptions/risks, subjected to only the most cursory analysis.

Partly in response to the challenges and frustrations of evaluating the cumulative contribution of development interventions (including those related to environment and disasters) based on analysis using the DAC Criteria and information organised around a Log Frame approach, theory-based approaches emerged as a new platform for complex evaluations. These attempt to outline and assess the interconnections among the activities of an intervention and its environment, which will be necessary to generate the desired contribution to change, taking into account such factors as timescales and sequencing.

Refining theory-based approaches

Although theory-based approaches rapidly gained traction across the evaluation community, they also soon ran into practical challenges and often appeared to promote confusion among different types and levels of development practitioners. Some symptoms of these challenges included:

- Theories generated at institution-wide or portfolio-wide level proved too all-encompassing to be evaluated
- Decision-makers became frustrated at the failure of theories to deliver concrete performance information
- Different levels and types of theory are needed for use by policy makers and for portfolio, programme and project managers
- Evaluators need the most detailed theories of all, to enable them to explore cause and effect of progress along intended "impact pathways".

Responding to such challenges, evaluators and practitioners moved towards an approach in which different levels of theory could be developed for empirical investigation and placed within an (eventually) over-arching theory of change for an intervention or set of interventions. This approach became identified as the use of "nested theories of change", as illustrated in Table 4.3.

When approaching the evaluation of any complex intervention, whether at policy, strategy, programme or project level it is therefore critical to first focus on one main "level" of theory of change, appropriate to the key issues being addressed. For example, the evaluation may be of a programmatic intervention, with the theory of change primarily addressing this level. However, the "environment" surrounding the programme is also likely to influence the achievement of its objectives. Such "environmental" influences on the programme may come from a "higher" level, (such as the Global Development Architecture), from a thematic level (such as

TABLE 4.3 The Use of "Nested Theories of Change" to Help Evaluate Different Types of Issue

Level for "nested ToC"	*Type of Issues Covered*
Global ToC	Linkages poverty, CC and disasters in Global Development Architecture
Institutional/Corporate ToC	Policies, objectives, strategies, resource allocation, overall performance
Thematic ToC	Gender mainstreaming, social safeguards, capacity development
Sectoral/Focal Area ToC	Disaster Risk Reduction, Climate Mitigation, Climate Change Adaptation
Programme/Portfolio ToC	Specific Funds (e.g. Special Climate Change Fund), Country Programmes
Project ToC	Individual projects within or across countries

gender mainstreaming) or from a "lower" level, such as individual projects, which derive from or are supported by the programme. In addition to its detailed examination of progress along expected development pathways of its main theory of change, in this case for the programme, the evaluation should therefore also consider at a less detailed level the inputs and influences on it from other levels of the nested TOCs. For example, was an expected piece of legislation delayed or abandoned, with adverse effects on the programme? It should also consider the outcomes and influences from the focus programme into other levels of the nested theories. For example, has the programme influenced gender mainstreaming in the area targeted; such as CCA, DRR or poverty reduction? Has it enabled new projects to be conceived and implemented, based on its achievements?

By using this "nested theory" approach, evaluators can avoid the temptation to develop "mega-theories" of such scope and complexity that they can scarcely be conceived, still less evaluated. Such approaches hinder the production of usable evaluation conclusions and recommendations and make the derivation of lessons for the future extremely difficult. In turn this can lower the perceived "value added" of evaluation for practitioners operating in complex development fields. Given the increasing understanding of the interactions between poverty, climate change and disasters, the use of a "nested theories" approach offers evaluators a valuable tool to explore the different levels and types of issues, which have contributed to achievements and progress.

Notes

1 https://www.mdgmonitor.org/, accessed 24th October 2019.
2 https://www.un.org/en/sections/issues-depth/poverty/, accessed 24th October 2019.
3 See, for example, https://sustainabledevelopment.un.org/sdg13, accessed 24th October 2019.
4 https://sustainabledevelopment.un.org/sdg13, accessed 24th October 2019.

5 "Leave no One Behind. Disaster Resilience for Sustainable Development". Asia-Pacific Disaster Report 2017. P. v. United Nations ESCAP, Bangkok.
6 Source: Asia-Pacific Disaster Report 2017, Table 1-1, P3.
7 Source: Asia-Pacific Disaster Report 2017, Figure 1-1, P4.
8 "Disaster Risk Reduction Including Climate Change Adaptation Over South Asia: Challenges and Ways Forward", in International Journal of Disaster Risk Science (2019) 10:14-27. Rajesh K. Mall, Ravindra K. Srivastava, Tirthankar Banerjee, Om Prakash Mishra, Diva Bhatt, Geetika Sonkar.
9 Mall et al, P15.
10 "Disasters without borders—Regional resilience for sustainable development". Asia-Pacific disaster report 2015. UNESCAP Bangkok 2016.
11 Mall et al., op.cit.
12 Mall et al., P21.
13 *Climate Resilience Strategy*, P1, Caribbean Development Bank, 2012.
14 Evaluation of The Caribbean Development Bank's 2009 Disaster Management Strategy and Operational Guidelines. Final Report. Office of Independent Evaluation, July 2018. P12.
15 CDB. Op.cit. P13.
16 *Climate Resilience Strategy*, 2012-2017. CDB. 2012.
17 CDB, op.cit. P42.

References

Caribbean Development Bank. *Climate Resilience Strategy*, 2012–2017, Barbados, 2012.

Gutierrez, Miren, McFarland, Will, Fonua, Lano. *Zero Poverty, Think Again*. Overseas Development Institute (ODI), London. 2014.

Mall, Rajesh K, Srivastava, Ravindra K, Banerjee, Tirthankar, Mishra, Om Prakash, Bhatt, Diva, Sonkar, Geetika. "Disaster risk reduction including climate change adaptation over South Asia: Challenges and ways forward", *International Journal of Disaster Risk Science* (2019) 10:14–27.

Office of Independent Evaluation, Caribbean Development Bank. "Evaluation of the Caribbean Development Bank's 2009 disaster management strategy and operational guidelines. Final Report.", Barbados. July 2018.

United Nations. "Disasters without borders—Regional resilience for sustainable development". *Asia-Pacific disaster report 2015. UNESCAP Bangkok*, 2016.

United Nations. "Leave no one behind: Disaster resilience for sustainable development". *Asia-Pacific Disaster Report* 2017. UN ESCAP, Bangkok. 2017.

United Nations. Sendai framework for disaster risk reduction 2015—2030. UNISDR, Geneva, 2015.

Websites

https://www.mdgmonitor.org/, accessed 24 October 2019.

https://www.un.org/en/sections/issues-depth/poverty/, accessed 24 October 2019.

https://sustainabledevelopment.un.org/sdg13, accessed 24 October 2019.

PART II

Approaches and challenges in evaluating environment and sustainable development

5

USING BIG DATA AND GEOSPATIAL APPROACHES IN EVALUATING ENVIRONMENTAL INTERVENTIONS

Anupam Anand and Geeta Batra

Introduction and background

Big data is commonly distinguished by volume, velocity, and variety (Goodchild 2013). A large portion of these data is georeferenced and therefore carries spatial information. This subset of spatial data is referred to as "big (geo) data." Geospatial data and methods, in particular the application of satellite remote sensing, have been used in the monitoring and assessment of environmental processes for the past four decades, based on its ability to provide synoptic, time-series data for various earth system processes (Spitzer 1986; Melesse et al. 2007; Awange and Kyalo Kiema 2013). However, its application in the field of evaluation to assess the relevance and performance of environmental programs has gained traction in the last two decades. Evaluators typically used GIS mainly for visualization during early applications in evaluation. Renger et al. (2002) describe how GIS data and analysis are used for visualization, change detection, and in conjunction with other evaluation data. Evaluators have also discussed the usefulness of spatial data for measuring baselines, outputs, and in observing the results of interventions over time (Azzam 2013; Azzam and Robinson 2013). Quasi-experimental designs (Ferraro and Pattanayak 2006; Andam et al. 2008; Buchanan et al. 2018) leveraging geospatial data were used to conduct impact evaluations in forestry and biodiversity interventions. Recently, geospatial analysis has also been used in randomized control trials (Jayachandran et al. 2017).

Further, the role of geospatial science is increasingly being recognized by several major environmental and development policy conventions and institutions as countries move toward more evidence-based policy decisions and practice. For example, the United Nations Convention to Combat Desertification (UNCCD) has endorsed the use of indicators obtained from remote sensing to monitor progress toward reversing and halting the degradation and desertification of land (Minelli et al., 2017). The United Nations Framework Convention on Climate Change (UNFCCC) and the Convention on Biological Diversity (CBD) also endorse the use of objective indicators, many of which are derived through geospatial methods.

Three main factors have influenced the uptake of geospatial data, and the "new data revolution." First, there has been a remarkable increase in the availability of geospatial data. Currently, there are more than 1950 operating satellites in space (World Economic Forum 2019), of which 382 were launched in 2018 (UNOOSA). Private investments in space technology have also increased substantially and such investment increased from US$0.5 billion in 2011 to US$5.8 Billion in 2019, making 2019 the most significant year on record for investment in space (Space Investment Quarterly: Q4 2019).

Second, the availability and accessibility to high-performance computational power have made such complex data sets efficient and affordable to process. Cloud-based platforms such as Google Earth Engine, the Sentinel Hub, ESRI, Amazon Web Services, etc. have made the processing and analysis of "big" data possible at a planetary scale (Lech et al. 2018). Moreover, recent developments in statistics and data science have led to novel algorithms based on the principles of machine learning and artificial intelligence that are "data-hungry" and therefore work efficiently with high volume and complex data structures.

The third factor is the growing demand for reliable and transparent data for various purposes – for business intelligence, environmental management, infrastructure planning, navigation, disaster risk management, etc. Global initiatives such as SDGs with a proposed list of about 230 indicators have further provided opportunities to seek data that is globally consistent and locally relevant.

Geospatial data and methods can help address common methodological challenges observed in evaluation, such as the lack of baseline data, sampling bias, difficulties in selecting appropriate counterfactuals, and account for the impact of multiple scales and contexts on processes and interventions. These new data and methods can complement other commonly used quantitative and qualitative evaluation approaches. Therefore, the timing is right for us to leverage the availability of such data, which can potentially change the way we collect evaluative evidence on environmental and other development interventions.

In the next section of this chapter, we illustrate the usefulness of geospatial data in evaluation through examples of specific applications to assess the relevance and impact of environmental interventions by the Global Environment Facility (GEF).

Applications of geospatial analysis in environmental evaluation

The Independent Evaluation Office (IEO) of the GEF is responsible for assessing the performance and effectiveness of GEF interventions. The IEO has applied geospatial methods to complement other evaluation methods to answer pertinent evaluation questions on the relevance, effectiveness, efficiency, and sustainability of

GEF interventions, in three focal areas: biodiversity, land degradation, and climate change. We present a few examples which demonstrate the application of remote sensing and geospatial approach in these thematic areas to answer questions based on standard evaluation criteria.

Case 1. Geospatial analysis to assess the relevance of GEF support to protected areas

Support to protected areas is a core component in strategies for biodiversity conservation (DeFries et al. 2005). The Aichi Targets and the associated Target 11 aspire to effectively and equitably manage 17% of terrestrial and inland water, and 10% of coastal and marine areas by 2020, thereby signifying the importance of protected areas in biodiversity conservation and management of ecosystem services. As the financial mechanism for the UN CBD, the GEF's Strategy is consistent with the CBD's Strategic Plan and is reflected in its support to protected areas over the past 26 years. Between 1991 and 2015, the GEF provided $3.4 billion in grants to 618 projects, matched by $12.0 billion in co-financing, to help protect almost 2.8 million km^2 of the world's non-marine ecosystems (GEF IEO 2016a).

Setting area-based targets for conservation through the establishment and management of protected areas is crucial. However, to maximize the return from conservation investments, interventions should be designed for ecologically representative biodiversity-rich sites with high biodiversity values. This is not always the case; for example, 49% of Important Bird Areas and 51% of Alliance for Zero Extinction sites for biodiversity conservation remain unprotected. However, the GEF biodiversity strategy prioritizes the conservation of protected areas based on significant and endemic biodiversity. Hence, in the evaluation of GEF Support to Protected Areas and Protected Area Systems (GEF IEO 2016a), conducted in collaboration with the IEO of the United Nations Development Programme (UNDP), we used geospatial analysis to assess the relevance of GEF interventions at global, country, and site levels. This impact evaluation also assessed the conservation outcomes as well as other co-benefits.

We carried out a spatial overlay analysis to determine the biodiversity significance of GEF-supported protected areas. The analysis involved a feature overlay of the GEF-supported protected areas with the areas of significant biodiversity presence and conservation importance such as Key Biodiversity Areas (KBAs) and Ramsar sites. The analysis demonstrated that 58% of GEF-supported protected areas were located in KBAs; 31% met other conservation designations such as a Ramsar site, a WWF priority area, a Conservation International biodiversity hotspot, an Alliance for Zero Extinction site, or a U.N. heritage site; 11% of GEF-supported protected areas were significant at the local or national level from a country perspective (Figure 5.1). The overall results from this study provided evidence that the GEF was allocating its resources into globally significant sites with high biological diversity or "hot spots."

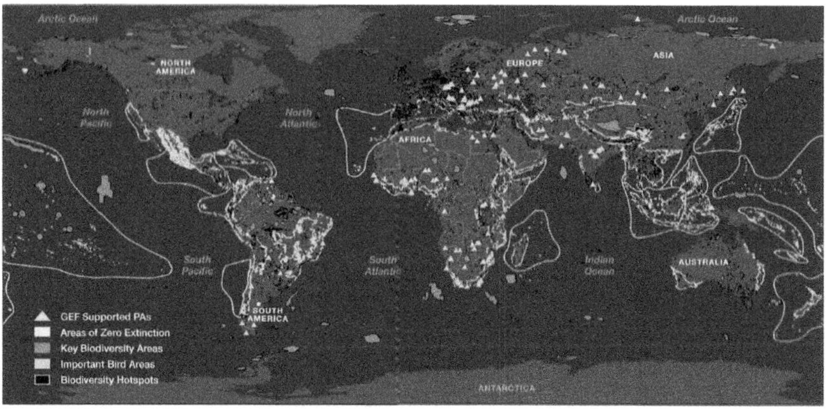

FIGURE 5.1 Globally Distributed Gef-Supported Protected Areas were Overlaid with Sites of Conservation Importance

Case 2. Geospatial analysis to assess socio-economic co-benefits of GEF-supported interventions

Despite extensive research over the past few decades, evidence on the socio-economic impacts of initiatives designed to influence environmental outcomes remain limited and inconsistent (Spitzer 1986; Melesse et al. 2007; Awange and Kyalo Kiema 2013). Studies that have tried to address this gap have various limitations, such as the varying nature of co-benefits attributable to environmental initiatives and the data and approaches used to assess co-benefits. The difference in methodological approaches and in temporal and spatial scales also presents a challenge in drawing general conclusions from these assessments (Naidoo et al. 2019; Alpízar and Ferraro 2020).

More recently, studies utilizing geospatial analysis have demonstrated how satellite-based data sources can be leveraged for assessing environmental and socio-economic outcomes. In the case of the GEF, the socio-economic co-benefits of its environmental interventions had never been evaluated before. Building on recent development in research and impact evaluation, the IEO conducted an evaluation to estimate the global and local level socio-economic co-benefits of GEF initiatives to support the environment.

We used a geospatial approach to determine the socio-economic benefits associated with GEF-supported interventions in Sustainable Forest Management (SFM). Since its establishment in 1992, the GEF has provided support to improve the sustainability of forestry resources to increase environmental benefits and deliver socio-economic co-benefits; yet these co-benefits had never been measured. Through this evaluation, we assessed the impacts of GEF-supported SFM interventions on biophysical and ecological variables, co-benefits measured in terms of socio-economic indicators, and the estimated monetary values of ecosystem services applying the principle of natural capital accounting.

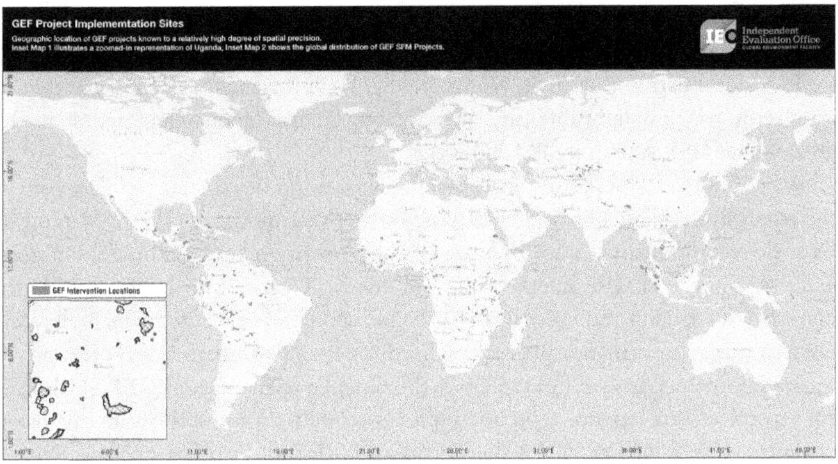

FIGURE 5.2 Geocoded Location Information for GEF Project Implementation Areas Inset Map 1 (Bottom) Illustrates a zoomed-in representation of Colombia

Data used included the geographic locations of GEF SFM projects and measurements on environmental outcomes based on indicators suggested by the Convention on Biological Diversity (CBD, 2016) and the United Nations Convention to Combat Desertification (UNCCD, 2015). To examine the socio-economic effects of GEF interventions, we used both a portfolio-wide approach (Figure 5.1) (based on night light activity[1]), as well as a single-country case study. The case study was in Uganda, where data from the World Bank's Living Standards Measurement Survey (LSMS) provided in-country household survey information.

A causal tree approach helped us understand the factors which have a significant effect on deforestation, vegetation density, and nighttime lights and to estimate the above-ground carbon sequestration attributable to each GEF SFM project location. Air temperature, precipitation, population, road networks, etc. were some of the variables included in the causal tree, several of which were significantly associated with the outcomes. The evaluation approach then compared geospatial regions with GEF projects with those regions with no GEF projects based on a set of similar attributes, and the differences in outcome were used to estimate the impact of the GEF intervention. Details of this approach can be found in Annex of the report (GEF IEO 2019a), as well as in the value for money analysis of land degradation projects of the GEF (GEF IEO 2016b).

The portfolio level global-scope analysis suggested a small, positive impact on socio-economic benefits indicated by nighttime light intensity. We found evidence that projects implemented since 2010 demonstrated a positive effect on nighttime lights (+0.24), a proxy for economic development, and which was not discernible in preceding periods. In the absence of precise geographic information, these findings may represent an under-estimate of the actual impacts across the GEF SFM portfolio since locations without any recorded high precision geographic data in project descriptions were not included in our analysis. We realized that the results from the nighttime lights at the portfolio level were not clear, suggesting the need for local-level data and analysis. Nighttime lights limit accuracy in measurement in areas with very low light intensity such as forest environments which represent the areas where GEF supports SFM initiatives.

We conducted a local-scale analysis in Uganda using survey data to fill the gap in the portfolio-level analysis and to explore further the impact of GEF SFM projects on socio-economic outcomes, by assessing the correlation between household assets and the presence of GEF interventions. We divided Uganda into an area-based grid consisting of smaller multiple units 10 square kilometers each, for which all satellite and survey information was generalized for analysis (Figure 5.3). For every 10 square kilometers, as seen in Figure 5.3, the distance to the nearest GEF SFM project was calculated. Further, total household assets in 2009 and 2011 were calculated using the LSMS data to detect the impact of GEF projects on proximate (within 50 km) households. The local analysis helped limit the interpretation to areas with significant degrees of change that are unlikely to be attributable to error. Further details of this approach are in the original evaluation report (GEF IEO 2019a).

The results showed that GEF SFM projects are associated with an increase in household assets. By matching LSMS locations proximate to GEF interventions to those further away from GEF interventions, we found that GEF SFM projects

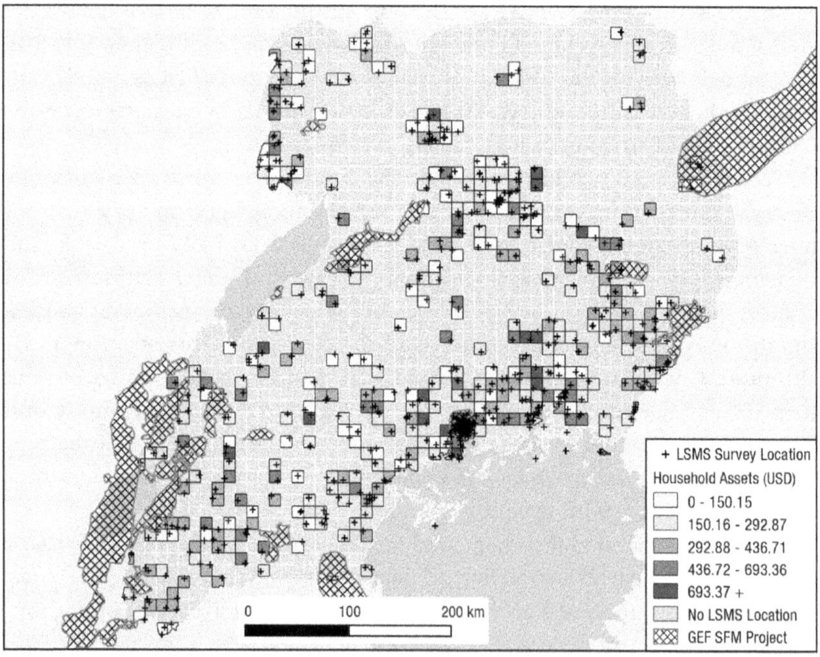

FIGURE 5.3 Data Used in the Uganda Case Study. The Light Gray Shade Indicates Areas with No LSMS Data, Hashed Areas Indicate GEF SFM Projects, and Square Grids with Black Boundaries Indicate Areas where LSMS Data was Available

are associated with an increase in household assets between $163 and $353 (within 40–60 km respectively). The study showed that households proximate to a GEF implementation site tended to have, on average, an increase in assets approximately $310 (within 50 km) higher than those not proximate to a GEF implementation site.

Case 3. Geospatial analysis in measuring the sustainability of environmental outcomes in the Ba Be protected area

Donors are increasingly interested in the long-term sustainability of project outcomes, and not just in the attainment of outcomes. An IEO evaluation found that the outcomes of several GEF projects are sustained during the post-completion period, and a higher percentage of projects achieve environmental stress reduction than had been determined at completion (GEF IEO 2019b). Assessing the sustainability of outcomes continues to be a challenge since sustainability at project closure is assessed as a "likelihood of sustainability" and is seldom re-evaluated during the post-completion period using primary data sources. It takes time to achieve sustainability of outcomes, and it takes significant resources to measure sustainability at post completion. Geospatial methods are useful in evaluating post completion sustainability efficiently. In an IEO study, using geospatial tools, we assessed the long-term sustainability of environmental outcomes of a GEF-supported protected area in Vietnam, for biodiversity conservation – "Promotion of Sustainable Forest and Land Management in the Vietnam Uplands."

One of the main sites of the project was the Ba Be/Na Hang Conservation Complex in the hilly Bac Kan Province in north-eastern Vietnam rich in biodiversity. The park supports the population of several nationally and globally threatened species. It also supports the only significant natural mountain lake in Viet Nam – a RAMSAR site – which is the most important wetland in the country's protected area system. Agriculture, forestry, and livestock production are the primary sources of income and sustenance. The main threat to the biodiversity in the area is the fragmentation of habitat, conversion of forest land for large-scale infrastructure and agriculture, livestock grazing, illegal hunting, and overuse for non-timber forest products. The project focused on working with rural upland communities for better management of land and forests: interventions included improved systems for animal husbandry and conservation of sloping areas, bio-energy applications; a voluntary payment for ecosystem services and small-scale private tourism enterprise development, participatory approaches to forest land allocation and protection; and, support for the implementation of protected area management plans.

We primarily used satellite-based data to assess the sustainability of environmental outcomes. Our analysis focused on the trends in the change of forest cover and vegetation productivity in Ba Be National Park (Figure 5.4). We compared the loss in forest cover for different periods (before, during, and after the post-project) to those in areas outside the protected area, as well as with the overall national trends in forest cover loss. Remote sensing was used to regenerate the baselines as well as measure environmental outcomes.

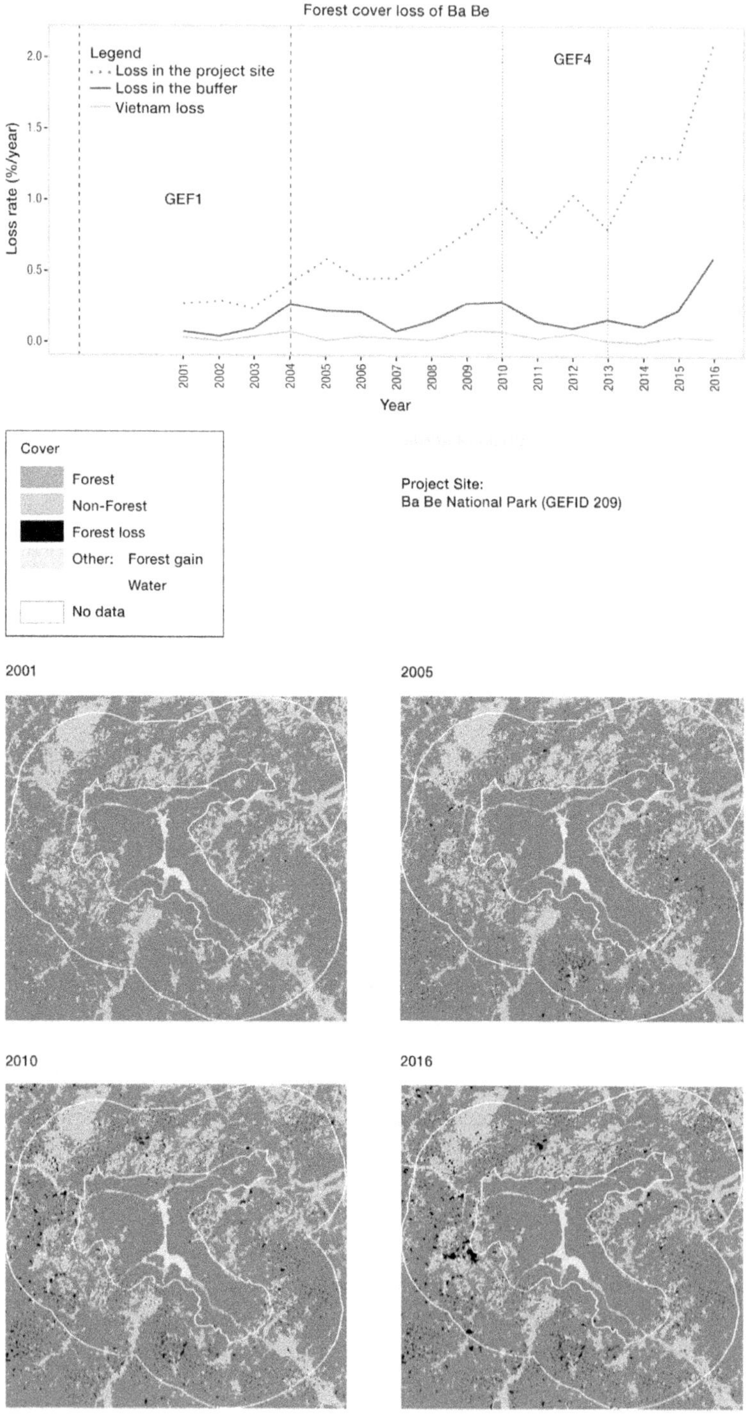

FIGURE 5.4 Trends and Comparison: Forest Loss Did Not Increase Despite an Unprecedented Increase in the Buffer and at Country Level

The findings from the remote sensing analysis showed that forest cover in Ba Be forest was maintained for several years after project completion. The forest loss in Ba-Be did not increase despite an unprecedented increase in forest loss in the adjacent area and more broadly at the country level. The post-project loss for the protected area was 0.1% compared to 0.55% in the buffer area and 2% at the national level in 2016, three years after project completion. Interviews with project staff and some beneficiaries indicated that project outcomes were sustained by community participation in project design and implementation including buy-in from local communities, attention to income generation activities, and continued support from provincial governments.

Case 4. Geospatial analysis in ecological forecasting in Kenya

An important decision for any multilateral institution such as the GEF is where to allocate scarce resources with the objective of maximizing overall environmental benefits. We partnered with the NASA DEVELOP team housed at Goddard Space Flight Center) to first measure land cover changes in GEF-supported protected areas in Kenya, and then developed a forecasting framework to estimate the future changes in land cover and carbon sequestration benefits, as returns on GEF investments.

GEF supported protected areas in Kenya

In Kenya, GEF projects have supported activities in approximately nineteen protected areas. These projects were accurately identified through the review of project documents. The protected areas spread over an area of 5,035 km^2 with a broad range of land cover types and designations, including montane forests, coastal mangrove forests, deserts, grasslands, and shrubs. We examined twelve of the terrestrial protected areas (Figure 5.5) comprising two national parks, one marine national reserve, five forest reserves, three national reserves, and a community conservancy. The largest protected areas is Mount Kenya NP (2,714.5 km^2), and the smallest is Mrima Forest Reserve (3.9 km^2). The study timeframe covered two time periods representing the past and the future: 1995–2016 and 2020–2030.

Deforestation is a major environmental issue that is detrimental to biodiversity conservation and increases the threat to the number of endangered species facing extinction (Brooks et al. 2006). Kenya loses an average of 12,000 hectares (ha) of forest and 33,500 ha of open woodland per year, equivalent to an annual loss of 2 million metric tons of carbon, with agriculture, and public or private development projects causing the most deforestation (KFS 2010).

We used NASA Earth observations for the remote sensing analysis to assess the effectiveness of PAs throughout Kenya for the study period of 1995–2016. Landsat 5 TM, Landsat 7 ETM+, and Landsat 8 OLI Level 1 products were acquired through Google Earth Engine (GEE). This is a cloud computing system that is open for non-commercial use. We used Landsat images because of their extensive historical

FIGURE 5.5 Study Area Map of the 12 PAs within Kenya Included in the Analysis

archive, open access, and suitable spatial resolution to analyze both large and small protected areas. We used Google Earth Engine for data acquisition and analysis. Freely available ancillary data sets were used for data on variables including temperature and precipitation, roads and waterways, human and livestock density estimates, and digital elevation, to project future land cover changes.

Carbon stock estimation tools are used for measuring the carbon balance and for estimating the likely greenhouse gas mitigation benefits as a result of project interventions. The most widely used carbon stock estimation tool is EX-ACT (EX-ante Appraisal Carbon-balance), a land-based accounting system developed by FAO. EX-ACT is a useful, cost-effective tool to measure carbon stocks and stock changes per unit of land and requires minimum data inputs. It is used for ex-ante assessments of the impact of agriculture and forestry interventions on carbon-balance.The tool helps to estimate economic and climate change mitigation benefits and thereby assists in prioritizing project activities.

Although tools such as EX-ACT are valuable for ex-ante measurements and analysis, and are easy to learn and deploy, these tools have certain limitations.They are not spatially explicit, their use is limited in identifying areas for interventions, and they do not account for contextual factors driving land use and land cover change.The primary input for these tabular models is area and type of land cover pre-intervention mainly derived from official records or information from processed satellite imagery.The main output of the tool is limited to carbon balance (GHGs) expressed in terms of $tCO2e/ha$ and year resulting from project activities.

Spatially explicit ecological forecasting models address the limitations of, and complement appraisal systems such as Ex-ACT.The primary inputs for such models are land cover maps that are often produced within the same suite of tools that take raw satellite data or readily available classified land cover data. The land cover data generated can also serve as baseline data for other simple carbon balance tools. This approach also provides the capability to model and estimate future land cover change, based on the factors driving the change.

For our study, we used land-use change analysis, ecological forecasting, and ecosystem service estimation in terms of carbon stocks. Carbon stock was calculated using the national and regional coefficient as per the IPCC guidelines. Additionally, a mixed-methods approach combining remote sensing with field validation visits to project sites around Mount Kenya provided us with an in-depth review of the GEF-funded projects at multiple spatial and temporal scales.

At the Kakamega Forest Reserve site, our results showed that vegetated land cover had increased between 1999 and 2015 (Figure 5.6). The annual average Normalized Difference Vegetation Index (NDVI – middle panel, Figure 5.6) illustrates the increasing reflectance of near-infrared light, consistent with increasing "greenness" of the vegetated surfaces. We found that within Kakamega, areas that were previously mainly agricultural have been transitioning back to forest. Our results also found that forested areas have noticeably expanded, particularly in the southern half of the forest reserve, further confirmed through the visit to the site. Shrub has also expanded into previously non-vegetated areas along the western edge of the forest. As reforestation occurs, more plant biomass is accumulated in the above-ground stocks. The above-ground carbon estimates in the Kakamega Forest Reserve increased throughout the study period and in the projections for 2020 and 2030 as well. This carbon sequestration (bottom panel, Figure 5.6) reflects the additional co-benefits from the biodiversity project.

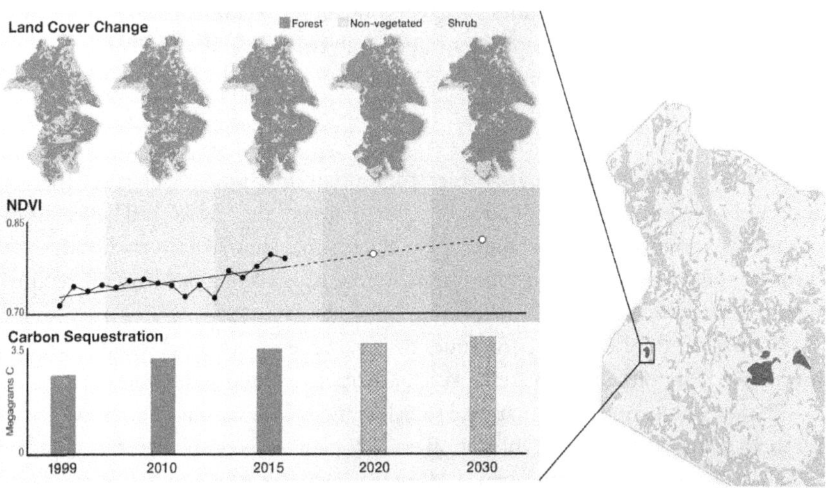

FIGURE 5.6 Land Cover Classifications for the Reserve Were Produced Using Landsat Imagery and Show the Progression of Vegetation for 1999, 2010, and 2015. The Forest Reserve Experienced Revegetation Following GEF-Funded Projects

Conclusion

The cases presented in this chapter demonstrate the broad applications and advantages in using recent big data sets, methodologies, and computing platforms in evaluating the outcomes of environmental interventions. In the protected area evaluation presented in case study 1, we utilized Google's cloud computing platform using forest cover data (Hansen et al. 2013), which reduced the processing time significantly. In assessing the socio-economic co-benefits of GEF-supported interventions in SFM, we applied machine learning algorithms driven by geospatial data and econometric analysis, which allowed us to work with a high volume of data, and also provided us with insights into the factors associated with the outcomes. To evaluate the outcome sustainability of GEF interventions around Ba Be, we used decades of dense time-series data to assess the results and their sustainability. The IEO experience is based on evaluations conducted on environmental interventions; however, the approaches discussed here are applicable across a broad range of evaluation topics including disaster risk management, infrastructure and urban development.

Geospatial tools have greatly enhanced our ability to evaluate efficiently and cost-effectively at project, national, global, and ecologically meaningful scales. Big data from satellites are capable of revealing patterns that are not otherwise apparent. The results of our analysis are reproducible and have generated an objective evidence base while complementing other evaluation methods. We have also used geospatial tools in disseminating evaluation results through both static and interactive dynamic maps and visualizations. These innovative approaches to presenting and communicating evaluation results has made a significant difference in conveying complex information in a more lucid and efficient way.

With the increase in the type, volume, and availability of data, geospatial tools have presented new opportunities to access quantitative information on environment and development interventions and analyze their impacts. Technical skills, high computing capacity, and multidisciplinary expertise are needed to analyze and interpret data and results. The accuracy and reliability of contextual variables often vary widely across countries and sites, so geospatial approaches need to be complemented by field verification and other appropriate methods to interpret the data and to be able to provide qualitative insights to answer the "how" and "why." Some of the data and resource constraints in using geospatial approaches may be addressed through collaborations with institutions that have access to big data and the required infrastructure for use.

As the field of big geodata continues to advance, evaluators will need to explore innovative technologies such as blockchain, artificial intelligence, deep learning, the Internet of Things and computational social science, alongside traditional evaluation methods. Geospatial data and analysis offer an efficient and complementary approach to monitoring and evaluating new and increasingly complex evaluative topics and questions. The potential for mixed-method and multi-method approaches drawing upon different disciplines is immense, and we in the evaluation community have just embarked on this exciting journey.

Acknowledgments

The authors gratefully acknowledge the role of the IEO partners – the Global Land Cover Facility at the University of Maryland AID DATA and NASA DEVELOP, AidData and the College of William and Mary, who contributed to the various evaluations presented in this chapter. The material presented in the case studies is based upon completed evaluations.

Note

1 Night lights are used as a proxy for socio-economic growth as studies have demonstrated that night time lights is highly correlated with economic activity, population, and establishment density (Mellander et al. 2015).

References

Alpízar, F. and Ferraro, P.J. (2020), "The environmental effects of poverty programs and the poverty effects of environmental programs: The missing RCTs", *World Development*, Vol. 127, p. 104783.

Andam, K.S., Ferraro, P.J., Pfaff, A., Sanchez-Azofeifa, G.A. and Robalino, J.A. (2008), "Measuring the effectiveness of protected area networks in reducing deforestation", *Proceedings of the National Academy of Sciences*, Vol. 105 No. 42, pp. 16089–16094.

Awange, J.L. and Kyalo Kiema, J.B. (2013), "Environmental monitoring and management", in Awange, J.L. and Kyalo Kiema, J.B. (Eds.), *Environmental Geoinformatics: Monitoring and Management*, Springer Berlin Heidelberg, Berlin, Heidelberg, pp. 3–16.

Azzam, T. (2013), "Mapping data, geographic information systems", *New Directions for Evaluation*, Vol. 2013 No. 140, pp. 69–84.

Azzam, T. and Robinson, D. (2013), "GIS in evaluation: Utilizing the power of geographic information systems to represent evaluation data", *American Journal of Evaluation*, Vol. 34 No. 2, pp. 207–224.

Brooks, T.M., Mittermeier, R.A., Fonseca, G.A.B. da, Gerlach, J., Hoffmann, M., Lamoreux, J.F., Mittermeier, C.G., et al. (2006), "Global biodiversity conservation priorities", *Science*, Vol. 313 No. 5783, pp. 58–61.

Buchanan, G. M., Parks, B. C., Donald, P. F., O'Donnell, B. F., Runfola, D., Swaddle, J. P., Tracewski, Ł., & Butchart, S. H. M. (2018). The local impacts of World Bank development projects near sites of conservation significance. *The Journal of Environment & Development*, 27(3), 299–322.

DeFries, R., Hansen, A., Newton, A.C. and Hansen, M.C. (2005), "Increasing isolation of protected areas in tropical forests over the past twenty years", *Ecological Applications*, Vol. 15 No. 1, pp. 19–26.

Ferraro, P.J. and Pattanayak, S.K. (2006), "Money for nothing? A call for empirical evaluation of biodiversity conservation investments", *PLoS Biol*, Vol. 4 No. 4, p. e105.

GEF IEO (2016a), *Impact Evaluation of GEF Support to Protected Areas and Protected Area Systems*, Washington, DC, Global Environment Facility Independent Evaluation Office. (http://www.gefieo.org/evaluations/impact-evaluation-gef-support-protected-areas-and-protected-area-systems-pas-2016)

GEF IEO (2016b), *Value for Money Analysis for GEF Land Degradation Projects*, Washington, DC, Global Environment Facility Independent Evaluation Office. (http://www.gefieo.org/evaluations/value-money-analysis-gef-land-degradation-projects-2016)

GEF IEO (2019a), *Value for Money Analysis of GEF Interventions in Support of Sustainable Forest Management*, Washington, DC, Global Environment Facility Independent Evaluation Office. (http://www.gefieo.org/evaluations/value-money-analysis-gef-interventions-support-sustainable-forest-management-2019)

GEF IEO (2019b), *GEF Annual Performance Report 2017*, Washington, DC, Global Environment Facility Independent Evaluation Office. (http://www.gefieo.org/evaluations/annual-performance-report-apr-2017)

Goodchild, M.F. (2013), "The quality of big (geo)data", *Dialogues in Human Geography*, Vol. 3 No. 3, pp. 280–284.

Hansen, M.C., Potapov, P.V., Moore, R., Hancher, M., Turubanova, S.A., Tyukavina, A., Thau, D., et al. (2013), "High-resolution global maps of 21st-century forest cover change", *Science*, Vol. 342 No. 6160, pp. 850–853.

Jayachandran, S., Laat, J. de, Lambin, E.F., Stanton, C.Y., Audy, R. and Thomas, N.E. (2017), "Cash for carbon: A randomized trial of payments for ecosystem services to reduce deforestation", *Science*, Vol. 357 No. 6348, pp. 267–273.

Lech, M., Uitto, J.I., Harten, S., Batra, G. and Anand, A. (2018), "Improving international development evaluation through geospatial data and analysis", *International Journal of Geospatial and Environmental Research*, Vol. 5 No. 2, available at: https://dc.uwm.edu/ijger/vol5/iss2/3.

Melesse, A.M., Weng, Q., S. Thenkabail, P. and Senay, G.B. (2007), "Remote sensing sensors and applications in environmental resources mapping and modelling", *Sensors (Basel, Switzerland)*, Vol. 7 No. 12, pp. 3209–3241.

Minelli, S., Erlewein, A. and Castillo, V. (2017), "Land degradation neutrality and the UNCCD: From political vision to measurable targets", *International Yearbook of Soil Law and Policy*, 2016, pp. 85–104.

Naidoo, R., Gerkey, D., Hole, D., Pfaff, A., Ellis, A.M., Golden, C.D., Herrera, D., et al. (2019), "Evaluating the impacts of protected areas on human well-being across the developing world", *Science Advances*, Vol. 5 No. 4, p. eaav3006.

Renger, R., Cimetta, A., Pettygrove, S. and Rogan, S. (2002), "Geographic information systems (GIS) as an evaluation tool", *American Journal of Evaluation*, Vol. 23 No. 4, pp. 469–479.

Spitzer, D. (1986), "On applications of remote sensing for environmental monitoring", *Environmental Monitoring and Assessment*, Vol. 7 No. 3, pp. 263–271.

6

MULTIPLE ACTORS AND CONFOUNDING FACTORS

Evaluating impact in complex social-ecological systems

Aaron E. Zazueta and Jeneen R. Garcia

The GEF and its support in the South China Sea[1]

The GEF is a financial mechanism that provides grant and concessional funds to 183 participant countries for projects and activities that help the countries fulfil their commitments to global environmental conventions.[2] From its inception in 1992 to the time the evaluation began in 2010, GEF support for coastal and marine-related concerns in the South China Sea was delivered through 34 GEF projects ($112 million) and 150 small grants ($3 million). This support was provided to seven littoral countries that were eligible for GEF funding – Cambodia, China, Indonesia, Malaysia, the Philippines, Thailand and Viet Nam. The projects were implemented at different times by various GEF partner agencies, which include the Asian Development Bank, United Nations Development Programme, UN Environment (formerly UN Environmental Programme) and the World Bank.

The main objective of the impact evaluation was to assess the extent to which GEF support contributed to, or is likely to lead to, changes in policies, technology, management practices or other behaviours that will address the priority trans-boundary environmental concerns.[3]

The geographical focus of the evaluation included the Gulf of Tonkin and Gulf of Thailand as part of the South China Sea. The marine area covered by the evaluation stretches in a south-west to north-east direction with a southern border between South Sumatra and Kalimantan (Karimata Strait), and a northern border at the Strait of Taiwan between the northern tip of Taiwan and the Fujian coast of mainland China.

The South China Sea – as is the case with other, large marine ecosystems – is characterized as a complex social-ecological system due to its inextricably linked and constantly interacting natural and human systems (Anderies 2004; Liu et al. 2007; Ostrom 2009). As a complex system, any interventions in the South China Sea are subject to non-linear processes that often make prediction of outcomes difficult (Holling 2001; Taleb 2007).

First, the time scale at which interventions take place (typically five to seven years) is often disproportionate to the time scale at which the ecosystem responds. Ecosystem responses may be immediate or may span one to several decades. Second, the geographical scale at which interventions take place (typically a local site, municipality or country) is likewise often disproportionate to the geographical scale of the ecosystem boundaries, or the boundaries within which the environmental concern being addressed originates and extends its impact. Ecosystem boundaries often transcend municipal or country boundaries, while environmental concerns may cut across economic and social system boundaries. Interventions implemented at a local scale may be affected by events and other factors interacting at the national, regional or global scales, such as market forces.[4] Third, the factors and actors at play influence each other and therefore make it difficult to trace the chains of causality from the observed change back to the intervention being assessed. Even if changes can be ascertained, and links between any given intervention and an observed change can be made, multiple actors and other confounding factors make it difficult to attribute causality to any specific intervention (Sanderson 2000; Davies 2004; Mee, Dublin and Eberhard 2006).

Thus, impact evaluation in complex systems requires close attention to the ways in which an intervention interacts with other elements of the system to influence the observed changes. To understand the impact of GEF support in the South China Sea, the evaluation drew on scientific literature on complex systems to guide the lines of inquiry that would (1) help assess the extent of change in environmental conditions, (2) establish causal links between interventions and the observed changes and (3) identify the specific contributions of GEF support to these observed changes within the context of other actors' contributions, and the influences of confounding factors.

Assessing direct impact

Determining the extent of change

Determining the extent of change that took place since GEF support began was in some instances straightforward. In the case of the Livestock Waste Management Project in China, Thailand and Viet Nam (GEF ID 2138) that demonstrated new pollution control technologies, end-of-pipeline measurements before and after the introduction of the technology provided reliable measurements of nutrient loads prevented by the intervention. Other indicators of change were improvements in the smell in pig farms and reductions in incidents of red-eye disease among farmers in all three visited demonstration sites. In Ha Tay, Viet Nam, evidence of pollution reduction was that the wastewater could be used for agriculture – wastewater released into rice paddies no longer killed the plants.

In the case of mangrove ecosystem management interventions, one important indicator was change in mangrove cover. Changes in mangrove cover were determined from before-and-after data presented in terminal evaluations and annual project reports. Data were verified through field visits that included visual assessments of mangrove forest conditions and interviews with stakeholders on the extent to which changes had taken place. To fill in information gaps and triangulate evidence from these information sources, the evaluation team carried out remote sensing analysis to compare mangrove cover at the sites across different years. Evidence confirmed that in most sites where the GEF had provided support, mangrove cover had increased over a period of about five years.

Given the nature of the concerns that GEF-supported interventions address, time lags of such magnitude (i.e. five years) or greater are necessary before changes in environmental status become evident. The higher the scale[5] of the system being addressed, the more slowly it tends to respond and, consequently, the longer it takes to begin shifting to an improved social and environmental state (Gunderson and Holling 2002). Further, several interventions may need to take place before a tipping point is reached, triggering a cascade of effects in the social-ecological system (Gladwell 2000; Kinzig et al. 2006). These unpredictable time lags between interventions and responses in the social-ecological system require that impact evaluation not only focus on changes that are directly observable in the social-ecological system (i.e. income of the local population or pollution levels) but also on indicators or markers of future change that allow an assessment of the extent to which interventions are likely to lead to the desired impact.

For example, numerous studies have shown that coral reef ecosystems may take decades to centuries before the effects of overfishing are observed (Jackson et al. 2001; Folke et al. 2004; Dulvy, Freckleton and Polunin 2004; Babcock et al. 2010). The evaluation found that while coral cover had been maintained or was slightly increasing in GEF-supported marine protected areas (often referred to as MPAs) over the course of at least five years, larger fish species and giant clam abundance had decreased in the Con Dao and Phu Quoc marine protected areas in Viet Nam. Although evidence indicates that marine protected area initiatives have positive results for hard corals, scientific research shows that declining fish populations may soon be followed by coral reef decline at the ecosystem level (Pandolfi et al. 2005). Thus, to better assess the likelihood of an intervention's impact on coral reef ecosystems, indicators tracking fish and benthic organisms (bottom-dwellers) must be measured. On this basis, the evaluation concluded that though GEF projects had often been able to protect coral cover from physical destruction, impact has been limited and insufficient to prevent the degradation of coral reefs targeted by these projects.

Establishing a chain of causality

In cases in which interventions were highly targeted and change could be measured immediately and in a straightforward manner, such as in the reduction of nutrient pollution, causality is easy to establish. However, interventions more commonly do not have a one-to-one or linear relationship with a desired effect (Stern et al.

2012). In cases where interventions were implemented at higher scales (e.g. national and regional) and sought to address non-linear processes, causal links between interventions and observed changes were often more difficult to establish.

A critical starting point for impact evaluation in such cases is to develop a sound understanding of the human and natural dynamics inherent to each of these interacting systems. This understanding enables the evaluation to identify the geographical boundaries of the specific system in which the intervention needs to create an impact; the system's inherent characteristics defining the extent of change that can take place, and the types of interventions that are most likely to result in change, given the patterns of causality in the specific system.

Mismatches between the scale at which the intervention is implemented and the scale at which the environmental concern manifests are common when the system's geographical boundaries are not well understood. This has often resulted in administrative or management boundaries not being aligned with ecosystem boundaries (Folke et al. 1997, 2002; Cash et al. 2006). For example, migratory fish stocks typically transcend national boundaries, requiring the countries concerned to agree on and create management boundaries that better approximate that of the fish stocks.

In the South China Sea, the evaluation found that while countries were aware of this, they historically have tended to not enter into binding multilateral agreements, especially when it came to environmental concerns. Of the 27 multilateral and bilateral regional instruments pertaining to coastal management in force in the South China Sea, only four bilateral agreements were legally binding. A comparative assessment of regional mechanisms in similar large marine ecosystems around the world also showed that even after more than 20 years, most regional mechanisms still relied heavily on external donors when low- to middle-income countries comprised the majority of the membership.[6]

Considering the countries' unwillingness to enter into binding regional environmental agreements, the relatively short time frame and the wide differences in country incomes, GEF support in the South China Sea region could not be expected to facilitate the ratification of a regional convention such as those present in other regional seas.

Evidence from scholarly research, however, indicates that in systems in which no single central actor disproportionately influences the behaviour of others (such as the South China Sea region), collaborative adaptive behaviour among independent actors tends to be more prevalent where good communication exists, especially when collaborative behaviour is expected across multiple administrative or ecological scales (Brondizio, Ostrom and Young 2009; Ostrom 2010). Therefore, one way to measure GEF's contribution towards regional environmental governance was to assess the extent to which GEF support fostered better communication, and the extent to which indicators of cooperative behaviour among countries could be linked to GEF support.

GEF-supported regional interventions included multidisciplinary workshops, steering committee meetings, task forces and expert networks that provided many new opportunities for interaction across the region among countries, local governments, regional organizations, civil society (including academic and research institutions) and the private sector. These activities allowed information exchange, joint fact-finding and regional priority setting and planning. Social network analyses of regional environmental actors carried out by the evaluation team based on available reports, online surveys and key informant interviews revealed that GEF support helped increase the connectivity between national and regional actors.

Furthermore, the evaluation team used interviews and document analyses to establish that new collaborative agreements were adopted as a direct result of GEF projects. This finding further strengthened evidence of causal links between GEF-supported communication-related activities and collaborative adaptive behaviour among independent actors, which in the case of the South China Sea is the most critical outcome given the region's inherent characteristics. Among these collaborative agreements are the memorandum of agreement between the provinces of Kien Giang (Viet Nam) and Kampot (Cambodia) signed in 2008 to jointly manage transboundary seagrass beds; the engagement of all littoral countries, including China, in the elaboration and approval of a Strategic Action Programme for the South China Sea; the Gulf of Thailand Joint Statement and Framework Programme for Joint Oil Spill Preparedness and Response, signed by Cambodia, Thailand and Viet Nam and supported by the private sector and international organizations; and the adoption of the Sustainable Development Strategy for the Seas of East Asia (SDS-SEA) by 11 East Asian countries and 19 non-country partners.

Although all these actions were taken by governments and other independent actors, stakeholder interviews and document analyses clearly indicated that these collaborative agreements would have been very unlikely at the time they took place had GEF support not been present. These accomplishments are particularly significant considering the tensions that exist among the littoral countries and the slow progress that had been made in multilateral processes related to the environmental management of the South China Sea. Based on these pieces of evidence analysed within the region's contextual conditions, the evaluation concluded that the GEF had provided the appropriate type of support at the regional scale, leading to outcomes that were critical to achieving long-term impacts.

As the analysis progressed, it became increasingly clear that the direct results of GEF projects tended to be strikingly similar within and across the different scales. Thus, GEF support was found to have a somewhat recursive nature across scales in as far as projects supported three broad types of interventions, including: generating and expanding information and knowledge (including raising awareness and developing mechanisms for information sharing and access); developing institutional capacities (including policy and regulatory frameworks, administrative structures and processes for trust building); and testing implementation strategies (including introducing technologies and approaches, implementation mechanisms and bodies and financial instruments).

The evaluation also found that the GEF has provided considerable support to initiating processes that facilitate the broader adoption of implementation strategies introduced by project demonstrations. Based on these findings, the evaluation developed a framework that was used to identify and classify project results and to establish chains of causality between GEF support and the observed changes. This framework proved to be very useful during the evaluation as a tool to compare and establish links of GEF engagement at different scales, regardless of the project type country or implementing agency.

Discounting rival hypotheses

Discounting rival hypotheses entails assessing which feasible causes or alternative explanations account for the change observed, and which do not. Most important, it establishes that the intervention being evaluated is one of the feasible causes, and that the observed change can be attributed to it. The evaluation used several approaches to discount rival hypotheses, depending largely on the extent to which there were confounding factors at play and the extent of information available. The first task was to assess if there were rival hypotheses with merit. For example, attributing nutrient pollution reduction to the new technology introduced in livestock farm demonstrations was straightforward, as the causal link was clear and field visits and interviews confirmed that no other plausible explanations could account for such a sharp decrease in nutrient loads in wastewater.

In the case of activities that supported mangrove management, a rival hypothesis with merit was that widespread policy changes could account for, or at least significantly contribute, to the change in the mangrove cover trends in the demonstration sites. Counterfactual analysis (i.e. comparison of results in similar sites where mangroves had not benefited from an intervention such as that provided by GEF projects) would have been desirable to assess the extent to which broader factors affected local trends in demonstration sites. But given the various socio-economic and environmental factors affecting mangrove growth, compounded by the lack of environmental monitoring data in both GEF and non-GEF sites, it was difficult to determine the counterfactual.

In the absence of information on counterfactuals, the evaluation compared trends in mangrove cover data at the demonstration site to more readily available data on national- and regional-scale trends. In most cases, it was found that GEF-supported sites showed some recovery, whereas national and regional trends continued to decline, albeit at a slower rate. This indicated that interventions at GEF-supported sites were indeed resulting in positive change compared to the rest of the region and countries that had not received these types of interventions. However, the trends also showed that widespread policy changes were contributing to this decline in mangrove cover slowing down across the region.

The evaluation also considered ongoing processes and other contextual factors that could have contributed to the observed changes to better assess the extent of GEF contributions. From remote-sensing analysis and interviews, the evaluation found that in most cases, mangrove cover was already increasing before GEF support began. In Trat, Thailand, for example, the process was driven by local communities as well as national economic conditions as early as 10 years before any GEF projects took place. GEF support, however, allowed communities in conflict to develop rules for mangrove use that then encouraged cooperative protection of a greater area of the mangrove forest. The impact of GEF support then was not increasing mangrove cover per se, but sustaining and increasing the momentum of community and government support for mangrove protection that otherwise might have fizzled out with no follow-up funding during that critical period.

At the regional scale, where cases were more complex, and plausible rival hypotheses grew in number or were more entangled, the analysis of context was even more important. The evaluation team made historical analyses of actions, programmes or events that took place before, during and after GEF support. For example, when assessing the impact of GEF support on the regional environmental architecture related to marine and coastal matters, the evaluation started by determining the results of efforts to establish regional mechanisms that predated GEF support. The evaluation also assessed the ways in which previous attempts to establish regional mechanisms affected GEF-supported initiatives.

Among the contextual factors, the Rio processes related to the summits on sustainable development that have taken place in the last three decades since 1992[7] were found to be key to raising awareness on environmental issues among policy makers, as these coincided with a cluster of regional and national environmental initiatives being implemented at specific periods. The Rio processes also implied a set of commitments to which countries signatory to the global conventions agreed to meet, often using their own resources but also drawing on resources provided by donors and multilateral financial institutions.

In the context of this multiplicity of actors and conditions affecting country decisions, it became a challenge to assess what had been the GEF's contributions to achieving desired impacts that often had not yet manifested. Thus, at the regional scale, the evaluation's approach was to determine the extent to which the GEF helped create the conditions and contributed to regional processes that in the causal chain are expected to lead to environmental stress reduction and improved environmental status.

To determine if the GEF had a unique contribution or niche in the mix of all these actors, the evaluation carried out a comparative assessment of the support provided by the GEF and other donors to marine and coastal initiatives in the region using information from a global donor database, historical records, project documents and donor reports. The idea was to place GEF support in the context of the financial support landscape in the East Asian seas over the last 25 years. The analysis found that the GEF was by far the biggest donor when it came to marine and coastal initiatives at the regional scale. Interviews and desk reviews of other regional organizations' reports also showed that the GEF was the only actor that linked its initiatives at local, national and regional scales. An important GEF contribution, this enabled actors to interact more effectively and allowed the processes necessary for environmental stress reduction in the South China Sea to progress in parallel at different scales. Furthermore, the regional mechanisms that the GEF supported had provided a framework that linked the initiatives of other donors and actors mainly working at a national scale to existing regional efforts.

Social network analysis was used to compare the current interactions among regional actors with GEF support present to a scenario without GEF support. The evaluation found that several of the organizations that GEF supported had over the years become more central to the network of regional environmental actors. With GEF support, some of the long-active organizations were able to expand their activities to include regional-scale coastal and marine initiatives. In general, more links among organizations existed in the presence of GEF support compared to the hypothetical scenario without GEF support, where some actors were completely cut off from the regional network. This affirmed the finding that one of the GEF's important contributions to the regional environmental architecture was the linking of initiatives and actors across local, national and regional scales to address priority regional transboundary concerns.

In both of the examples on the impacts of GEF support on mangrove cover at the local scale, and the environmental governance architecture at the regional scale, the evaluation team triangulated different information sources and analytical methods in order to augment the lack of available information, and to account for confounding factors or limitations imposed by the social-ecological system's inherent characteristics. In the absence of counterfactuals, the task of impact evaluation is to develop approaches to discount rival hypotheses that, although not able to attribute changes solely to the intervention being assessed, are nevertheless able to make a clear link between the intervention's contributions and the observed outcomes (Mayne 2011).

Assessing progress towards impact

The undertaking of the three tasks of impact evaluation showed that the GEF had helped countries improve capacities and identify approaches that resulted in positive environmental changes. However, the evaluation also determined that much of the accomplishments were found to have taken place at a relatively small scale or in specific conditions in which the GEF-supported demonstrations had been implemented. Despite this progress, the gains were insufficient to address the full range of challenges in the sustainable management of the South China Sea, GEF's goal in the region.

Fully achieving impacts requires that the boundaries of the intervention match the boundaries of the system or the environmental concern being addressed. For example, the evaluation found that GEF-supported demonstrations protecting seagrass and coral reefs were often effective in addressing local-scale stressors and helped slow down rates of environmental degradation in the short term. However, the evaluation also found that GEF support during that period was less successful in addressing stressors that originated beyond these localities, such as siltation from the watersheds in which the protected areas were situated or encroachment by commercial fishers from neighbouring countries with lower environmental awareness and a lower interest in protecting the local resources.

These larger-scale drivers have inevitably resulted in continuing trends of degradation. It is not realistic to expect that the type of support provided by the GEF or other agencies can by itself counteract the numerous factors driving environmental degradation in the South China Sea, such as global demand for natural resources, population growth and increasing standards of living in the region. Larger-scale changes will have to be initiated at the scale of the countries and the broader consumer markets if positive environmental impact is to be sustained over the long term.

Thus, GEF support is intended to catalyse processes leading to these large-scale changes, with the engagement of country governments, private sector, civil society organizations, local communities and other stakeholders that, with time, will result in an improved environment (van den Berg and Todd 2011). Reaching this larger goal will, among other things, require a much broader adoption of the approaches demonstrated with GEF support. Though these processes may be initiated during a project's lifetime, such broader adoption is not expected to take place until perhaps decades after GEF support has ended.

In this context, a central concern of impact evaluation is to assess not only direct, immediate impacts, but also – and more important – the progress made towards achieving impact at the scale of the targeted system by assessing the extent to which broader adoption has begun, will continue or is likely to take place beyond project completion. Particularly important is assessing which approaches are truly effective, how broader adoption occurs, under what circumstances and why (Pawson and Tilley 1997; Pawson, Greenhalgh and Walshe 2005).

The evaluation found that broader adoption took place through three main processes. One was through mainstreaming, by which information, lessons or specific results of GEF projects were incorporated into broader stakeholder mandates and initiatives such as laws, policies, regulations and programmes. This might occur not only through governments but also within communities, other development agents and the private sector. Another process was through replication, by which GEF-supported initiatives were reproduced or adopted at comparable administrative or ecological scales, often in another geographical area or region. The third process was scaling-up, by which GEF-supported initiatives were expanded to cover larger geographical scales, often including new aspects or concerns that might be political, administrative or ecological in nature. Scaling-up allows the integration of concerns that cannot be resolved at lower scales and allows the spread of GEF contributions to areas contiguous to the original project sites.

These three processes of broader adoption may be at work in any combination at the same time for a given project and may take place simultaneously at different spatial and temporal scales, in different degrees of intensity and importance. Often, one process may have to occur for another process to take place. Assessing the effects of GEF support at a broader scale entails assessing evidence of these processes occurring as they relate to the broader adoption of technologies and approaches that have been shown effective in improving management of marine and coastal resources.

Contextual factors directly and primarily affected the differences in the extent of broader adoption and the extent or likelihood of long-term impact of GEF support. For example, although GEF support to the integrated coastal management (often referred to as ICM) approach was fairly consistent across the East Asia region and mostly appropriate for the demonstration sites that had been selected, scaling-up or replicating ICM beyond demonstration sites has greatly advanced mainly in countries such as China and the Philippines. In these countries, national policies of decentralization were more robust and local economic conditions and institutional absorptive capacities in the expansion areas were more developed. This is in contrast to processes taking place in countries such as Viet Nam or Thailand, where national decentralization policies were not as robust and where local conditions in the areas were not as conducive to ICM expansion.

Another factor at play was the extent to which the specific approach introduced was an appropriate response to the environmental concerns that were relevant to the locality. In Thailand, for example, it was found that the ICM approach is well suited for addressing the planning needs of Sriracha, a port city, as well as its adjacent coastal municipalities in Chonburi province. But it is not as well suited for dealing with livestock and agricultural waste, which is a non-point source pollution originating from the province's upland areas. Thus, although scaling-up from the demonstration in Sriracha to the entire coastal area of Chonburi was found to improve wastewater management in the area, developments in the upland areas were found to take place at a much slower rate. The evaluation therefore concluded that progress towards impact was taking place in the coastal municipalities and would likely result in large-scale impact in the long term; on the other hand, GEF support would be more effective if replicated or scaled up in similar coastal areas rather than scaling up the approach to upland areas where evidence of progress towards impact was not observed.

Conclusion

The evaluation found that in most areas where GEF support has taken place, evidence of positive direct and indirect change could be observed at the local, national and regional scales. At the local scale, in cases where evidence was available, most of the technologies and approaches demonstrated through GEF support directly contributed to reducing environmental stress and, in some cases, resulted in improvements in environmental status. At the regional scale, GEF-supported initiatives that encouraged collaboration and communication and trust-building across different scales; communication and trust serve as enabling conditions to regional environmental cooperation where several sovereign countries are involved. Most important, the triangulation of evidence showed that GEF support had a unique role in the region that linked interventions at multiple scales, which has resulted in significant contributions that no other actor could have made.

However, at the time of evaluation, these positive changes were a far cry from the impact that GEF support aims to achieve in the large marine ecosystem as a whole. Many environmental and socio-economic drivers had not been addressed due to the highly localized nature of many of the interventions. Perhaps even more important, not enough time had elapsed for more significant changes to manifest, especially at the regional scale. Under these conditions and given the larger GEF goals, the immediate or direct impacts observed merely indicated the extent to which the supported technologies and approaches were effective in addressing a specific concern in a particular context.

To evaluate the extent to which the GEF is meeting its broader goal, it is critical to assess not only the direct impacts that can be observed but also, more important, the likely intended long-term effects and indirect impacts of an intervention. To determine the catalytic or transformational contributions of any given programme or intervention, the evaluation must thus assess the extent to which there is progress in establishing the processes and conditions that will likely result in improved environmental conditions in the larger system.

This assessment is only possible if the evaluator has a sound understanding of the system being targeted by the intervention. This includes a good understanding of the system components, system boundaries and the chains of causality through which changes in the system take place. It is based on this sound understanding that the evaluator can assess if current interventions are contributing to conditions that are likely to lead to desired changes in the distant future. Understanding the system and how the system develops over time also provides the evaluator with a sense of the extent of change that is possible within a particular context, regardless of the ambitious objectives set by projects in their proposals. Similarly, through the better understanding of the chains of causality across geographical and temporal scales, the evaluator can assess which major gaps remain in the conditions necessary for change, and which critical ones need to be addressed to increase the likelihood of impact at a broader scale.

Postscript, 2020

Nearly ten years after the evaluation was completed,[8] the authors had the opportunity to undertake a post-completion evaluation aimed at assessing the sustainability of outcomes generated by the cluster of projects linked to the establishment of the Partnerships in Environmental Management for the Seas of East Asia (PEMSEA). PEMSEA, a regional organization that itself was an outcome of the GEF-supported cluster of projects, was envisioned as the main catalyst for the broader adoption of integrated coastal management (ICM) in the region. This unusual opportunity to revisit our evaluand allows us to verify some of our assumptions about the conditions that catalyse progress towards impact. This has also allowed us to reflect on our understanding of what evaluations can and cannot assess in interventions that aim for long-term, large-scale impact in complex systems.

Below we examine three of our key conclusions and related assumptions against our updated findings from the post-completion evaluation. Afterwards, we offer an alternative approach to evaluating interventions in large complex systems.

Initiatives to increase communication among governments and other stakeholders will foster collaborations to address regional environmental challenges. The Sustainable Development Strategy for the Seas of East Asia (SDS-SEA), intended as a regional framework and platform for collaborative action among the East Asian countries and its non-country partners, was updated in 2015 with continuing GEF support. From its original membership of 12 countries in 2003, the SDS-SEA signatories now number 11 countries, with its non-country partners increasing from 19 to 21. Included among the non-country partners are NGOs, multilateral organizations and private sector enterprises. Partners continue to meet every three years at the ministerial and technical levels through the East Asian Seas Congress; a smaller Executive Committee meets twice a year to oversee implementation of the SDS-SEA. Partner countries report on their progress during the meetings, exchange learning from their experience and discuss future directions.

The PEMSEA Network of Local Governments (PNLG), a mechanism for communication, learning and exchange among local governments that was created with GEF support in 2001 has continued to grow. Since 2011, its membership has doubled to 50 local governments in 10 countries, with a self-sustaining secretariat in Xiamen, China. The Gulf of Thailand oil spill preparedness initiative, signed by Cambodia, Thailand and Viet Nam in 2006, has evolved into an organization with a secretariat based in Thailand. The three countries have agreed on the coordinated implementation of the Gulf of Thailand Strategic Action Plan (2017–2021). Based on these developments, it appears that GEF support for communication initiatives has indeed contributed to countries continuing to work together, with the progress aided by uninterrupted grants over more than 25 years.

Broader adoption and significant environmental change at a regional scale is not expected to take place until decades after GEF support has ended. The updating of the SDS-SEA in 2015 included the adoption of a target to have 25% – previously 20% – of the coastline of participating countries under ICM by 2021. The extent and thoroughness of ICM adoption differs among countries; nonetheless, all the GEF project recipient countries except one had exceeded the 25% target by 2018.[9]

Currently all participating countries have ICM sites with intersectoral committees at the provincial level, and local staff to manage the ICM process. In total, 43 provinces across eight countries have ICM learning sites. An additional 76 sites are in various stages of ICM development and for which there is little information available.

The most aggressive adoption of ICM has taken place in China (32 sites), the Philippines (32 sites), Thailand (24 sites) and Viet Nam (14 sites). These developments challenge the evaluation's conclusion that broader adoption of ICM can only take place in highly decentralized countries such as China and the Philippines, rather than in Thailand and Viet Nam. According to country representatives interviewed for the post-completion evaluation, the ICM approach has been useful for addressing multiple intersectoral issues, and not just coastal or environmental.

In this case, it appears that time was the main constraint in the speed of ICM adoption rather than the inappropriateness of the approach.

However, technical and human resources continue to be a limitation that has slowed ICM adoption. Common across the GEF-supported countries was how PEMSEA-trained government staff eventually take on more financially attractive career opportunities in more urban locations. This relatively frequent staff turnover requires local governments to periodically hire and train new staff. Another common factor found to slow ICM adoption in most countries was the interruption of financial and political support for ICM by election cycles and corresponding changes in administrative priorities. This has required PEMSEA staff to also periodically re-orient government officials and try to convince them to continue their predecessor's priorities to improve the environment.

The updated findings on ICM scaling-up and replication show that while broader adoption has taken place more quickly than we expected, environmental change at the regional level is still elusive after more than 25 years of support. This is partly because a larger geographical scale requires a corresponding larger temporal scale for significant change to be detected. At the same time, progress on ICM implementation has differed from case to case. ICM has not been fully adopted in many sites, and in many cases is resource-constrained, as mentioned above. In China where much time, effort and resources have been invested in ICM, improvements in water quality have been observed over the last decade (e.g. Zeng et al. 2019); it is reasonable to conclude that such significant investments have contributed to reducing environmental stress along the China's coast.

Key to measuring ICM's contributions is having systems in place for monitoring and reporting environmental change. Evidence of ICM's positive impacts has been reported at the local level, but some are anecdotal. Many sites lack the infrastructure and human capacities to monitor water quality. At the regional level, there is no overall system to track social and environmental trends related to ICM implementation. Despite several GEF-supported initiatives promoting monitoring and reporting systems in the region, these initiatives have been adopted partially or sporadically by participating governments. For example, in 2008, PEMSEA introduced the State of the Coast (SOC) Report, a self-reporting scorecard consisting of legal, institutional, economic and environmental indicators that have now been adapted for the municipal, provincial, national and regional levels. PEMSEA has been assisting ICM sites in putting together SOC reports, but many remain in various stages of development (Padayao 2018); only a few sites have published more than one report to track changes over time.

Broader adoption of local-scale interventions by stakeholders at different scales is necessary so that large-scale drivers are addressed. At the time of the evaluation in 2011, ICM was being gradually replicated from pilot sites to neighbouring municipalities or scaled up at the provincial level; the adoption of national regulations in support of ICM was in its early stages. Many of the countries that had gained broad endorsement of ICM from the executive branches of national government then are now in the process of getting ICM-related laws approved by the legislative branches. In some countries, implementing mechanisms, such as intersectoral committees, are already being established. Key to this development is that most member countries have drawn on the experience of pilot ICM sites established in the first 10 to 15 years of GEF support to adopt legal, regulatory and institutional reforms that facilitate ICM adoption at a larger scale.

In China, lessons from the pilot sites have been leveraged through the China-PEMSEA Sustainable Coastal Management Cooperation Center (CPC), which provides training and support for ICM expansion in all coastal cities. Other countries such as Cambodia, Thailand and Indonesia are considering establishing similar centres. However, widespread geographical expansion of ICM does not automatically address large-scale drivers, many of which originate beyond coastal areas.

At least three ICM sites – also three of the longest-running ones supported by the GEF – have aimed to expand the geographical reach of the intervention to better match the ecological boundaries of the problem, which in this case is coastal pollution originating from both coastal and non-coastal areas.

One site is Xiamen in China where the local government linked with the existing Jiulong River Watershed Project (JRWP). Together they established a system to control pollution discharges in the river that supplied water to the city and discharged in Xiamen Bay. Using a payment-for-environmental-services (PES) arrangement, Xiamen transferred funds to the upstream municipalities in exchange for clean water. Ten years later in 2020, the PES system is still functioning and continues to result in improvements in the river's water quality. The second site is Manila Bay, where PEMSEA helped expand ICM in the cities surrounding the bay. The Manila Bay ICM initiative is currently linked with the country's River Basin Control Office to address pollution sources in the two major river basins of Pampanga River and Pasig River-Laguna de Bay through integrated basin management, stakeholder engagement and information management.

In the province of Chonburi in Thailand, the ICM programme expanded to include all 26 coastal municipalities from 2005 to 2009; by 2010, the 73 non-coastal municipalities had signed on to implement a Provincial Coastal Development Plan seeking to address upland pollution from pig and agricultural farms.[10] The city of Sriracha, Thailand's ICM pilot site, provided training in non-coastal municipalities. Clusters of municipalities were to prepare ICM plans for consolidation into the provincial ICM plan. However, due to logistical constraints and the large number of local governments involved, only the 26 coastal municipalities developed ICM action plans; ICM practices, particularly in solid waste management, continued to be applied throughout the entire province, coordinated by the provincial government. An interagency and multi-sectoral Provincial Marine and Coastal Resources Management Committee was established in 2015, having jurisdiction over both coastal and non-coastal municipalities. An informal survey of the heads of 25 coastal and 21 non-coastal municipalities in 2015 showed that ICM for them created a "platform for intermunicipal dialogue and exchange of information" (Barnette and Wiwekwin 2018). We were, however, unable to reach local government officials to get an update on what has happened since.

While we do not have complete information on environmental outcomes in these three ICM sites, based on the developments post-evaluation, it appears that it may indeed be possible to address large-scale drivers by scaling up a local-scale intervention such as ICM. In turn, implementation at higher scales has been made possible by the existence of enabling conditions at the corresponding higher scales, such as the regulations and intersectoral committees gradually established at the national and provincial levels after many years of learning from pilot sites.

From evaluating static long-term goals to evaluating development trajectories

The three main assumptions examined in this postscript remain mostly valid. However, the analytical model used in the evaluation had other misleading assumptions that have become evident in retrospection. First, in the introduction of the chapter, we stress the importance of assessing the progress made towards achieving impact. This assumes that "impact", which is the goal of the intervention and assumed to take place sometime in the distant future, would remain unchanged. Second, the model adopted by the evaluation assumes that a successful intervention would put in place a set of conditions that, once achieved, would over time enable the achievement of the desired long-term goal.

However, interventions concerned with large complex systems such as the East Asian seas are better understood as efforts to steer such large systems towards a development trajectory that enhances the likelihood that desired benefits or services are generated. This trajectory is constantly influenced by multiple actors and factors, which introduces a high degree of uncertainty into the process. Over time, the predetermined conditions for success might no longer contribute to sustaining the desired benefits and services. Shifting circumstances and new information generated during implementation will require periodic reassessment of the conditions that are assumed to enable long-term change and, if necessary, a redefinition how "impact"—the long-term objective of the intervention—is defined. Since the system is inherently unpredictable, it is therefore more pragmatic to track its trajectory in providing benefits and services desired, rather than just the extent to which the pre-specified enabling conditions have been established.

The environmental problems of the South China Sea and the other East Asian seas are far from solved. Even after more than 25 years of GEF support, it may not be realistic to expect a dramatic improvement in the environmental health of these water bodies. Nevertheless, there is considerable anecdotal evidence that the types of adaptive approaches and models supported by the GEF help to steer the region towards a development trajectory that enhances the delivery of valued environmental and economic services.

PEMSEA's long-term goals have not remained static. To ensure the desired level of environmental services, the overall regional goal was increased from 20% to 25% of the region's coastline placed under ICM. Similarly, ICM practices were scaled up to address stresses originating from non-coastal municipalities. The conditions targeted for ICM adoption to enable long-term change have gradually been adapted to specific local and national circumstances, and are increasingly incorporating new approaches, sectors and stakeholders.

What we have yet to see is a better understanding of the extent to which the many local success stories translate into a broader development trajectory that will ensure the sustainability of the desired services at a regional scale in the East Asian seas. Systematic and regular State of the Coast reports at multiple scales could provide valuable information to assess the broader trajectory and make adjustments if necessary.

As we say in our conclusion almost ten years ago, the evaluator needs a sound understanding of the system; it is clear now that it is also important to understand how the system develops over time. However, it is not realistic to expect that we will ever have perfect knowledge to predict when, how and what long-term impacts will take place due to the unpredictable nature of complex systems. Often we may not see the outcomes we wanted or expected in the time that we predicted. After more than 25 years of GEF support, we expected to see some large-scale environmental changes in the region by now, yet there is no counterfactual region to allow us to say if the system's pace of change would have been faster or slower without this continuous long-term support. In this sense, trying to predict when long-term goals might finally be achieved is an almost futile exercise. More useful may be to periodically assess changes in the system and the extent to which interventions have adapted in ways that support the development trajectory towards desired benefits and services – which themselves could also change over time.

Notes

1 This sea is called the "South Sea", 南海, Nánhǎi in China and the "East Sea", Biển Đông, in Viet Nam. In September 2012, the president of the Philippines issued Administrative Order No. 29, renaming the "maritime areas on the western side of the Philippine archipelago as the West Philippine Sea", to cover the areas within the Philippines' Exclusive Economic Zone. "South China Sea" is the international name for this area as recognized by the International Hydrographic Organization and is therefore the name used throughout this evaluation.

2 These are the Convention on Biological Diversity, United Nations Framework Convention on Climate Change, the UN Convention to Combat Desertification, Stockholm Convention on Persistent Organic Pollutants and the Minamata Convention on Mercury. For more information on the GEF, see https://www.thegef.org/about-us.

3 The GEF strategy for the international waters focal area is largely focused on facilitating cooperative action among governments that derive benefits from a shared water body, such as a large marine ecosystem, lake, river or aquifer. The initial approach is the undertaking of a transboundary diagnostic analysis, through which threats to the shared water body that cross or extend beyond national jurisdictions (i.e. are transboundary) are identified based on available scientific data. The countries then jointly prioritize which of these environmental concerns to take action on. The priority environmental concerns and actions with which to address them are formalized through the countries' agreement to a regional Strategic Action Programme.

4 Scale in this context is to be understood as the spatial, temporal, quantitative or analytical dimensions used to measure and study any phenomenon (Gibson et al. 2000).

5 A higher scale implies a greater geographical scope, and a greater number and types of interacting elements, such as ecosystems and social, political and economic sub-systems.

6 A list of large marine ecosystems similar to the South China Sea and Gulf of Thailand in terms of ecological, political and socio-economic characteristics was derived from Mahon et al. (2010).
7 These were the 1992 United Nations Conference on Environment and Development (the Rio Earth Summit) in Rio de Janeiro, the 2002 World Summit on Sustainable Development in Johannesburg and their precursor, the 1972 United Nations Conference on the Human Environment (Stockholm Sustainable Development Conference) in Stockholm.
8 The Impact Evaluation of GEF Support to International Waters in the South China Sea and Adjacent Areas was undertaken from 2010 to 2012.
9 Various figures have been published in 2018 and 2019 PEMSEA reports and proceedings of the project steering committee.
10 In the case of Chonburi, there was no major river draining into marine water bodies, only small streams and canals.

References

Anderies, J. M., M.A. Janssen, and E. Ostrom, 'A framework to analyze the robustness of social-ecological systems from an institutional perspective', *Ecology and Society*, 9(1): 18–36, 2004.

Babcock, R.C. et al., 'Decadal trends in marine reserves reveal differential rates of change in direct and indirect effects', *Proceedings of the National Academy of Sciences*, 107(43): 18256–18261, 2010.

Barnette, P. and N. Wiwekwin, 'Integrated coastal management implementation and scaling up in chonburi province, Thailand, In: Chua, T.-E., L.M. Chou, G. Jacinto, S.A. Ross, and D. Bonga, eds., *Local Contributions to Global Sustainable Agenda: Case Studies in Integrated Coastal Management in the East Asian Seas Region*. Partnerships in Environmental Management for the Seas of East Asia (PEMSEA) and Coastal Management Center (CMC), Quezon City, Philippines, 469–482, 2018.

Brondizio, E., E. Ostrom and O.R. Young, 'Connectivity and the governance of multilevel socioecological systems: The role of social capital', *Annual Review of Environmental Resources*, 34: 253–278, 2009.

Cash, D.W. et al., 'Scale and cross-scale dynamics: Governance and information in a multilevel world', *Ecology and Society*, 11(2): 8–20, 2006.

Davies, R., 'Scale, complexity and the representation of theories of change', *Evaluation*, 10(1): 101–121, 2004.

Dulvy, N., R.P. Freckleton and N.V.C. Polunin, 'Coral reef cascades and the indirect effects of predator removal by exploitation', *Ecology Letters*, 7: 410–416, 2004.

Folke, C., S. Carpenter, T. Elmqvist, L. Gunderson, C.S. Holling and B. Walker, 'Resilience and sustainable development: Building adaptive capacity in a world of transformations, *AMBIO: A Journal of Human Environment*, 31: 437–440, 2002.

Folke, C., L. Pritchard Jr., F. Berkes, J. Colding and U. Svedin, 'The problem of fit between ecosystems and institutions: Ten years later, *Ecology and Society*, 12(1): 30–42, 1997.

Folke, C. et al., 'Regime shifts, resilience, and biodiversity in ecosystem management', *Annual Review of Ecology, Evolution, and Systematics*, 35: 557–581, 2004.

Gibson, C.C., E. Ostrom and T.-K. Ahn, 'The concept of scale and the human dimensions of global change: a survey', *Ecological Economics*, 32(2): 217–239, 2000.

Gladwell, M., *The Tipping Point: How Little Things Can Make a Big Difference*, Boston, Little Brown, 2000.

Global Environment Facility (GEF), '*Impact Evaluation of GEF Support to International Waters in the South China Sea and Adjacent Areas*', Global Environment Facility Independent Evaluation Office (GEF IEO), Washington, DC, 2012.

Gunderson, L.H. and C.S. Holling, eds., *Panarchy: Understanding Transformations in Human and Natural Systems*, Washington, DC, Island Press, 2002.

Holling, C.S., 'Understanding the complexity of economic, ecological, and social systems', *Ecosystems*, 4: 390–405, 2001.

Jackson, J.B.C. et al., 'Historical overfishing and the recent collapse of coastal ecosystems', *Science*, 293(5530): 629–638, 2001.

Kinzig, A. P., P. Ryan, M. Etienne, H. Allison, T. Elmqvist and B.H. Walker, 'Resilience and regime shifts: assessing cascading effects', *Ecology and Society*, 11(2): 20–43, 2006.

Liu, J. et al., 'Complexity of coupled human and natural systems', *Science*, 317: 1513–1516, 2007.

Mahon, R., L. Fanning, P. McConney and R. Pollnac, 'Governance characteristics of large marine ecosystems', *Marine Policy*, 34(5): 919–927, 2010.

Mayne, J. 'Contribution analysis: Addressing cause and effect, In: R. Schwartz, K. Forss, and M. Marra, eds., *Evaluating the Complex*, 53–97, New Brunswick, NJ, Transaction Publishers, 2011.

Mee, L. D., H.T. Dublin and A. A. Eberhard, 'Evaluating the global environment facility: A goodwill gesture or a serious attempt to deliver global benefits?', *Global Environment Change*, 18(4): 800–810, 2006.

Organisation for Economic Co-operation and Development (OECD), 'Glossary of key terms in evaluation and results based management, 2002, available at http://www.oecd.org/development/peer-reviews/2754804.pdf, accessed August 18 2013.

Ostrom, E., 'A general framework for analyzing sustainability of social-ecological systems', *Science*, 325 (5939): 419–422, 2009.

Ostrom, E., 'Beyond markets and states: Polycentric governance of complex economic systems', *American Economic Review*, 100: 1–33, 2010.

Padayao, D. 'Enhancing accountability in environmental governance through the state of the coasts reporting system, In: Chua, T.-E., L.M. Chou, G. Jacinto, S.A. Ross, and D. Bonga, eds., *Local Contributions to Global Sustainable Agenda: Case Studies in Integrated Coastal Management in the East Asian Seas Region*. Partnerships in Environmental Management for the Seas of East Asia (PEMSEA) and Coastal Management Center (CMC), Quezon City, Philippines, 219–234, 2018.

Pandolfi, J. M. et al., 'Are U.S. coral reefs on the slippery slope to slime?', *Science*, 307(5716): 1725–1726, 2005.

Pawson, R., T. Greenhalgh, G. Harvey and K. Walshe, 'Realist review – A new method of systematic review designed for complex policy interventions', *Journal of Health Services Research and Policy*, 10(suppl 1): 21–34, 2005.

Pawson, R., and N. Tilley, (1997). *Realistic Evaluation*, London, Sage, 1997.

Sanderson, I., ' Evaluation in complex policy systems, *Evaluation*, 6: 433–454, 2000.

Stern, E., N. Stame, J. Mayne, K. Forss, R. Davies and B. Befani, '*Broadening the Range of Designs and Methods for Impact Evaluations*', London, Department for International Development, 2012, available at http://r4d.dfid.gov.uk/pdf/outputs/misc_infocomm/DFIDWorkingPaper38.pdf, accessed May 24 2013.

Taleb, N. N., *The Black Swan: The Impact of the Highly Improbable*, Second Edition, New York, Random House, 2007.

van den Berg, R. and D. Todd, 'The full road to impact: The experience of the Global Environment Facility fourth overall performance study', *Journal of Development Effectiveness*, 3(3): 389–413, 2011.

Zeng, J., Yin, B., Wang, Y., and Huai, B. (2019). Significantly decreasing harmful algal blooms in China seas in the early 21st century. *Marine Pollution Bulletin*, 139, 270–274.

7

ASSESSING PROGRESS TOWARDS IMPACTS IN ENVIRONMENTAL PROGRAMMES USING THE FIELD REVIEW OF OUTCOMES TO IMPACTS METHODOLOGY

David Todd and Rob Craig

Impacts in the context of environmental programmes and projects

The GEF Evaluation Office impact evaluation programme's main objective was to evaluate the long-term results of interventions several years after GEF support had concluded – to assess the sustainability and replication of results and draw out lessons learned. An earlier GEF evaluation, *The Role of Local Benefits in Global Environmental Programs*[3] had demonstrated that social means must be used in order to deliver environmental results. This is because human behaviour towards the environment is a critical factor in achieving sustainable natural resource management. Examples include biodiversity (the interactions between the local human population and natural resources), climate change (the role of domestic and industrial energy use), international waters (damage caused by overfishing, nutrient spill and pollution) and land degradation (the importance of changing land and water use practices in farming systems).

These insights on the importance of using social means to achieve environmental ends were combined with the use of cause and effect chains as a theoretical basis upon which to assess progress towards long-term objectives. The result was a specific fieldwork-based evaluative approach, known as the 'Review of Outcomes to Impacts'(ROtI). This was used to evaluate progress towards project impacts in a series of studies, one of which is described in detail here: The Seychelles Marine Ecosystem Management Project (SEYMEMP).[4]

The elements of a Theory of Change for environmental interventions

The Theory of Change for a project is the logical sequence of conditions and factors that are necessary to deliver its ultimate impact. A basic project Theory of Change starts with activities and develops through a means-ends hierarchy until finally reaching a project's impacts. Project Terminal Evaluations implicitly assess against a basic Theory of Change as far as outcomes, but do not usually go further in assessing the crucial last steps towards impact. The Review of Outcomes to Impacts assessment takes up where Terminal Evaluations leave off and focuses on developing and assessing a detailed Theory of Change between outcomes and impacts, referred to as *outcomes–impacts pathways*.

Key elements in the outcomes-impacts pathways are Intermediate States, impact drivers and assumptions; these are defined in Table 7.1 and illustrated in Figure 7.1. If project outcomes are assessed to be successfully delivered and the key elements of the Theory of Change between outcomes and impacts are in place, then it is reasonable to conclude that there is indirect evidence that the impact has been or will be achieved with time.

TABLE 7.1 Definitions of Theory of Change Elements in the Outcomes-Impacts Pathways

Theory of Change terms	*Definition*
Outcomes	Short- to medium-term behavioural or systemic effects result from outputs designed to help achieve the project's impacts (e.g. capacities developed).
Intermediate States	The transitional conditions between a project's outcomes and impacts that must be achieved in order to deliver the intended impacts.
Impact drivers	The significant factors that, if present, are expected to contribute to the ultimate realization of project impacts and that are within the ability of the project to influence.
Assumptions	The significant factors that, if present, are expected to contribute to the ultimate realization of project impacts but that are largely beyond the power of the project to influence or address.

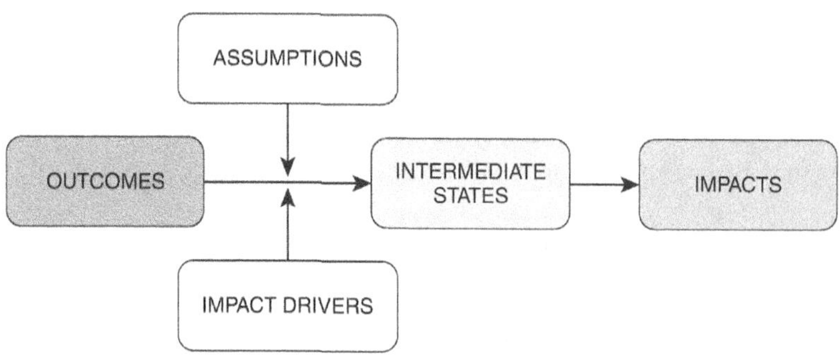

FIGURE 7.1 The Relationship between the Key Elements in a Project Theory of Change

The field Review of Outcomes to Impacts methodology

One of the methods developed and practised by the GEF Independent Evaluation Office[5] to assess progress towards impacts of completed GEF-assisted activities is the 'field Review of Outcomes to Impacts'.[6] This uses a combination of different information collection methods, as shown in Figure 7.2. It begins with a desk review, proceeds with consultations with key project stakeholders and concludes (when possible) with fact-finding at the project site or sites. Ideally, field investigation is followed by further consultation with key informants and additional desk research to confirm information and project documentation facts that were collected in the field.

During the assessment process, it is necessary to gradually develop an understanding of the status of the Intermediate States, impact drivers and assumptions through a combination of the steps shown in Figure 7.2. On this basis, the evaluator is able to draw conclusions and establish a set of qualitative and/or quantitative findings. Specifics of the key methodological steps are discussed in the following.

Desk research

As far as possible, all relevant documentation is consulted during the initial desk research step. This includes previous evaluation documents, the project outputs/terminal reports and any subsequent reports relating to the sustainability or follow-up to the project. At a minimum, a thorough understanding of the project document and Terminal Evaluation is an essential foundation for undertaking the subsequent steps of a field Review of Outcomes to Impacts assessment. A useful output of the initial desk research step is a 'key issues checklist' that summarizes the key information that the assessment needs to focus on in order to validate and assess the project Theory of Change.

Key informants

The consultation with key informants provides an opportunity to obtain additional documents, either produced for or resulting from the project, that assist in cross-checking and validating the assessment. Consultations are conducted in the following order:

1. Officials: The consultation process should start with the officials involved in the project, for example, officials from participating government departments and representatives of project implementing agencies.

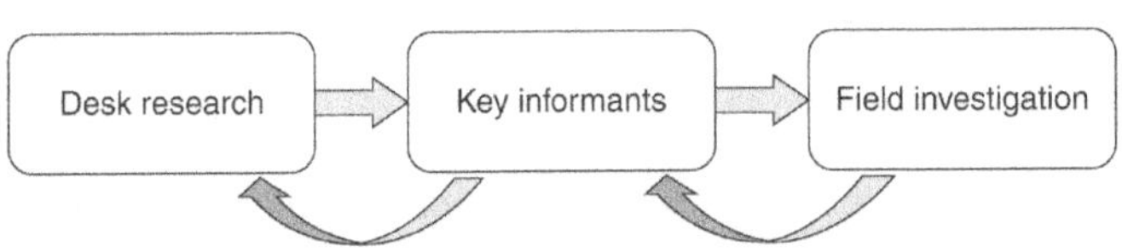

FIGURE 7.2 Steps in the Field-Based Review of Outcomes to Impacts Assessment Process

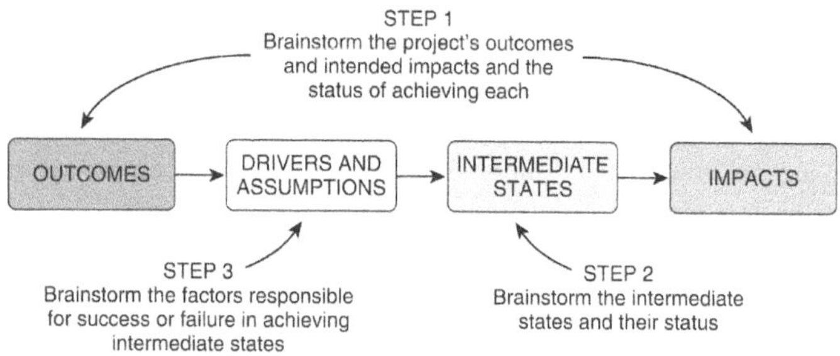

FIGURE 7.3 Steps in Conducting a Field Review of Outcomes to Impacts Analysis with Group or Individual Key Informants

2. Focus groups: The Review of Outcomes to Impacts field assessment exercise is ideally conducted as a group exercise with a cross-section of individuals that were responsible for the design and implementation of the specific project being assessed. In some cases, it is necessary to hold more than one focus group for a particular project depending on the logistics and the politics of bringing various individuals together. In other cases, it is not possible to convene focus groups; in these instances, it is necessary to discuss the relevant section of the Theory of Change with each individual or institution in turn.
3. Individual experts: After the focus group exercise, it is often necessary to follow up and cross-check findings with key individuals who were not able to attend the focus group meetings.

The basic order of activities to undertake during the Review of Outcomes to Impacts Exercise[7] with the focus group and individual experts is illustrated in Figure 7.3.

Step 1: Validating project logic

This is done by presenting the outcomes and impacts identified during the desk review stage and asking the focus group to validate and comment on them. Key questions to ask are

- What was the project ultimately trying to achieve (i.e. project impact)?
- What did the project actually achieve at completion (i.e. project outcomes)?

Step 2: Assessing Intermediate States

The focus group then identifies the Intermediate States and the results are compared with those from the desk review. Questions to ask in identifying and assessing the Intermediate States are

- What has already been achieved since project completion to contribute to impacts?
- What else needs to happen to deliver the intended impacts?

Step 3: Assessing the impact delivery process

Once an understanding has been developed of the achievement or otherwise of the intermediate state, it is then possible to look at the factors that may have resulted in this situation by examining the presence or absence of the identified impact drivers and assumptions. The basic question to ask is

- What were the reasons for successes or failures in delivering the Intermediate States?

The Review of Outcomes to Impacts exercise with the focus groups (and to a lesser extent with individual experts) uses visualization techniques to present the elements of the Theory of Change and to facilitate a collective process of thinking.

The end result is the establishment of a stakeholder consensus on the outcomes–impacts Theory of Change model for the specific project, plus a more detailed understanding of the status of the project's outcomes–impacts pathways and the key underlying factors responsible for success or failure. Annex 1 shows the specific Theory of Change model developed by the focus group exercise for the Seychelles Marine Ecosystem Management Project (SEYMEMP).

Field investigations

The project Theory of Change models and the initial assessments given during the key informant focus groups and consultations are then cross-checked through field visits to former project sites and discussions with relevant beneficiary institutions and communities. This also provides a good opportunity to gather available field data to back up the overall assessment findings. These findings should then be further cross-checked with the key informants and available literature collected during the process.

Reporting of the assessment findings

The field Review of Outcomes to Impacts rating system provides a simple score that gives a summary indication of progress towards the project's expected impact (see Table 7.2). The rating system is applied at the different hierarchical levels of the Theory of Change – namely at the individual Theory of Change element level

TABLE 7.2 Field Review of Outcomes to Impacts Rating System

Rating	*Description*
0	Not achieved
1	Poorly achieved
2	Partially achieved
3	Fully achieved

(outcomes, Intermediate States, impact drivers and assumptions), at the overall strategy level and at the overall project level.

Below the rating, scores are elaborated with descriptions of the general interpretations implied from a theoretical and/or delivery perspective. These descriptions are provided as guidance for scoring; it is recognized that projects are extremely complicated and that evaluators need to use value judgements in order to score projects.

Not achieved – (0)

From a *theoretical perspective*, the Theory of Change aspect is not explicitly or implicitly identified by the project, and/or from a *delivery perspective*, very little progress has been made towards achieving the Theory of Change; the conditions are not in place for future progress.

Poorly achieved – (1)

From a *theoretical perspective*, there are no appropriate mechanisms set out to achieve the Theory of Change aspect after GEF funding ended, and/or from a *delivery perspective*, little progress has been made towards achieving the Theory of Change aspect; the conditions are in place for future progress.

Partially achieved – (2)

From a *theoretical perspective*, the Theory of Change aspect is explicitly recognized and the mechanisms set out to achieve it are appropriate but insufficient (e.g. there is no clear allocation of responsibilities for implementing the mechanisms after GEF funding ends). From a *delivery perspective*, moderate and continuing progress is being made towards achieving the Theory of Change aspect, although there is not yet a strong basis for the eventual delivery of the intended global environmental benefits.

Fully achieved – (3)

From a *theoretical perspective*, the Theory of Change aspect is explicitly recognized and appropriate and sufficient mechanisms to achieve it are apparent (e.g. specific allocation of responsibilities after GEF funding ended), and/or from a *delivery perspective* substantial progress has been made towards achieving the Theory of Change aspect and a strong basis is in place for eventual delivery of the intended Global Environment Benefits.

The reporting of the Review of Outcomes to Impacts assessment is initially done for each strategy, assessing the individual Theory of Change element level comprising the strategy (i.e. the outcomes, impact drivers, assumptions and Intermediate States). The assessment for the Intermediate States, by virtue of the means-ends logic of the Theory of Change model, is based both on a direct assessment of the intermediate state itself and on the individual assessments of the relevant outcomes, impact drivers and assumptions. This is necessarily an inexact measurement, based on the evaluator's considered judgement of the achievement of the intermediate state rather than on any definitive measure of achievement.

Background: the Seychelles Marine Ecosystem Management Project

The Seychelles Marine Ecosystem Project was a medium-sized GEF/World Bank project that was implemented from August 2000 to March 2004. The $1.25 million project fell under the Coastal and Marine Biodiversity Operational Programme of the GEF Biodiversity Focal Area. GEF provided $0.67 million in funding; the Government of the Seychelles co-financed the remainder. The stated goal of the project was the 'successful management of Seychelles' unique and threatened marine ecosystems in light of recent global and local changes in particular coral bleaching'. Its overall objective was 'identify, monitor, manage and rehabilitate remnant ecosystems by the removal of critical barriers including lack of skills, scientific understanding and conservation management knowledge and direction'.

At closure, the project was favourably rated by its Terminal Evaluation, with the delivery of project outcomes considered to have been 'satisfactory' and the probability of sustainability assessed to be 'likely'.

This chapter presents a Review of Outcomes to Impacts that seeks to answer whether the completed project has in fact contributed to achieving lasting and beneficial environmental impacts.

The impacts towards which the SEYMEMP would contribute

The starting point for the SEYMEMP Review of Outcomes to Impacts assessment was to identify the project's intended environmental impacts, which for GEF projects is the delivery of global environmental benefits. These are defined in the Review of Outcomes to Impacts manual as 'lasting improvements in the status of an aspect of the global environment that safeguards environmental functioning and integrity as well as benefiting human society'. The SEYMEMP project identified four key aspects of the marine environment that provided the justification for GEF support to this project and which formed the project's intended global environmental benefits. The benefits are lasting improvements in the status of hard coral reefs, reef fish assemblages, marine turtles and whale sharks (see Table 7.3).

It is important to have a clear understanding of the desired final impact of an intervention, since this provides the foundation for the development of an appropriate outcomes–impacts Theory of Change. To characterize the SEYMEMP global environmental benefits further, Table 7.3 provides the rationale for their selection according to their documented global significance, lists the key attributes essential for their long-term survival and identifies the main threats to attainment of the global environmental benefits.

TABLE 7.3 Global Environmental Benefits (to Biodiversity) for the SEYMEMP Project

Global environmental benefits	*Rationale for global significance*	*Key attributes*	*Threats*
Lasting improvement in the status of:			
Hard coral reefs of the Western Indian Ocean	The Seychelles coral reefs are listed as an area of 'rich to very rich species diversity'.* In addition, the comparative lack of scientific information of the coral reefs makes it an important area for international scientific research in future	• Recruitment • Water quality • Water temperature	• Grazing organisms, e.g. Crown of Thorns starfish/urchins • oral bleaching and diseases • Pollution • Sedimentation/landslides • Nautical activities
Reef fish assemblages	Important indicators of reef structure and composition	• Diversity • Abundance of key species • Size of key species	• Fisheries • Pollution • Sedimentation/landslides
Whale sharks	Listed on the Convention on International Trade in Endangered Species Appendix II, as data deficient by the International Union for the Conservation of Nature, and in Annex 11 of the Convention on Migratory Species	• Numbers • Reproduction rates • Sex ratios	• Nautical activities • Elevated water/beach temperatures (global warming)
Marine turtles	One of the five largest remaining global populations of critically endangered hawksbill turtles (Eretmochelys imbricata) and a significant population of endangered green turtles (Chelonia mydas)	• Availability of forage (coral reef, sponges and seagrass) • Breeding sites • Reproduction rates • Sex ratios	

Outlining the outcomes–impacts Theory of Change for SEYMEMP

The development of the SEYMEMP outcomes–impacts Theory of Change was based on a review of project documentation and discussions with key informants. Principal consultations with key informants were conducted as a focus group exercise using visualization techniques (as explained earlier and in detail in the GEF Review of Outcomes to Impacts Manual).[8] The resulting overall project outcomes-impacts Theory of Change is presented in Table 7.4 and in the chapter Annex 1. The Theory of Change sets out what was intended to occur after project completion in order to eventually achieve the intended project impacts. In combination, the three Intermediate States would deliver direct actions to address threats to global environmental benefits (Intermediate State 1), an effective Marine Protected Area (MPA)[9] system to protect key marine sites (Intermediate State 2) and an enabling policy environment to ensure national and regional compliance and cooperation (Intermediate State 3). Together, the review considered these three states to be sufficient to achieve the intended impact.

Evaluating progress against the Theory of Change

According to the Theory of Change, achieving the three Intermediate States is necessary (although not necessarily sufficient) in order to achieve the intended impact. Therefore, the Review of Outcomes to Impacts assessed, in detail, the progress that was made since project completion along each of the cause and effect pathways from the four outcomes (already assessed in the project Terminal Evaluation) towards the three Intermediate States. However, in order to keep this chapter to a reasonable length, only one of the pathways (towards Intermediate State 3) is examined in detail. In the original review,[10] all pathways were comprehensively reviewed to provide the evidence necessary to draw conclusions on progress towards impacts.

Assessment of progress towards Intermediate State 3: implementation and mainstreaming of enabling marine policies at national and regional levels

Theory of Change overview

The third intermediate state, 'implementation and mainstreaming of enabling marine policies at national and regional levels', was considered necessary to ensure that support and commitment for marine protection is maintained and scaled up through the formulation and enactment of enabling policies and laws. These would provide incentives and support mechanisms for marine ecosystem users (e.g. fisheries and tourism sectors) to comply, cooperate and become active partners in marine conservation. This intermediate state includes the neighbouring countries in the Indian Ocean in order to seek regional cooperation in protecting the greater ecosystem on which the Seychelles marine environment depends.

TABLE 7.4 The SEYMEMP Outcomes-Impacts Theory of Change

Outcomes	*Impact drivers & assumptions*	*Intermediate States*	*Impacts*
What was the situation at the end of the project?	What key factors were responsible for delivery (or non-delivery) of the Intermediate States?	What has happened since the project ended, or still needs to happen, to achieve impacts?	What was the project ultimately aiming to achieve?
Outcome 1: Seychelles marine ecosystems and their values are better understood	Impact driver: Research and monitoring methodology integrated into ongoing initiatives and institutions Impact driver: Research and monitoring capacity built in Seychellois institutions responsible for marine protection	Intermediate state: Coping mechanisms addressing major threats to marine ecosystems are rolled out nationally	Reduced human and natural threats to Seychelles' fragile marine ecosystem habitats; fauna
Outcome 2: Coping mechanisms that directly address marine ecosystem degradation introduced	Impact driver: Coping mechanisms integrated and funded by existing structures		Enhanced conservation status of four marine global environmental benefits

Outcome 3: Integrated marine protected area system operationalized	Impact driver: Accountability and transparency in decision-making Impact driver: marine protected area network is adequate to protect key ecosystem functioning Impact driver: Financial sustainability of marine protected area network is established Assumption: Government/Department of the Environment has a clear vision of what it wants from plan and takes leadership role Assumption: There is sufficient buy-in and common ground between stakeholders	Intermediate state: marine protected area network is being managed effectively to achieve conservation goals
Outcome 4: Broad stakeholder involvement and cooperation in the implementation of regional marine conservation programmes	Impact driver: Policies and Regulations established, understood and enforced Impact driver: There are sufficient incentives for marine users to participate in programmes Assumption: Political leadership is committed to prioritizing marine issues	Intermediate state: Implementation and mainstreaming of enabling marine policies at the national and regional levels

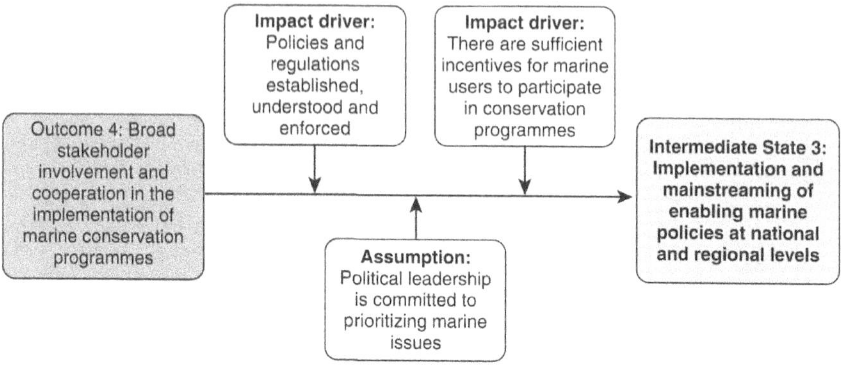

FIGURE 7.4 Theory of Change for Intermediate State 3

The project outcome that leads towards Intermediate State 3 is Outcome 4 (see Figure 7.4). This outcome focused on public education about the marine environment and on obtaining broad stakeholder inputs through institutional involvement and partnerships. Such partnerships included links with other regional marine conservation initiatives.

In order for the intermediate state to be achieved, the review identified two impact drivers and one external assumption, as shown in Figure 7.4. The first, 'policies and regulations established, understood and enforced', is critical to achieving the intermediate state, because clear rules and effective enforcement of regulations protecting the marine environment are the foundations for obtaining broad compliance from marine users for ensuring conservation. The second impact driver, 'there are sufficient incentives for marine users to participate in conservation programmes', seeks to complement law enforcement through education and tangible incentives to encourage marine users to proactively conserve the ecosystem. The external assumption, 'political leadership is committed to prioritizing marine issues', is critical to realizing the enabling policies and incentive schemes of the impact drivers.

The next section assesses the extent to which this element of the Theory of Change has been realized by examining the achievement of its components, starting with the outcomes and finishing with the intermediate state 3. Table 7.5 provides a summary of this analysis.

Theory of Change assessment

Outcomes

The review agreed with the Terminal Evaluation that good progress was made in delivering the project's fourth outcome. The project successfully delivered awareness-raising activities, particularly through using local media and workshops to educate coral reef users (e.g. boat handlers, divers) and encouraging public participation

TABLE 7.5 Outcomes-Impacts Assessment Findings for Intermediate State 3

Theory of Change component	*Qualitative Assessment*	*Rating*
Outcome #4: Broad stakeholder involvement and support	Good level of public awareness-raising activities (workshops, local media, and publicity) In addition to the project executing agencies (Ministry of Environment, Marine Conservation Society of Seychelles and Marine Parks Authority), the project also involved the Ministry of Land Use and Habitat, Seychelles Fishing Authority and the Seychelles Islands Foundation to encourage wider stakeholder participation and build local capacities Limited evidence that the above partnership led to significant local capacity building and inadequate links made with regional initiatives (e.g. integrated coastal area management process)	2 (partially achieved)
Impact Driver: Policies and regulations established, understood and enforced	Based on the SEYMEMP research findings, the government declared the whale shark as a protected species under the Wild Animals and Birds Protection Act (S.I. 1 of 2003) and the whale shark programme is now a national programme of action The Government of the Seychelles endorsed the RAMSAR Convention in 2005, along with the enactment of the Wetlands Policy, which provides clear regulations and a mandate to the Wetlands Unit. The unit has successfully policed illegal activities (dumping/ reclamation) and ensured that major new developments undertake environmental impact assessments and comply with guidelines. However, capacity in the unit is not yet sufficient to enforce guidelines at the household level	2 (partially achieved)
Impact Driver: There are sufficient incentives for marine users to participate in conservation programmes	Limited progress has been made in getting the tourism or fishing industry to adopt mooring installations and to support other initiatives to reduce marine degradation. However, the new UNDP/GEF Mainstreaming Biodiversity Management into Production Sector Activities should address this issue. Through education awareness, the Wetlands Unit has had success in getting schools and hotels to look after their wetlands (e.g. establishment of the Hotel Babarons' wetland boardwalk), although enforcement is still the most effective tool	1 (poorly achieved)

(Continued)

TABLE 7.5 (Continued)

Theory of Change component	*Qualitative Assessment*	*Rating*
Assumption: Political leadership is committed to prioritizing marine issues	The government is committed to the marine environment, but lacks financial resources, especially since the tightening of government spending under the new International Monetary Fund-supported economic reform programme and the reduction of international donor support for the environment coming to the Seychelles The government has not taken the critical leadership role needed to overcome the impasse in agreeing to and implementing an integrated marine protected area system plan with devolved responsibility for implementation	1 (poorly achieved)
Intermediate State #3: Implementation and mainstreaming of enabling marine policies at national and regional levels	Awareness is certainly in place, and some policies are in place at the national and regional levels. However, there is a need for policies and actions to protect the behavioural aspects of marine life, e.g. migratory routes, corridors and spawning areas, which are not covered under the current marine protected area system New initiatives, such as the European Union-funded Regional Programme for the Sustainable Management of the Coastal Zones of the Indian Ocean Countries and the new set of UNDP/GEF projects are focusing on mainstreaming existing policies	1 (poorly achieved)

in monitoring of turtles, whale sharks and aspects of the coral reef programme. The project also involved the Ministry of Land Use and Habitat, the Seychelles Fishing Authority and the Seychelles Islands Foundation in order to encourage wider stakeholder participation and build local capacities. However, an over-reliance on overseas consultants (coupled with limitations on their time) meant that local capacity-building activities were not given the attention or time needed to make a difference. In addition, intended partnerships with broader initiatives (such as the integrated coastal area management project) were not realized. The partial delivery of this outcome provided some basis for the eventual achievement of Intermediate State Number Three, depending on the status of the impact drivers and assumptions.

Impact drivers/external assumptions

The review found evidence that the first impact driver, 'policies and regulations established, understood and enforced', was partially delivered. The project made effective contributions towards strengthening environmental policy and regulations in the Seychelles. A major accomplishment was towards modifying the Wild Animal and Birds Protection Act to include whale sharks (S.I. 1 of 2003). This government decision was based on the project's whale shark programme research findings and has since become a national programme of action. Another significant piece of enabling policy to which the project contributed concerned wetlands management, with the government's endorsement of the 1971 Convention on Wetlands of International Importance (the RAMSAR Convention) and its enactment of the Wetlands Policy in 2005. These have provided the Wetlands Unit with the regulations and mandate to police against illegal activities (such as dumping and reclamation) and to ensure that major new developments comply with wetlands guidelines. This should have the long-term effect of reducing contamination and damage to the marine environment and coral reefs. However, this impact driver was not considered to be fully delivered because the regulations approved do yet not offer full coral reef protection and the capacity to enforce the existing and new regulations remains limited.

The review found that the second driver, 'there are sufficient incentives for marine users to participate in conservation programmes', has been poorly realized. The lack of progress since project closure to create incentives for marine users (such as tour operators and the fisheries industry) to participate in conservation programmes can, in part, be attributed to the reduction in available environmental funding. This was due to the decrease in international donors supporting the Seychelles and the recent implementation of the International Monetary Fund–supported economic reform programme. The lack of effective cooperation between government and non-governmental organizations and the lack of capacity retained in government institutions also played a role.

However, newly funded initiatives have recently been launched that have the potential to overcome these barriers to realizing this impact driver. In particular, there are new United Nations Development Programme (UNDP)/GEF projects: The Mainstreaming Biodiversity Management into Production Sector Activities project, which will focus on the fisheries and tourism sector, and the Capacity Development for Sustainable Land Management project, which will build on the SEYMEMP work on wetlands management. There is also a UNDP/GEF marine and terrestrial protected area project in the proposal development stage. In addition to GEF projects, there is a European Union–funded Regional Programme for the Sustainable Management of the Coastal Zones of the Indian Ocean Countries that is in its early stages of implementation, which should help to encourage broader community participation and links with other countries in the western Indian Ocean.

The review assessed that the assumption, 'political leadership is committed to prioritizing marine issues' has been poorly realized. Although the government is, in principle, committed to the marine environment, it lacks the financial and human resources to fully realize its leadership role.

Overview of progress towards Intermediate State 3

The Review of Outcomes to Impacts concluded that this Intermediate State remains at an early stage of delivery. Most notably, progress has been made in promoting enabling policies and there is greater awareness concerning the marine global environmental benefits. In addition, new initiatives, such as the European Union–funded Regional Programme for the Sustainable Management of the Coastal Zones of the Indian Ocean Countries and the new set of UNDP/GEF projects are providing opportunities for mainstreaming many of the issues raised by the SEYMEMP project. However, the current lack of government leadership, intersectoral cooperation and participation of marine users has meant that this intermediate state has not yet been significantly delivered. Policies and other sectors' involvement are still needed to protect the behavioural aspects of marine global environmental benefits (e.g. migratory routes, corridors and spawning areas), which are not covered under the current marine protected area system or by regulations. In conclusion, the overall assessment for the delivery of Intermediate State Number Three is *poorly achieved*.

Assessment of progress towards Intermediate State 1: coping mechanisms addressing major threats to marine ecosystems are rolled out nationally[11]

Theory of Change overview

The review considered the first intermediate state, 'coping mechanisms addressing major threats to marine ecosystems are rolled out nationally', to be an essential (necessary) ingredient to delivering the intended impact: improved conservation status of the Seychelles coral reef ecosystem and globally endangered marine species. The coping mechanisms are a series of direct actions that provide long-term protection against human-induced threats (e.g. coral damage by boats or pollution entering the ecosystem), as well as protection against detrimental natural events (e.g. the coral bleaching events of 1998 that destroyed a large percentage of the corals in the Seychelles islands). To minimize the threats to the ecosystem, it is essential that there is sufficient sustainable financing and capacity within local institutions (government, non-governmental organizations and the private sector) to enable appropriate responses to emerging threats to be launched as and when necessary.

The study team identified Outcomes 1 and 2 as important for delivering this intermediate state (see Figure 7.5). The research and monitoring activities undertaken to deliver Outcome 1 are essential for testing, adapting and scaling up the coping mechanisms piloted under Outcome 2.

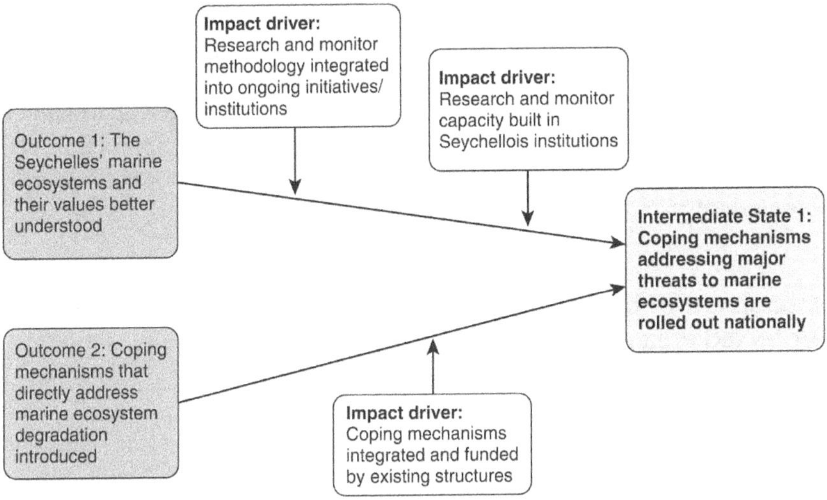

FIGURE 7.5 Theory of Change for Intermediate State 1

The review identified three impact drivers necessary to bridge the gap between the project outcomes and the delivery of the intermediate state (see Figure 7.5). The first, 'research and monitoring methodology integrated into ongoing initiatives and institutions', is necessary to ensure that the research and monitoring findings and methodologies of the project are utilized by all marine research bodies active in the Seychelles. This would help ensure the necessary continuity to build understanding of the ecosystem and to better inform the development and application of coping mechanisms. The second impact driver, 'research and monitor capacity built in Seychellois institutions', is related to the first driver but specifically relates to marine institutions' capacities to implement the research and monitoring programmes initiated under Outcome 1 (e.g. sufficiently trained personnel). The final driver, 'coping mechanisms integrated and funded by existing structures', is regarded as fundamental for the successfully piloted coping mechanisms of Outcome 2 to be more broadly applied across the marine ecosystem. The review did not consider there to be any major external assumptions underpinning the achievement of the intermediate state.

Overview of progress towards achieving Intermediate State 1

The review found evidence that the intermediate state had begun to be delivered. In particular, the project-initiated research findings have led to important decisions regarding marine protection at the national level (such as controls on fisheries in sensitive marine areas) that are expected to deliver a lasting improvement to the conservation status of the overall Seychelles marine ecosystems. In addition, the formation of the Seychelles Centre for Marine Research and Technology-Marine Parks Authority (SCMRT-MPA) following project closure provides a better institutional mechanism for linking marine research with management actions. However, to date, the limited research and monitoring capacity built into government institutions with responsibility for the Seychelles marine ecosystem and the lack of funding mechanisms for rolling out marine protection activities have formed a barrier to fully delivering the scaling up of coping mechanisms needed to achieve the intended impact. In summary, the overall assessment for the delivery of Intermediate State 1 is *partially achieved*.

Assessment of progress towards Intermediate State 2: marine protected area network is being managed effectively to achieve conservation goals

Theory of Change overview

The intermediate state, 'Marine Protected Area (MPA) network is being managed effectively to achieve conservation goals', was the second key ingredient necessary to contribute towards delivering the intended project impact. As the understanding of the Seychelles marine ecosystem improves, it is becoming apparent that existing marine protected area coverage is inappropriate and insufficient to conserve all the ecologically important and sensitive areas, both in terms of global environmental benefits and the ecosystem functions and processes supporting them.[12] An effectively managed Seychellois MPA network would adapt its coverage where appropriate and feasible and would ensure that each MPA is managed as part of an integrated system rather than as an individual, isolated entity. When such an integrated MPA system is in place, the review considers that conservation goals and impacts will have been achieved. This intermediate state is focused on enhancing the conservation status of the threatened marine species.

The study team identified Outcome 3 as critical for delivering this intermediate state (see Figure 7.6). Outcome 3 sought to lay the foundation necessary to run an integrated MPA network, in particular by planning and agreeing to the long-term arrangements and institutional modalities for implementing such a network.

The review identified two impact drivers and two external assumptions as being necessary to bridge the gap between the delivery of Outcome 3 and the achievement of Intermediate State 2 (see Figure 7.6). The first impact driver, 'MPA network is adequate to protect key ecosystem functions and processes', is regarded as an important consideration that should be asked periodically of all protected area systems, based on current scientific understanding, to ensure that they are adequately protecting the ecosystem processes that sustain the associated impacts (e.g. global environmental benefits). The second driver, 'financial sustainability of MPA network is established', underpins the ability to manage, enforce and coordinate activities within and between MPAs and is therefore fundamental to the successful delivery of this intermediate state.

Regarding the external assumptions, the first, 'government has a clear vision for the MPA network and takes the leadership role for its development', is considered crucial for achieving the intermediate state, because government is the only stakeholder with the mandate and authority to expand or alter protected area system coverage and

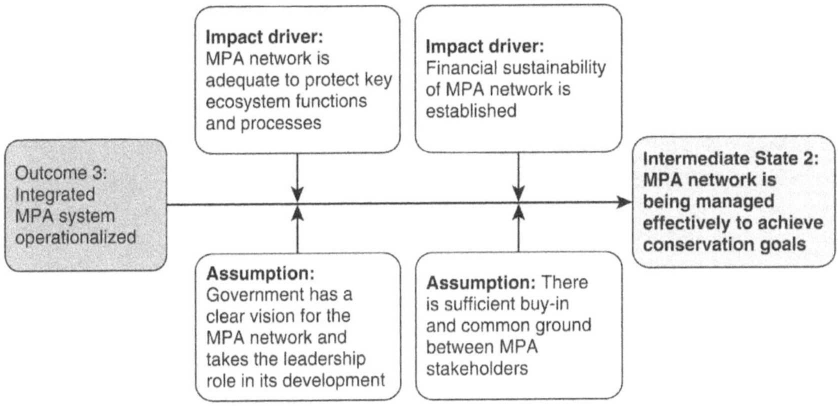

FIGURE 7.6 Theory of Change for Intermediate State 2

adjust, where necessary, the associated management regimes. The second assumption, that 'there is sufficient buy-in and common ground between MPA stakeholders', is also considered critical. This is because diverse actors (e.g. parastatal bodies, non-governmental organizations and the private sector) are involved in effectively managing an MPA network, and without transparency, accountability and willingness to pool resources together it is unlikely that such a network will be effectively managed.

Overall, the review found limited evidence to show that the second intermediate state had been delivered. Due to the lack of an agreed strategy for developing a more integrated MPA network, no substantive progress has been made to improve the coverage of MPAs to capture the critical coral refugia and other representative ecosystem components identified by the project as being outside of the existing system. Although informal collaboration between the Seychelles Centre for Marine Research and Technology-Marine Parks Authority and the Seychelles Fisheries Authority over the management of spawning grounds has been initiated, no significant progress has been made to improve management efficiency between organizations dealing with Marine Protected Areas. In conclusion, the overall assessment for the delivery of Intermediate State Number Two is that it has been *poorly achieved.*

Current status of progress towards the intended impacts

The Review of Outcomes to Impacts did not undertake a direct assessment of the status of the intended global environmental benefits that formed the intervention's intended impacts. However, project documentation was reviewed to collate existing information about the global environmental benefits and their conservation status. Table 7.6 provides a summary of the information that the review acquired.

The research reports emerging from the SEYMEMP project assessed the ecological status of the coral reef and reef fish assemblages following the 1998 coral bleaching event, which generally showed slow but steady recovery, and monitored the ecological status of whale shark and turtles, which, although providing a good

TABLE 7.6 Available Information on Global Environmental Benefit Status

	Change in status	
Global environmental benefit	*At project end (2004)*	*Since 2004*
Coral Reef of the Western Indian Ocean	Hard corals had shown a slow but accelerating recovery. There was no overall loss of coral biodiversity, but the corals are still very vulnerable to ecological disturbances.	No information available
Reef fish assemblages	Project recorded significant increases in the abundance of some twenty fish categories between 2002 and 2003, which seems to relate to increased recruitment resulting from favourable conditions (which may not be sustained in the future).	No information available and no figures on sustainable off-take of commercial reef fish
Whale sharks	Exploratory research revealed that whale sharks around the Seychelles Granitic island population consist almost entirely of male juveniles, which migrate in when plankton is available.	No data seen by study team, although the Marine Conservation Society of Seychelles is still conducting research
Marine turtles	Hawksbill: between the early 1980s and 2003, estimated numbers have declined by approximately 25%. But at unprotected sites the decline has been approximately 60%. Population in early 2000s was estimated at 625. Green turtles: numbers of nesting turtles in the inner islands have remained less than 50 animals from the early 1980s to 2002–2003. Increases in population are only evident on four privately managed islands of Cousin (571%), Aride (167%), and Cousine and Bird islands, for which no specific estimates could be obtained.	No data seen by the study team, although Turtle Action Group and other non-governmental organizations are still conducting monitoring and research

baseline, did not provide any clear trends in status. The review was unable to obtain information on the ecological status of the global environmental benefits following project completion. Although certain non-governmental organizations are continuing to gather data, particularly regarding marine turtles and whale sharks, the analysis of these data (if collected) are not publicly available.

Regarding the status of threats to the global environmental benefits, the review did not undertake threat assessments. However, discussions with stakeholders indicated that the threats are likely to be increasing, with more hotels in and around MPAs in the inner islands. Although the outer islands used to be protected due to their isolation, recent developments in the region (e.g. increased reach of fisheries due to larger vessels with greater cruising ranges and the market for more remote nature-based tourism activities) have made these threats more likely.

A direct assessment of global environmental benefits would require a separate study to compile and assess the monitoring data being collected by various institutions, which was beyond the scope of a Review of Outcomes to Impacts. In the case of the Seychelles, the review felt that the Seychelles Centre for Marine Research and Technology-Marine Parks Authority would be well positioned to coordinate an annual assessment on the status of these and other potential global environmental benefits, which could feed into the further development/expansion of the integrated Marine Protected Areas network.

Overall conclusions on progress towards impacts of the SEYMEMP

The study team used the Theory of Change methodology to assess that to date, only poor to partial success has been achieved in delivering the intended global environmental benefits/impacts (see Figure 7.7). Based on the continued monitoring and protection activities of individual institutions (e.g. the Marine Conservation Society of Seychelles, Whale Shark Programme and the Turtle Action Group monitoring), and the enacting of more enabling policies, the review team assessed that the conservation status of whale sharks and turtles has remained stable or improved following project closure. However, the review did not find any evidence of an improvement in the conservation status of the coral reef and reef fish assemblages, as the overall marine protected area system has not yet been expanded to protect the emerging patterns of hard coral distribution and abundance. Furthermore, the project's coral protection measures have not been scaled up (e.g. mooring installations and maintenance), and in some cases, these activities have been discontinued (e.g. programme to remove coral grazing organisms).

The Review of Outcomes to Impacts assessment concluded that the limited progress in delivering impacts has been mainly the result of the lack of institutional capacity, leadership and collaboration in further developing and integrating the management of the Seychelles' marine protected area network.

The lack of national-level coordination and leadership capacity for marine research and monitoring seems to have partly resulted from the over-reliance of the project on external consultants to undertake key aspects of the project. As identified in the project brief and Terminal Evaluation report, the national Marine Unit was envisioned to be the focus for developing research capacity and leadership in improving marine protected area management. But the unit relied heavily on a project adviser and other institutions and consultants to conduct the research and did not develop sufficient internal capacity and long-term funding sources during the project. As a result, the future of the marine unit appears to be unsustainable and a different institutional arrangement is needed to provide leadership.

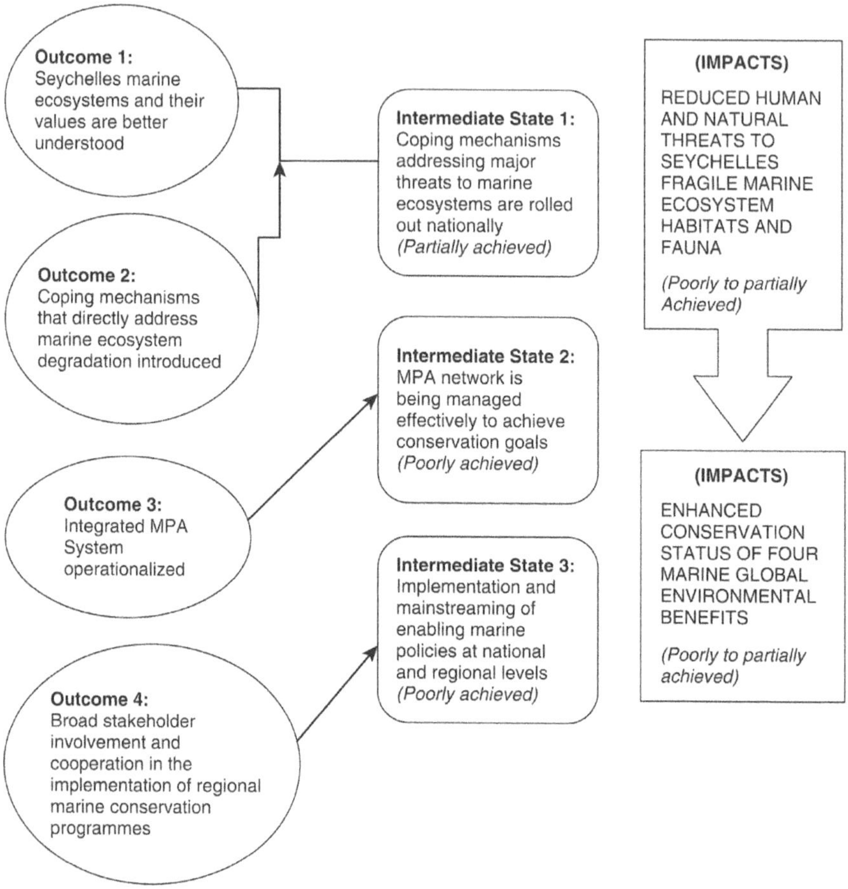

FIGURE 7.7 Overall Review of Outcomes to Impacts Assessment of SEYMEMP Progress towards Impacts

The diverse institutions involved in marine conservation require a clear framework for coordination of research and management and the adoption of a systematic approach to the further expansion of a more representative and integrated marine protected area network. The failure to date to implement the project's Integrated MPA System Plan and the continued lack of an agreed plan or framework for cooperation has meant that the status of the protected area network has remained little changed since project closure, with no new protected areas gazetted and management effectiveness basically unchanged.

However, the review concluded that the intended impacts could still be achieved if this barrier of lack of institutional capacity, leadership and cooperation can be overcome. A development in this direction is the amalgamation of the Seychelles Centre for Marine Research and Technology with the Marine Park Authority to form the SCMRT-MPA in 2003. The SCMRT-MPA provides an appropriate institution to take over the role envisaged for the Marine Unit in coordinating marine research, feeding it into the Marine Protected Area management decision-making and championing the revival of the MPA System Plan or an equivalent for developing an integrated MPA network. SCMRT-MPA has already made progress on the research side, but has yet to take on the role of leading the process to develop a more integrated and expanded MPA system.

Overall conclusions on assessing progress towards impacts in environmental programmes using the field Review of Outcomes to Impacts (ROtI) methodology

This chapter gives an introduction to the use of the field Review of Outcomes to Impacts as a means of assessing progress towards the intended impacts of an intervention some years after formal project completion. The Review of Outcomes to Impacts begins with the project Terminal Evaluation and other key documents and creates a Theory of Change for the intended progression from the outcomes identified in the Terminal Evaluation towards the long-term impact objectives of the intervention.

The methodology explores the cause and effect chains of the pathway towards impacts, including the extent to which defined Intermediate States between outcomes and impacts have been achieved. This allows the assessment of progress, even in cases where the duration of the change process may be many years. By using the Review of Outcomes to Impacts method, it can be seen whether the necessary follow-up activities to an intervention have been commenced, and, if so, how far they have gone and with what results. In other words, are the intervention follow-up activities on track to eventually contribute towards the impacts for which the project was originally funded?

An important issue encompassed by the Review of Outcomes to Impacts methodology is the extent to which the original assumptions of the project proved accurate. For example, almost all project funding documents have the statement 'government will continue to prioritize this issue for funds and human resources'. If this does not prove to be the case, the original positive outcomes achieved may fade. The Review of Outcomes to Impacts explicitly assesses whether the assumptions have in fact held true in the longer term. In addition, the method looks at the impact drivers set in motion by the project – its champions and its support systems, which need to continue after the initial project support has gone. It assesses whether these remain sufficiently strong to keep the necessary activities and systems moving forward towards their objectives.

As shown by the example of the SEYMEMP field Review of Outcomes to Impacts, the method enables a sufficiently detailed picture to be built to give an overall assessment of progress towards impacts. It does so in a cost-effective manner, usually requiring about two person-weeks of in-country mission, most of which is spent with institutional stakeholders and with limited field-visit verification. It therefore represents an intermediate method between full impact evaluation (which requires far more resources) and desk review (which lacks the opportunity, in particular, to bring together groups of stakeholders to develop an interactive vision of what has actually happened since project closure).

The ROtI method has been found effective in various environmental sectors and for different timescales. For example, another detailed field ROtI was conducted in Jamaica for the GEF Energy Demand Side Management project in the field of climate change. A particularly interesting aspect of this review is that it was conducted a full ten years after project completion. A brief overview of its findings is provided in Box 7.1.

BOX 7.1 KEY FINDINGS OF JAMAICA DEMAND SIDE MANAGEMENT ROTI

Ten years after project completion, the project had partially achieved its intended progress towards impact and the expected Global Environment Benefits. After a post-completion period in which it appeared that the project's contribution might fade away (apart from the market transformation for Compact Fluorescent Lightbulbs (CFLs), as a result of the privatization of the main national energy supplier, there was a return of interest focused around Government's development of an Energy Policy. This has a component sub-policy on Energy Conservation and Efficiency that explicitly refers to the DSM project as part of its antecedents. The issues around Climate Change, Energy Efficiency and Demand Side Management have also, over time, been well incorporated at all levels of the national educational system, including at University level, which is a regional facility.

Furthermore, energy efficiency approaches have recently been supported by UNDP, both in terms of specific projects in the health sector and of support to the development of the Government's Energy Policy. The Inter-American Development Bank is also providing substantial support in this area. Thus, it appears likely that the progress of Demand Side Management/Energy Efficiency will continue and even expand in future. The DSM Project has clearly made an important contribution towards these trends, although it would not be possible to say exactly how much contribution.

Whereas the earlier World Bank-GEF Post-Implementation Impact Assessment, five years after Project Completion, focused mainly on attempting to quantify the contribution of reduced GHG emissions (and reduced energy costs), the ROtI after ten years has found that a 'second wave' of results, further along the Outcomes to Impacts pathways, has become evident. These results focus in the field of enhanced knowledge and expertise concerning Energy Efficiency/Demand Side Management promoted through all levels of the education system; and in the development of a detailed and coherent Government approach towards Energy and Climate Change, embodied in a new national Energy Policy, intended to focus national approaches until the year 2030.

Overall, the field Review of Outcomes to Impacts presents a valuable addition to the range of methods available to those seeking to assess progress from project results towards long-term impacts. Furthermore, since it was specifically developed for the realm of environmental interventions (notably for global environmental activities), it does not suffer from the difficulties commonly experienced in adapting methods of poverty-focused evaluation to the environment sector.

A. Annex 1: Overall SEYMEMP Theory of Change

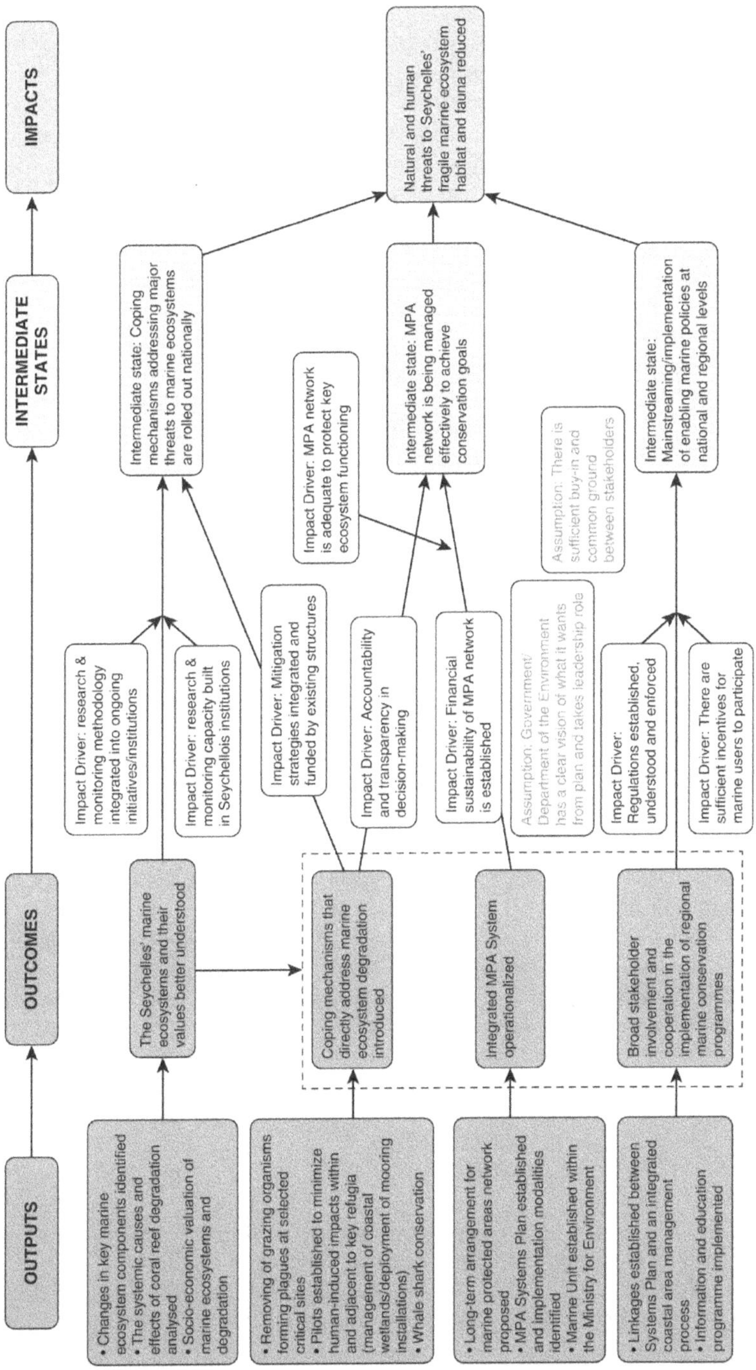

FIGURE 7.8 Overall SEYMEMP Theory of Change

Notes

1 See, for example, Leeuw and Vaessen (2009) and 3ie (2013).
2 Further details on this work are provided in R. van den Berg and D. Todd (2011).
3 See GEF Evaluation Office (2006).
4 See GEF Evaluation Office (2009a).
5 The range of approaches and methods used by the GEF Independent Evaluation Office is described on its website: https://www.gefieo.org/knowledge-methods.
6 There is also a desk review of Outcomes to Impacts, which uses only project documents to assess the fit between project design and delivery at completion and the intended pathway towards impacts.
7 Full details of the Review of Outcomes to Impacts methodology have been provided in a handbook. See GEF Evaluation Office (2009b).
8 See GEF Evaluation Office (2009b).
9 The acronym MPA refers to the Marine Protected Area system. A similar acronym, the SCMRT-MPA, refers to an institution, the Seychelles Centre for Marine Research and Technology – Marine Parks Authority.
10 See GEF Evaluation Office (2009a).
11 In order to keep the chapter to a manageable length, only a summary of the review process is provided for this intermediate state (the full method has been outlined for Intermediate State 3).
12 See Engelhardt (2004a, 2004b).

References

Engelhardt, U., '*The status of scleractinian coral and reef associated fish communities 6 years after the 1998 mass coral bleaching event*', Consultancy report by Reefcare International, Australia, 2004a.

Engelhardt, U., '*Seychelles integrated marine protected area system plan*', Consultancy report by Reefcare International, Australia. 2004b.

Global Environment Facility (GEF) Evaluation Office, *GEF Country Portfolio Study: Jamaica. Review of Outcomes to Impacts: Jamaica Demand Side Management Project* (*Volume* 2), Washington, DC, 2011.

Global Environment Facility (GEF) Evaluation Office, *The Role of Local Benefits in Global Environmental Programs*, Washington, DC, 2006.

GEF Evaluation Office, '*Seychelles Marine Ecosystem Management Project: Review of Outcomes to Impacts*', Nairobi and Washington, DC, 2009a.

GEF Evaluation Office, '*The Review of Outcomes to Impacts Handbook: Towards Enhancing the Impacts of Environmental Projects*', Nairobi and Washington, DC 2009b.

International Initiative for Impact Evaluation (3IE), 2013 '*Improving Lives Through Impact Evaluation: A Strategy for 3IE 2010–2013*', New Delhi, India available at http://www.3ieimpact.org/media/filer/2012/05/17/3ie_strategy_report_2010-13.pdf, last accessed September 12 2013.

Leeuw, F. and J. Vaessen, *Impact Evaluations and Development: NONIE Guidance on Impact*, , Network of Networks for Impact Evaluation, Washington, DC2009.

van den Berg, R. and D. Todd, 'The full road to impact: The experience of the Global Environment Facility fourth overall performance study', *Journal of Development Effectiveness*, no. 3, 2011.

8

META-ANALYSIS OF CLIMATE MITIGATION EVALUATIONS

Christine Wörlen

Introduction

In evaluating climate change mitigation interventions, a large number of questions revolve around the impacts of greenhouse gas mitigation (e.g. Did the intervention actually lead to greenhouse gas emission reductions? Who can claim credit for the reductions?). Although these questions are straightforward in some cases, for example where renewable fuels are directly substituting for fossil fuels, few climate change mitigation interventions in developing countries focus on such a direct switch.

Instead, mitigation interventions focus the majority of their effort on capacity building, policy frameworks, consumer awareness or training of technicians. This complicates the challenge of measuring the impacts, and the challenge of attribution: assessing the relative contribution of each such activity requires a clear understanding of the answers to complex questions, such as why and in what situation which technology is used and what effected a change.

Market and behaviour change can be measurable, but not attributable to the intervention, because factors outside of the intervention also contributed to the change in market conditions. In order to identify an interventions' impact in a given context, it is useful to use a framework to clarify which barriers to the use of the 'better' technology were actually limiting the change for the better in the first place, and if these were addressed effectively by the intervention. Such a framework would constitute an important step towards solving the attribution question in climate change mitigation. Without such a framework, evaluations typically give limited weight to capacity building and policy interventions and most greenhouse gas benefits are attributed to investments.

This study presents the 'Theory of No Change', an 'inverted' theory of change for climate mitigation interventions and a tool for assessing situations why projects fail. The core theory is a scheme comprising the barriers that prevent the broader diffusion of a product or keep users and consumers from making more climate-friendly choices. Based on empirical analysis, it was possible to identify a closed set of such barriers, which in their sum are close to representing a full programme theory, the Theory of No Change.

With the help of this framework, we are able to assess whether or not an intervention contributed to a more favourable framework for a sustainable energy technology's market development. This allows a deeper and more useful analysis of an intervention's impacts and potential avenues for improvement than the standard practice of using output-based evaluation.

The Climate Change Evaluators Community of Practice, hosted by the Evaluation Office of the Global Environment Facility (GEF), sponsored this work. The Community of Practice facilitates knowledge exchange, mutual help and inspiration among climate evaluators. It has compiled a library of almost 500 climate change mitigation and adaptation evaluations at the project, programme, policy and portfolio levels. After a number of more formal summaries (e.g. Matambo and Griebenow 2010), this chapter takes a first stab at a fundamental challenge of mitigation evaluations – the quest for a common programme logic of climate mitigation interventions. It can be used as an evaluation framework tool for attributing causality. The framework was first published in a longer version by the Community of Practice (Wörlen 2011a). The author is grateful to the Community of Practice for the support of this work.

Some persistent climate mitigation evaluation questions

Climate change mitigation initiatives attempt to minimize changes to the global climate by limiting greenhouse gas emissions. Most mitigation efforts have been undertaken in the energy sector, where most interventions strive to replace fossil fuels with non-emitting energy sources or to reduce energy consumption. Many donors, national institutions and private entities undertake projects to that end.

These projects, almost irrespective of whether they take place in developing or developed countries, suffer from a persistent tension – perceived or real – between greenhouse gas-related and developmental objectives. Growth often leads to rising greenhouse gas emissions. Therefore, avoiding greenhouse gas emissions is often put on par with limiting growth. Mitigation projects in the development realm need to reconcile these seemingly contradictory objectives.

Few development interventions directly reduce emissions. Greenhouse gas reducing interventions attempt to facilitate the switch from existing technologies to less- or zero-emitting technologies or fuels. With the exception of the Clean Development Mechanism (CDM), few development-oriented activities help to make that switch directly. Instead, non-CDM climate mitigation initiatives often help build supply chains, policy frameworks, informed demand, technical skills and other types of local capacity, thus enabling the actual users of the greenhouse-gas-emitting technologies to use cleaner alternatives. Directly replacing them is not typically part of project activities. Rather, most interventions conduct or support activities that cause changes in target groups' behaviour. Projects often educate users about the new technologies, build the new technologies' supply chains or make available financing to buy and operate these technologies. The end users themselves might not even be part of the intervention (e.g. when interventions work with policy makers on regulatory changes or with financiers on the development of financial products).

Thus, most interventions work on a more fundamental level, apply a more indirect programme logic and intend to provide more catalytic impacts towards a climate-friendly way of living. This presents a challenge for results measurement and attribution. Projects' impacts on greenhouse gas emissions are often assessed based on outcome indicators that relate to emission-relevant behaviour (e.g. energy consumption). A number of assumptions are necessary for drawing conclusions regarding the causal link between project activities and greenhouse gas impacts. The basis for these conclusions is necessarily a conceptual model of the relationship between project outputs and outcomes and between outcomes and objectives. Although this is a well-documented challenge for results-based evaluations, the logical chain between a project's interventions and the ultimate objective of climate preservation is particularly long and weakly formulated in many mitigation projects.

This is compounded by the fact that a project's formulation or its underlying conceptual model frequently fails to discuss a large number of preconditions. For example, there is no common understanding on the right set of preconditions for climate-friendly behaviour, appropriate indicators (and on which levels they should be measured), standardized data, data sources and data quality requirements. Often, the mix of preconditions is described as general 'lack of capacity', which hardly clarifies what should be done about it. In addition, mitigation interventions do not start with a blank slate or exist in a static environment. The context in which an intervention takes place and its development over time are highly relevant to the interventions' success. However, contexts are hard to acknowledge, to fully describe and for which to account.

A theory of change that accounts for an intervention's context is the necessary basis for assessing an intervention's results. This theory of change needs to go beyond the linear project logic of any single component. It should also serve as a model for aggregating the outcomes of different activities that might take place at the same time, which can generate synergistic effects, counteract each other or remain independent. They might take place with completely different stakeholder groups, interventions, instruments and on such different time scales that, in evaluations, they are hard to bring into relation to each other.

One challenge in particular compounds this issue: many climate change mitigation interventions will only result in reduced carbon emissions sometime after the project's end and after its final evaluation. The evaluator can only examine intermediary outcomes; conclusions about a project's ultimate impacts with respect to the climate mitigation objectives will need to be drawn based on these interim observations. Necessarily, these evaluations will have preliminary character and the findings will remain clouded with significant uncertainty as to the project's ultimate impacts. Improving the underlying theory that links the intermediary outcomes with the ultimate objectives might reduce this uncertainty.

Objective and methodology of the meta-analysis

A large number of challenges persist in climate mitigation evaluations. One reason for a number of these challenges is that there is no agreed-on programme theory of change regarding how to transform unsustainable energy use into more sustainable use of energy (e.g. by substituting renewable energy for fossil fuels or by shifting towards more energy-efficient, less polluting equipment). Having a clear conceptualization of what is required for behavioural changes to take place would address a significant number of the challenges mentioned – it would help clarify the roles that non-investment-related activities play and how different interventions interact with each other, so that context can be better analysed. The meta-analysis set out to compile theories of change from a large number of evaluations of climate mitigation interventions, to distil a common theory of change.

Such a theory of change can not only form the basis for formulating systematic outcome indicators that reflect the full set of necessary enabling conditions but can also help identify the full scope of evaluations that look for reasons for a project's success or failure (not only in the projects proper, but also in their context). Such a concept would not only be helpful for the evaluation of projects, programmes and policies, but it would also have some predictive power and would be able to support project design and monitoring.

There are a number of necessary preconditions for a market to physically switch towards sustainable energy technologies: the technology needs to be available, local users need to be aware of and create demand for it, they need to understand the new technology and might need some kind of supply chain for maintenance services. Larger investments might require loan financing, as sometimes the amounts of money to be initially invested might be simply unaffordably high despite an investment's long-term cost-effectiveness. Further, in some development contexts an energy-efficient cook stove costing just few dollars might represent a significant outlay to the target demographic. In other cases, policy frameworks might be necessary to level the economic and regulatory playing field between new and traditional technologies. Developing such frameworks requires that policy makers are aware of the benefits of a sustainable energy technology and know-how to create policy frameworks that leverage these benefits. All of these capacities need to be in place.

They refer to a number of different stakeholders which need to be considered when analysing mitigation interventions, in particular those interventions that intend to trigger market development for sustainable energy technologies. After analysing a large number of climate mitigation evaluations, the study on which this chapter is based concluded that for sustainable market development, four main groups of stakeholders play a role: users of the technology, the supply chain (i.e. shops and maintenance technicians), policy makers and local financial institutions.

Each of these groups typically encounters a number of barriers that keep them from using or supporting the sustainable energy technology. This chapter catalogues the barriers for the relevant stakeholder groups and puts them together in a Theory of No Change, which helps identify why a desired change is not happening. Analysing barriers with the theory can serve to design activities for removing the barriers to change.

The model uses Tokle and Uitto (2009) as the basis for drafting a full set of barriers to be included in the Theory of No Change. For testing, two case studies were undertaken on the basis of evaluations from the Climate-Eval library (Wörlen 2011b, 2011c). The Thailand case study selected projects that come from the traditional realm of market transformation approaches and tried to analyse whether the Theory of No Change could completely represent the market barriers and their relationship with the ultimate objectives. The second case study, for Poland, worked on the public investment sector (district heating and boiler replacement) and analysed to what degree the market transformation concept and the barrier-oriented Theory of No Change helped to understand processes in the transformation of a larger, bulky investment. These case studies help extend the versatility of the concept and formulate recommendations for evaluative practice and future research needs.

Programme logic for climate change mitigation: the Theory of No Change

Typical climate mitigation interventions include public awareness campaigns, capacity building for technicians, advisory services for policy makers, provision of information and demonstration projects. Very few climate change mitigation interventions of, for example, the GEF, address direct greenhouse gas emissions on a significant scale. Many more are targeted towards providing an enabling environment for the deployment of energy efficient technologies or renewable energy use. This means that the theory of change for these interventions is necessarily somewhat indirect and hard to express in strong causalities or even quantitative indicators.[1]

The evaluation framework of Tokle and Uitto (2009)

The challenge is to come up with a strong description of the logic that leads from enabling environments to greenhouse gas reductions. Tokle and Uitto (2009) propose an evaluation framework that illustrates a possible programme logic for such a market transformation intervention (see Figure 8.1). It shows that an enabling environment consists of five different capacities that need to be in existence locally:

- Enabling policies, strategies, standards and certification in place
- Adequate financing available
- Adequate business infrastructure
- Awareness created
- Innovation and technology diffused

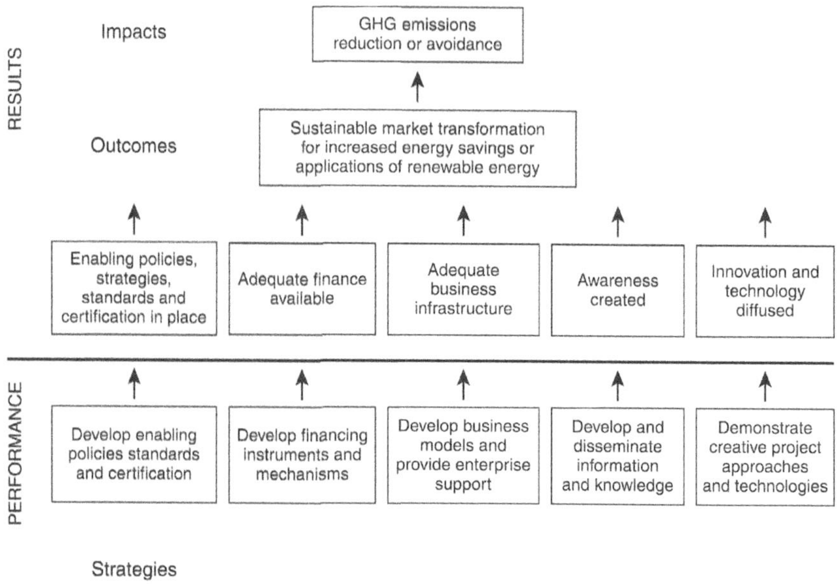

FIGURE 8.1 Evaluation Framework of Tokle and Uitto (2009)

Tokle and Uitto (2009: 143) emphasize that 'normally all these capacities must be in place in order to provide the enabling environment for sustainable development and growth of a market, with supply and demand infrastructure for renewable energy technologies. Market development and removal of barriers to adoption of climate friendly technologies are a continuous process'. When these capacities are in place, the authors describe the intermediate outcome of a climate mitigation intervention as a sustainable market transformation for increased energy savings or applications of renewable energy.

These statements also imply that an intervention addresses only one of these aspects (e.g. it works only with policy makers, financiers or the training of technicians), risks not leading to market change or sustainable energy utilization, as they might neglect other important preconditions. This limits the intervention's potential overall impact. If an intervention chooses to focus on only one small part of the necessary capacities, but still intends to achieve significant greenhouse gas impacts, it needs to ensure that the other capacities either are already in existence or are addressed through other interventions.

Project strategies often work towards one or more of these results (see Figure 8.1). For example, awareness campaigns, technical training, policy formulation assistance or development of energy efficiency standards are all typical activities within climate mitigation projects. Their evaluations, however, will typically remain intervention specific, pay little attention to the context in terms of the other necessary preconditions and thus not be able to analyse all of the previously mentioned attribution and aggregation challenges. Further, the evaluations will not be able to reflect the context of the local market situation in terms of the other necessary preconditions, as there is no baseline and no absolute standard of 'how it should be'.

In their framework, Tokle and Uitto (2009) implicitly acknowledge that a multitude of stakeholders are involved in market transformation. For example, consumers, businesses, financial intermediaries and policy makers all constitute relevant target groups. Policy makers are responsible for providing the necessary policy framework; banks and financiers need to be available for financing the energy transformation; service providers and technology companies need to install, sell, operate and/or maintain the new energy equipment; and all these groups and individuals need to be well informed and aware of the new technologies and opportunities. Figure 8.2 maps which strategy can apply to which stakeholder group.

Evaluation framework

Figure 8.2 illustrates that the stakeholders find themselves in different positions in Tokle and Uitto's (2009) framework. In terms of sustainable energy use, important agents include the users of energy or energy-using equipment; the supply chain of sustainable energy technologies, fuels and maintenance services; the financiers for both supply chain enterprises and users of energy technologies; and policy makers (in the widest sense of the word) who need to provide conducive framework conditions for deploying sustainable energy technologies and services. For each group of agents, it is important to identify the reasons why he or she does not yet behave in

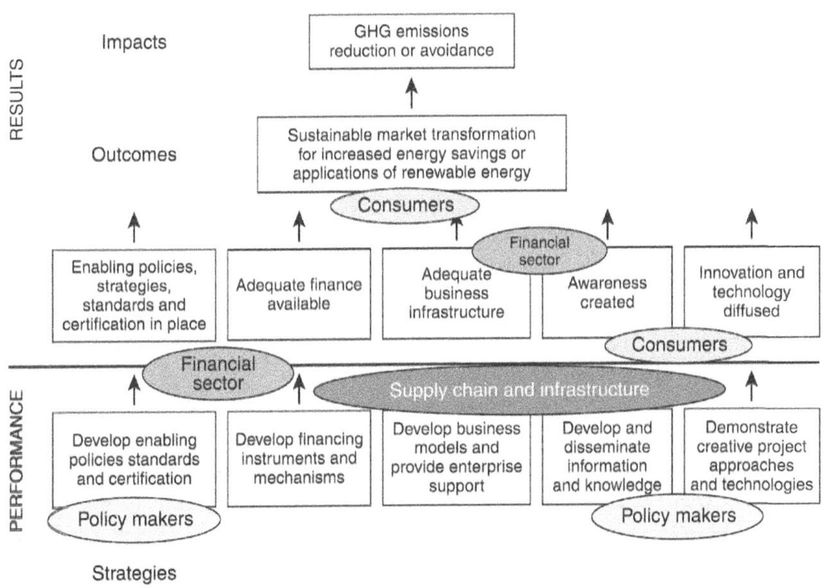

FIGURE 8.2 Evaluation Framework of Tokle and Uitto (2009) with Stakeholder Groups

an climate-friendly manner (i.e. does not yet use the sustainable energy technology in question, foster it with supportive policy schemes, finance investments into this technology or selling or servicing that technology). These reasons can be understood as the barriers to climate-friendly behaviour and sustainable energy systems.

Mapping stakeholders onto the Tokle and Uitto (2009) framework makes it possible to rearrange the strategies from a focus on enabling capacities towards a focus on removing barriers: if all stakeholders play their respective role with respect to the strategies, the desired outcome of greenhouse gas savings ensues. By turning this around, we can identify strategies along the lines of the stakeholders and find the reasons why a situation might not change.

The absence of enabling capacities poses a barrier to market development that can be measured in a more generalizable and standardizable way for a larger number and scale of interventions. If the barriers are gone – the enabling capacities are present – the situation is going to change and gravitate to the desired behaviour or market situation. This 'Theory of No Change' thus formulates a framework describing the complete set of conditions that might be barriers to more efficient behaviour for all relevant stakeholders.

An abstract description of the potential barrier types

Analysing a large number of evaluations for two sectoral developments (energy efficiency in Thailand and district heating in Poland, both over almost two decades; Wörlen 2011b, 2011c) has enabled the identification of seven generic barriers that can be observed for almost all stakeholder groups:

1. **Ignorance:** Stakeholders might not know that a technological alternative exists. This is a particularly obvious barrier for consumers and users – if they do not know that an alternative to their current unsustainable behaviour exists, they cannot use it. However, all the other market stakeholders also need to be aware of the more sustainable alternative in order to play their respective role in the market. In terms of Figure 8.1, awareness needs to be created throughout the market that is to be changed.
2. **Lack of expertise:** Even if people know about the technologies, actually using, marketing or servicing them might require specific technical knowledge or skills. In this analysis, *expertise* is defined for each stakeholder group as the specific skills that are required in the transformed market. Training of technicians is particularly important for the supply chain, and many technology programmes in developing countries and technology suppliers provide it. In addition, policy makers need some expertise in order to provide a supportive policy framework, and financiers need to have the skills to evaluate a new technology in its context.
3. **Lack of access to technology:** Even if sufficient people are trained in using the technology, the technology might not be available in the local market. That

might be an expression of insufficient capacity along the supply chain, which might or might not be caused by a lack of financing or one of the other barriers to building up a sustainable supply chain. However, in many cases it is related to policies in unrelated domains (e.g. terms of trade, taxes, tariffs, administrative procedures and other policy areas). This barrier is important for users and for the supply chain.

4. **Lack of motivation:** Even if the technology is accessible, people are aware of it and know how to use it, and even if it might be cost-effective compared to the conventional alternative, people might still not be interested in using, supplying, financing or politically supporting it. Reasons for this might lie in the image connected with the old technology, in the realm of prejudices, or perceived risks or bad experiences with the new technology. A lack of motivation might also be associated with an overall resistance to change. Lack of motivation can affect all stakeholder groups (with the possible exception of financiers).
5. **Lack of cost effectiveness:** One barrier is that on a total cost of ownership basis, the technology might be more expensive than the established technology. This can be due to a number of factors, such as fossil fuel subsidies or the newness of the technology. Barring substantial technological advances, using hydrogen fuel cells for self-consumption instead of subsidized grid electricity might be more expensive in both the long and short run, and will therefore not be a popular choice.
6. **Lack of affordability:** Even if a technology is cost effective under total-cost-of-ownership considerations, sustainable energy technologies are often associated with high upfront costs and low operating costs. For example, wind turbines entail a large investment but have no fuel costs so that in good wind locations the production of a unit of wind power might be cheaper than coal power. However, if no investment financing for these technologies is available (e.g. in the form of investment capital, equity or loans), the technology will not be deployed. This lack of working capital is a barrier for both consumers and supply chain actors. In addition, financiers might have issues in providing loans due to their own liquidity issues. Policy makers may want to finance incentives but not have the fiscal means to do so.
7. **Lack of demand/business model:** For some products, it is necessary that the market reaches a specific size in order for the supply chain to build up or for financiers to become available. If this is not the case, innovative business models could reduce this barrier. For example, energy service companies can use innovative loans or rental schemes (leasing or exclusive-use contracts) so that stakeholders in a niche market can pioneer the technology.
8. Projects, policies and programmes in the climate mitigation area typically try to remove one or more of these barriers. As discussed, the same barrier might apply to different stakeholder groups. For example, policy makers, financiers and users all might not trust new technologies in terms of their technical performance. For these generic barriers, the same barrier removal strategy – and

sometimes even the same activity – can be used, tailored to the respective stakeholder group. The more comprehensive the programme, the more barriers are addressed. In the best of worlds, all barriers that exist in a specific context are identified at the project design phase and comprehensive barrier removal strategies are designed accordingly.

The stakeholder–barrier matrix

If every stakeholder group encountered every barrier, a matrix with 28 barriers would result. However, not all barriers are relevant for all stakeholders. The following section discusses what barriers can be eliminated by theoretical considerations in order to reduce the number of barriers that are necessary to draw the full picture.

For example, for financiers and policy makers, it makes no difference whether they have access to the technology as they will not use it themselves – they will only provide the financing or regulatory frameworks for it. The concept of a 'business model' should also not be applied to policy makers. Excluding these irrelevant barriers allows us to draw a reduced stakeholder–barrier matrix (see Table 8.1).

For users, the different business cases result in different cost-effectiveness and are therefore subsumed under cost-effectiveness. For now, another barrier disregarded in the next stages of discussion is the supply chain and financiers' potential lack of interest and motivation – here it shall be assumed that the supply chain consists mostly of organizations that strive to increase their business and will not need extra motivation if they see a new business opportunity or can expand their product offerings. It is also assumed that a lack of liquidity with financiers constitutes the same barrier to financiers' engagement as a lack of cost effectiveness. Excluding these irrelevant barriers allows the drawing of a reduced stakeholder-barrier matrix (see Table 8.1).

A case study based on ten evaluations of energy efficient market transformations in Thailand was used to test whether this set-up of stakeholder groups and barriers is able to reflect the situation in the market. The model was tested for the number of stakeholder groups to be included: consumers/users of equipment, the supply chain that delivers hardware and maintenance services, policy makers who create the enabling policy framework and the financiers that provide for the necessary financial liquidity.

One test was whether the implementing agency should be part of the model. This was rejected as barriers are only relevant for those stakeholders that play a role in the functioning market after project implementation. If implementing agencies are not active in one of the markets in one of the four roles mentioned earlier, their barrier situation is irrelevant for the actual functioning of the market. Once the market is sustainably operating, there is no need for further activities of the implementing agency or a special role in the barrier circle. Their activity is expressed

TABLE 8.1 Example for Barrier Removal Strategies

Stakeholder group	Barrier	Barrier removal strategy, project activity
Consumer/user	Ignorance	Awareness campaign, pilot project
	Lack of expertise	Product design
	Lack of access	Build-up of supply chain
	Lack of affordability	Subsidy
	Lack of interest/motivation	Awareness campaign
	Lack of cost-effectiveness	Product design
Supply chain	Ignorance	Awareness campaign, pilot project
	Lack of expertise	Training
	Lack of access	Trade facilitation
	Lack of affordability	Facilitating finance through special or mainstream financial intermediaries
	Lack of cost effectiveness	Support policies
	Lack of business model	Support for business model development, demonstration and marketing
Policy maker	Lack of motivation	Awareness campaign, pilot project
	Misinformation w.r.t. abatement options	Training
	Lack of expertise	Advisory support
	Lack of fiscal affordability	Financial transfers
Financier	Ignorance	Awareness campaign
	Lack of expertise	Training
	Lack of cost-effectiveness	Training, financial support facilities (e.g. guarantees, concessions)
	Lack of business model	Support for business model development, demonstration and marketing

in the project mapping. Thus, it is not helpful to include them in the stakeholder groups of the Theory of No Change.

A number of barriers might apply only to specific subgroups of the stakeholder groups or specific product markets. For example, in the market transformation from incandescent light bulbs to compact fluorescent light bulbs, users do not need any additional expertise in using the light bulbs (their functionality is exactly the same for both products). The case study in Poland used examples from a number of large investment programmes in energy efficient heating and district heating. In district heating, consumers often do not have a choice. Heat is provided by a utility, and supporting services might be provided by a private sector supply chain. So, depending on the project set-up or the market complexity, it might be necessary to adjust the TONC, e.g. by splitting the stakeholder group of supply chain actors into several subgroups. And again, not each stakeholder group faces all barriers. In the case studies on Poland for example, three more barriers were found to be irrelevant for these particular groups.

Across all market situations studied in Thailand and Poland, two barriers were consistently found to not significantly impede market development. These were 'access to technology' for the supply chain and 'ignorance' for policy makers. It reflects well on the projects that these two barriers were not relevant in the country cases studied. 'Access to technology' was possible for the supply chain in these cases, which meant that international technology markets were effectively supplying the countries with the necessary technologies. For the most part, the implementing agencies sufficiently included policy makers in the interventions in order to make them aware of the technologies and energy efficient options that were available. Where it can be assumed that this will be the case for most countries and most energy technologies (except nuclear power) it might be possible to shorten the concept by these two barriers.

Barriers might not be independent. For example, whenever 'lack of affordability' for the supply chain was an issue at the project outset (only in the cases of coal to gas and geothermal in Poland), the 'lack of business model/demand' barrier was a dispositive barrier to market development. When the 'lack of demand' barrier was removed, the suppliers were also able to afford the investment into these new lines of business. In those cases in which lack of affordability for the supply chain is observed the barrier can be reflected on the financiers' side. However, this might not apply in other areas. For example, in the area of off-grid electrification, higher electrification rates can only be reached with higher capital infusions. Therefore, one of the two barriers could be taken out, and in later applications of the Theory of No Change, we have mostly left out the barrier of 'lack of business model/demand' as it was shown to be a compound of other barriers, and its inclusion did not lead to additional analytical power.

Other barriers appear to have had a negligible impact on market development in the case studies. In particular, the lack of motivation for policy makers has not effectively hampered market development in these cases. However, government support is part of the decision-making system of most official development assistance bodies, and therefore, it is not surprising that in all the projects analysed here, the government was motivated to support market development. If these were private sector- or civil society-driven market changes, governments' motivation might have been a barrier. Therefore, it is not recommended to generally leave out this barrier but be judgemental about that.

A mapping tool for barriers and interventions

An underlying assumption of the barrier discussion for market transformation is that all relevant barriers need to be removed in order for market transformation to take place. This can be addressed with a checklist. A visualization tool has been developed that illustrates barrier intensity with traffic light colours (see Figure 8.3). It can be combined with a visualization of the project intervention (see Figure 8.4) so that the line-up of the intervention with the barriers can be assessed at one glance (see Figure 8.5).

The barrier circle

Figure 8.3 represents the market as a circle with four segments representing the four stakeholder groups (users/consumers, supply chain, local financiers and policy makers). The barriers, according to Table 8.1, are represented by small elements labelled with the name of the barrier. Each element can be coloured according to the strength of the barrier in a specific market situation. This colour code follows the globally accepted colour scheme of a traffic light, but with two intermediate steps (yellow and orange) instead of only one. Green is a situation that is favourable to market change. Yellow is a situation that is not necessarily favourable, but there is no significant barrier. Orange and red are barriers that impede market change (orange is the colour for a situation that significantly slows down market change; red is the colour for a barrier that can bring market development to a halt). As long as there is a red barrier for any single factor, the market will not change in any meaningful way.

The example in Figure 8.3 is taken from the case studies and relates to a market where the financiers' activities, attitudes and awareness levels do not fully stop, but do slow down the change in the market, particularly due to a 'lack of business model' (i.e. they did not encounter enough demand to develop a financial product). This is symbolized by the yellow and orange wedges in the financiers' part of the circle in the lower right segment. Policy makers – the lower-left segment of the circle – know of the opportunity (as indicated by the green of the 'ignorance' barrier), are motivated to put in place the appropriate policies and frameworks (as indicated by green of the 'lack of interest/motivation' ring segment) and have the fiscal means to do so – indicated by the green colour of the 'lack of affordability' ring segment. However, policy makers do not know which would be the right policies or how to implement them. Thus, 'lack of expertise' is coloured orange: it constitutes a significant barrier to market change. None of these barriers would necessarily be an absolute bar to market change without an intervention. But as shown in Figure 8.3, the consumers' ignorance and the lack of cost effectiveness of an engagement

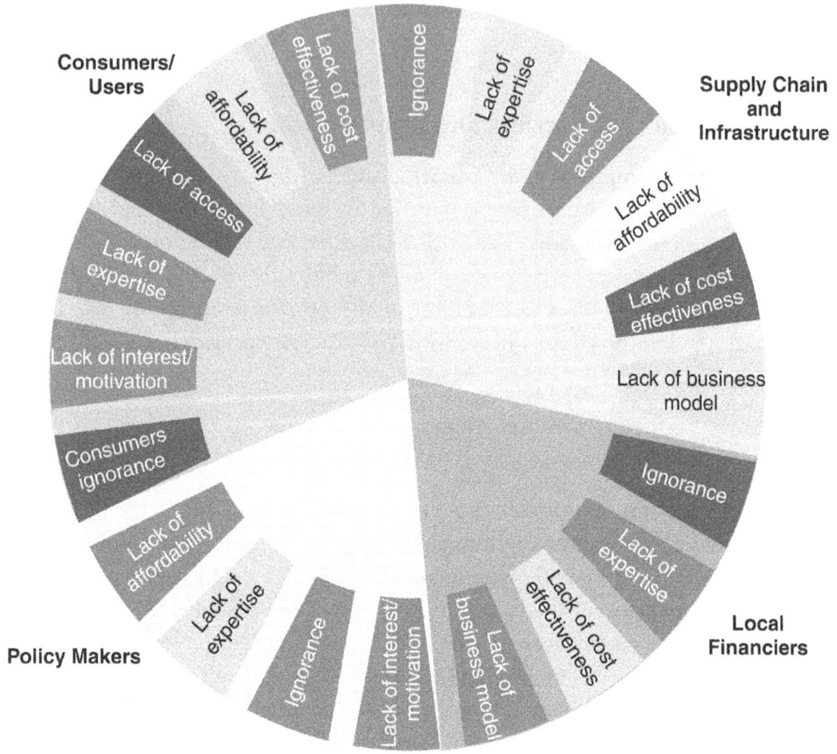

FIGURE 8.3 Example for Mapping the Barriers in the Barrier Circle Diagram

of the supply chain in the market are red, indicating that they are absolute barriers preventing a functioning market for energy-efficient products from developing.

The barrier circle can be used for project planning up front and can help identify the relevant barriers and design the appropriate barrier removal strategies. Comparing the barrier circle is drawn for the situation before and after the project illustrates the barrier removal impact of a project.

The intervention circle

Figure 8.4 presents an example from the case studies of the second part of the visualization tool, the intervention circle. The spikes on the spider web point in the same as the direction as the barrier they are designed to address. The axis signifies the intensity of the intervention: the farther out the points lie on the spider web, the more intense is the project's focus on these activities. The intensity of the barrier removal activities is ranked on a scale from zero to five. So far, no methodology can serve to calibrate the intensity of the barrier removal activity as compared to the intensity of the barrier. Therefore, the relative rank of the activity relates to its

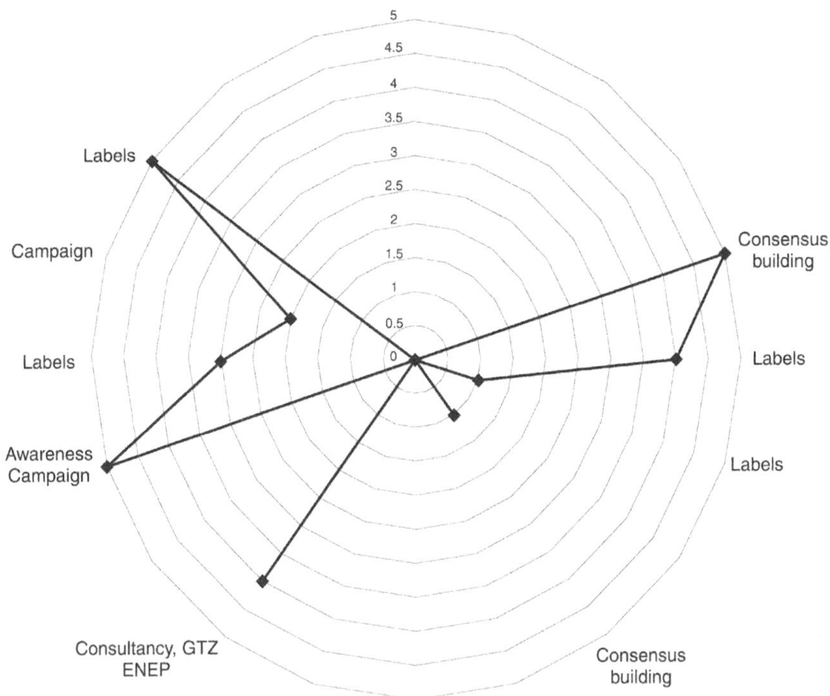

FIGURE 8.4 The Intervention Circle

importance within the intervention. The most important element of an intervention is given the highest ranking of five. Other, less important parts of the intervention received lower rankings, in relation to their relative importance within the intervention.

In the example presented in Figure 8.4, the project consisted of several activities: a consultancy helped policy makers develop expertise on smart policies, in this case a labelling policy for energy efficient appliances. The project built a consensus on the labelling system among manufacturers of these systems so that a joint move towards more market transparency through the labels created a business case for the suppliers to produce and distribute more efficient appliances. An awareness campaign helped consumers understand the energy efficient product and the energy efficiency labels. A part of the awareness campaign worked on the motivational barrier, by making it 'the cool thing' to buy the appliance with the energy efficiency label. Side effects of these activities were that financiers also started to understand the market for energy efficient appliances (through the labels) and found it a cost-effective market opportunity (through the consensus building exercise whose primary target group were the manufacturers).

Thus, with the help of the intervention circle, each project is illustrated as a characteristic fingerprint of barrier removal activities. If interventions or intervention components cannot be mapped on this circle, their contribution to market development might be limited or at least unconventional. On the other hand, the intervention circle does not distinguish between projects carried out by different actors, stakeholder groups or agencies. It can also capture the activities of several projects and interventions going on in parallel. All of them can be mapped onto a single spider web diagram which highlights potential synergies and complementarities (as well as potential conflicts) at a glance.

Putting the two together

Figure 8.5 illustrates how the two tools shown in Figures 8.3 and 8.4 can be combined to illustrate an intervention's match with the existing barriers in a market. A simple overlay of the two diagrams illustrates the degree to which the activities align with the barriers. In the example presented here, the consensus achieved with the supply chain and the energy efficiency labels directly addressed the lack of awareness for this not-yet-cost-effective product and created a new business model, consisting of selling energy efficient appliances in addition to the original appliances. This improved consumers' access to the energy efficient appliance. The awareness campaign informed consumers and users about the energy efficient option, and the labels motivated consumers to buy the more energy efficient appliance. Another

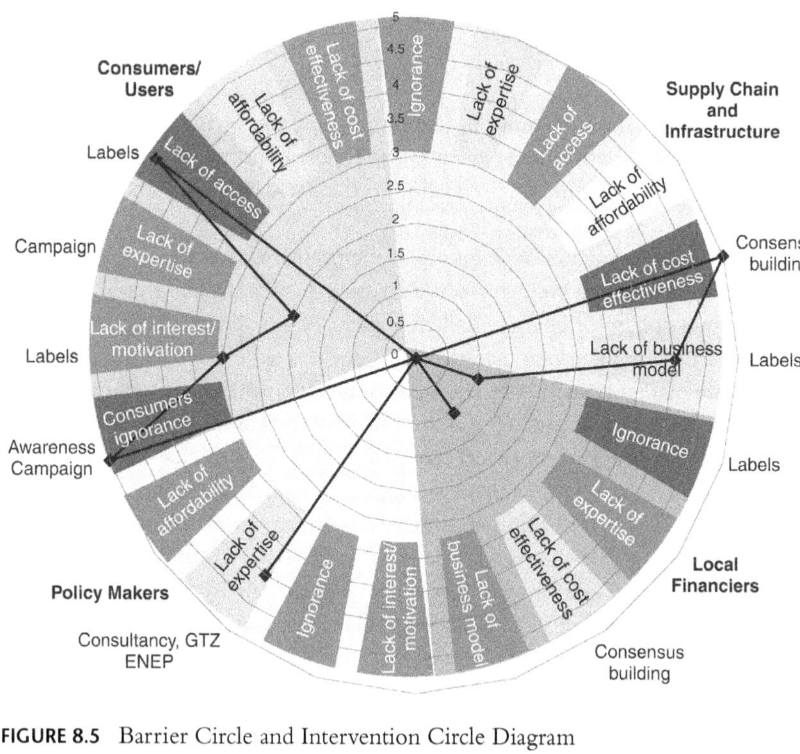

FIGURE 8.5 Barrier Circle and Intervention Circle Diagram

project component assisted policy makers in becoming smarter about energy efficiency labelling policies, their development and their enforcement. However, the overlay of the diagrams also shows that a number of yellow and orange barriers were not addressed by project activities. It seems that these barriers were not removed successfully through the intervention. If they are not in place after the intervention anymore, this would have to be attributed to other factors that were not part of the project.

This example illustrates how, together, the barrier circle and the intervention circle can give an indication of the likelihood for success of an intervention at the design stage of a project. When used in evaluation, the direction of the lines in the Intervention Circle will be aligned with those barriers that they actually addressed (even if they might have been designed to address other barriers or without an explicit barrier removal consideration). The tool is able to illustrate the sector in a holistic manner and reflect that barriers are sometimes not independent. It also reflects the barriers in their relative importance: If an intervention is designed on the basis of a sound barrier analysis, it will typically strive to remove the red barriers. If the red barriers are removed, the market might grow to some degree but market transformation most likely will be slowed down if orange barriers remain. As markets develop, new barriers that used to be orange will then come up and become 'red lights'. New barriers can also be created by external factors such as changes in government, financial crises, failure of technical infrastructures or new technological developments. The traffic light system will reliably indicate these barriers in updated analyses.

Summary and outlook

Effective climate change mitigation requires a long-term fundamental transformation of almost all energy-consuming processes in society. In order to reach a climate-compatible energy system – and this is true for many other areas of greenhouse gas emissions as well – we need a close-to-complete transformation of the way we provide and use energy. Project designers are aware that their efforts can only be small steps on this long path. Thus, most projects strive for some catalytic or transformative impacts that would trigger changes beyond the actual scope of the interventions. Most of the project documents formulate this explicitly as part of their motivation or even as their objective. Their mission is to contribute to an altered way of energy use by creating an enabling environment, rather than replacing every light bulb.

The larger goal of reduced emissions is many causal steps removed from whatever a project can achieve. This creates a significant attribution challenge. In order to better define the logical linkages between the steps and the goal, this chapter has developed a programme theory for climate mitigation intervention that allows assessing contributions to the larger goal. It looks not at positive contributions but at effects of removing barriers – where they exist nothing happens. When they are removed, change can take place.

This concept gave the programme theory its name: Theory of No Change. The concept has been developed on the basis of three sources: The online library of mitigation evaluations of the Climate Change Evaluation Community of Practice, the Evaluation Framework of Tokle and Uitto (2009) and the concept of market transformation for energy efficient consumer goods.

It has then been tested on two case studies (energy-efficient products in Thailand and district heating in Poland), for which a large number of evaluations were available. In these, four types of stakeholders played a role: consumers who constitute demand, suppliers who satisfy it, financiers who provide the financial liquidity in the market and policy makers who set the framework conditions. These groups of stakeholders typically encounter a number of barriers that keep them from using or supporting the sustainable energy technology. Seven generic barriers have been identified (not all of which apply to all stakeholders).

This resulted in a full programme theory for market development, and as such the Theory of No Change is able to assess whether or not an intervention has been contributing to a more favourable framework for market development for a sustainable energy technology. Rather than a positive log-frame-type theory of change, the Theory of No Change reflects the relevant context for change and provides a theory for what might have been limiting the success of the intervention. This is also important in order to identify to what degree the contribution was really decisive for change. Was the project really effecting change, or was an impact only perceived because it took place together with other changes in the market – changes that might have been even more decisive in spurring a change in market conditions? By including context into the analysis, the Theory of No Change is a step towards solving the attribution question in climate change mitigation, which will typically limit the importance given to capacity building and policy interventions and attribute most of greenhouse-gas benefits to investments.

Further research is needed in testing the Theory of No Change in other mitigation fields beyond retail products and heating systems so that a Generalized Programme Theory for Climate Change Mitigation can arise step by step. This will help identify where a more flexible approach is needed and how it can be formulated. If a general specification can be found, it can be used not only in project evaluation but also in monitoring and project design. As the Theory of No Change is able to reflect the context, it can also be used for policy evaluations as well as project planning.

As the barrier circle includes almost 20 barriers, this analysis requires some effort. It can potentially be reduced by identifying SMART[2] elegant outcome indicators or comprehensive analysis methods (e.g. surveys). Some further analysis is required in order to reduce the necessary empirical effort, for example, through more standardized outcome indicators for barrier removal activities.

Discussions with evaluators from other areas have demonstrated that the Theory of No Change can be applied to other areas of evaluation, policy making and change management. Whenever we are concerned with effecting change in people's behaviours, in theory, we can ask ourselves what it is that keeps people from behaving in a beneficial way and then remove the barriers to 'better' behaviour.

Notes

1 The notable exception to this are the project-based Kyoto mechanisms, such as the Clean Development Mechanism, in which each project needs to prove direct greenhouse gas emission reductions. They also rely to a significant degree on other interventions for project identification and development.
2 That is, Specific, Meaningful, Attainable, Relevant, Time-Bound.

References

Matambo, S. and G. Griebenow, 'Report on the inventory of climate change evaluations, 2010', Unpublished manuscript.

Tokle, S. and J. Uitto, 'Overview of climate change mitigation evaluation: What do we know?' In: R. van den Berg and O. Feinstein, eds., *Evaluating Climate Change and Development, World Bank Series on Development*, Volume 8, New Brunswick, NJ, and London, Transaction Publishers, 2009.

Wörlen, C., 'Meta-evaluation of climate mitigation evaluations', *Study for the Climate Change Evaluation Community of Practice*, 2011a, available at http://www.climate-eval.org/www.climate-eval.org/?q=system/files/studies/Meta-Evaluation%20of%20climate%20mitigation%20evaluations.pdf, last accessed September 12 2013.

Wörlen, C., 'Meta-evaluation of climate mitigation evaluations: Case study: Transforming markets for energy efficient products in Thailand', *Study for the Climate Change Evaluation Community of Practice*, 2011b, available at http://www.climate-eval.org/www.climate-eval.org/?q=system/files/studies/Meta-Evaluation%20-%20Thailand%20Case%20Study.pdf, last accessed September 12 2013.

Wörlen, C., 'Meta-evaluation of climate mitigation evaluations: Case study: Poland's heat sector', *Study for the Climate Change Evaluation Community of Practice*, 2011c, available at http://www.climate-eval.org/www.climate-eval.org/?q=system/files/studies/Meta-Evaluation%20-%20Poland%20Case%20Study.pdf, last accessed September 12 2013.

9

A PROGRAMME THEORY APPROACH TO EVALUATING NORMATIVE ENVIRONMENTAL INTERVENTIONS

Segbedzi Norgbey and Michael Spilsbury

Introduction

In the lead-up to Rio+20, many countries commented on the 'Institutional Framework for Sustainable Development' and articulated the need to promote a better balance among its environmental, social and economic pillars. Despite the difficulties experienced in finding common agreement on *how* to take this idea forward in practical terms, it is now well accepted that there needs to be a greater focus placed on the interlinkages among these pillars in responses to global sustainable development challenges.

Global governance frameworks for environmental issues are fragmented. The last 40 years have seen a proliferation of multilateral environmental agreements. Individually, each has been a step forward in strengthening governance responses to environmental concerns, yet collectively, their provisions have lacked coherence. As such, country efforts to comply with an ever-increasing number of conventions and their related requirements are unlikely to lead to optimal sustainable development solutions – resources will continue to be allocated to piecemeal responses. Simplifying global governance structures will present opportunities to bring about a greater integration of environmental, social and economic objectives in policy-making at the country level in order to move beyond sector-specific responses (i.e. the strengthening of international environmental governance).

A significant portion of the United Nations Environment Programme's (UNEP) work is geared towards influencing these international and national policy-making processes; the agency regards environmental sustainability as a key foundation upon which sustainable development rests. This work is often described as being largely normative in nature.

In this chapter, the authors argue that there are no clear differences between the methods used to evaluate *normative* aspects of development work and the methods used to evaluate more *operational* (or 'on the ground') activities. Any perceived differences are in the relative lengths and complexities of the causal chains leading from the intervention to the desired results and impacts.

The arguments articulated in this chapter are founded on theory-based approaches to evaluating development interventions. They are based on the realization that development interventions, whether designed with clear intervention logic or haphazardly/opportunistically formulated, have an underlying intent – to produce change from one state or condition to another. Thus, development interventions are embodiments of theories.[1] Inherent in this assertion is the idea that not only is there a clear underlying logic or theory on which the interventions (new programmes or policy) are based, but also that given stated or unstated assumptions the interventions' outcomes can be traced back to the activities undertaken. Indeed, in the United Nations (UN) system (as well as in many international development agencies), the most commonly used approach to planning development interventions is the logical framework matrix, which has the intentionality of proposed interventions at its core.

If one views development interventions as a set of activities with causal intent, it is possible to deploy theory-based approaches to explore the intended changes and determine whether the interventions have, indeed, produced the expected changes (and explore whether interventions yielded unexpected changes). This chapter describes approaches to evaluating the environmental aspects of international development with particular reference to UNEP work in general, and its normative aspects in particular.

The nature of normative environmental work

The UN defines *normative work* to include support to the development of norms and standards in conventions, declarations, regulatory frameworks, agreements, guidelines, codes of practice and other standard setting instruments, at global, regional and national levels. Normative work may also include support to the implementation of these instruments at the policy level, that is, their integration into legislation, policies and development plans (UNEG 2014).

In order to effectively address environmental issues, governments and institutions need to understand, evaluate, predict and respond to emerging needs. Providing information for decision-making is a key role performed by UNEP in international environmental governance processes. As part of its mandate to 'keep the world environment situation under review', UNEP places considerable emphasis on supporting and building assessment capacity at the global, regional and national levels. Developing policy guidelines and providing support to establishing global and regional environmental agreements is one of the key means by which UNEP catalyses action among governments.

In order to achieve this goal, UNEP provides support to the development of institutional and legal frameworks, especially at the national level, through efforts that include building capacities in the fields of institution-building and environmental law. UNEP's activities in this area also include enhancing the ability of developing country governments and countries with economies in transition to participate, in a meaningful way, in the negotiation of multilateral environmental agreements and in meeting their obligations under these agreements. UNEP provides intellectual leadership and acts as a catalyst for environmental action by disseminating environmental information and promoting public participation through the forging of partnerships with non-governmental organizations, the private sector and civil society groups.

The 2010–2013 UNEP Medium Term Strategy states the organization's mandate as comprising five overall, interrelated areas:

1. Keeping the world environmental situation under review;
2. Catalysing and promoting international cooperation and action;
3. Providing policy advice and early warning information, based upon sound science and assessments;
4. Facilitating the development, implementation and evolution of norms and standards and developing coherent inter-linkages among international environmental conventions; and
5. Strengthening technology support and capacity in line with country needs and priorities.

The organization's scope of work is broad, extensive and *predominantly normative*. It relates to the development of guidelines, norms and standards; to the support to conventions, international agreements and policy development processes; to the support to the development of legislative frameworks, capacity building and technology support; and to the assessment of global environmental trends.

Even when UNEP project and programme activities are implemented 'on the ground', the focus has been predominantly normative; pilot and demonstration sites are often intended to feed back into broader policy formulation and improvement. Project activities often include developing norms, standards, strategic action plans, policy options and strategies to address the environmental dimensions of poverty alleviation. Interventions frequently aim at strengthening communication, information and research networks on environmental issues; promoting cleaner production and sustainable resource use through developing guidelines and policies; and demonstrating and promoting the use of improved technologies as practical approaches for policy improvement or development. UNEP interventions frequently feature mainstreaming environmental considerations (within and across various sectoral policies, legislation, programmes and projects), and strengthening institutional capacities for disaster and conflict prevention and preparedness in high-risk areas.

Evaluation approaches

Discussion of evaluation methods

Development evaluation literature is replete with categorizations and classifications of approaches to evaluating international development interventions. Evaluations can be classified as **deductive** or **inductive**.

Deductive methods draw out the intervention's implications and assess evidence that the intervention's design achieved its anticipated outcomes. Deductive approaches often use theory-based methods that use logic models to describe the intervention logic. Commonly used terms and approaches include 'Theory of Change', 'causal pathway analysis', 'programme theory', 'impact pathway analysis', 'outcome mapping', 'results chains' and 'systemic evaluation' (Chen 2005; Bamberger, Rugh and Mabry 2006; GIZ 2011). Theory-based methods are not new; indeed, they are at the core of the long-accepted logical framework approach. However, in contrast to a logical framework, a full theory of change allows consideration of multiple pathways and better captures the actions required and possible risks at various stages along the causal pathways from activities towards intended results.

In contrast, inductive methods involve qualitative analysis oriented towards explorations, discovery and inductive logic (Patton 1987). These evaluation approaches are inductive to the extent that the evaluator makes no assumptions about prior intentions, except at the broad level of general goals. When an inductive approach is used, meaning is constructed after the event out of reflections on past events, including changes that may or may not be seen as achievements or that may or may not have been anticipated (Davies 2003). The approach begins with the evaluator making specific observations and builds towards general patterns. The nature and dimension of analysis required are often derived from observation as the evaluator gains a greater understanding of existing programmes or projects (Patton 1987; Bamberger, Rugh and Mabry 2006; Thomas 2006).

Patton (1987) notes two other ways that evaluation approaches can be inductive. Within a programme, an approach can be inductive if it involves exploring programme participants' and stakeholders' individual experiences through structured or unstructured interviews and questionnaires. Among programmes, the inductive approach looks for the characteristics of each programme that make them unique. *Goal-free* evaluation is the most commonly used inductive approach.

In goal-free methods, the evaluator starts with the changes that are evident and investigates whether the programme being evaluated has played any substantive role in the observed change. Approaches based on stakeholder participation are built on the principle that stakeholders should be involved in all stages of evaluation, including determining objectives and impacts, identifying and selecting indicators and participating in data collection and analysis (Leeuw and Vaessen 2009).

Evaluations have been classified as theory-driven and atheoretical. Theory-driven approaches formulate programme elements, rationale and causal linkages. The atheoretical approach to evaluation, at the extreme end, is characterized by 'a step-by-step cookbook method of doing evaluations' (Chen 1990: 18). The atheoretical approach tends to focus on the relationship between inputs and effects (black box evaluations) without taking into account the transformational processes that are inherent in the programmes being evaluated. Claims of success based on such input-effect models generate conclusions about programmes that policy makers may find difficult to apply. For example, if a simple input/output evaluation shows that eliminating chlorofluorocarbons will reduce climate change without providing information on the underlying mechanisms and processes, the consequences of the policy prescriptions on the economy and environment will not be known and policy makers will have extreme difficulty in designing policy options.

Furthermore, conclusions from input-effect models that indicate programme failure may be misleading. It is possible that models or evaluations that follow this approach may not explain which was flawed – the logic on which the intervention was based or the processes used to implement the intervention. In other words, such evaluative approaches provide limited information to assist managers to improve programmes.

In practice, evaluations are neither wholly inductive nor deductive. Some evaluation questions are left for inductive analysis based on direct observation; others are determined deductively. Patton (1987: 16) argues that there is often a 'flow from inductive approaches to find out what the important questions and variables are (exploratory work), to deductive hypothesis-testing aimed at confirming exploratory findings'. Similarly, the methods evaluations apply are seldom wholly naturalistic or experimental, theoretical or atheoretical.

Evaluation methods have evolved significantly beyond simple *black box* approaches, and a consensus has emerged among evaluators that evaluations must deal with multiple values in which different methods can be deployed that are tailored to unique situations. Depending on the specific questions or objectives of a given evaluation, some methods have advantages over others. Particular methods or perspectives may complement one another in providing a more complete picture (Leeuw and Vaessen 2009).

Impact evaluations are 'focused on quantifying the lasting and significant changes that occurred in the short or long term, direct or indirect, produced by an intervention or a body of work, or to which the same has contributed'.[2] Impact evaluations attempt to establish whether an intervention has caused the observed effects and explain *how* the effects were caused to satisfy the operational improvement/learning objective of evaluation. Establishing causation without explanation of the processes limits the utility of evaluation findings; a strong theoretical underpinning is essential both for intervention design and for evaluation.

Although not routinely undertaken, impact evaluations are in great demand by the donor community. The primary reason for the increased demand is that many outside of development agencies believe that the results achieved from the expenditure of international development resources have been poor or not adequately documented. Changes expected from development interventions are not evident after the interventions have come to an end, and donors wonder if the interventions made any difference (Leeuw and Vaessen 2009). Impact evaluations provide the evidence to demonstrate that the interventions have 'made a difference' and often quantify how large the impacts are. However, evaluating impacts is a complex and costly exercise, often fraught with methodological difficulties and therefore undertaken selectively.

Theory-based approaches: causal pathways – theory of change

Environment and sustainable development issues are complex and deal with overlapping and interrelated biophysical, economic, social and political systems, often at multiple scales. Designing and evaluating interventions must both define and bound the unit of intervention and the evaluative analysis. Models, as simplified representations of reality, are needed to focus on interventions' design and/or to provide a framework for the evaluation. Causal pathway analysis or Theories of Change provide a means for this.

A Theory of Change depicts and describes (i.e. provides a simple model of) the causal processes through which changes occur as a result of interventions. There are many published resources that provide guidance on the development and use of theory of change approaches and logic models (Bamberger et al. 2004; Chen 2005; University of Kansas 2013). Theories of change or causal pathway diagrams should be regarded as conceptual frameworks that summarize sequences of planned, desired or observed change. As such, they can be usefully applied to aid project design, monitoring and evaluation.

Figure 9.1 shows a graphical representation of generic set of causal pathways for an intervention. The pathways are comprised of the standard result levels used in project logical frameworks: outputs, outcomes and objectives.[3] The pathways represent causal relationships and, when elaborated in detail, help identify or clarify

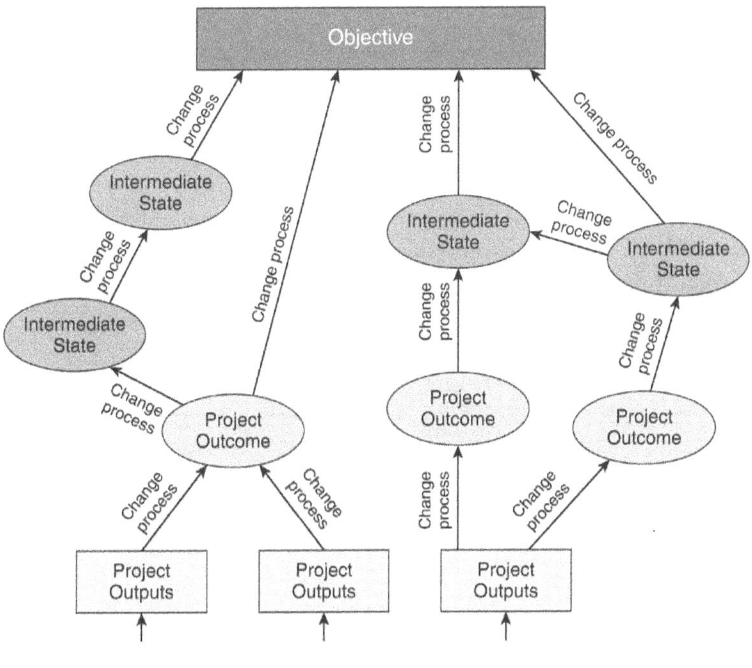

FIGURE 9.1 A Set of Generic Results Chains, which can also be Termed 'Causal Pathways', 'Impact Pathways' or a 'Theory of Change'

the assumptions in the intervention logic of a project or programme. From the schematic diagram, it can be observed that more than one output and change process may be required to achieve a certain outcome or, alternatively, one single output may be required for more than one outcome (via different change processes). In addition, there may be further outcome stages (termed 'intermediate states' in the diagram) between the immediate project outcome and the desired objective. The figure shows six different pathways from the outputs to the objective, but activities to produce outputs and promote/foster change processes are not shown. When specified with additional detail, in particular including the key users of outputs, description of the change processes (represented by the arrows in Figure 9.1) including externalities (assumptions), 'impact drivers' and details of performance indicators (for either processes or result levels or both), causal pathway analysis can be invaluable as a tool for both project/programme planning and for evaluation. Figure 9.2 takes one of the six pathways from Figure 9.1 and shows a single generic causal pathway with impact drivers and assumptions.

It should be stressed that the activities in a results-oriented intervention are not restricted to a level prior to or below outputs as they are often presented in a logical framework. Rather, activities also feature in the processes that link outputs to outcomes and those outcomes to higher-level results. Intervention designs should describe the activities needed to produce the outputs and those activities needed to ensure that the outputs will lead to outcomes and higher-level results. Project and programme activities should therefore feature in or complement the impact drivers (see Box 9.1).

Similarly, evaluation considers the observed changes and attempts to establish whether the intervention played a role in causing them. There are often several pathways that lead to results in a single project or programme intervention, and though multiple pathways can be captured in logical frameworks they are often more difficult to interpret in that form. Logical frameworks seldom provide sufficient detail in relation to the change processes that link one result level to the next. Pathways that do not form part of the intervention do not readily feature in logical frameworks. In contrast, casual pathway analysis can incorporate pathways (change processes) that are external to the intervention.

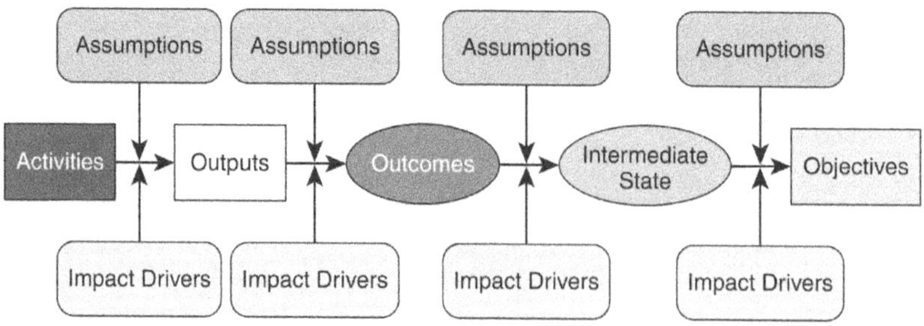

FIGURE 9.2 A Schematic Single 'Impact Pathway' Showing Intermediate States, Assumptions and Impact Drivers

BOX 9.1 IMPACT DRIVERS AND ASSUMPTIONS

Impact drivers are the significant factors that, if present, are expected to contribute to realizing the intended impacts and can be influenced by the project, by project partners and by stakeholders. They are often referred to as a project's critical success factors.

Assumptions are the significant factors that, if present, are expected to contribute to realizing higher-level results but are largely beyond the control of the project and its partners and stakeholders. The likelihood that the assumptions will not hold is the risk of not achieving results.

Impact drivers and assumptions are often key factors affecting project sustainability.

Does the linear nature of Theory of Change constrain its validity and application?

A common criticism of both Logical Frameworks and Theory of Change logic models is that they assume linear cause and effect relationships, which limits their utility and validity (Cooperative for Assistance and Relief Everywhere [CARE] 2012). Critics point out that the majority of real-life development interventions with environmental dimensions are complex; there are many interrelated and interacting factors with multiple and often nested feedback loops that involve non-linear relationships that, as such, are not scalable (Mayne and Stern et al. 2012; Vogel 2012a). It is commonly argued that linear models are inappropriate in such situations.

However, all models are simplified representations of reality, with the utility of any model being highly dependent upon its purpose. If any given change process is studied in more detail, it may be found to be highly complex with multiple actors and external factors affecting the change from one level to the next and with feedback relationships between levels. This reality does not invalidate the original Theory of Change, but merely highlights that it is a simplified representation of reality. Similarly, it does not imply that an evaluation using a Theory of Change approach has adopted the assumption that all the change processes are linear. 'The logical sequencing aspect often means that people mistakenly interpret theory of change as a linear sequence of change. Building development impact is not a linear process' (Vogel 2012b: 14).

This discussion also highlights the trade-offs between presenting too fine a level of detail and oversimplifying causal pathways within a theory of change. When too much detail is presented, the big picture can get lost in the complexity of multiple interrelationships. If oversimplified, however, clusters of outputs and outcomes may end up being lumped together and important interconnections and change processes could be overlooked.

To illustrate the similarities and differences between normative work and more direct forms of intervention, consider the following example: an intervention's desired results are defined in terms of quantifiable changes to a specific measure of environmental status (e.g. reduction in greenhouse gas emissions). An intervention that directly affects that environmental status is likely to be readily planned, monitored and evaluated. Another intervention that aims to achieve the same change in environmental status, but does so more indirectly via, say, a policy change process, followed by formalization of regulations and some form of enforcement 'on the ground', is relatively more challenging to plan, monitor and eventually evaluate because there would be several change processes each with associated actors and factors to consider. The number of steps in the causal chain between the initial interventions and the desired end result of changed environmental status would be quite different. A large portion of UNEP work is normative in nature and is akin to this latter situation. It is imperative, therefore, that the multiple, often long and indirect, causal pathways for interventions are clearly articulated at both project and programmatic levels.

This guides realistic intervention design, effective implementation and facilitates robust evaluation. But why would UNEP focus on normative work if the causal pathways to results on the ground are indirect? Beyond the fact that such work is a key part of the mandate of the organization, it is often the case that more direct pathways to environmental benefits operate at smaller scales. For example, an intervention to improve forest management is unlikely to have the resources to be able to engage each and every forest manager in a country or continent, whereas normative work on forest management standards and regulation processes (such as certification) can change the way legal and regulatory systems function, and these, in turn, can have downstream effects at much larger scales (albeit indirectly).

Application of the Theory of Change approach to evaluating normative environmental projects and programmes

This section gives a brief overview of the use of Theory of Change/causal pathway analysis in the evaluation of different types of environmental interventions at UNEP. Examples are chosen to highlight trends and lessons.

The 'Synergies Decisions' of the Stockholm, Basel and Rotterdam conventions

The Decisions (BC.Ex-1/1, RC.Ex-1/1 and SC.Ex-1/1; the... 'omnibus decisions'), were adopted by the Conferences of the Parties to the Basel, Rotterdam and Stockholm Conventions, respectively, at their simultaneous extraordinary meetings in February 2010. Parties decided that they would review the arrangements adopted pursuant to the 'Synergies Decisions',[4] in particular actions taken by the Secretariats of the Convention to merge and conduct joint activities, joint managerial functions and joint services in order to determine how far they had contributed to achieving the following objectives:

1. Strengthening of the implementation of the three Conventions at the national, regional and global levels;
2. Promoting coherent policy guidance;
3. Reducing administrative burdens;
4. Maximizing the effective and efficient use of resources at all levels; and
5. Protecting human health and the environment for the promotion of sustainable development.

The decisions further called upon the Executive Director of UNEP in consultations with the Director General of Food and Agriculture Organization of the United Nations to undertake an independent evaluation and to prepare reports of the evaluation for consideration by the Conferences of the Parties. The evaluation was to focus primarily on the extent to which the synergies process among the chemicals and waste-related conventions has contributed to improving cooperation and coordination at the global, regional and national levels. A Theory of Change (Figure 9.3) was developed prior to initiating the main data-gathering phase of the evaluation from a desk review of convention documents that outlined the aims of the 'Synergies Decisions'. The Theory of Change sets out the causal intent of the synergies decisions and provides a conceptual framework for the evaluation's implementation phase, guiding the data collection necessary for assessing performance indicators. The Theory of Change framework was used to structure interview questions with key stakeholders (e.g. Secretariat Staff and Parties to the Convention), which aided in identifying assumptions and threats that were key to assessing the likelihood of contributions being made to higher level objectives.

Assumptions were identified as the following:

1. **Leadership is actively committed to the synergies process:** The synergies process involves merging and restructuring the Convention Secretariats into one cohesive team serving all three Conventions, particularly on substantive/technical activities. This requires leadership commitment to the process at the highest level (Executive Secretary) and mid-tier management buy-in to the process of change management and joint-delivery of services to Parties;
2. **Accountability and incentive structures are in place to support synergies:** Responsibilities and roles are structurally and individually aligned to carry out synergies process and to support teamwork within the restructured secretariat (e.g. job descriptions, operating procedures, functions and processes for teams and clear reporting lines). Appropriate incentives (rewards and sanctions) are in place to underpin delivery of services internally and to Parties;
3. **Synergies restructuring is accepted and supported by all staff:** The synergies process and actions need to be accepted and supported by all staff and at all levels of the secretariat organization to be successful;

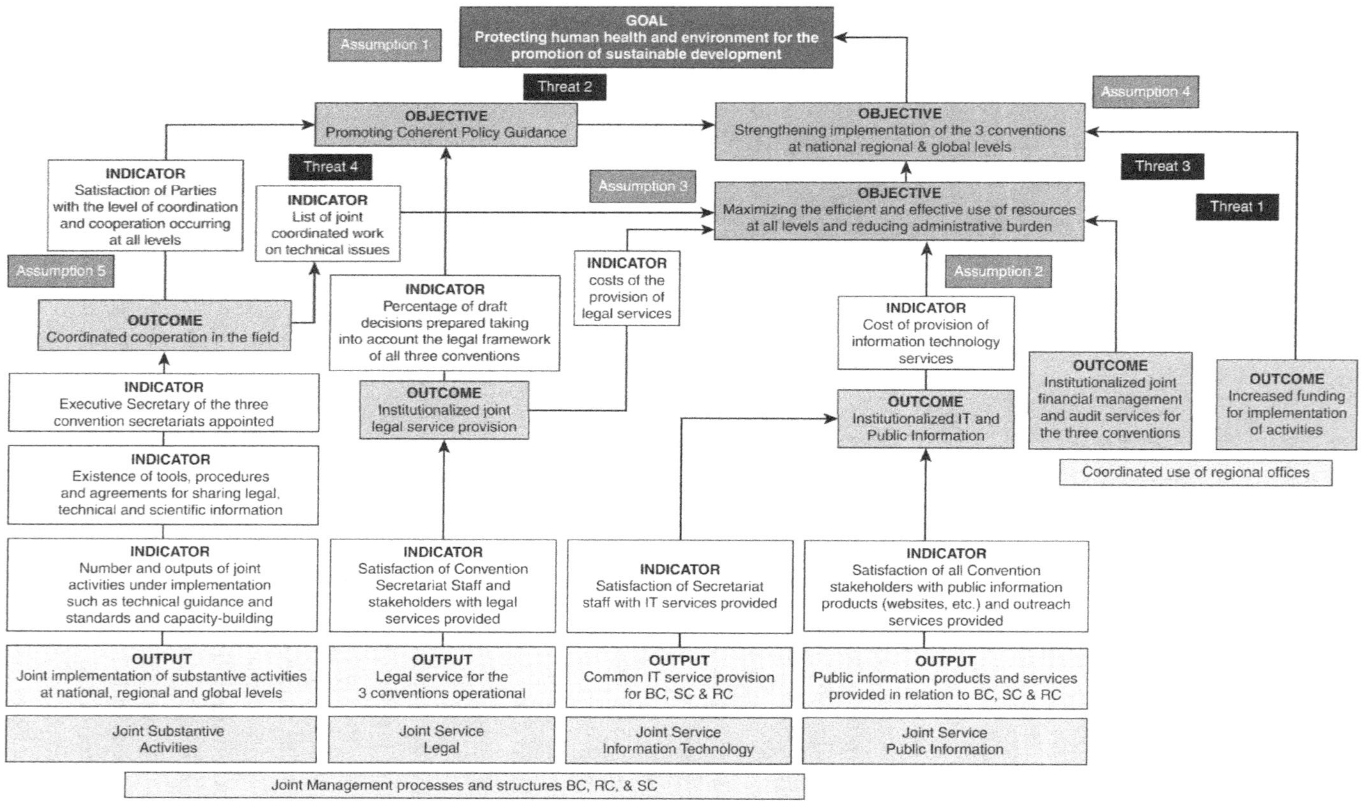

FIGURE 9.3 'Synergies Decisions' Theory of Change (Shown in Part)

4. **Synergies restructuring is cost-neutral and will lead to improved efficiency in implementing the Conventions:** The restructuring and merging of the Secretariats (while preserving the legal autonomy of each Convention) and delivery of joint services and substantive activities to Parties will lead to improved efficiency; and
5. **Parties are supportive of synergies and carry out the necessary institutional and organizational changes at the national level to promote cooperation and coordination:** For the strengthened implementation of the three Conventions and progress towards protecting human health and the environment, it is assumed that Parties will support the synergies process and pursuant actions and take actions at the national level (supported by the Secretariat/UN agencies and other relevant bodies). This will include, *inter alia*, improved systemic and institutional capacities to improve enforcement of the three Conventions, inter-ministerial coordination (including cooperation between focal points)[5] and bringing responsibilities for implementation under one ministry (e.g. one focal point for all chemicals Conventions).

Threats to the achievement of outcomes were identified as the following:

1. **Cost of synergistic actions rise, leading to decreases in party interest and support:** If Assumption 4 (cost neutrality and improved efficiencies) does not hold, then Parties may decide to abandon or limit the synergies process;
2. **Potential conflicts between managers, leading to poor delivery of services:** Managers may have conflicts over human and financial resources if managerial controls, responsibilities and roles lack clarity within the new matrix structure;[6]
3. **No increases in funding for implementation of activities to support the strengthening of the Conventions:** A lack of financial support is likely to be a significant threat to the realization of synergies in terms of delivery of substantive activities by the secretariat and implementation of synergies at the national and regional levels; and
4. **National cooperation and coordination fails:** Parties are unable to forge operational synergies at the national level due to lack of enabling policy, capacity or mandate disagreements between ministries (e.g. lack of communication and institutional structures that can facilitate regularized coordination). Implementation of synergies actions fails.

In this case, Goal (e) of 'protecting human health and the environment for the promotion of sustainable development' is intended to result from 'strengthening the implementation of the three conventions at national, regional and global level', that is, changes in third-party behaviours within countries acting in compliance with national regulatory requirements that stem from Convention provisions. Although reducing threats to human health through the convention mechanisms features in the overall goal, it would be unrealistic to attempt to measure the downstream effects of changed management arrangements in Convention Secretariats at that level. The locus for measuring performance in the normative work, in this situation, is not feasible at the level of changes in environmental status/condition, because the causal linkages are indirect and weak and so any observed effects are difficult to attribute to the upstream change in question. This implies that evaluation of the effects of the synergies decisions are best captured at the outcome level and viewed as contributions to higher-level intended objectives.

The Global Environment Facility joint geothermal imaging project

The evaluation of the Joint Geothermal Imaging project and a follow-up study undertaken by the Global Environment Facility (GEF) Evaluation Office made use of Theory of Change and provided another example of normative research work – the development of ways to combine data from different imaging methods for site identification of geothermal wells. The potential to establish linkages between site identification and environmental benefits in terms of CO_2 emissions avoided was identified during the Terminal Evaluation[7] of the project, and UNEP developed the Theory of Change as a contribution to the follow-up study undertaken by the GEF Evaluation Office. The Theory of Change shows the pathways from imaging method development, scientific capacity-building and training events (often considered as normative activities) through to the resulting benefits expressed as CO_2 equivalents avoided from the use of geothermal electricity generation (rather than the 'business as usual' scenario, which would have resulted in fossil fuel CO_2 emissions) (see Figure 9.4).

The points to note in this example are that many development projects contain normative aspects, and it is not unusual for the causal pathways from project activities to the desired development objectives to be somewhat indirect. In this case, tracing the actual results of the project along the causal pathways leading towards the intended objectives highlighted the fact that the application of the imaging technology could be linked to quantifiable improvements in energy-generating efficiency of geothermal wells, which can be expressed in terms of CO_2 emissions avoided. Routine application of Theory of Change approaches can aid in identifying projects that have potential for more detailed impact evaluations, because causal pathways that may have high 'attributive ease' can be identified.

Forest certification: normative work leading to quantified benefits through a regulatory framework

Forest certification provides an example of an evaluation – using Theory of Change as a guiding framework – of normative work on improving the criteria and indicators used for assessment and certification of sustainable forest management through scientific testing. An example of a previous evaluation[8] has applications for several UNEP projects, including one UNEP-Global Environment Facility (GEF) project[9]

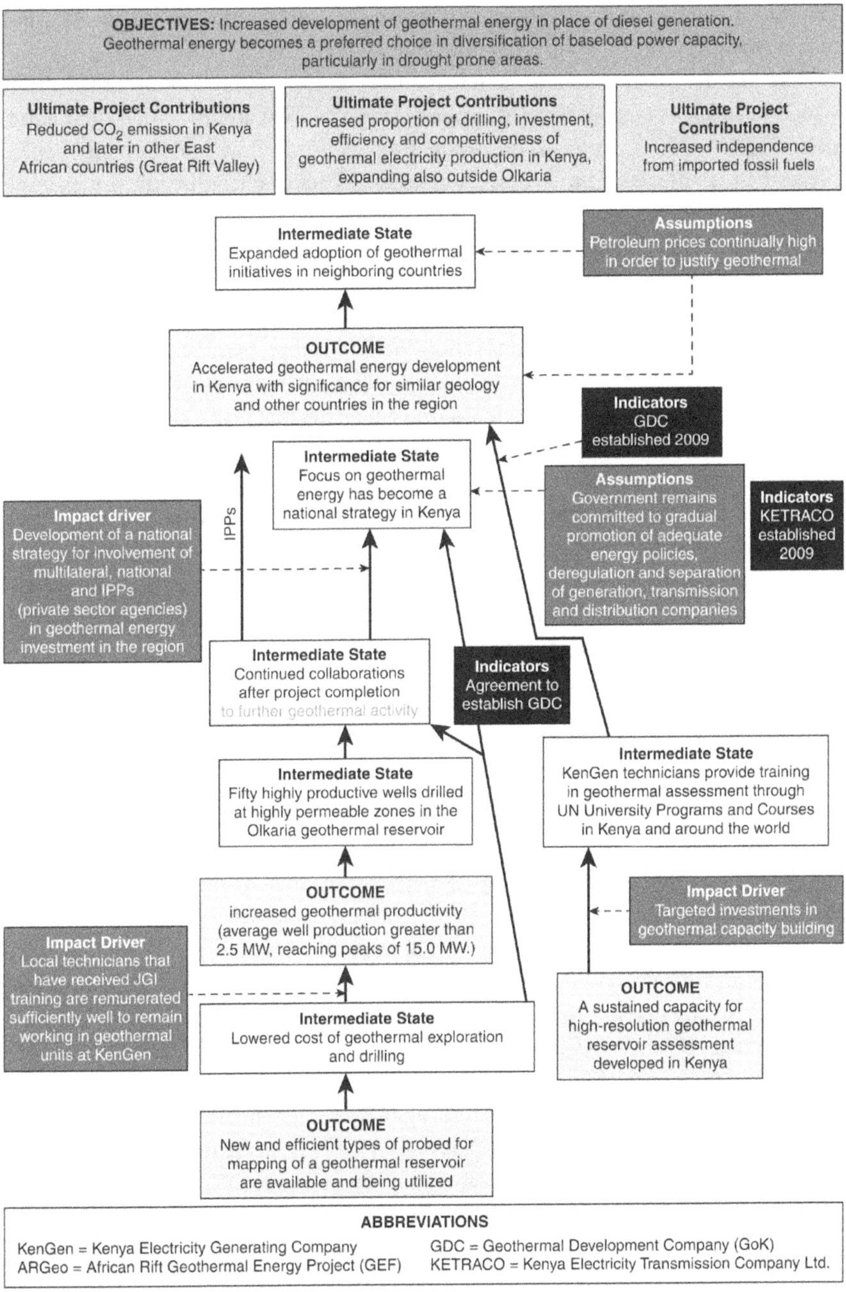

FIGURE 9.4 Theory of Change – Joint Geophysical Imaging Methodology for Geothermal Reservoir Assessment

that was a follow-up to the original Centre for International Forestry Research investigation.

The impact of research is generally more readily appraised in situations in which new science-based innovations are clearly defined and in which their adoption directly affects patterns of production, consumption and human welfare. Nevertheless, impacts from science may also be achieved indirectly, for example through influencing policies, decision-making processes, management assessment processes or development assistance strategies. When research leads to developing new technologies for use directly by land mangers (e.g. farmers/forest managers), the magnitude of the impact often depends on the number of adopters and the land areas over which the research innovation yields an improvement (i.e. a cumulative effect). However, there are other types of impact pathways in which a small number of adoption events (or even a single event) can change the way a system or a process functions, for example, national governance processes or a regulatory system (such as forest certification); more normative pathways create a systemic effect.

The research criteria and indicators for sustainable forest management generated information rather than finished technologies. However, utilizing information from research (to a greater degree than with finished technologies) is not a binary phenomenon (i.e. uptake or no uptake). The use of information from research may be symbolic, conceptual or instrumental, and often there is no straight-line cause and effect between providing information and outcomes leading towards intended environmental effects and benefits. Additionally, information may be only partially applied, further increasing the difficulties of determining the level of adoption and concomitant linkages to any changes on the ground.

The criteria and indicators for sustainable forest management developed through the Centre for International Forestry Research analysis were intended to be of relevance for application at individual Forest Management Units to improve forest management across a wide range of countries and settings. The criteria and indicators were also intended to have relevance for broader forest-related initiatives at both national and regional levels. Although the criteria and indicators were intended for application at the Forest Management Unit level, a range of pathways leading to improved forest management were anticipated. In fact, achieving the desired outcomes of widespread improvement in forest management at the Forest Management Unit level was thought to be less likely through a series of independent, direct (and cumulative) adoption events among multiple, separate and widely geographically dispersed forest management entities. Widespread impact was thought to be more likely to occur through using criteria and indicators in regulatory processes (e.g. national legislation and regulation and voluntary certification) (see Figure 9.5).

The uptake (and impact) strategy for the criteria and indicators work was based on the premise that collaborative research and engagement of key stakeholders would effectively generate interest in, and ownership of, the research findings among key user groups. It was anticipated that the work would be used by forest certification bodies, accreditation agencies, development assistance agencies, national forestry

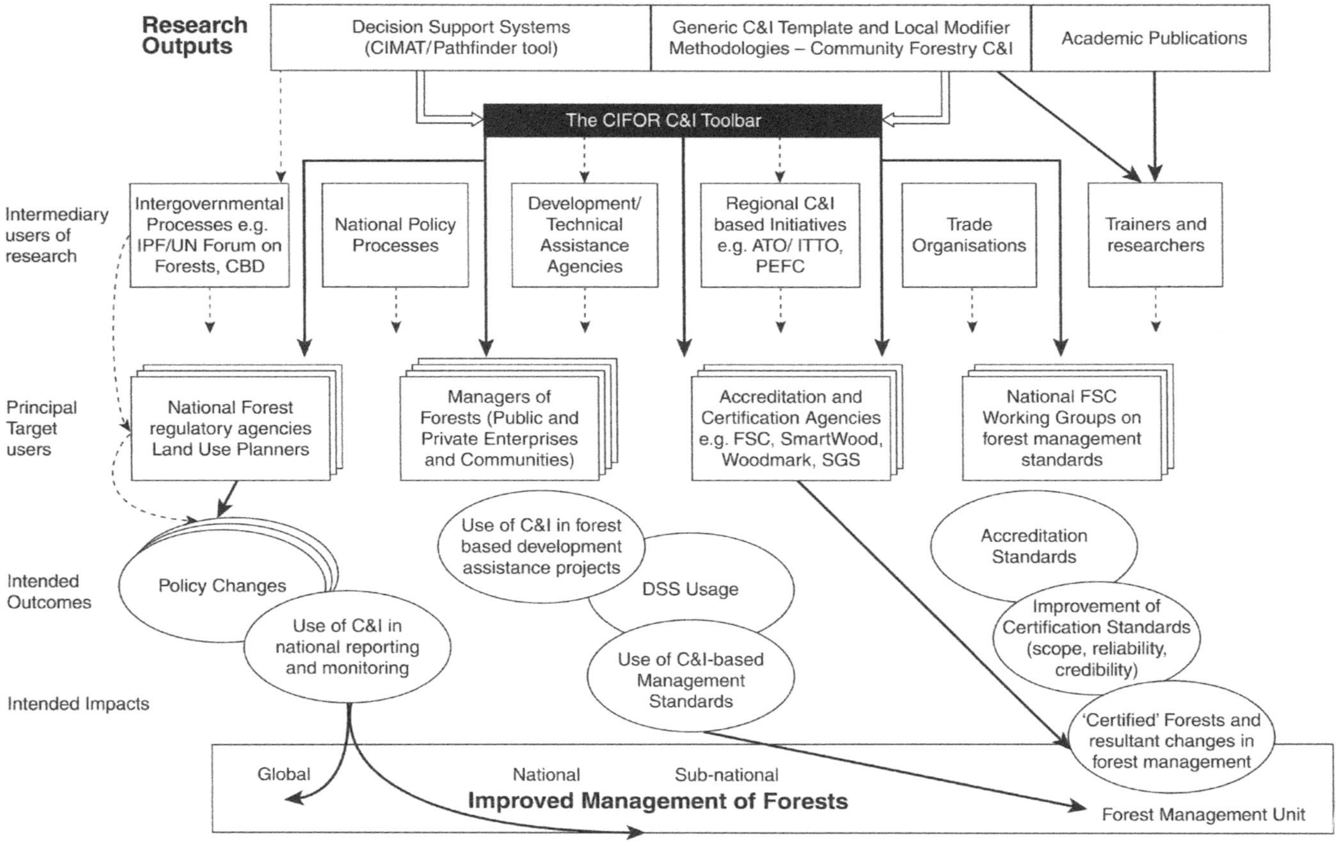

FIGURE 9.5 A Generalized Representation of Impact Pathways Relating the Centre for International Forestry Research Criteria and Indicators Project. Source: Spilsbury (2005)

authorities and regional and national criteria and indicators development processes in order to help assimilate current best practices. The research also helped to orient existing criteria and indicators-related trends and initiatives in the right direction.

In the detailed evaluation of this project,[10] evidence of causal changes was traced along multiple pathways in the Theory of Change. However, the pathways that passed through certification processes presented an opportunity to link uptake (by certification bodies into their certification standards) of the normative research to changes in management practices in certified forests through the regulatory chain of independent certification audits that applied the revised standards to different forest management enterprises across the world (see Figure 9.6).

It is possible to examine the causal effects of Forest Stewardship Council certification in terms of changes to on the ground forest management by examining the specific improvements in forest management that forest owners/managers were

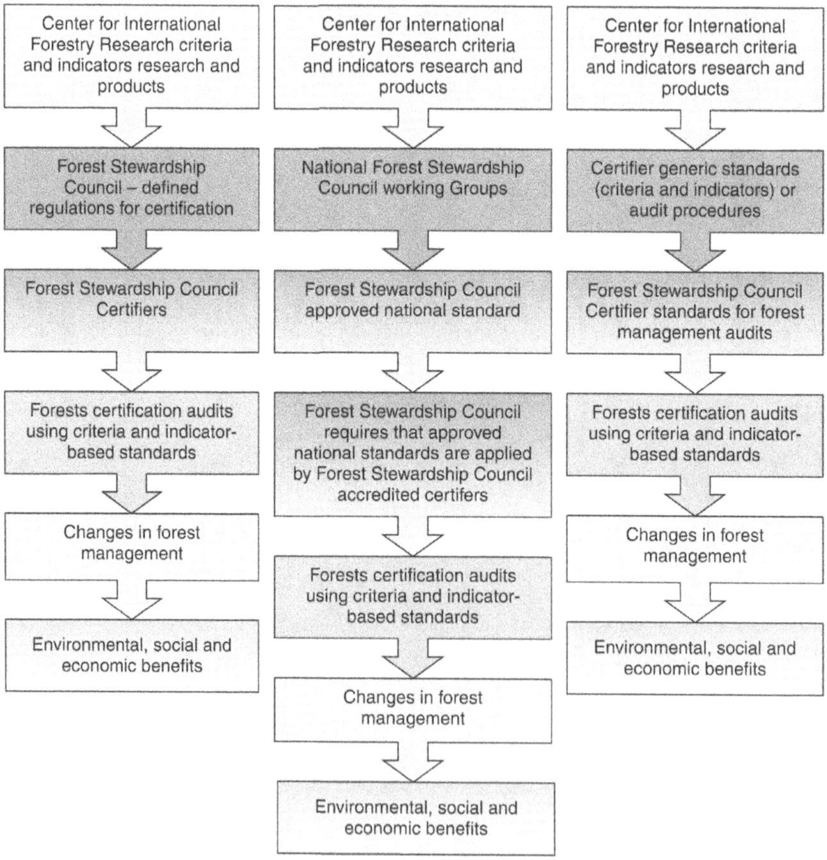

FIGURE 9.6 Major Impact Pathways through Forest Stewardship Council Certification Processes. Source: Spilsbury (2005)

required to make in response to the certification auditing process. These provide a means of examining before-and-after situations in certified forests.

The Forest Stewardship Council forest certification audit process requires independent third-party certifiers to assess forest management against consistent criteria and indicators-based standards, highlighting which management aspects are in compliance and, critically, where standards are not met.

Non-compliance with the certifier's standards or failure to adequately meet the certification standard's forest management performance criteria results in the issuance of a corrective action requests, which outline what needs to be improved in order to bring the operation into compliance. Corrective action requests are specified in publicly available Certification Assessment Reports[11,12] and define aspects such as forest production, environmental, social and economic issues the operation is required to address in order to attain certification.

The certification regulatory system, which includes follow up audits, ensures that forest management entities improve their management with regard to these corrective action requests in order to become compliant and receive or retain their official certified status. Thus, any forest management entity that achieves a certified status must have successfully addressed any corrective action requests that were issued during the certification process. If the corrective action requests are checked against, and correspond to, the specific criteria and indicators in the new standards that the research work improved, then a credible causal link between normative research and changes in the on the ground management of multiple forest enterprises that have been certified can be established. Early identification of causal pathways through Theory of Change analysis during project design and implementation proved invaluable in identifying possibilities for robust evaluation.

Programme theory and results-based monitoring and evaluation

Results-based monitoring and evaluation systems are designed to address the 'so what' question in project or programme implementation. A results-based system provides feedback on the actual outcomes and goals of organizational interventions. 'Results-based monitoring is a continuous process of collecting and analyzing information to compare how well a project, program, or policy is being implemented against expected results' (Kusek and Rist 2004: 16). Key elements of results monitoring include collecting the baseline information that describes the existing situation before the intervention, defining outcome indicators, collecting information on outputs and intermediate states (or milestones) to determine if they contribute to achieving outcomes, systematic quantitative and qualitative reporting on progress made towards achieving outcomes, collecting information on stakeholder perceptions and collecting information regarding the success of the partnership strategy adopted. Results-based monitoring and evaluation is often undertaken collaboratively with strategic partners.

A critical point to note is that monitoring and evaluation of development interventions can be meaningfully undertaken only when the interventions' intended outcomes are stated as explicitly as possible. The explicit statement of outcomes becomes the key to developing appropriate indicators that measure success because the outcomes will ultimately lead, particularly in the case of UNEP, to environmental benefits. Developing a system to monitor and evaluate development interventions is essentially 'a deductive process in which inputs, activities, and outputs are all derived and flow from the setting of outcomes; indicators, baselines, and targets, all crucial elements of the performance framework, are derived from and based on the setting of outcomes' (Kusek and Rist 2004: 57).

Within UNEP's planning framework, project activities are designed to deliver certain outputs that are intended to lead to certain predefined results, which are expected to contribute to the expected accomplishments (immediate outcomes). Within project-, programme framework- and sub-programme strategy documents, the intervention logic is captured both in logical frameworks and project narratives. As many projects within UNEP's larger organizational work plans have a normative nature, applying the Theory of Change approach to evaluating higher programmatic levels is instructive and reveals a number of strategically significant findings. A Formative Evaluation of the UNEP Programme of Work 2010–2011 (UNEP 2011) analysed the causal relationships embedded in all UNEP planning documents that contributed to the Programme of Work in order to understand whether project designs were optimally linked to higher-level results. Such feedback was aimed at inducing adaptations to programme implementation in order to enhance the likelihood of success in achieving the intended results and to improve future UNEP work planning processes.

The evaluation noted that performance indicators for outcomes are normally defined within project documents. Projects, however, are often designed separately (despite efforts to promote greater collaborative design). Project-specific outcome indicators, even among sets of closely linked projects within a programme, usually have quite different metrics (depicted by tinted triangles in Figure 9.7), and outcomes often cannot be aggregated. This poses challenges for assessing aggregate performance at the level of programmatic outcomes. Programmatic outcomes are often more broadly defined outcome statements in higher-level planning documents than project-specific outcomes. In many organizations, including UNEP, higher-level planning processes are 'top down' in the sense that they derive the higher-level results statements from official mandates of governing bodies and longer-term programmatic strategies. In effect, programmatic outcomes define a 'set' or category intended to encompass several project-specific outcomes. Most organizations face challenges in both monitoring and evaluating performance at this level.

Analysis of Theories of Change at higher organizational levels shows that programme designs can contain inherent weaknesses that pose problems. For example, in UNEP's Programme of Work 2010–2011, outcome indicators were not suitable for assessing performance across the contributing projects. In addition, there were often temporal problems in using such indicators to monitor progress in programme implementation. It was often the case that achieving project-level outcomes was neither linear nor incremental. Outcomes of normative international work may frequently involve a change in national policies that are discrete events, not ones that

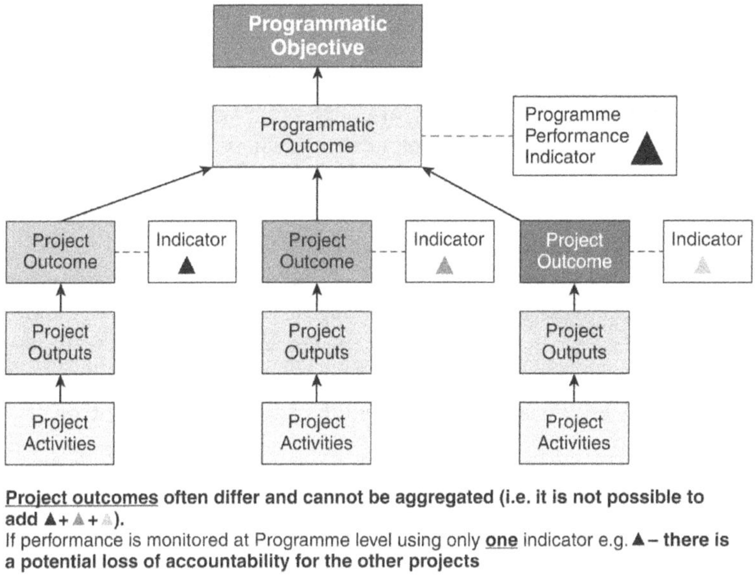

FIGURE 9.7 Theory of Change – Common Problems in Capturing Performance at the Programme Level

gradually accrue over time. Monitoring such outcomes would repeatedly record 'no change' until such time as a policy change occurred – often anticipated towards the end of (or considerably beyond) project implementation.

The utility of directing highly aggregated monitoring information as results-based feedback into lower level management processes is extremely limited. Monitoring should focus on verifiable milestones that chart progress towards desired result levels. Milestones capture progress from project initiation to achievement of outcomes, and should be specified as activities, sub-outputs needed to deliver key outputs, the key outputs themselves or activities or events needed to ensure that outputs lead to outcomes. Milestones will usually be closely linked to the outputs and impact drivers identified in a Theory of Change and should be activities or deliverables for which clear accountability can be specified.

This is the crux of results-based management – the interface between sound causal logic, results frames and individual accountabilities within organizational management structures. Organizations can aspire to achieve outcomes (and the benefits that stem from them). However, individuals within an organization cannot be held directly accountable for outcome achievement. An outcome involves a change in behaviour beyond the direct control of a project or intervention. Thus, individuals cannot reasonably be held accountable for a change in someone else's behaviour, although they can (and should) be held accountable for doing all the things that are necessary and feasible to maximize the likelihood that an outcome will be achieved. These activities should form a standard component of work planning and performance appraisal. For example, though UNEP projects cannot be held directly accountable for the promulgation and implementation of national climate change policies, they can facilitate policy development processes by presenting workshops, providing technical support, ensuring the engagement of relevant government institutions and civil society in policy processes, enabling access to good practice examples and fostering of high levels of ownership.

Project milestones should be used to track the progress of project implementation through outputs and onwards to outcomes to immediate objectives. The Formative Evaluation of the UNEP Programme of Work 2010–2011 (UNEP 2011) found that the overwhelming majority of project milestones in approved project documents were pitched at or below the output level. In a few cases, milestones referred to external events that would have happened anyway. Very few milestones captured processes and achievements further along the intended causal pathways towards higher-level results in the organization's Medium-Term Strategy.

Evaluating the cost-effectiveness of normative work

Although it is possible to track progress towards achieving outcomes and impacts through theory-based approaches, one of the more problematic evaluative issues in normative work is how to determine cost-effectiveness. Often, donors and governments are unsatisfied with the simple answer that outcomes have been achieved. Invariably, they seek an answer as to whether the intervention represents value for money. Determining value for money involves analysing cost-effectiveness, which should measure the cost of achieving intended programme outcomes and impacts and should compare the costs of alternative ways of producing the same or similar benefits.

In general, although it may be feasible to document programme or project costs, estimating the environmental and other benefits further along the results chain often presents a much more complex problem and is seldom attempted. Environmental benefits stemming from project outcomes are less amenable to measurement because they are often not easily quantifiable and are frequently only partially attributable to the intervention. Comparing alternative ways of producing the same or similar benefits involves benchmarking for which data are frequently unavailable. For normative environmental work, therefore, the difficulties related to determining outcomes and impacts that occur further along the results chain (as well as attribution issues) make cost-effectiveness analysis at that level an almost intractable exercise.

Given the difficulties associated with undertaking cost-effectiveness analysis within the context of limited evaluation resources, the authors are of the view that initiating any effort to determine value for money for development interventions of a normative nature, especially as it relates to environmental activities, should focus on assessing cost-efficiency. Cost-efficiency relates to how well inputs are converted to outputs. Expected benefits should be set out along the results chain found in well-prepared logframes and causal pathway/Theory of Change analysis. Outputs (and sometimes outcomes) are often clearly defined in planning documents and their achievement is often better documented and more readily verifiable.

Conclusion

Our experience from evaluations of a wide range of environmental activities leads us to conclude that the causal logic that undergirds the theory-based approach provides a robust method for understanding development interventions and facilitates the evaluator's ability to clearly map progress towards the results of development interventions. Although the approach does not guarantee that impacts can be readily identified and irrefutably attributed to particular development interventions, it nevertheless facilitates contribution analysis and the identification of impact drivers and intermediate states that, from both a planning and adaptive management perspective, can increase the likelihood of attaining impacts. From an evaluative perspective, such approaches increase the clarity and rigour of assessments. Contrary to some commonly expressed views in the evaluation community, we see no clear differences in methods used to evaluate normative as opposed to operational activities. Normative interventions do not define a separate category but are part of a continuum from very indirect to more direct (on the ground) interventions. The differences relate to the relative lengths/complexities of the causal pathways to impact with associated attribution issues.

The bulk of the work undertaken in UNEP has a normative character, and hence the various causal pathways to ultimate impact are often quite long – which presents challenges for assessing ultimate impacts. Theory of Change analysis, however, improves the clarity of evaluative analysis with regard to achieving the immediate outcomes and their causally linked intermediate states in order to enhance the analysis of performance.

It is our view that because project logical frameworks do not often provide comprehensive information on the processes by which project outputs yield outcomes and eventually lead, via intermediate states, to impacts, causal pathways need to be carefully examined and the following questions addressed:

- Are there other causal pathways that would stem from the use of project outputs by other potential user groups?
- Is each pathway complete? Are there any missing intermediate states between project outcomes and expected accomplishments?
- Have the key impact drivers and assumptions been identified for each step in the pathway?

Our experience shows that it is possible, within a programmatic framework, for an evaluation to map the causal pathways for sets of related projects in order to clarify how projects intend to deliver project outputs, achieve outcomes and contribute to higher-level results. Within the context of evaluations, a Theory of Change approach can provide the conceptual framework for detailing the relationship among explicit (planned) and implicit outcomes and impacts or to set clear targets and reconstruct indicators of success where they are not readily available. The analysis can identify whether interventions, by design, are mutually reinforcing and converge and synergize with one another to deliver the intended higher-level results. At the same time, the analysis can highlight possible interlinkages between related programmes. The approach is sufficiently flexible to incorporate analysis of causal pathways that were not foreseen in interventions' initial planning. Indeed, comparing the causal pathways from the initial project designs to the pathways that evaluative evidence highlights as being the most effective can offer insights into project/programme adaptive management processes.

The use of Theories of Change or causal pathways aids project design, implementation and evaluation by clarifying causal logic and identifying performance measures and key impact drivers. This information can also help define or refine appropriate monitoring approaches and provide feedback to help guide results-oriented adaptive management. It is also the key guiding framework for results-oriented evaluations.

Notes

1. See Leeuw and Vaessen (2009), Chapter 3, p. 15.
2. Adapted from Organisation for Economic Co-operation and Development (OECD) DAC (2002).
3. Logical frameworks show some variation from one agency to another – outcomes are sometimes termed 'purpose', some logical frameworks include 'immediate objectives' and 'development objective' and/or 'goal'.
4. See Decision BC.IX/10 (June 2008), RC.4/11 (October 2008), and SC.4/34 (May 2009), available at http://www.brsmeas.org/Implementation/DecisionsandDocuments/Decisions/tabid/2616/language/en-US/Default.aspx.
5. For example, among ministries of agriculture, environment, health, industry, customs and excise and trade.
6. See Proposal from the Executive Secretary of the Basel, Rotterdam and Stockholm Conventions for the Organization of the Secretariats of the Three Conventions, December 2011.
7. See https://www.unenvironment.org/resources/terminal-project-evaluations/terminal-evaluation-unep-gef-project-joint-geophysical.
8. See Spilsbury (2005, 2007).
9. GEF Project No. 1897, Improved Certification Schemes for Sustainable Tropical Forest Management.
10. See Spilsbury (2005, 2007)).
11. For Public Certification Summaries, see:www.rainforest-alliance.org/programs/forestry/smartwood/public-summary-reports.html; www.qualifor.sgs.com/home_qualifor/forest_management_certification/forest_management_reports.htm; and www.scscertified.com/forestry/forest_certclients.html.

References

Bamberger, M., J. Rugh and L. Mabry, *Real World evaluation: Working under budget, time, data and political constraints*, Thousand Oaks, CA, Sage, 2006.

Chen, H.T., *Theory-driven evaluations*, Thousand Oaks, CA, Sage, 1990.

Chen H.T., *Practical programme evaluation: Assessing and improving planning, implementation and effectiveness*, Thousand Oaks, CA, Sage, 2005.

Cooperative for Assistance and Relief Everywhere (CARE) International UK, '*Peace building with impact: Defining theories of change*', London, 2012.

Davies, R., '*Network perspectives in the evaluation of development interventions: More than a metaphor*', *EDAIS conference*, New directions in impact assessment for development methods and practice, Manchester, UK, 2003.

German Agency for International Cooperation (GIZ) '*Systemic approaches in evaluation: Documentation of the conference on 25–26 January 2011*', German Federal Ministry of Economic Cooperation and Development, 2011, available at http://www.evaluation-conference.de/en/index.html, accessed August 23 2013.

Kusek, J. Z. and R.C. Rist, *Ten steps to a results-based monitoring and evaluation system: A handbook for development practitioners*, The World Bank, Washington, DC, 2004.

Leeuw, F. and J. Vaessen, '*Impact evaluations and development: NONIE (The Network of Networks on Impact Evaluation) Guidance on Impact Evaluation*', 2009, available at http://siteresources.worldbank.org/EXTOED/Resources/nonie_guidance.pdf, accessed August 23 2013.

Mayne J. et al., Position paper on impact evaluation of CGIAR NRM research programmes: A broader view, Prepared for the NRM-Impact Community of Practice, 2012.

Organisation for Economic Co-operation and Development (OECD)/Development Assistance Committee (DAC), '*Glossary of key terms in evaluation and results based management*', Paris, 2002.

Organisation for Economic Co-operation and Development (OECD) DAC, *Glossary of key terms in evaluation and results based management*, Paris, UNEG Task Force on Impact, 2002.

Patton, M.Q., *How to use qualitative methods in evaluation*, Thousand Oaks, SAGE Publications, 1987.

Spilsbury, M.J., '*The sustainability of forest management: Assessing the impact of CIFOR criteria and indicators research*', CIFOR Impact Paper No 4, Bogor Indonesia, 2005, available at http://www.cifor.cgiar.org/publications/pdf_files/Books/BSpilsbury0503.pdf, accessed May 20 2013.

Spilsbury, M.J., 'CIFOR. The sustainability of forest management: Assessing the impact of CIFOR criteria and indicators research'. In: H. Waibel and D. Zilberman, eds., *International research on natural resource management: Advances in impact assessment*, 217–245, Food and Agriculture Organization of the United Nations and CAB International, Rome, Italy, and Oxfordshire, UK, 2007.

Thomas, D.R., 'A general inductive approach for analyzing qualitative evaluation data', *American Journal of Evaluation*, 27(2): 237–246, 2006.

United Nations Environment Programme (UNEP), *Formative Evaluation of the UNEP Programme of Work 2010–2011*, United Nations Environment Programme, New York, 2011.

United Nations Environment Programme (UNEP) '*2010–2013 medium-term strategy: Environment for development*', United Nations Environment Programme, New York, 2007.

United Nations Evaluation Group (UNEG), '*UNEG handbook for conducting evaluations of normative work in the UN system*' (http://unevaluation.org/document/detail/1484).

University of Kansas, 2013 *Community Tool Box, 'Developing a framework or model of change'*, available online at http://ctb.ku.edu/en/dothework/tools_tk_4.aspx, last accessed September 11 2013.

Vogel, I., '*Review of the use of theory of change in international development*', Review Report for UK Department of International Development (DfID), London, 2012a.

Vogel, I, *'Ecosystem Services for Poverty Alleviation (ESPA) guide to working with Theory of Change for research projects', Report for DfID*, National Environment Research Council and Economic and Social Research Council, London, 2012b.

10

FROM EVALUATION OF JOINT PROGRAMMES TO JOINT EVALUATION OF SDGs-READY INTERVENTIONS

Lessons from the Joint GEF-UNDP Evaluation of the Small Grants Programme

Carlo Carugi and Heather Bryant

Introduction

The signatories to the 2030 Agenda for Sustainable Development resolved not only "to free the human race from the tyranny of poverty and want" but also to "secure our planet" (UN 2015). The 17 Sustainable Development Goals (SDGs) that constitute the Agenda integrate and recognize the indivisibility of the three dimensions of sustainable development: the economic, social and environmental. At least three goals are considered to be "environmental", 39 of the targets are directly related to the environment (Elder and Olsen 2019) and 93 of the 244 indicators – spread across almost all goals – have an environmental dimension (UNEP 2019). However, while the SDGs have brought the social, the economic and the environmental closer to each other in discourse, development practice, monitoring and evaluation do not equally address or integrate these dimensions. For example, while approximately half of all SDG indicators are classified as Tier 1,[1] only 27% of the environment-related indicators are in this category.[2] With respect to evaluation, Uitto (2019) observes that the profession has primarily focused on the human dimensions of development while neglecting the environmental, while Rowe (2019) points out that evaluations usually take a "single system perspective" where, for example, evaluations addressing conservation concerns in a natural system tend to be unconcerned with effects on the human system, and evaluations focused on a human system concern do not consider effects in the natural system.

Joint programming (where different agencies bring complementary expertise to address complex development problems) and joint evaluations (where different evaluation offices combine diverse skills to evaluate development interventions) offer opportunities to better integrate and understand the social, economic and environmental dimensions of development programming and results. In the UN system, joint programming has been encouraged since the beginning of the century, with the adoption of Guidelines on Joint Programming in 2003, and given new impetus through the creation of the Millennium Development Goals (MDGs) Achievement Fund which funded 130 joint programmes between 2007 and 2013 (UNDP 2014). Building upon the experience and lessons learned of the MDG Achievement Fund, the Sustainable Development Goals Fund was created, acting as a bridge in the transition from the MDGs to the SDGs, providing concrete experiences on how to achieve a sustainable and inclusive world post-2015 through integrated and multidimensional joint programmes. This fund represents a concrete response to SDG 17's call for strengthening the means of implementation and revitalizing the global partnership for sustainable development, implicitly promoting partnering in joint programmes.

In the first edition of this book (2014), Bodemann-Ostow and Gallego Piñero explored the opportunities and challenges of evaluating environment joint programmes, based on lessons from the MDG Achievement Fund. They analysed 28 evaluations of joint programmes under two funding windows that addressed climate issues: environment and climate change and water governance. The authors sought to draw lessons from the review to help evaluators and programme teams develop effective tools to evaluate joint programmes, discussing challenges but also benefits of evaluation processes. They noted that a central feature of the Fund's development programmes was the application of a multi-sectoral approach, based on the Fund's view of the MDGs not as a set of individual targets, but rather closely interconnected ones. The evaluations of the Fund's joint programmes thus considered, among others, whether a joint programme's objectives and overall design had been holistically designed. This meant, for example, in the environment and climate change and water governance thematic windows, that "issues of environmental infrastructure, entrepreneurship promotion and environmental education, for example, were considered jointly with capacity building, local empowerment and gender mainstreaming" (p. 257).

Bodemann-Ostow and Gallego Piñero found, among others, that the evaluation processes had significant implications for the programmes themselves, with "positive effects on programme cohesiveness, management and decision making, on programme partner coordination and on ownership and stakeholder commitment to programme objectives" (p. 270). They also highlighted common challenges the evaluators faced, such as the lack of cohesion between individual programme components to their overall objective, weak monitoring and evaluation frameworks, and the fact that geographic dispersion, time limitations and frequent national counterpart staff turnover created information gaps (pp. 273–274). These are challenges common to many programmes and their evaluations, whether joint or not.

The evaluations analysed by Bodemann-Ostow and Gallego Piñero were not "joint"; the evaluations were commissioned and managed by the Fund's Secretariat, and generally carried out by a single evaluator or teams of two. This chapter picks up where Bodemann-Ostow and Gallego Piñero left off and argues that joint evaluation, where diverse institutions bring together their corporate skills, data, technical knowledge, expertise and experience to the assessment of the social, economic and environmental dimensions of development initiatives, is well suited to assess development interventions in the SDG era. Joint evaluation however also brings its own challenges. Lessons from a joint evaluation by the Independent Evaluation Offices (IEOs) of the Global Environment Facility (GEF) and the United Nations Development Programme (UNDP) of the Small Grants Programme (SGP) point to both advantages and potential pitfalls of such an approach.

This chapter begins with an overview of joint evaluations and some of the lessons learned, followed by a short reflection on the SDGs and joint evaluation. Then follows an introduction to the joint evaluation of the SGP and a discussion of the lessons from this evaluation, including both practical aspects of carrying out a joint evaluation and reflections on how this evaluation examined multiple dimensions of the SGP and on potential lessons for future "two system" evaluations.

Overview of joint evaluations

Joint evaluations are not a recent phenomenon. The OECD DAC evaluation network considered them "at almost every meeting" in the 1980s (OECD-DAC 2013: 17). In the 1990s, members of this evaluation network undertook a number of important joint evaluations, one example of which is an evaluation of the international response to conflict and genocide in Rwanda, led by Denmark with several OECD members and UN Agency partners (OECD-DAC 2005). In the late 1990s, the DAC Working Party on Aid Evaluation began focusing on joint sector evaluations in selected developing countries. The group observed that "in the medium term this will be particularly relevant for monitoring progress towards achieving the goals of 'Shaping the 21st Century' " (OECD-DAC 1998), an OECD-DAC precursor to the MDGs. In 2000, the MDGs were adopted, and in 2006, the UN Secretary General convened a panel on UN system-wide coherence. In his remarks on the panel's report, he stated that, "It will be essential that we swiftly modernize and achieve full compatibility on processes for resource planning, human resources, common services and evaluation, as these are important drivers of coherence in the United Nations system (UN 2006, para.17)." As discussed in Bodemann-Ostow and Gallego Piñero, evaluation of joint programmes was an important component of the MDG Achievement Fund.

Joint evaluations are not without their challenges, and the OECD DAC observed in 2013, "a bit of a backlash to joint evaluations" (OECD-DAC 2013: 24). Data on UNDP evaluations also shows that the number of joint evaluations peaked in 2013 and then decreased (Carugi and Bryant 2019). Various papers published over the past several years have highlighted benefits and challenges of joint evaluations. On the positive side, several of them emphasize the importance of joint evaluations in a context of common, multidimensional development goals that can only be achieved through partnerships (OECD-DAC n.d.) with specific reference to the MDGs (Feinstein and Ingram 2003; OECD-DAC 2005; UNEG 2014). Joint evaluations allow expansion of the scope and the number of evaluation questions that can be addressed with combined resources (OECD-DAC n.d.). They may also "facilitate a sense of the bigger picture within which a programme or set of joint activities is situated" (UNEG 2014: 24). Joint arrangements have the potential to yield higher quality, more credible evaluations (Feinstein and Ingram 2003; OECD-DAC n.d.; OECD-DAC 2005; UNEG 2014). Analyses, findings, conclusions and recommendations of joint evaluations are based on broader knowledge and a wider range of inputs and contributions (OECD-DAC 2005). They also benefit from joint rather than individual scrutiny and quality assessment procedures (UNEG, 2014). There is a greater likelihood that a variety of methods for data collection and analysis will be used in a joint evaluation, as different agencies may have different types of data available, and experiences using different approaches (OECD-DAC 2005; UNEG 2014). Similarly, interviews can be more easily conducted with a wider range of stakeholders, allowing for better triangulation (UNEG 2014). Several of these sources emphasize that joint evaluations typically carry more weight and are less easy to ignore than a single agency evaluation as they reflect the views of multiple partners (Feinstein and Ingram 2003; OECD-DAC 2005; UNEG 2014). It is also argued that joint evaluations reduce transaction costs for the evaluand and the stakeholders consulted, as the total number of missions with a joint evaluation is less than if each donor carried out its own evaluation (Feinstein and Ingram 2003; OECD-DAC 2005; UNEG 2014). Joint evaluations also reduce multiple messages, and the risk of conveying conflicting evaluation messages to partner countries (OECD-DAC 2005; UNEG 2014). Joint evaluations result in a reduced financial burden through cost sharing (Feinstein and Ingram 2003; OECD-DAC n.d.). Another benefit, it is also postulated, is that joint evaluations foster mutual capacity development and peer learning, as agencies learn from each other and share evaluation techniques, and partners come to understand better the different perspectives, mandates and approaches of each of the institutions involved (Feinstein and Ingram 2003; OECD-DAC n.d.; OECD-DAC 2005; UNEG 2014).

However, these papers also highlight a number of challenges with joint evaluations. Developing comprehensive and yet manageable terms of reference that meet each partner's needs may take time and require compromises (OECD-DAC n.d.; SADEV 2008; UNEG 2014). Joint evaluations are typically characterized by complex management, communications and governance arrangements, and generally require more time to carry out, which in turn may result in being more costly than individual agency evaluations (Feinstein and Ingram 2003; OECD-DAC n.d.; OECD-DAC 2005; SADEV 2008; UNEG 2014). Methodologies can also become an area of contention and reaching agreements on methods may also extend the time frame of the preparatory phase (OECD-DAC 2005; SADEV 2008). Other challenges may include power differentials between partners and different needs and accountability requirements of the partner organizations (UNEG 2014).

SDGs and joint evaluation

These reflections on the advantages and disadvantages of joint evaluations are relevant as the adoption of the SDGs in 2015 is leading to renewed interest in joint evaluations. First, the 2030 Agenda gives greater recognition to evaluation than did the Millennium Declaration. Paragraph 74 of the 2030 Agenda states that "follow-up and review processes at all levels will be guided by the following principles: ... they will be rigorous and based on evidence, informed by country led evaluations..." (UN General Assembly 2015). Second, new commitments such as the "funding compact" between Member States and entities of the UN Sustainable Development Group highlight that

> the objective of pursuing joint activities, notably in the areas of analytical work and the formulation of operational support and policy options for acceleration and evaluation of progress towards the achievement of the Sustainable Development Goals, is to ensure that United Nations support is coherent and efficient across economic, social and environmental issues (UN 2019, para. 30).

And third, the UN Secretary is establishing a dedicated capacity to coordinate system-wide evaluations and advance shared learning and accountability for the 2030 Agenda (UN 2020). This new office will be tasked with conducting evaluations designed to complement the evaluative work of UN entities, focusing on "joint activities that cannot adequately be addressed through other existing UN accountability mechanisms" (UN 2020, para 111). Joint evaluations serve an intermediary purpose – addressing issues that can be better addressed together rather than by a single evaluation entity, but which may not require a system-wide evaluation. The Evaluation Cooperation Group (ECG) (whose members are multi-lateral development banks) is also giving increased attention to joint evaluations, discussed at the ECG Fall 2018 and Spring 2020 meetings. During the last discussion, joint evaluations were proposed among the ideas for future collaboration on upcoming priorities in response to the Covid-19 pandemic crisis, a global public health issue that is strongly related to environment and socio-economic interlinkages. The UN Evaluation Group, equally cognizant of the burdens multiple evaluations may pose on programme countries, is seeking ways to increase joint evaluations and other forms of evaluation cooperation between the UN evaluation units.

To understand progress in the context of the SDGs, evaluation needs to go beyond examining results in a single dimension and carefully look at trade-offs and synergies between the economic, social and environmental dimensions to assess how different outcomes can be valued. In this line, Uitto (2019) highlights the importance of mixed methods approaches and the need for interdisciplinary teams to evaluate at the nexus of the environment and development. Similarly, Rowe (2019) argues for "sustainability-ready evaluation" that addresses coupled human and natural systems, recommending that expertise from "both systems" be present in an evaluation team.

One way to bring the interdisciplinarity needed to assess the integrated nature of the SDGs is for specialized institutions to partner in joint evaluations, each contributing their respective corporate skills and technical knowledge as well as their institutional expertise, data and experience on the issues under scrutiny. The discussion on partnering for addressing the integrated nature of the SDGs is particularly relevant to the GEF, one of the few international institutions based on partnership. A special challenge is posed in adequately monitoring and evaluating the achievements of the GEF, accounting for the activities of all partners in a consistent and coherent manner.

In 2015, the IEOs of the GEF and the UNDP carried out a joint evaluation of a unique programme, the SGP. While the evaluation itself pre-dated the SDGs, the experiences not only nourish the ongoing discussion of challenges and opportunities of joint evaluations but also bring new insights with respect to the need to integrate multiple dimensions into evaluations in the context of the SDGs.

The joint GEF-UNDP evaluation of the Small Grants Programme

The GEF is a financial mechanism for international cooperation that addresses global environmental concerns while supporting national sustainable development initiatives. The GEF operates through a large partnership involving 183 countries, 18 agencies and a large network of civil society organizations and private sector entities. The GEF created the SGP in 1992 with the aim of developing community-led and -owned strategies and technologies for reducing threats to the global environment while addressing livelihood challenges. Implemented by UNDP, the SGP awards small grants—up to a maximum of $50,000—to needy communities to support the use of practices and technologies that benefit the global environment. Since its start up, the SGP has provided about 23,990 small grants with a total of $653 million in grants (as of June 2019; GEF IEO and UNDP IEO 2020) to communities in more than 125 countries. The SGP cannot be considered a joint programme as it is implemented by only one agency, the UNDP. However, it incorporates the social, economic with the environmental at the local level, in full alignment with the SDG philosophy. To note, UNDP is the largest GEF Agency in terms of both number of projects and funding. UNDP is also one of the very first three GEF implementing Agencies and has been implementing the SGP since 1992.

The SGP has been jointly evaluated by the IEOs of the GEF and UNDP twice, in 2008 (GEF IEO and UNDP IEO 2008) and in 2015 (GEF IEO and UNDP IEO 2016). The 2008 joint SGP evaluation was an important milestone for the SGP. Overall, the evaluation found that the SGP is a cost-effective way for the GEF to generate global environmental benefits while addressing country priorities and responding to the needs of local populations. It also found that the SGP management model had reached its limits and was not suitable for a new phase of growth: the SGP governance and audit procedures needed to be strengthened. The 2015 joint SGP evaluation assessed the extent to which the most important recommendations from the 2008 evaluation had been implemented and the extent to which these recommendations and Council decisions remained pertinent. The evaluation also reported on the SGP's current role and results in terms of achieving global environmental benefits while addressing livelihoods, poverty, and gender equality; broader adoption of grant-level results; the SGP's strategic positioning; and monitoring and evaluation.

Lessons from the joint evaluation of the SGP

Experiences from the recent Joint GEF-UNDP evaluation of the SGP further illustrate many of both main advantages and challenges of joint evaluations. Lessons from this experience add to the lessons provided by Bodemann-Ostow and Gallego Piñero on evaluation of MDG-funded joint programmes. The evaluations of MDG-Fund joint programmes, often conducted by one consultant, did not benefit from the full spectrum of advantages inherent to joint evaluations such as the Joint GEF-UNDP Evaluation of the SGP.

The following discusses the lessons learned from conducting this joint evaluation in the approximate order encountered in the evaluation process. First, practical and often challenging aspects like partnership arrangements, timing and management structure are described. More substantive aspects follow, including scope, methods and analysis, where the advantages and benefits of joint evaluations become more apparent.

#1 Deciding on a joint evaluation

The decision to carry out a joint evaluation is made within a political or institutional context. In the case of the SGP, the decision to conduct a joint evaluation was straightforward. The GEF funds the SGP, and UNDP implements it, making the two institutions natural partners for a joint evaluation. Both the UNDP and GEF evaluation offices are independent and have considerable scope in determining their work plans. A precedent had been set with the 2008 joint evaluation. For the two institutions, this specific context was conducive to the decision of conducting a joint evaluation.

Moving forward, the decision to undertake a joint evaluation may also be informed by Rowe's call for SDGs-ready, two-system evaluations, where the necessary capacities to assess the socio-economic and its interlinkages with the environmental are brought in by the participating institutions. Nevertheless, there are practical challenges: while partnering to carry out a joint evaluation may be an ideal way to approach "two system" evaluations, the programming and/or financial cycles of each participating institution do not always coincide; and timing an evaluation to meet the different institutional needs can be a challenge, as discussed below.

#2 Partnership arrangements

The SGP experience suggests that institutions working as equal partners enhance joint evaluation success. It has been observed that there are often power differentials at play in joint evaluations, where one agency may end up dominating the evaluation process, either because it has invested more funding, has a stronger position in the management structure or because it has an agenda it wishes to pursue (UNEG 2014). The last point is particularly important. The political dimension can be a strong derailing force in any evaluation, and joint evaluations are no exception. For example, one institution may be seeking to terminate or exit from a programme, while the other may wish to continue. In such cases, the independent nature of the evaluation function within each institution mitigates such political interferences by bringing partnering agencies to the table together and reiterating the need to maintain focus on evidence-based responses to evaluation questions.

The SGP evaluation was carried out by the two IEOs as equal partners. The different mandates of the two institutions, development for UNDP and environment for the GEF, did mean the two had slightly different interests in the evaluation. This led to significant debates during the evaluation (see below on the scope of the evaluation), but these were debates between equal partners. Looking forward, the SGP experience – where the GEF and UNDP offices ensured both the environmental and the human dimensions of the evaluation were given appropriate weightage – suggests equal partner arrangements may help achieve balance and synergy when evaluating interventions in a two-system approach.

Partnership for joint evaluations includes agreeing on financial arrangements. A success factor of this joint evaluation – of potential interest to practitioners if not specific to the SDGs context or the question of two-system evaluations - was the approach adopted to co-financing. This is important in consideration of the fact that not only the share of co-financing from each participating institution but also the funding management modalities may influence the power dynamics in a joint evaluation. The joint SGP evaluation was co-financed by the IEOs of GEF and UNDP in equal shares, and by the SGP itself, from the SGP budget allocated for an Operation Phase 5 terminal evaluation. A key aspect of the co-financing for the evaluation was that the two offices agreed to share costs equally while avoiding complicated fund transfers between two institutions, each with its own financial, administrative and operational rules and procedures. The budget for the evaluation was designed with each institution taking responsibility for the funding of different components, with regular consultation to ensure the cost split remained equal. The trust built through the previous experience of joint work by the two offices facilitated the budget sharing arrangement.

#3 Timing

Following the decision to conduct a joint evaluation and establishment of adequate partnership arrangements, the next practical consideration for a successful joint evaluation is timing. Timing is important in several respects. First, the evaluation process may be influenced by different reporting time frames of partnering institutions. In the case of the Joint Evaluation of the SGP, the timing of the evaluation was dictated by institutional programming time frames, rather than the state of the programme implementation or its results. More specifically, timing considerations led to a decision to conduct the evaluation in two phases. The first phase served the GEF IEO's need for information on the adoption and implementation of the 2008 recommendations within a fairly short time frame in order to contribute to the Fifth Overall Performance Study of the GEF (OPS5). The second phase was an opportunity to build on the first phase findings by addressing additional issues at the heart of the UNDP mandate, particularly related to livelihoods, poverty reduction and gender/inclusion. In practice, opportunities for a joint evaluation should be seized whenever possible and the evaluation process adapted as needed to meet organizational requirements.

A second aspect of timing is the length of time required to complete an evaluation. Joint evaluations typically take longer than a single-agency evaluation, and the SGP evaluation was no exception. The data collection and analysis phases (six months from approval of the terms of reference to submission of the draft report to the evaluation's joint steering committee) were no different than they would have been in a single agency evaluation, but convening the steering committee to review the drafts and agree on issues, followed by finalization of the report and obtention of final approval of the report by the steering committee took four months in the first phase, and seven months in the second phase, considerably longer than the usual time to finalize a single agency report. With reference to the SDG context and multi-sectoral interventions, the extended time line of joint evaluations as referenced in the literature and as experienced in the present case may present challenges to relevance and use of the final evaluation results, as conditions and interactions between dimensions are constantly changing on the ground.

A third element of timing that should be considered when looking at evaluations covering both human and environmental systems is the different time scales for environmental (usually long term), social and human development (shorter term) outcomes to materialize and become observable (Uitto 2019). For example, evidence from recent GEF IEO evaluations indicates that a lag time of 4.5–5.5 years was an important inflection point at which impacts of land degradation projects were observed to be larger in magnitude (GEF IEO 2016). To garner and maintain people's support for these initiatives, they are often accompanied by shorter-term livelihoods interventions. In the case of the SGP evaluation, given the nature of the small grant projects, it was often possible to observe initial changes in the natural environment (e.g. new plantings in a reforestation project or waste management improvements in villages) as well as in new socio-economic arrangements, such formations of cooperatives that not only engaged in conservation activities but also undertook income generating activities to provide economic benefits in the short term.

#4 Management structure

Designing an appropriate management structure and developing adequate communication mechanisms are important for successful implementation of a joint evaluation. Joint evaluations have typically been characterized by complex management and governance arrangements. This was also the case of the present joint evaluation, with a three-tier management structure, including a top-heavy apex body. The challenges of the structure were partially mitigated by the communication strategies adopted by the evaluation managers. The management architecture and roles and responsibilities included a Steering Committee, a Management Team and an Evaluation team. The Steering Committee was co-chaired by the two offices' directors and included senior staff members from each office. The Committee proved to be an unwieldy decision-making forum, the convening of which required careful coordination of the members' respective busy agendas to avoid delays.

The Management Team, formed by two evaluation co-managers took care of the selection, hiring and supervision of consultants in accordance to mutually agreed Terms of Reference and institutional procedures; coordinated the evaluation activities carried out by both offices, quality-controlled evaluation deliverables and processes; and ensured the timely delivery of evaluation products. The quality of the collaboration between co-managers was key to the success of the joint SGP evaluation. Frequent communication, including short chats over Skype on specific issues significantly contributed to effective co-management.

The Evaluation Team included the management team complemented by one lead consultant, nine regional or national consultants and research assistants from both UNDP and GEF evaluation offices assigned to the evaluation. In addition to a long and diversified experience in evaluation (including joint evaluation), both evaluation co-managers had complementary skill sets. The UNDP IEO task manager has experience in poverty, livelihoods, gender and inequalities; the GEF IEO task manager in environment, natural resource management, and sustainable development. The lead consultant was an expert in evaluation and climate change.

The SGP evaluation structure did not include an Evaluation Reference Group, which was a feature of the joint programme evaluations discussed in Bodemann-Ostow and Gallego Piñero, where representatives from each of the participating UN agencies and their national counterparts came together. Given the multi-layer management structure of the SGP evaluation, the addition of another formal mechanism would have been a burden. Key is ensuring that the management structure and evaluation process foster ownership and learning: at the country level, the MDG-Fund evaluation reference groups gave government counterparts a voice in the evaluation process (Bodemann-Ostow and Gallego Piñero 2014: 24). In the case of the SGP evaluation, ad hoc briefing sessions were held with key corporate level stakeholders to gather feedback and strengthen ownership of the recommendations before the evaluation report was finalized.

#5 Scope

Determining the scope of an evaluation – balancing the potential interest in answering a wide range of questions with the available resources – is critical for any evaluation. One of the main benefits of joint evaluations cited in the literature is the potential to broaden the scope and the number of questions to be answered given combined resources, provided it is kept at a manageable level. This is of particular interest if one is seeking to conduct a "two-system" evaluation, where there will necessarily be questions on both the environmental and the human spheres.

This was reaffirmed with the SGP evaluation, where the scope was broader than it might have been had only one agency conducted the evaluation. The 2015 evaluation broadened the scope beyond that of the 2008 evaluation, to not only examine environmental benefits but to include a more in-depth look at SGP's role in improving livelihoods, reducing poverty and contributing to gender equality and women's empowerment. Thus, the evaluation looked not only at the environmental but also at the interactions between the environmental, social and economic, the three dimensions at the heart of the 2030 Agenda.

Agreeing on the scope in the context of a two-system evaluation may generate debate. In the case of the SGP evaluation, expanding the scope beyond environmental considerations sparked numerous debates throughout the conduct of the evaluation. One reason was that different programme and evaluation stakeholders had differing interests. For example, the SGP programme manager (UNDP) saw one of the values of the programme as its ability to "reach the most vulnerable", whereas many environment specialists and GEF stakeholders challenged the claim, some arguing that it is virtually impossible to work with the most vulnerable as they do not have the necessary capacities to engage in development initiatives or are themselves a threat to the environmental benefits the programme seeks to secure. Some GEF stakeholders questioned UNDP's interest in examining SGP's socio-economic benefits in detail. The relevance of these questions and tensions is illustrated by the fact that one of the evaluation recommendations refers to the need to clarify the SGP's long-term vision, including the balance between global environmental benefits and socio-economic objectives.

A risk of joint evaluations with their potentially broader scope is however that the number of evaluation questions becomes unmanageable, as each agency has its own requirements, needs and interests. Again, this risk may be particularly relevant to two-system evaluations. In the case of the SGP evaluation, the scope was overly ambitious in the beginning. For example, the original terms of reference included a key question for the second phase of the evaluation, asking, to what extent the SGP, through its work with non-governmental and civil society organizations alike, facilitated civic engagement in the local and/or national policy arena, especially in post-conflict and fragile states. UNDP was interested in this aspect of the programme, given its mandate on governance and peacebuilding issues (which, in terms of the five "Ps" of the 2030 Agenda, would have added "peace" to the elements of "people, planet and prosperity" already captured by the focus on the social, environmental and economic aspects of SGP). However, the question was not of primary interest to GEF, and the evaluation management team also came to realize that there was a need to narrow the scope of the second phase of the evaluation, given resource constraints. Thus, maintaining the dual focus on environmental and socio-economic benefits required choices on the extent to which the latter could be addressed.

#6 Multidimensional analysis

Another feature and important benefit of this joint evaluation was the strengthened multidimensional analysis, composed of environmental and socio-economic research issues which drew on the strengths of the two partner evaluation offices highlighted earlier and which illustrates the interest of joint evaluations in the SDGs context. The GEF aims at achieving global environmental benefits. While not directly targeting socio-economic co-benefits, it welcomes when the initiatives it supports manage to achieve them too. UNDP focuses more on poverty reduction, livelihoods and gender, while the environment is a theme that cuts across UNDP's main strategic and operational pillars. The mandates of the two organizations overlap, but they are not identical, which can lead to differences in approach or emphases to programming, and by extension, to evaluation (Uitto, 2016). This joint evaluation however, in terms of evaluation purpose, objectives and key questions, was designed with a high degree of complementarity. Gender equality and livelihoods are both components of the SDG sustainability and resilience principles. The 2015 evaluation added a stronger emphasis on livelihoods, poverty reduction and gender results than the 2008 evaluation.

#7 Methods and tools

Uitto (2019) argues that in most cases, a mixed methods approach is needed for sustainable development evaluation, with methods that capture changes in both the natural and human systems, further stating that "interdisciplinary teams are the gold standard" (p. 52). Earlier discussions on advantages of joint evaluations point to the potential for methodology development and the use of a greater variety of methods for data collection and analysis (UNEG 2014) brought to the table by the partner agencies. In the case of the SGP joint evaluation, many of the evaluation methods and tools were built upon and adapted from the ones developed and used in the 2008 joint evaluation. The team modified these tools to align with the new evaluation questions. New tools were also introduced. For example, 12 country studies were conducted, with field verification of 144 small grants projects. The team used the same tool that had been developed for the 2008 joint evaluation to assess grant project effectiveness in terms of economic benefits (also allowing for comparison with the 2008 evaluation results). Inspired by UNDP's "gender marker", the team developed new rating tools to assess the contributions of the grant projects to gender equality and women's empowerment as well as to the reduction of poverty, inequality and exclusion, allowing for more in-depth analysis of these aspects. More generally, data were collected through several additional complementary methods and tools: a global online survey reaching out to almost 2500 programme country stakeholders; an in-depth literature review of SGP documentation at all levels, from global to national; a meta-analysis of 30 randomly selected SGP country programme strategies and 50 evaluations covering SGP interventions; a portfolio review of performance and financial data for 18,000 small grant projects; and several key stakeholder interviews and focus groups at central level as well as in the countries visited during the evaluations. These tools generated a huge amount of both quantitative and qualitative data that could be used for generating solidly triangulated findings using techniques developed by the GEF team (Carugi, 2016) in response to each evaluation question.

This joint evaluation benefited from complementarity of skills and professional experience from UNDP – stronger than GEF in gender and livelihoods – and from the GEF, strong in environment. In addition to this complementarity, the experience offered an opportunity for peer learning, confirming one of the most common benefits of joint evaluations reported in the literature. Each component was designed together bringing diverse experience to bear on each section. The multidimensional analysis improved as a result, fitting perfectly to the nature of the evaluand, a global programme tasked with achieving both environmental and socio-economic benefits at the local level. In other words, the nature of the SGP calls for this kind of integrated analysis, which makes this experience informative in the context of the discussion on joint evaluation for the SDG 2030 Agenda.

#8 Reducing multiple messages while multiplying use

Recognized advantages of joint evaluations also include the potential for reducing multiple (and potentially conflicting) messages and broadened ownership of findings and recommendations (UNEG, 2014). The joint evaluation of the SGP examined several strategic and controversial (within the SGP universe) questions and, after extensive consultations including presentations of preliminary findings and recommendations to stakeholders, provided a single set of messages to both the GEF and its Council and UNDP (and by extension its Executive Board). This also contributed to evaluation use. The joint SGP evaluation led to structural changes in both organizations, a clear benefit. The evaluation recommended revitalization of the global SGP Steering Committee as a forum to provide high-level strategic direction and clarity of purpose to the programme, for example in terms of balancing the contributions to global environmental benefits and to other socio-economic benefits, which is central to SDGs' call for attention to dual-systems thinking in sustainable development interventions. Revitalization of the Global SGP Steering Committee also addresses the political/balance of power dimension related to two partnering institutions with complementary yet very diverse aims – the environmental and the human – both in terms of time (short vs long term) as well as scale (global vs local). The GEF Council, to which the GEF IEO reports directly, issued a corresponding decision addressed to the GEF Secretariat. UNDP also adopted recommendations regarding management of different SGP country programmes at different levels of maturity within a single unit to ensure coherence. Had the evaluation not been joint, detailed recommendations may not have been made to both institutions at the highest level. For example, UNDP alone could not have made recommendations to the GEF Council, and the GEF ensured that recommendations related to global environmental benefits were included, which might not have been the case had UNDP undertaken the evaluation by itself.

Looking at this in a broader context, the 2030 Agenda emphasizes the importance of multi-stakeholder partnerships to support achievement of the SDGs. Joint evaluations can facilitate, as did the SGP evaluation, formulation of common messages to stakeholders working in different "systems", the environmental and human, with the potential to lead to meaningful change.

Conclusions

Bodemann-Ostow and Gallego Piñero (2014), in their chapter in the first edition of this book, sought to draw lessons to help evaluators and programme teams develop effective tools to evaluate joint programmes, discussing challenges but also benefits of evaluation processes for improved programme coherence and results. This chapter has broadened the discussion on these opportunities and challenges to look at joint evaluations in the new context of the SDGs, where the social, the economic and the environmental have been brought closer together in development discourse.

Joint evaluations have been the subject of several guides and analyses over the past two decades (Feinstein and Ingram 2003; OECD-DAC n.d.; OECD-DAC 2005; SADEV 2008; OECD-DAC 2013; UNEG 2014), producing many lessons in terms of advantages and disadvantages as well as "do's and don'ts". Many of these were confirmed by the 2015 SGP evaluation discussed in this chapter. Joint evaluations have seen highs and lows over the years, with a backlash and resistance to these evaluations due to high transaction costs and heavy coordination requirements observed in the period leading up to 2015. The year 2015, however, represented a shift in the international development agenda with the adoption of the SDGs. The implications of the SDGs for multi-stakeholder approaches and integrated programming need to be incorporated into the evaluation agenda. As argued by Uitto (2019) and others, despite the increasing awareness of environmental threats to ecosystems that support human life and society, the evaluation profession has focused primarily on the socio-economic dimensions of development. This chapter has illustrated that joint evaluations – despite their challenges – offer significant advantages that can lead to important institutional and strategic changes with a view to strengthening development results in both the human and environmental spheres.

The literature and the 2015 SGP evaluation have shown that, for example, joint evaluations are suited when all institutions involved have a stake in the scope covered, provided the scope remains sufficiently delimited so that the key evaluation questions are kept to a manageable number. The temptation to add evaluation questions is likely to increase when looking at multiple dimensions – the environmental, the social and the economic – and thus must be carefully managed. Institutional arrangements for joint evaluations can easily become cumbersome, and care should be taken to keep institutional architecture of the evaluation as simple as possible, especially at the joint steering committee level. Joint evaluations will inevitably have transaction costs for the partnering evaluation units, but these can be minimized with appropriate architectures and regular communication. Joint evaluations have the potential to bring together institutions and evaluators with complementary expertise and professional experience, facilitating the creation of an interdisciplinary evaluation team, which is important when evaluating at the nexus of the natural and human systems (Uitto, 2019).

In summary, the experience of the Joint SGP Evaluation supports the findings of earlier studies that the greatest advantages of joint evaluations include the potential for broader scope than single-agency evaluations, increased multidimensionality in the analysis and a single set of coherent messages addressed to multiple partners. The Joint SGP evaluation also illustrates how complementary tools can be used to examine results of a common intervention through different lenses, the environmental, the social and the economic. This is very relevant in the context of the SDGs, where interactions and linkages between goals and targets are increasingly analysed, and the need for integrating different sectoral programmes and to develop cross-sectoral policy is increasingly recognized (e.g. Mainali et al. 2018). Joint evaluations such as the SGP evaluation facilitate the expansion of scope beyond a traditional single sector, bringing together partners with different knowledge and skill sets to foster cross-sectoral analysis, examine trade-offs and highlight synergies and to craft meaningful messages for actors in multiple spheres.

Notes

1 "Indicator is conceptually clear, has an internationally established methodology and standards are available, and data are regularly produced by countries for at least 50 per cent of countries and of the population in every region where the indicator is relevant." https://unstats.un.org/sdgs/iaeg-sdgs/tier-classification/.

2 Analysis based on the classification of environment-related indicators by UNEP 2019 and 11 December 2019 updated tier classification https://unstats.un.org/sdgs/iaeg-sdgs/tier-classification/.

References

Bodemann-Ostow, N. and Gallego Piñero, R. (2014). Opportunities and challenges of evaluating environment joint programmes. Lessons from the millennium development goal achievement fund. In J.I. Uitto (ed.), *Evaluating Environment in International Development*. London, Routledge, pp. 256–276.

Carugi, C. (2016). Experiences with Systematic Triangulation at the Global Environment Facility. *Evaluation and Program Planning*, 55, 55–66.

Carugi, C. and Bryant, H. (2020). A Joint Evaluation with Lessons for the Sustainable Development Goals Era: The Joint GEF-UNDP Evaluation of the Small Grants Programme. *American Journal of Evaluation*, 41(2), 182–200.

Elder, M. and Olsen, S.H. (2019). The Design of Environmental Priorities in the SDGs. *Global Policy*, 10(Supplement 1, 70–81.

Feinstein, O. and Ingram, G.K. (2003). Lessons Learned from World Bank Experiences in Joint Evaluation. *Room Document No. 3*. Paris: Development Assistance Committee Working Party on Aid Evaluation.

GEF IEO & UNDP IEO (2008) Joint Evaluation of the Small Grants Programme. *Evaluation Report No. 39*.Washington, DC: GEF Independent Evaluation Office.

GEF IEO and UNDP IEO. (2016).*Joint GEF-UNDP Evaluation of the Small Grants Programme. Evaluation Report No. 97*. Washington, DC: GEF Independent Evaluation Office.

GEF IEO and UNDP IEO. (2020). Third Joint GEF-UNDP Small Grants Programme Evaluation, Approach Paper, Carilo.

Mainali, B., Luukkanen, J., Silveira, S., and Kaivo-oja, J. (2018). Evaluating Synergies and Trade-Offs Among Sustainable Development Goals (SDGs): Explorative Analyses of Development Paths in South Asia and Sub-Saharan Africa. *Sustainability*, 10, 815.

OECD-DAC. (1998). *Annual Report by the Chair of the DAC Working Party on Evaluation. DCD/DAC/EV(99)1*. Paris: Organization for Economic Co-operation and Development – Development Assistance Committee.

OECD-DAC. (2005). Joint Evaluations: Recent Experiences, Lessons Learned and Options for the Future. *DAC Evaluation Network Working Paper*. Paris: Organization for Economic Co-operation and Development.

OECD-DAC. (2013). *The DAC Network on Development Evaluation – 30 years of strengthening learning in development*. Paris: Organization for Economic Co-operation and Development - Development Assistance Committee.

OECD-DAC. (n.d.). *Effective Practices in Conducting a Multi-Donor Evaluation*. Paris: Organization for Economic Co-operation and Development – Development Assistance Committee.

Rowe, A. (2019). Sustainability-Ready Evaluation: A Call to Action. In G. Julnes (Ed.), *Evaluating Sustainability: Evaluative Support for Managing Processes in the Public Interest. New Directions for Evaluation*, 162, 29–48.

Swedish Agency for Development Evaluation (SADEV). (2008). Challenges, Opportunities and Approaches for Increasing Joint Donor Programming of Evaluations. *SADEV Report 2008:8*. Karlstad: SADEV.

Uitto, J.I. (2016). The Environment-poverty Nexus in Evaluation: Implications for the Sustainable Development Goals. *Global Policy*, 7(3), 441–447.

Uitto, J. I. (2019). Sustainable development evaluation: Understanding the nexus of natural and human systems. In G. Julnes (Ed.), *Evaluating Sustainability: Evaluative Support for Managing Processes in the Public Interest. New Directions for Evaluation*, 162, 49–67.

United Nations Economic and Social Council. (2015). *Thematic evaluation of monitoring and evaluation for the Millennium Development Goals: lessons learned for the post-2015 era*. E/AC.51.2015/3*. 18 March 2015.

United Nations Environment Programme (UNEP). (2019). *Measuring progress: Towards achieving the environmental dimension of the SDGs*. Nairobi: United Nations Environment Programme.

UN General Assembly. (2006). *Note by the Secretary-General* transmitting report of the High-Level Panel on UN System-wide Coherence in the Areas of Development, Humanitarian Assistance and the Environment. A/61/583. 20 November 2006.

UN General Assembly. (2013). Resolution adopted by the General Assembly on 21 2012. A/RES/67/226. 22 January 2013.

UN General Assembly. (2015). Transforming our world: the 2030 Agenda for Sustainable Development, A/RES/70/1. 21 October 2015.

United Nations General Assembly Economic and Social Council. (2019). Implementation of General Assembly resolution 71/243 on the quadrennial comprehensive policy review of operational activities for development of the United Nations system: funding compact, A/74/73/Add.1 – E/2019/14/Add.1 2019. 2 April 2019.

UN General Assembly Economic and Social Council. (2020). Report of the Secretary General, Implementation of General Assembly resolution 71/243 on the quadrennial comprehensive policy review of operational activities for development of the United Nations System (QCPR), A/75/x-E/2020/7. 24 April 2020 (advance unedited version)

United Nations Development Group (UNDG). (2014). *Guidance Note on Joint Programmes*, New York" UN Development Operations Coordination Office.

UNEG. (2014). *Resource pack for joint evaluations*. New York: United Nations Evaluation Group.

11

EVALUATING THE POVERTY–ENVIRONMENT NEXUS IN AFRICA

Michael Stocking[1]

Background

The idea that poverty and environmental degradation are linked has been discussed, debated, rediscovered and reinvented numerous times. An early published manifestation came from Thomas Malthus who saw the main threat to 'the intention of the Creator that the earth should be replenished' being 'an unhealthy, vicious and miserable population' (Malthus 1826: XXIV). Colonial powers in Africa and Asia ensured continuity of the thesis. The entire discourse of increasing populations of poor and desperate people undermining the integrity of the natural environment is imbued with hidden messages, not least of which is that rural peasantry equates with poverty, poverty with ignorance and ignorance with environmental stupidity.

Since the 1992 Earth Summit, the concept of sustainable development has renewed interest into the poverty–environment debate (Gray and Moseley 2005). Popularizing the concept, the Brundtland Report described how 'poor people are forced to overuse environmental resources to survive from day to day, and their impoverishment of their environment further impoverishes them' (World Commission on Environment and Development [WCED] 1987). Influential organizations have perpetuated the link between the condition of the environment and the state of poverty, especially via issues such as food security and health. For example, the International Food Policy Research Institute has stated unequivocally 'the condition of the world's natural resource base in the year 2020 largely depends on whether poverty has been eradicated' (Pinstrup-Andersen and Pandya-Lorch 1995). The basis for such assertions is the presumed coexistence of areas of poor people with areas of severe environmental degradation, leading to the assumption that poverty drives people to use their resources unsustainably; the evidence, however, is weak.

Indeed, such has been the pervasive nature of the sustainability concept that poverty (along with population) and the environment have become so inextricably associated that they have earned the epithet 'nexus' – that is, a set of mutually reinforcing links between poverty and environmental damage (Ekbom and Bojö 1999; Dasgupta et al. 2005). Nexus is particularly used in the context of it being one of the main challenges to achieving the Millennium Development Goals (MDGs; United Nations Economic and Social Commission for Asia and the Pacific [UNESCAP] 2003). There is a compelling body of evidence, both biophysical and socio-economic that the environment is one of the core building blocks for pro-poor economic growth (UNDP-UNEP Poverty-Environment Facility 2008). The predominant school of thought argues that poverty is a major cause of environmental degradation. If policy makers want to tackle environmental issues, then the nexus discourse states they must first address the poverty problem (Duraiappa 1998). Poverty, it is argued, undermines environmental sustainability through a number of complex drivers, not least of which is that the poorest in their desperation to sustain their lives have to undermine their environment (Lufumpa 2005). Deforestation, land degradation, low agricultural productivity, water scarcity, threats to biodiversity and the impact of civil conflicts are all frequently cited as negative impacts resulting from the close linkages between poverty and environment (Lufumpa 2005).

This chapter describes the challenge of evaluating such a broad and complex concept as the poverty–environment nexus. It reports on the 'Evaluation of UNDP Contribution to Environmental Management for Poverty Reduction: The Poverty-Environment Nexus. Final Report' (hereinafter the Poverty–Environment Nexus), an evaluation commissioned by United Nations Development Programme (UNDP) to examine how the organization handles on the one side its core mandate (addressing poverty in the developing world) and environmental sustainability on the other side (an issue that is more often seen as the concern of other agencies and, by many developing countries, not a high priority (EO of UNDP 2010). The evaluation had to accommodate a number of theoretical and practical questions, the first of which was why should poverty and the environment be linked; is it just received – and assumed – wisdom that UNDP should be addressing environmental issues as a way of achieving poverty reduction targets? Or would the ready availability of finance for the environment through the Global Environment Facility (GEF) dictate a focus on poverty–environment linkages without embedding the intellectual underpinnings of the nexus in the organization? These and other issues are addressed in the following sections that describe the methods and principal findings of the evaluation, with a special focus on Africa.

Why might poverty and environment be linked in Africa?

Poor people live more intimately with their biophysical environment, depending much more directly on the natural resource base for their food, energy, water and shelter. They till the soil, collect wood for the fire, fetch water in buckets and construct their houses from local materials. Their livelihood is spatially and temporally tied to the condition of their natural resources. Therefore, if the resources are degraded, poverty ensues; if poverty is endemic, resources are degraded. The media reinforces this two-way link. Images of starving people in the Ethiopian famine of 1984 were always seen against a backdrop of treeless desert or bare fields. When their survival is at stake and alternatives are impossible, it is argued that people will overuse their resources. Desperate hunger leads to desperate strategies for survival. Future welfare has to take a back seat when sheer survival is in question.

Nevertheless, a direct link between poverty and environment is contested. One study of two adjacent farming blocks in central Zambia found that the more prosperous commercial farming block was far more subject to environmental degradation than the adjacent block of small subsistence farms (Stocking 1983). Indeed, affluence may enable greater investment in land use technologies that intensify farming practices and more readily degrade the soil of its organic and nutrient content. In contrast, the more elaborate and complex practices of smallholders are less damaging to the environment and may even mimic nature.

Linkages are, however, complex and involve secondary influencing factors. In Kenya, the now (in) famous Machakos study, *More People, Less Erosion* (Tiffen, Morimore and Gichuki 1994), showed how – under certain conditions – increasing population can provide opportunities for better control of soil erosion and the development of sustainable small-holder production systems. It helped by providing empirical evidence that the closely related *population*-environment nexus is not necessarily true (Tiffen, Mortimore and Gichuki 1994). The influence of nearby urban markets stimulated intensive but integrated land use practices, while at the same time supporting three times the population. The status of the environment improved almost beyond recognition with the innovation spurred by secondary factors. Access to credit and technologies to practice environmentally sustainable agriculture, plus the gaining of land entitlements, all combined to heal what had been an extremely degraded part of Kenya that supported only a low density of very poor people.

Property rights can be a major influence on the status of the environment. Not only does security of tenure lead to increased investment in the land, but it also encourages longer-term environmentally beneficial investments such as tree planting and soil conservation structures.[2] In Africa, communal tenure and common-property resources are often the norm, where, it is argued, there is little incentive for the individual to conserve for the good of the community. Africa is, therefore, the continent in which the poverty–environment nexus is most widely discussed; it is also the location for the largest global programme that addresses the nexus, the UNDP-UNEP Poverty–Environment Initiative (PEI 2012).[3] The case of Malawi is instructive, where a 2011 PEI study calculated that unsustainable – and therefore, degrading – practices costs the country 5.3% of its gross domestic product annually, substantially more than its total funding of education and health (UNEP 2013). If this loss of gross domestic product translates to increasing rural poverty in agriculture, fisheries, forestry and wildlife (as PEI claims the government of Malawi now believes), than there is a powerful argument for a development strategy that targets sustainable practices as a way out of poverty.

Why evaluate the poverty–environment nexus?

A prevailing view among some development professionals is that investments in UNDP's core mandate may have to allow for some environmental damage. Even more common is the view that investments in environmental conservation, such as national parks and forest reserves, need not worry unduly about their impact on local people. Land alienation and restricted access are issues that have been hotly debated in Africa since colonial times.[4] An evaluation should not only identify whether these views were entrenched, but should also seek empirical evidence as to whether investments in the poverty reduction or environmental conservation areas had beneficial unintended effects for the other area (and, if so, what aspects of project design contributed to the co-benefits?). Given UNDP's reliance on Global Environment Facility funding of environmental issues, it was especially important that UNDP could demonstrate co-benefits for both the global environment and for local development.

The hypothesis behind the poverty–environment nexus evaluation is that there is a set of closely linked issues – the nexus – that affects two major goals of United Nations developmental and environmental agencies: poverty alleviation and environmental protection. The nexus stems in particular from evidence that development schemes often sacrifice longer-term environmental sustainability for short-term economic and job creation benefits, and that over-exploitation of natural resources adversely affects ecosystem health (and, in time, reduces economic output). The Millennium Ecosystem Assessment, completed in 2005, the largest review of such linkages to date, produced compelling evidence at the global, national and local scales that *inter alia*, human health and welfare depends on the sustainable functioning of ecosystems and that these ecosystems are vulnerable to depletion by overuse that is often driven by the needs of poor people. For example, the Millennium Ecosystem Assessment found that 'over 1 billion people lack access to safe water supplies; 2.6 billion people lack adequate sanitation. This has led to widespread microbial contamination of drinking water. Water-associated infectious diseases claim up to 3.2 million lives each year, approximately 6% of all deaths globally. The burden of disease from inadequate water, sanitation and hygiene totals 1.7 million deaths and the loss of more than 54 million healthy life years' (Corvalan et al. 2005). It is the poor that are selectively and adversely impacted – it is also the poor who largely contribute to the microbial contamination. However, as this example illustrates, the links are by no means direct or uncontroversial. An evaluation should assist UNDP in building empirical evidence of how investments in poverty reduction might benefit the environment and, if they do, what multiple co-benefits may arise that would further justify gains in productivity bringing environmental benefits.

The rural poor disproportionately depend on the availability of natural resources for their subsistence livelihoods. Efforts to protect ecosystems and address other environmental factors can affect poor people's access to resources. Conversely, reducing poverty can affect the environmental systems' sustainability. There should, therefore, be a substantial poverty dimension to environmental protection, and a substantial environmental dimension to poverty reduction. Public support for these efforts is a critical factor, as efforts to reduce pollution and conserve natural resources are unlikely to succeed if they unfairly restrict opportunities for local people to work and feed their families. Taken together, these dynamics suggest that integrated programming is necessary to simultaneously improve livelihoods for the poor while protecting the environment. An evaluation must identify not only whether integration is built into project design, but also how it is practised.

Scope and method of the poverty–environment nexus evaluation

The Evaluation Office of UNDP conducted the evaluation and assigned two senior officers specifically for it. A team of three consultants undertook much of the interviewing and analysis and drafted the final report. The team was led by a senior developing country professional and former Minister of the Environment with leadership experience in a number of high-profile international organizations. A professional evaluator with World Bank experience and an academic with Global Environment Facility and substantial project experience supported the team leader. All three met with staff from the Evaluation Office of UNDP at least three times in New York. UNDP assigned two support staff for research and data analysis. In addition, 21 national consultants were contracted for detailed case studies. The whole exercise took just over one year to complete.

At an early stage, it was decided that the evaluation should be both retrospective and prospective – it should take stock of the past while looking into the future. The latter is especially important given UNDP's leadership roles, being the most prominent agency sponsoring poverty reduction and, in many countries, the leading sponsor of environmental projects. Additionally, UNDP coordinates multi-agency donor support in many countries and has specific responsibilities regarding the United Nations reform processes.[5]

In terms of timeframe, the evaluation acknowledged that activities involving poverty–environment linkages have been ongoing since the 1992 United Nations Conference on Environment and Development. However, the evaluation's focus of analysis was limited to after 2004, covering the Second Multi-Year Funding Framework (2004–2007) and the strategic plan 2008–2011[6] implementation periods. This narrower timeframe conforms to the period after the Johannesburg summit, when the Poverty–Environment Partnership[7] and the UNDP-UNEP Poverty–Environment Initiative (PEI)[8] were established. It also conforms to the period when the then newly appointed UNDP Administrator articulated a 'vision for UNDP to be widely acknowledged as a world class, knowledge based development organization which helps developing countries make transformational change and helps channel the strengths of the entire United Nations (UN) development system to that end'.[9]

The evaluation took an approach that built from standard evaluation criteria (relevance, effectiveness, efficiency and sustainability (UNDP 2009), organized around a set of broad evaluation questions (see Box 11.1). *Relevance* assessed the extent that poverty–environment interventions met the mandates of UNDP, other agencies that UNDP works with and its recipient countries. UNDP's core focus on poverty reduction was vital here, but so were the more recent priorities of UNDP on the Millennium Development Goals, climate change and donor coordination. *Effectiveness*, a measure of the extent to which an aid activity attains its objectives, was tested with how far the nexus of poverty–environment issues was factored not only into the UNDP poverty and environment practice areas, but also in other practice areas such as crisis prevention, governance and gender. In addition, effectiveness was evaluated in the extent to which UNDP persuaded its agency and country partners to include poverty–environment issues in their work. *Efficiency* measured the outputs – qualitative and quantitative – in relation to the inputs in two principal ways in this evaluation. First, it looked at country requests and how these better link poverty and the environment, and second, it addressed internal UNDP structures to see if they were responsive to the poverty–environment nexus. This last question on the internal barriers to cross-disciplinary issues such as poverty–environment proved to be very important. Finally, *sustainability* examined how well poverty–environment linkages are embedded in the organization and are likely to continue.

BOX 11.1 EVALUATION QUESTIONS AGAINST UNDP STANDARD CRITERIA OF RELEVANCE, EFFECTIVENESS, EFFICIENCY AND SUSTAINABILITY

Relevance

What is the relevance of addressing poverty–environment linkages in UNDP work and activities, in relation to its overall mandate and the needs of programme countries?

- Is explicitly dealing with these linkages of high importance to achieving UNDP's strategic objectives, including support for MDG achievement?
- Is the poverty–environment nexus a critical aspect in the global effort to reduce and mitigate the effects of greenhouse gas emissions and assist in adapting to climate change?
- How does dealing with the nexus relate to UNDP's relationship with other United Nations agencies, the World Bank and other donors?

Effectiveness

Have UNDP efforts to link poverty and environment been 'generally acceptable' and have they achieved results?

- Do the poverty and environment practice areas at global, regional and country levels focus attention on this nexus of issues?
- Are poverty and environment-related priorities being factored into UNDP strategies and activities in other practice areas, such as crisis prevention and recovery, and governance?

(Continued)

- Is UNDP having success in encouraging country government partners to implement policies and programmes that harmonize poverty alleviation and environmental protection priorities?
- Has UNDP succeeded in establishing successful partnerships with other United Nations and international agencies in support of efforts to more closely link poverty alleviation and environmental protection?
- What approaches have been most successful, and what improvements should be made to enhance UNDP effectiveness?

Efficiency

Have the programmes and projects developed to better link poverty and environment issues been carried out efficiently?

- Has the effort enabled UNDP to respond more efficiently to country requests for assistance on sustainable development issues?
- Are there internal structural and financial aspects that have a significant bearing on UNDP efforts to improve poverty–environment programme linkages?

Sustainability

How well are the results of UNDP's work to more closely link poverty alleviation and environmental protection policies being sustained?

- What are the contributions of UNDP in this regard to the long-term benefits to people's well-being?
- Is there adequate support in UNDP's structure and financial basis to continue addressing the nexus where there is further need and demand?

The evaluation employed a variety of data collection methods, including desk reviews, stakeholder interviews and country case studies. It was conducted in accordance with Evaluation Office of UNDP guidelines and methods, as well as standard evaluation practices such as the triangulation principle and the validation of facts and findings with relevant stakeholders. The evaluation team decided not to use questionnaires because of past experience with limited responses and the difficulty of obtaining clear responses on this conceptual topic without face-to-face interaction.

Because poverty and environment issues are so country-specific and vary so enormously between regions and between countries within regions, the evaluation team decided to use as large a sample as resources and time would allow. Therefore, the Poverty–Environment Nexus evaluation included detailed case studies for nine countries, four of which are African (Mali, Morocco, Rwanda and Tanzania), telephone interviews with personnel in 29 other countries, 8 of which are African (Botswana, Cameroon, Ghana, Kenya, Mozambique, Senegal, South Africa and Tunisia) and regional consultations including UNDP offices in Nairobi and Pretoria and with key partner organizations. The telephone interviews were a departure from previous evaluations and proved to be rewarding. Country Offices telephoned took these interviews seriously, often as conference calls with several of their staff made available. Other telephone interviews were with individuals and were conducted by one of the core consultants. English, French and Spanish languages were used in these interviews. Responses in this format were often candid and sometimes surprising. Individuals appeared to be willing to give detailed and often critical information, sometimes asking that responses be taken confidentially. The team respected such wishes and anonymized all reporting, although it would probably have been possible for views to have been traced back by anyone with close UNDP experience.

The detailed case studies were contracted to local consultants who were given a standard format for reporting. The case study outputs provided less useful information than had been hoped for, tended to repeat large amounts of data on poverty and environment information already in the public domain and were somewhat light in analytical rigour. Criticism of the organization of Country Offices, the barriers to uptake on poverty–environment nexus issues and difficulties with individual projects were muted. In retrospect, the contracted consultants chosen for their local knowledge were perhaps being careful to avoid undue criticism of their subjects, given their reliance in the future on building good relationships for potential further consultancies. Nevertheless, the core consultants were able to use these studies to give empirical backing to views and opinions expressed in the telephone interviews and other face-to-face meetings. The methodological approach enabled the team to sample a wide variety of opinions, engage stakeholders in more substantive discussions and probe country-specific issues.

Challenges and limitations

Cross-cutting topics such as poverty and the environment present major challenges to agencies with a singular or thematic focus. There is little incentive under such conditions for professionals to work together. With the exception of the PEI, few results frameworks or baseline indicators are available to assess efficiencies and effectiveness. Consequently, many of the findings are subjective and rely on participants' and stakeholders' views. Therefore, the PEI was given special attention along with UNDP's role as an implementing agency for GEF, the largest funder worldwide of projects to improve the global environment. From 2006 to 2010, UNDP assisted partner governments to secure a total of US$1.146 million in funding from the GEF, an average of US$286 million per year. GEF funding has comprised roughly 50% of UNDP annual environment and energy expenditures. As part of its GEF implementation responsibilities, UNDP also administers the Small Grants Programme, which focuses on local environmental issues and is especially pertinent to the poverty–environment nexus.

However, the emphasis on PEI and the GEF brought challenges and limitations to the evaluation. PEI was (and still is) a somewhat isolated outpost of UNDP, both geographically (Nairobi) and thematically (cross-disciplinary). Being jointly run by the two UN agencies has meant that its survival in times of budgetary crisis was continually in question, with financial priorities usually assigned to mainstream practice areas. The GEF provides the 'increment' or top-up to development projects in order to deliver global environmental benefits such as biodiversity conservation, climate change mitigation and protection of international waters.

In many GEF projects, the increment is no more than one-twentieth of total project expenditure. Three challenging outcomes arise from this model of project funding: (1) the environmental components assume a far lower priority than developmental components; (2) a particular slant is imposed on the environmental component to gain what are accepted as global environmental benefits, rather than domestic or national environmental issues such as soil conservation or agricultural sustainability; and (3) the availability and relatively easy access to GEF funding enabled UNDP to become dependent on GEF for environmental funding, thereby allowing its core resources to be more concentrated in its other practice areas. The poverty–environment nexus evaluation used these points initially to interrogate some of the difficulties of the GEF model of project funding as applied to UNDP and encourage a more holistic and integrated approach by UNDP.

Findings: country case studies

This section summarizes the findings from the evaluation's four country-based case studies conducted in Africa (out of nine worldwide). By most criteria, the Mali, Rwanda and Tanzania case studies provide situations of substantial rural poverty alongside considerable environmental degradation. Hence, they could be expected to be country cases where the poverty–environmental nexus would not only be prominent but also a high priority for development agencies and country ministries. The evaluation used these case studies as an important source of evidence to support its findings. Each case study involved a review of relevant documents and interviews with key individuals. The documents reviewed included major national policies and strategic frameworks as well as UNDP country programme documents (such as the United Nations Development Assistance Framework [UNDAF] and the country programme action plan) plus specific documents related to the poverty–environment nexus.

Mali

Mali ranked 184th out of 189 countries in the 2019 UNDP Human Development Report (UNDP 2019), with a Human Development Index rating of 0.427. Just under half of its population (49.7%) earns less than US$1.25 per day (UNDP 2019).[10] The annual birth rate is projected at 2% through 2014, and the adult literacy rate is 33.1%. Mali's economy is primarily based on agriculture and agropastoralism, with agriculture accounting for more than 35% of GDP and 80% of livelihoods (FAO 2017). More than 80% of rural and urban household energy requirements are met by wood fuel and biomass resources.

The country's geographical location, small percentage of arable land (14%) and low level of economic development leave Mali vulnerable to climate change. Almost three quarters of the population (73%) lives in rural areas under extreme poverty. Sustainable land management is a major concern, with the economy largely dependent on the primary sector, notably agriculture and farming.

Given the seriousness of both the status of poverty in Mali and the condition of its environment, it was not surprising that the evaluation found high levels of political and public awareness of the nexus. UNDP has been a major partner in the effort to mainstream natural resources and environment into the country's Strategic Framework for growth and Poverty Reduction and the National Policy for the Protection of the Environment. It has also been a partner in implementation of the PEI, which included several diagnostic studies, including the development of indicators. Two thirds of the Country Office programme budget is committed to activities directly related to the poverty–environmental nexus under the UNDP country cooperation framework 2008–2012, most of it (54%) to poverty reduction and achieving the MDGs (only 12% went to environment and energy). The main results of the PEI project included greater awareness and knowledge on poverty and environment linkages at national level, establishment of tools and mechanisms to integrate environment into national development planning and decentralization frameworks and enhanced national capacity to integrate environment into national development planning and decentralization processes.

Yet, problems remain in mainstreaming the nexus as opposed to poverty and environment as single issues into UNDP practice areas. A PEI evaluation concluded that the initiative in Mali has not achieved all its intended results (Bass and Renard 2009). Problem areas related to the structure and composition of project management committees and delays in fund disbursements, a weakness identified generically in the marginal structural position of PEI in the UNDP portfolio. In contrast, the GEF Small Grants Programme successfully supported communities in developing and implementing poverty–environment community projects through linked environmental conservation and income-generating activities.

Underlying the weaknesses in the poverty–environment nexus in Mali is that UNDP staff has limited understanding as to what constitutes the poverty–environment nexus in practical terms. This leads to operational issues such as delays in release of funds, institutional issues (e.g. coordination) and structural issues that inhibit collaboration between units. Lessons from PEI implementation in Mali included the need for a stronger project management unit at country level to ensure greater impact on national and local planning processes and stronger advocacy with national decision makers. The best way forward was considered to be community-based demonstration projects on sustainable environmental management and improved living conditions to support decentralization of environmental management

Morocco

In 2018, Morocco had an annual per capita income of US$3,273 (UNSD 2018) and a population of approximately 36.03 million people.[1] From 2001 to 2020, relative poverty declined from 15.3% to 4.8% nationally,[2] while for the same period, vulnerability decreased from 22.8% to 17.5%. The data indicate that 3.9% of people were subjected to undernourishment in Morocco between 2015 and 2017 compared to 5.7% in the period between 2004 and 2006 (FAO et al. 2018). However, 4.8% of the population still live below the national poverty line in 2018 (UNDP 2019).

Morocco has three principal ecosystems: the mountain forest ecosystem; the oasis, desert, semi-desert ecosystem; and the Mediterranean coastal and marine ecosystem. Each zone experiences different forms of land use, providing important environmental goods and services. Some of these land uses are vital to the national economy (e.g. phosphate mining, tourism) and also to the livelihoods of the rural poor (e.g. rain-fed and irrigated agriculture, pastureland, water for irrigation). One of the major concerns in Morocco therefore relates to degradation of environmental resources (land, water, biodiversity), which also poses a threat to the livelihoods of communities that depend on these goods and services. There is, however, little information on the current status of environmental degradation.

Given the middle-income status of Morocco and the low profile on environmental issues, it might be expected that the poverty–environment nexus issues are relatively muted in their inclusion in country strategies for Morocco. Unsurprisingly, Morocco had only one policy framework relevant to the poverty–environment nexus: the national initiative for human development policy statement, which the king promulgated in 2005. The national initiative for human development encapsulates the poverty–environment nexus principles of participatory local development. This is the means by which progress towards achieving the MDGs is being driven. At the time of the evaluation, a poverty strategy was being formulated but had not entered into force.[11] At the project level, the evaluation found several projects that could be said to be 'poverty–environment nexus compliant', such as integrated rural development.

There is public awareness of poverty–environment nexus issues, as indicated by the large number of domestic Non-governmental organizations undertaking relevant activities with communities. The UNDP Country Office, in its position as trusted strategic partner with the government, is playing a role in promoting the coherent implementation of the poverty–environment dimension of sustainable development in Morocco. Nevertheless, constraints to effectively integrating poverty–environment nexus issues include limited understanding of the concept, need for indicators/guidelines, lack of criteria for nexus and the clustering of programmes as either 'poverty' or 'environment'. For this middle-income country, there is some way to go before it could be said that the poverty–environment nexus informs the design and implementation of country projects for sustainable development.

Rwanda

Rwanda ranks 157th out of 189 countries in the 2019 Human Development Report; its Human Development Index is 0.536 (UNDP 2019), which is below the average of 0.541 for countries in Sub-Saharan Africa (UNDP 2018). Consequently, poverty is a priority issue in Rwanda's development policy. The structural dimensions of poverty and vulnerability, particularly demographic pressures and environmental degradation, exacerbate an already complex situation. Population density in Rwanda is the highest in Africa, with more than 415 persons per km^2 [highest compared to neighbouring countries such as Burundi (333), Uganda (173) and Kenya (73)], and the approximate population growth rate is 2.6% per year. In addition, 83% of the nearly 10 million people live in rural areas, with livelihoods dependent on the natural environment (NISR 2012).

The significance of environmental management to the government's policy objectives is underscored in several strategic documents, including the Environment and Natural Resources Sector Strategic Plan (2009), the Environment and Climate Change Strategic Plan and the National Biodiversity Strategy and Action Plan (Government of the Republic of Rwanda 2009a, 2009b and 2003). A key goal of the government to be achieved by 2020 is integrating environmental objectives into all policies and programmes pertaining to economic and social development as well as all decision-making processes. Strategic inclusion of the poverty–environment nexus in Rwanda is, therefore, significant.

Nevertheless, barriers remain, not least of which is the persistent separation of environmental from poverty issues. The United Nations Development Assistance Framework 2008–2012 addresses poverty and environment as two separate issues. Outcome 4 of the component on energy and the environment for sustainable development is 'management of environment, natural resources and land is improved in a sustainable way', and Outcome 5 of the component on achieving the MDGs and poverty reduction is 'Rwandan population benefits from economic growth and is less vulnerable to social and economic shocks'.

The 2008–2012 UNDP country programme document proposed a total contribution of US$41 million, with US$9.5 million earmarked for programmes related to the poverty–environment nexus (US$8.5 million to environment; US$1 million to poverty). The country programme document also treats environment and poverty as separate issues for budgeting and programming purposes. This indicates that UNDP, in its discussions with a country partner, has not yet embraced the poverty–environment nexus concept at the planning or operational levels.

UNDP has a special role in Rwanda, as the country was one of only eight chosen to pilot the Delivering As One concept to achieve 'a more effective, efficient, coherent, coordinated and better performing United Nations country presence'.[12] The UNDP Country Office is promoting implementation of the poverty and environmental dimensions of sustainable development in Rwanda, particularly in the context of the United Nations Development Assistance Framework and the One UN programme. Yet indications are that the poverty–environment nexus has not taken root in the Development Framework, and the country programme document still addresses poverty and environment as separate issues. This points to the need for concerted efforts to develop the tools (e.g. manuals, brochures and guidelines) for awareness raising and targeted training of UNDP staff who are expected to manage poverty–environment nexus–related programmes. It also calls for commitment, determination and consistency by the UNDP Country Office to support national priorities and initiatives.

The United Republic of Tanzania

Poverty in the United Republic of Tanzania can be considered within the context of three fundamental realities. First, about 80% of the country's poor lives in rural areas (UNDP 2017). Second, these rural people overwhelmingly depend on agriculture and other natural resource uses for their livelihoods. Third, the economy is based largely on land and natural resources, particularly forests, biodiversity and agriculture. Thus, poverty and the environment are intrinsically linked, and the poverty–environment nexus is a central consideration in all sustainable development policies and strategies.

The government displays a clear political will to address the poverty–environment nexus at the national level. This is demonstrated by the development of poverty–environment indicators.[13] Tanzania is one of the few countries into a second generation of poverty-reduction strategy papers, supported by UNDP. The agency plays a key role in supporting programmes and projects to mainstream poverty and environment issues in government policies, strategies and programmes at all levels. The PEI project has promoted awareness of the linkages between poverty and environment, and it continues to contribute to understanding and development of poverty–environment nexus tools and indicators. Key results include the establishment of a national environment education strategy; development of poverty–environment indicators and reviews of the Poverty Reduction Strategy process and Poverty Monitoring System. UNDP continues as a trusted partner with government as the lead authority on sustainable development, promoting coherent implementation of the poverty–environment dimension.

Even in Tanzania, almost a model country in terms of sensitivity to poverty–environment linkages, the evaluation identified limitations to both the inclusion and practice of the poverty–environment nexus. UNDP staff had limited understanding as to what constitutes the nexus in practice. Definition, guidelines and criteria for the nexus and guidance in how to assess progress in achieving operational targets regarding the nexus were absent.

In government agencies, policies and legislation on benefits and cost-sharing arrangements through ecosystem payment mechanisms were weak or non-existent. For example, few benefits of big projects on biodiversity and ecosystem conservation and protection trickled down to local populations, a disincentive to participation in the poverty–environment nexus. Joint programming and funding of the nexus will remain a major challenge.

Development partners of UNDP continue justifiably to have policies that dictate their preferences on thematic areas, different proposal approval and funding cycles and/or different monitoring and evaluation and reporting requirements. This has to be appreciated in the promotion of even cross-cutting issues such as the linkages between poverty and the environment. Harmonizing and coordinating joint programming for the poverty–environment nexus will, therefore, remain a challenge. Country Office experience suggests that integrating environment into the policies, strategies and plans should continue at the 'upstream' level. However, there is a need to extend integration and mainstreaming to implementation, particularly to projects at community level.

Despite the promotion of the poverty–environment nexus from UNDP headquarters and elsewhere, the Country Office continues to cluster programmes as either poverty or environment. This creates difficulties for gaining credence for the nexus and for fostering its true integration into projects and programmes.

Overall findings: the retrospective

The country case studies from Africa – and indeed from Asia and South America – revealed a reasonably consistent set of findings for the evaluation. Weaknesses in UNDP dealing with poverty–environment nexus issues arise from a poor understanding of what the nexus means and how it can be practically implemented, entrenched views among staff that activities are either poverty focused or environment focused, lack of incentive to develop poverty–environment nexus projects across practice areas and the marginalization of the topic itself and lack of partners' awareness of the poverty–environment nexus (including other agencies and donor governments). The practice structure of UNDP was often seen as inimical to cross-disciplinary initiatives: 'silos' were mentioned frequently, meaning that careers, promotion and plaudits from headquarters depended more on how well an individual developed his or her practice (or focus) area in UNDP, than on how well he or she cooperated with other practice areas.[14]

Interviews with agencies, telephone interviews with Country Offices and meetings with professionals involved with the poverty–environment nexus corroborated the overall findings. Strategically, UNDP has embraced the poverty–environment nexus at the global, regional and national levels. Many countries have quite impressive strategies that emphasize the importance of nexus in achieving sustainable development. Yet, the poverty–environment nexus is a difficult and sometimes elusive topic that does not easily translate to meaningful actions. Most people agree it is vital to adopt an integrative approach, but when it comes to practice it is easier to develop single-practice projects that are 'poverty–environment nexus-compliant', in that the linkage is recognized but are not 'poverty–environment nexus-active' in terms of real activities on the ground.

The major findings, including for non-African countries, are outlined next.[15]

1. Within UNDP there is substantial recognition of a poverty–environment 'nexus' and of its importance for countries to achieve sustainable development.

However, the articulation of this awareness is uneven and somewhat haphazard throughout the organization.

At the field level, the linkages are generally understood to mean taking account of poverty issues in environmental work. At regional and headquarters levels, the understanding of the nexus is sometimes more sophisticated but is rarely translated into a consistent articulation of principles and practices in strategies or guidance. Where good practice is found and replicated, it more often than not arises from individual 'champions' and Country Office initiatives rather than a coordinated institutional approach.

1. UNDP's focus area structure promotes a 'silo effect' that makes cooperation across sectors difficult.

Because the nexus is not incorporated into UNDP's goals or measures of performance, there is no incentive for staff to take up integrative, cross-sectoral initiatives. Interviews and other evidence from the 38 Country Offices analysed in this evaluation show that in some Country Offices there has been very little coordination between the environment and poverty focus areas (e.g. Botswana, Costa Rica, India, Kenya), while in others they have worked together on an *ad hoc* basis (Malaysia, Mozambique, Papua New Guinea and Viet Nam).

In some Country Offices, a close working arrangement can be seen (Bangladesh, Dominican Republic, Ghana, Lao People's Democratic Republic, Sri Lanka, Thailand), whereas in others, the Country Offices have combined their focal-area structures to better address linkages (Cameroon, Senegal), or simply for greater programme management efficiency (Bulgaria, Syrian Arab Republic, Ukraine).

2. UNDP's dependence on external funding, especially for environmental activities, reinforces the institutional focus on area-specific work and makes it more difficult to articulate the connections among UNDP priorities.

Most donors do not provide incentives to address poverty–environment linkages, although many external funding sources for environment programmes tend to be receptive to their inclusion. The GEF has been seen in the past as an impediment to poverty–environment linkages due to its focus exclusively on global environmental benefits. This has been changing in its past two replenishment cycles. Strategic plans now acknowledge the importance of promoting sustainable livelihoods to build local support, and there has been an expansion of programmes (especially small grants and programmes addressing land degradation) that focus on local impacts. There is evidence that UNDP has influenced GEF policy with regard to mainstreaming global environmental and local development benefits, particularly in the biodiversity focal area.

3. A systemic impediment to effective integration of poverty and environment in UNDP's work is the absence of monitoring processes and indicators, which affects both the initiation and the design of programmes and projects and the determination of their results.

The lack of indicators to track poverty–environment linkages, either qualitative or quantitative, significantly diminishes attention to the related issues. Reduced ability to monitor progress also reduces incentives. This applies to both programme and project monitoring, as well as to performance reviews of Country Offices and staff. The absence of monitoring and evaluation eliminates the potential for sharing and learning from best practices, and there is less information to disseminate about what is being done related to the poverty–environment nexus.

4. UNDP's efforts to highlight the importance and potential of poverty–environment linkages have been mixed, with significant achievements but considerable variation in direction and priority.

In many cases UNDP has used the processes of donor coordination and development of the United Nations Development Assistance Framework to encourage greater attention to poverty–environment linkages. In Mexico, UNDP has convened multisector environmental consultative groups and established 'platforms for debate' at local, state and federal levels. In Dominican Republic, UNDP has taken the lead on environmental sustainability aspects of achievement of the MDGs and used this work to foster poverty–environment nexus issues in its interactions with government. In Sri Lanka, UNDP and the government have worked closely under the UNDAF to promote more attention to the nexus. In United Republic of Tanzania, UNDP has led the pilot 'Delivering as One' and UNDAF activities to expand coordination among donors and ministries regarding poverty–environment issues.

5. UNDP's cooperation with other institutions on the poverty–environment nexus varies based on opportunities and on the level of interaction between organizations in a particular context.

Globally, UNDP is a partner to the major multilateral accords and conventions related to development. At the country level, UNDP plays a pivotal role due to its extensive Country Office presence and its management role of the United Nations resident coordinator system. This enables it to lead donor coordination and promote integrative activities through the UNDAF. Inter-agency rivalry at country level has sometimes inhibited cooperation, except where co-funding and donor support have been sought, such as for a GEF project where such cooperation is mandatory. One specific partnership that formally integrates the two focus areas has exhibited high potential: the PEI, with UNEP.

6. Country studies and interviews have shown that when nexus issues are recognized as critical to achieving sustainable development, there is strong support to address them in programmes and projects.

Positive examples have been seen in GEF-funded projects, notably the Small Grants Programme, as well as recent programmes on climate change adaptation.

7. There is evidence that positive results at country level can be replicated.

Favourable outcomes of initial PEI projects in Rwanda and United Republic of Tanzania in 2005 led to a significant scaling up of the programme in 2007. Eighteen countries were involved, including several in Asia and Pacific and two each in Central Asia, Latin America and the Caribbean. A further expansion of the PEI is anticipated.

8. Country-specific circumstances regarding the nexus play a major role in how poverty–environment linkages are understood and addressed.

Results vary by country depending on the commitment of the government, degree of cooperation within the government, efficiency of UNDP advocacy and effectiveness of PEI implementation. When government officials have recognized their country's dependence on natural resource management as a means to reduce poverty, there is good receptivity to the PEI. In five of the seven case study countries where it is operative, UNDP Country Offices were found to be supportive of the projects. They were using this approach to promote cooperation among practice groups and integrate poverty and environment into their activities as well as into government planning. Significant progress has also been achieved in other countries where Country Offices have actively promoted taking account of the nexus (UNDP 2019a).

Conclusion: the prospect

At the outset, UNDP always intended that the evaluation would include a vision into the future as to how poverty and the environment could be better linked and how investments could yield simultaneous co-benefits from both. In part, this prospective desire was driven by the knowledge that the nexus was relatively little understood except in rather simplistic terms, as indeed the evaluation found. Evidence was sparse and experience of employing positive results for future projects was rare. The evaluators, however, felt that this somewhat negative perception could and should be remedied and that identification of good practice in the poverty–environment nexus should be promoted. These lessons will be valuable in making make generic recommendations based upon solid evidence from UNDP's own practices and that of others.

The evaluation identified five conclusions and articulated four recommendations for UNDP to encourage transformational change in the organization especially in breaking down some of the internal structural barriers to cross-disciplinary integration, an aspect over which UNDP should have full control itself as a learning agency (see Box 11.2).[16]

BOX 11.2 CONCLUSIONS AND RECOMMENDATIONS

Conclusions	*Recommendations*
1. Addressing the poverty–environment nexus is essential to achieving the UNDP mission. The linkages between poverty reduction, environmental sustainability and progress on achievement of the MDGs have been well established in analyses by UNDP and other major institutions. Poor people depend disproportionately on access to natural resources for their livelihoods, and development and poverty-reduction programmes have significant effects on the environment.	1. UNDP should ensure that practices follow principles. In addition to following policy and advocacy, UNDP needs to learn from good practices and replicate successes.
2. Strategic planning and advocacy on the poverty–environment nexus are occurring at UNDP, but policy is not yet systematically translated into practice. Conversely, examples of good practice and success at local and regional levels are not being effectively communicated and replicated.	2. The Poverty–Environment Initiative represents good practice and should be scaled up to provide a model of how UNDP does business at the country level. It should also be used as a model for working together with UNEP and other agencies.
3. UNDP's institutional and financing architecture serves as a barrier to integrated approaches. Particular problems are dependence on external financing and concentration of substantive capacity in headquarters focus area teams, not in Country Offices.	3. UNDP should provide guidelines and create verifiable indicators to further integrate poverty reduction and environmental protection into other UNDP operations. It must also invest in developing staff capacity.

(Continued)

Conclusions	*Recommendations*
4. UNDP efforts to integrate poverty alleviation and environmental protection programmes at country level depend on the interest of countries. All governments are committed to both poverty reduction and environmental sustainability. However, evidence suggests that many partner governments continue to believe there are major trade-offs between these goals. Given the wide variation in poverty and environment challenges faced by countries, UNDP can demonstrate how to minimize such trade-offs.	4. UNDP must overcome the functional silos that prevent cooperation and integration between focus areas. Analysis of poverty and environment priorities should be incorporated into governance and crisis prevention and recovery, as well as gender support activities and vice versa.
5. UNDP is ideally situated to strengthen partnerships within the United Nations system to coordinate action on poverty alleviation and environmental protection.	

Source: UNDP (2010)

As summarized in Box 11.2, the evaluation concluded that UNDP has made sporadic and patchy progress in the poverty–environment nexus; it recognizes that the issue has particular resonance for poor people and for its own operations (Conclusion 1). Consequently, UNDP should learn from the pockets of good practice at country, regional and global levels, build better communication and replication facilities (Conclusion 2) and spread these examples throughout the organization (Recommendation 1). One of UNDP's main roles is to enthuse its country partners and other UN agencies via donor coordination to prioritize the poverty–environment nexus (Conclusions 4 and 5). The joint UNDP-UNEP PEI is a model of the poverty–environment nexus practice worth both replicating and disseminating more widely; it should be brought more fully into the mainstream of UNDP operations (Recommendation 2). As part of picking up on good practice, UNDP should set the lead in developing guidelines and indicators for the poverty–environment nexus, as well as building staff capacity to handle the complex of issues (Recommendation 3).

One of the evaluation's principal findings is that UNDP's own structural architecture, including its operational and financing mechanisms, is not suited to cross-disciplinary initiatives (Conclusion 3). The practice-area 'silos' are too big and their foundations too entrenched. A first step towards breaking the barriers would be to ensure that poverty–environment nexus issues are also included in governance, crisis prevention and gender strategies, approaches and projects (Recommendation 4). A further step would be to take the examples of good practice, identifying where individual staff took strong leadership for integrating poverty and environment – the role of 'champion' – and then implementing cross-disciplinary practice based on how the individual 'champion' managed to overcome practice-area 'silos'. However, looking to the sustainability of the poverty–environment nexus within the organization will necessarily involve fundamental structural reform, an issue rather bigger and more controversial than this evaluation was mandated to address.

The poverty–environment nexus will always be harder to implement than standard mono-focal approaches because it will not only be more complicated but also will require people from different disciplines to work together and share a similar vision of poverty reduction being positive for the environment and environmental rehabilitation as positive for poverty reduction. The vision includes having the appropriate strategies and the practical means to identify poverty and environment synergies – and conversely, to exclude activities where poverty and environment may be in conflict. This will require good leadership, the promotion of 'champions for the poverty–environment nexus' at all levels and the agency-wide dissemination of good practices – all of which the evaluation found, but not sufficiently consistently or intensively.

Notes

1 Prof. Michael Stocking passed away in 2018. This analysis and argumentation in this chapter remains valid and consequently has not been revised. However, the country-specific statistics have been updated to the extent relevant (J.I. Uitto, ed.).
2 For an example from Ghana, see Besley (1995).
3 PEI is jointly run by UNEP and UNDP; see PEI (2012).
4 For an example from Ghana, see Amanor (1999).
5 For example, UNDP takes the lead role in partner countries in the 'Delivering as One' concept initiated by Kofi Annan in 2005 designed to capitalize on the strengths and comparative advantages of the different members of the UN family.
6 See http://web.undp.org/execbrd/undp-action-plan.shtml.
7 The PEP is an informal network of development agencies, which seeks to improve the coordination of work on poverty reduction and the environment.
8 PEI was launched in 2005 and scaled up in 2007; see https://www.unpei.org/.
9 Helen Clark, UNDP Administrator, Statement to the UNDP/UNFPA Executive Board, 24 June 2010.
10 Country specific information from UNDP HDR website: http://hdr.undp.org/en/data and http://hdr.undp.org/en/indicators/167106# (accessed 30 June 2020).
11 Morocco still has no Poverty Reduction Strategy. Tackling rural and urban poverty does, however, appear as a priority in the African Development Bank's Country Strategy paper, 2007–2011, for the Kingdom of Morocco.

12 See https://www.un.org/en/ga/deliveringasone/.

13 See Vice President's Office, Development of Poverty-Environment Indicators Report, August 2006.

14 UNDP practice areas include environment and energy, inclusive growth and poverty reduction, democratic governance, crisis prevention and recovery, HIV health and development, capacity development and women's empowerment.

15 Taken from the Executive Summary of EO of UNDP (2010). More details are in the full evaluation report at http://web.undp.org/evaluation/evaluations/thematic/pen.shtml.

16 UNDP claims to set importance on learning from current practices. It has a Learning Resource Centre providing online training to staff and a Virtual Development Academy, for example.

References

Amanor, K., *Global restructuring and land rights in Ghana: Forest food chains, timber and rural livelihoods, Research report no. 108*, Uppsala, Nordiska Afrikainstitutet, 1999.

Bass, S. And Y. *Renard, Evaluation of the UNDP-UNEP poverty-environment initiative (PEI)*, Report to the Norwegian Ministry of Foreign Affairs, London, 2009.

Besley, T., 'Property rights and investment incentives: Theory and evidence from Ghana', *Journal of Political Economy* 103 (5): 903–907, 1995.

Corvalan, C. et al., *Ecosystems and human well-being: Health synthesis. A report of the Millennium Ecosystem Assessment*, Geneva, Switzerland. World Health Organization, 2005.

Dasgupta, S., U. Deichmann, C. Meisner, and D. Wheeler, 'Where is the poverty-environment nexus? Evidence from Cambodia, Lao PDR, and Vietnam', *World Development* 33 (4): 617–638, 2005.

Duraiappah, A.K., Poverty and environmental degradation: A review and analysis of the nexus, *World Development* 26 (12): 2169–2179, 1998.

Ekbom, A. and J. Bojö, *Poverty and environment: Evidence of links and integration in the country assistance strategy process, Africa Region Discussion Paper, No. 4*, World Bank, Washington DC, 1999.

Evaluation Office of UNDP (EO). *Evaluation of UNDP contribution to environmental management for poverty reduction: The poverty-environment nexus*, Final Report, New York, 2010.

FAO, 2017 (http://www.fao.org/3/a-i7617e.pdf).

FAO, IFAD, UNICEF, WFP and WHO, *The State of Food Security and Nutrition in the World 2018*. Building climate resilience for food security and nutrition. Rome, 2018. (https://reliefweb.int/sites/reliefweb.int/files/resources/English___The_State_of_Food_Security_and_Nutrition_in_the_World_2018_-_Full_Report.pdf).

Government of the Republic of Rwanda, 'National strategy and action plan for the conservation of biodiversity in Rwanda', *Ministry of Lands Resettlement and Environment*, Kigali, 2003.

Government of the Republic of Rwanda, 'Environment and climate change strategic plan 2010–2011', Kigali, 2009a.

Government of the Republic of Rwanda, 'Environment and natural resources sector plan (2009–2013): Towards a green, clean, healthy and wealthy Rwanda', *Ministry of Natural Resources*, 2009b.

Gray, L and W. Moseley, 'A geographical perspective on poverty–environment interactions', *The Geographical Journal* 171 (1): 9–23, 2005.

Lufumpa, C.L., 'The poverty–environment Nexus in Africa', *African Development Review* 17 (3): 366–381, 2005.

Malthus, T.R., *An essay on the principle of population*, Sixth Edition, London, John Murray, 1826.

National Institute of Statistics of Rwanda (NISR), *Ministry of Finance and Economic Planning (MINECOFIN), Fourth population and housing census 2012*, Thematic Report – Population size, structure and distribution, Rwanda, 2012.

Poverty-Environment Initiative (PEI), *PEI Annual Progress Report 2011*, Nairobi, 2012.

Pinstrup-Andersen, P. and R. Pandya-Lorch, '*Poverty, food security, and the environment', Brief 29*, Washington DC, International Food Policy Research Institute, 1995.

Stocking, M.A., 'Farming and environmental degradation in Zambia: The human dimension', *Applied Geography* 3: 63–77, 1983.

Tiffen, M., M. Mortimore, and F. Gichuki, *More people, less erosion: Environmental recovery in Kenya*, London, John Wiley, 1994.

United Nations Development Programme *(UNDP), Handbook on planning, monitoring and evaluation for development results*, Second Edition, United Nations Development Programme, New York, 2009.

UNDP, *Social policy in the context of economic transformation, Tanzania Human Development Report 2017*, Tanzania, 2017

UNDP, *Beyond income, beyond averages, beyond today: Inequalities in human development in the 21st century, Human Development Report 2019*, New York, 2019a.

United Nations Statistics Division. *Gross domestic product 2018*. Country Profile, Morocco, 2018. Retrieved from https://unstats.un.org/unsd/snaama/CountryProfile

UNDP, *Beyond income, beyond averages, beyond today: Inequalities in human development in the 21st century, Human Development Report 2019*, New York, 2019b.

UNDP-UNEP Poverty-Environment Facility, '*Making the economic case: A primer on the economic arguments for mainstreaming poverty-environment linkages into development planning*', Nairobi, 2008.

Websites

1 https://worldpopulationreview.com/countries/morocco-population/.
2 https://www.moroccoworldnews.com/2017/12/236710/poverty-morocco-essaouira-stampede-illiteracy/.

12

SMALL GRANTS, BIG IMPACTS

Aggregation challenges

Sulan Chen and Juha I. Uitto

Introduction

'Think globally, act locally' refers to the argument that global environmental problems can be only properly and effectively addressed by considering the ecological, economic and cultural differences of our local surroundings. This approach is based on the premise that environmental issues are globally connected – that issues' complexities manifest themselves at the local level through physical, climatic and cultural contexts. Therefore, local actions designed for specific environmental issues are most effective in tackling global environmental issues. However, translating global thinking into local actions does not happen easily and smoothly, recognizing contextual complexities and local needs. Although local actions may effectively address issues at the small scale, employing such an approach to address global issues is often challenged by difficulties in scaling up successes to benefit more localities. One solution could be to duplicate the action in many other similar local sites, hence scaling up impacts through replication. Another solution is to scale up projects' authority, funding and coverage to achieve greater coverage, results and impacts. The result pathway of such approach is not clear-cut, linear and one-dimensional. Instead, results and impacts are achieved over a long time horizon, and sometimes randomly and unintentionally.

The complexities and difficulties of implementation of global thinking in local contexts also pose similar challenges to evaluating the global programs or projects that work at the local level. This chapter takes the Global Environment Facility (GEF) Small Grants Programme (SGP) as a case and discusses the management challenges of the programme in translating global policies to local actions, coordinating numerous small-scale activities to achieve coherent global objectives, and reconciling global and local interests. Further, this poses similar challenges to evaluate the programme comprehensively: aggregating numerous local actions for global results, assessing the relationships between global and local benefits and identifying the complex web of forces and factors of results. More fundamentally, SGP is a unique programme of GEF in that it is a corporate programme, is not time bound or limited to GEF replenishment cycles and is different from other projects funded by GEF, which set clear timelines, targets and indicators. The GEF global evaluation framework, which is geared towards projects, does not necessarily reflect the high complexities and variations a programme such as SGP faces and manages.

It is often difficult to distinguish the impacts of development interventions from the wider processes of which they are only a part. This is even more so for SGP, a global programme running almost like an international organization in itself in terms of its geographical coverage, reach and timeframe. Particularly, the number of projects is large and activities are scattered around the world. Specifically, first, how do evaluators gauge the collective impacts and results of numerous small-scale projects spread throughout the world, and furthermore, how do evaluators draw conclusions on the projects' aggregate effectiveness in addressing global issues? Second, how do evaluators assess the extent to which replication and upscaling are being carried out, and furthermore, how to attribute the indirect impacts (derived from replication and upscaling) to these small projects which might have inspired or contributed to such impacts?

This chapter presents the challenges of measuring SGP results and impacts. It argues that there is a tension between the global environmentally focused and sectoral approach of the GEF and the SGP's demand-driven, community-based approach. The scale and diversity of SGP projects makes it operationally difficult to aggregate and report according to the global framework, which was developed for government-centred projects that are orders of magnitude larger in scale and funding. This results in a large portion of the transformative changes that SGP has contributed to being left unaccounted for or not captured by the existing evaluation system. This chapter calls for an adapted, flexible and inclusive GEF approach to monitoring and evaluating SGP results and impacts. It suggests that a country programme level of analysis – rather than a global aggregation of individual projects – would provide a more appropriate picture of SGP impacts.

GEF small grants programme

The GEF was launched in 1991 as a pilot programme in order to assist developing countries and countries with economies in transition to protect the global environment and to promote sustainable development. The GEF also serves as financial mechanism for several conventions (the Convention on Biological Diversity, the Stockholm Convention on Persistent Organic Pollutants, the United Nations Convention to Combat Desertification, the United Nations Framework Convention on Climate Change, and the Minamata Convention on Mercury). The GEF, although not linked formally to the Montreal Protocol on Substances That Deplete the Ozone Layer, supports implementation of the Protocol in countries with economies in transition. GEF provides grants to various types of projects ranging in size from several thousand dollars to several million dollars through various modalities.[1]

The SGP, launched in 1992, is the oldest programme funded by GEF. It originally included more than a dozen countries, and then expanded to cover 125 countries presently. Like in the case of full-sized projects, the GEF Council's approval of funding for the SGP is based on a Project Document which sets forth the objectives and activities to be undertaken. SGP submits a Project Document to the GEF Council in each operational phase (every five years) to seek funding. These SGP Project Documents provide the framework for SGP operations in accordance with the GEF mandate, including specific benchmarks for expected project achievements. It also sets forth many of the programme and financial reporting requirements for which the United Nations Development Programme (UNDP) has responsibility as the implementing agency for SGP.

The SGP provides direct support to civil society organizations and local communities to take action in the areas of biodiversity, climate change, international waters, land degradation and sustainable forest management and chemicals. SGP supports community-level initiatives across the range of global environmental issues addressed by the GEF – with the added integration of actions that lead to poverty reduction and empowerment, in recognition that environmental issues cannot be dealt with alone without tending local needs. To date, SGP has funded more than 25,000 projects with US$625 million in 134 countries, having generated about US$800 million in co-financing. Table 12.1 presents the overall global portfolio of SGP by focal area.

SGP structure[2]

The structure of SGP is decentralized and country driven. Within the parameters established by the GEF Council and Secretariat and reflected in the Project Document for its Operational Phases, it provides for maximum country- and community-level ownership and initiative. This decentralization is balanced against the need for programme consistency and accountability across the participating countries for the achievement of the GEF global environmental objectives and the SGP's

TABLE 12.1 SGP Portfolio by Focal Area

Focal areas – total	*Number of projects*	*Grant amount*	*Co-financing in cash*	*Co-financing in kind*
Biodiversity	12,099	$293,699,380	$180,592,161	$214,923,856
Climate Change	6,197	$160,242,658	$101,039,167	$103,912,620
International Waters	1,183	$25,302,393	$15,674,692	$23,185,808
Chemicals and Waste	769	$19,280,855	$10,478,576	$10,878,890
Land Degradation	4,391	$100,125,065	$51,413,090	$68,400,429
Capacity Development	1,202	$26,123,431	$8,345,833	$10,747,492
Total	25,841	$624,773,782	$367,543,519	$432,049,095

particular benchmarks as stated in its Project Documents. In terms of management and execution, SGP is run by a team of about 200 staff members. Through the global management team, SGP reports to UNDP and the GEF Council on its achievements and results. Figure 12.1 includes SGP's management diagram.

Global-level management

A GEF Unit at the UNDP Headquarters in New York manages all of its GEF activities, including the SGP. The SGP Central Programme Management Team (CPMT), located in New York, is composed of the Global Manager, Deputy Global Manager, Programme Advisors, Knowledge Facilitator, Programme Assistant, and consultants as needed. The CPMT in New York is currently staffed with eight professionals and two support staff members. The CPMT is responsible for overall programme management; provides operational guidance and support to the country programmes, including identification and establishment of the SGP in new countries; and reports to the GEF Council. The United Nations Office for Project Services provides programme execution services and project management for SGP, such as financial management and audits, recruitment, procurement and other financial and administrative matters.

Country-level management

The SGP operates in a decentralized and country-driven manner through a National Coordinator and National Steering Committee (NSC) in each participating country, and with management, financial, and administrative support from UNDP Country Office. NSC is composed of voluntary members from national non-governmental organizations, academic and scientific institutions, other civil society organizations, the UNDP Country Office and government, with a majority of members coming from the non-governmental sector. It provides overall guidance and direction to the country programme and contributes to developing and implementing strategies for country programme sustainability. In collaboration with the National Coordinator, NSC helps to develop the country programme strategy in accordance with the global SGP Project Document and national environmental priorities, and oversees its implementation. NSC is responsible for selecting and approving projects, and for ensuring their technical and substantive quality.

The UNDP Country Office provides management support to the SGP country programme. The UNDP resident representative in each country assigns a senior staff person (typically the sustainable development advisor or environment focal point) to serve as the SGP focal point. The resident representative or the focal point as his/her delegate participates in NSC. Each UNDP Country Office also contributes to monitoring programme activities, usually through broad oversight by the designated focal point as part of NSC responsibilities, facilitating interaction with the host government and developing links with other in-country financial and technical resources.

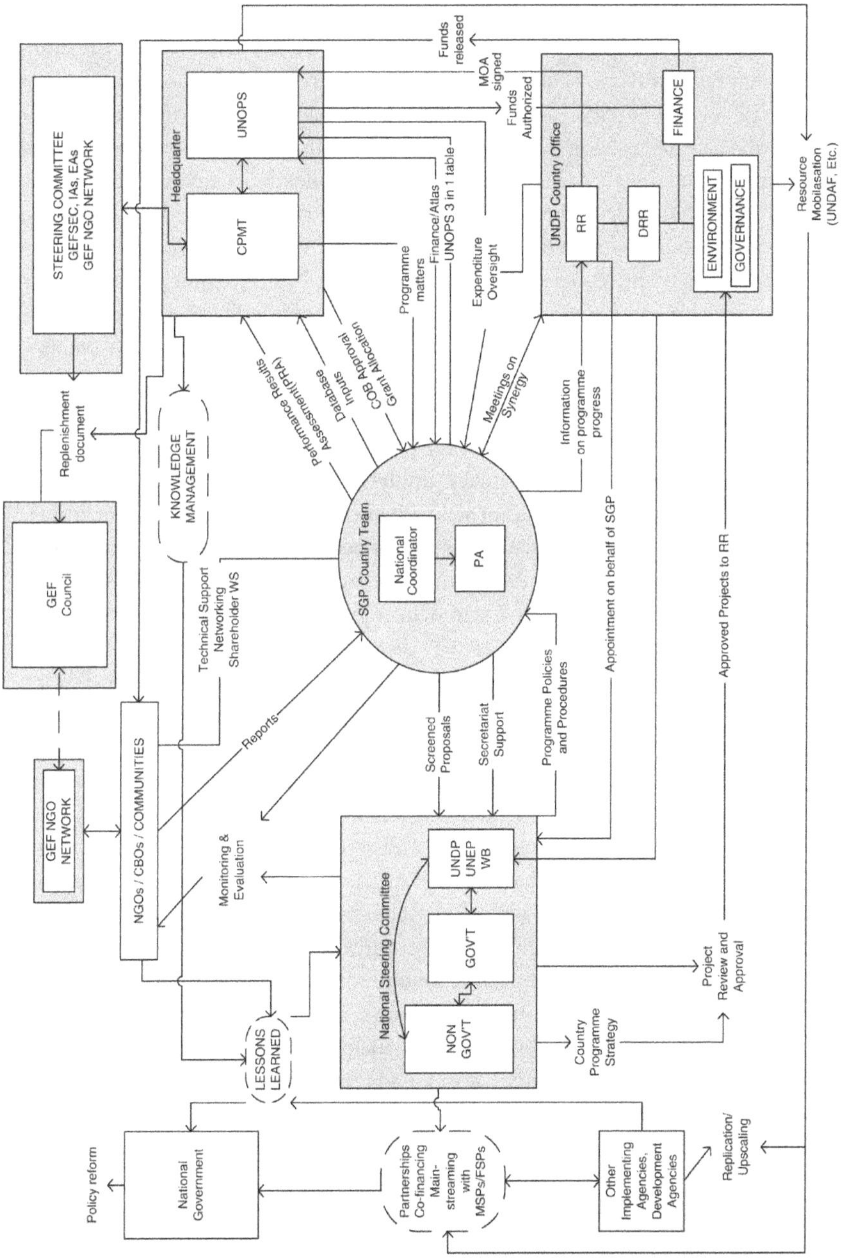

FIGURE 12.1 SGP Management Diagram

SGP operational challenges

Challenge to coordinate country programmes for coherent global objectives

SGP is a country-driven programme in the sense that key policies and decisions regarding strategic direction, funding eligibility and project selection are made at the national level. The NSC is the final decision-making body of country programme operations (as long as its decisions fall within SGP global Operational Guidelines, which allow for adequate innovation and flexibility for specific country contexts). NSC not only reviews and approves projects but also provides strategic direction and technical guidance and ensures strategic dissemination and utilization of SGP knowledge and experience. The majority of NSC members are typically from non-governmental organizations or chosen independently as individuals. The NSC is often composed of influential and accomplished persons in the country, which provides an effective interface between policy formulation processes and community development activities. However, NSCs are focused on national priorities and often put them ahead of global GEF priorities.

SGP country programmes are usually thinly staffed, often with only a national coordinator and a programme assistant who are in charge of the development, implementation, monitoring and evaluation of an average of about 100 projects over an SGP operational phase. Previous evaluations have noted that SGP country teams are often overloaded; their priority work is to deliver grants to communities, leaving limited time for other activities, such as strategy development, monitoring or evaluation.

The work to ensure global coherence and align with global objectives falls on the small CPMT team, which reviews and comments on country programme strategies to ensure technical soundness and policy alignment with GEF priorities, oversees country programming and operations, and communicates global policies and priorities to country programmes. Each SGP country program team submits annual reports to CPMT for global consolidation and reporting to the GEF Council and Secretariat. It should be noted that it is CPMT that plays the critical role in transmitting global GEF policies to national level actors (national coordinators, NSC and grantees), through whom the policies are further translated into local actions on the ground. When it comes to aggregating results from the ground up, CPMT is the global data-mining centre to collect information, consolidate it and report the results to the GEF. The challenges for CPMT include the large number of country programmes (each programme advisor in CPMT covers approximately 30 country programmes), limited face-to-face interactions with key stakeholders and limited travel and capacity-development budgets to train and coordinate country teams.

Tension between community needs and global environmental mandate

The communities SGP focuses on are often the poorest and most vulnerable, and typically have low levels of technical and institutional capacity to adequately address global environmental problems. More than 60% of SGP grants target poor communities in participating countries, which have the greatest need for assistance (GEF 2008). At least 15% of SGP grants target indigenous peoples (frequently amongst the poorest communities), who often have the knowledge and experience to create sustainable solutions to environmental challenges. More than a quarter of SGP grants specifically support women, who constitute another priority target group.

As these poor and vulnerable communities struggle for basic daily needs such as food, water, sanitation and education, it is hard for SGP to focus on effectively achieving global environmental benefits without investment in promoting these basic needs. The second independent evaluation report of SGP noted (Wells, Ganapin and Trempe 1998: 22):

> Access to and acceptance by communities – the GEF/SGP's principal clients – almost invariably requires an emphasis on activities which communities perceive are closely linked to their own immediate concerns, a characteristic by no means limited to poorer countries. Ask a low-income rural community in the developing world what their priority problems are, and the answer is unlikely to feature biodiversity or climate change. Few, if any, communities begin with an understanding or awareness of these terms.

To address the challenges to reconcile global environmental benefits and local benefits, SGP has three pillars in its comprehensive development approach: environmental protection, poverty reduction and community empowerment. This approach recognizes the intrinsic linkages between environment and development, particularly at the community level, and advocates for integrating environmental protection into development. The SGP approach is intended to leverage shifts towards environmentally sustainable livelihood options and increase education and awareness on environmental issues. The centrality of local development for SGP was demonstrated by a 2009 global survey by the CPMT, which estimated that SGP generated more than half a million jobs for local communities around the world. In a major study led by the GEF Evaluation Office (2008), SGP was found to address local benefits and needs while contributing to global environmental benefits. However, the importance of these local benefits are often neglected in the GEF Focal Area Results Frameworks (focusing on global environmental benefits), and sometimes are even considered 'non-GEFable',[3] leaving them unaccounted for or unappreciated.

Gaining communities' confidence and encouraging community members to participate in projects and modify their behaviour in ways that generate global environmental benefits is a long-term proposition. Such an ambitious task needs to be approached with considerable patience and restrained expectations. This was why, in the early stage of SGP, many activities were related to poverty reduction, sometimes with ambiguous linkages to global environmental benefits (Wells, Ganapin and Trempe 1998). Over the years, however, after developing the foundational capacities with communities, SGP was able to demonstrate its critical role in achieving global environmental benefits (GEF 2008). The challenge lies in managing the complex realities in the field and the expectations of GEF Council and Secretariat for the programme to deliver global environmental benefits. The GEF's operational phase-based funding replenishment cycle requires that SGP demonstrates immediate global environmental benefits in order to justify its continuous funding. At the community level, the environment is intrinsically intertwined with development. To achieve environmental results it is essential to address the urgent local development issues. The SGP joint evaluation (GEF 2008) concluded that SGP has a significantly higher sustainability rate than the full-sized projects. Although the evaluation did not give the reasons, it seems likely that SGP's integrated approach in the field is a contributing factor.

SGP evaluations

There have been five global evaluations of the SGP, conducted in 1995, 1998, 2002, 2007 and 2015. The three first ones were commissioned by the CPMT, while the latter two were conducted as joint evaluations by the Independent Evaluation Offices of the GEF and UNDP with CPMT involved only as an evaluand.[4] The 2007 evaluation noted that the previous three evaluations 'were primarily oriented toward improving SGP operations and design and toward distilling lessons' (GEF EO and UNDP EO 2008: 5). It further stated that the evaluation was 'not able to assess which global environmental benefits had been achieved, whether the programme was cost effective, or whether there were trade-offs between the SGP and other GEF projects' (GEF EO and UNDP EO 2008: 5).

It did conclude that 'SGP has contributed to numerous institutional reforms and policy changes in the recipient countries to address global environmental issues' (GEF EO and UNDP EO 2008: 27). The evaluation report cited a number of cases in which SGP influenced institutional reforms and policy changes.

The following joint evaluation that was presented by the two IEOs to the governing bodies of the GEF and UNDP in 2015 was able to go further based on thorough research that included portfolio review, extensive meta-analysis of existing country and project level evaluations, document and literature review, a global online survey sent to 2,449 program country stakeholders, focusing on the SGP's strategy and niche, broader adoption, gender, and poverty, and field work in 12 countries ranging from the longest running country programmes to several more recently established programmes, and covering the main geographical regions (GEF IEO and UNDP IEO 2015). The research used a mixed methods approach combining qualitative and quantitative approaches (see also Chapter 10 by Carugi and Bryant in this volume).

The evaluation concluded that the SGP continues to support communities with projects that are effective, efficient, and relevant in achieving global environmental benefits while addressing livelihoods and poverty as well as promoting gender equality and empowering women. The evaluation report stated: 'The SGP results are nevertheless impressive, given the high number of small-scale projects, the emphasis on innovation and piloting, the wide variety of intended outcomes, and the wide range of competencies of local project managers' (GEF IEO and UNDP IEO 2015: 5).

Referring to five transformational processes – sustaining, mainstreaming, replication, scaling-up, and market change – that have been found to lead to broader adoption in the GEF, the evaluation sought to verify cases where SGP action on the ground had led to broader adoption and the factors influencing such processes (GEF IEO and UNDP IEO 2015: 17–20). Although the formal expectations for the SGP to lead to broader adaptations of successful approaches pioneered by the small projects were quite new, the evaluation was able to confirm that 'broader adoption certainly occurs, particularly in the form of replication and scaling-up and at a local scale; and the SGP deserves recognition for its contribution to results that extend beyond the project level' (GEF IEO and UNDP IEO 2015: 19).

Aggregation challenges: measuring local actions through global lenses

There are some fundamental challenges to evaluate SGP and aggregate results and impacts from SGP projects. First, SGP reporting indicators were guided by the global SGP Project Documents with results frameworks extracted from the GEF Focal Area Results Frameworks, a thematically focused, government-centred approach that caters to full-sized development projects. These indicators may not fully and comprehensively reflect the impacts of SGP, because of SGP's comprehensive approach to environment and development that address not only the global environmental benefits but also attend foundational development needs at the community level. Second, the ongoing SGP global monitoring and aggregation system uses community projects as the unit of analysis and attempts to aggregate direct environmental benefits from numerous small projects to a global level. Such aggregation tends to overlook some major results and impacts that are not directly associated with the on-the-ground changes in the physical project sites. Third, some types of impacts are individual-country based and are difficult to measures, such as changes in attitude towards the environment, and therefore, they cannot easily be aggregated at the global level. Fourth, there are operational challenges in collecting, standardizing and aggregating data and information, such as the lack of baseline information, the lack of staffing and technical capacity, and application of a globally applied methodology to more than 120 country programmes.

Focal area-based environmental indicators versus inclusive community development

The challenges to evaluate SGP stem from the fact that it is a unique programme that does not neatly fit into GEF's project modalities and frameworks. SGP is a continuous programme with a rolling modality, but the funding is released based on a three- or four-year Project Documents submitted to the GEF Council. Overall, GEF technical work is built on focal area divisions covering biodiversity, climate change, chemicals, international waters, land degradation and sustainable forest management/REDD+. During the GEF replenishment process, each focal area produces a focal area strategy with a results framework to present to the donor governments the expected results during an operational phase. SGP, which is expected to deliver small-scale projects in all focal areas, therefore draws from these focal area results frameworks relevant to local and community work to form its own programme document for funding. This approach tends to oversimplify the real on-the-ground complexities and the processes through which the results and impacts are achieved.

The GEF focal area results framework provides clear operational guidance on what GEF focuses on and what GEF looks for in terms of results and impacts. GEF Secretariat focal area managers, working with national stakeholders, develop and review projects by following rigorously developed policies and strategies developed for each of the focal areas. Such focal area approaches have been successful in bringing global attention to thematic environmental issues and can enable project developers and managers to produce and generate immediate and comparable impacts and results by focal area for global consolidation and aggregation. Because GEF work is thematically organized, each focal area cluster within the GEF Secretariat and implementing agencies has a clear understanding of the specific objectives, outcomes, indicators and outputs in each focal area.

GEF's focal area results frameworks were developed to serve the needs of the majority of the projects GEF funds. The majority of these are single-country projects with a focus on a thematic focal area. SGP is a global programme intended to cover all GEF focal areas (except ozone depletion) and is operational in more than 120 countries. There is an inherent dilemma in measuring and reporting SGP results and impacts: GEF's focal area-based results framework cannot properly capture SGP's comprehensive approach to development. As the various evaluations have noted (Wells, Ganapin and Trempe 1998; Wells et al. 2003; GEF 2008), SGP's results and impacts are comprehensive, providing a whole package of community solutions that addresses not only environmental issues but also social and economic conditions. Environmental protection cannot be singled out as the only target and cannot be achieved without attention to the local context and immediate needs of local communities. Effective environmental actions must be embedded within specific social, economic, cultural and political conditions.

Using GEF focal area indicators to monitor and evaluate SGP leads to a fundamental contradiction. GEF focal area indicators are sector-based and focal-area specific, whereas SGP takes on an integrated approach that crosses focal areas and integrates other development efforts at the community level. SGP's bottom-up, demand-driven and comprehensive approach requires flexibilities to adapt to local conditions, while GEF, as the funder, has a global vision and develops global strategies that require more focused implementation by its projects or programmes. This leads to an inherent dilemma in designing SGP's global results framework: How to translate the global framework into local actions while capturing the diversity of local actions?

The thematic focal area approach poses a series of difficulties to SGP operations, monitoring and evaluation. First, the results framework was developed to cater to full-sized projects with a government-centred approach; it places limited importance on communities or non-governmental processes and results. For example, all GEF focal areas emphasize the development of national plans, policies and regulatory frameworks but lack concrete activities of implementation and specific measurement of the number of households, communities, vulnerable people, women or children who are reached by GEF initiatives. Second, to gather and consolidate results by focal area, SGP has to code its thousands of projects by focal area. Yet, the realities at the community level are a lot messier and complicated than one focal area.[5]

Furthermore, the focal area approach can have the unintended effect of fostering a fragmented approach to global environmental issues. As an ecosystem is non-divisible, attempting to address separate parts of the system in isolation does not fulfil the purpose of environmental management. Failing to take a comprehensive approach to the entire process and system risks overemphasizing the achievement of single focal area results. Projects may be designed, developed and implemented to artificially achieve focal area results, while neglecting overall ecosystem needs, interlocked environmental issues or degradation causes.

The focal area results framework approach places great barriers to adopting an integrated social, environment and development approach on the ground. The numeric outputs in each focal area (hectares of protected areas or reduced CO_2 emissions) may satisfy the needs of donors who are looking for immediate and concrete results to justify continued funding of the GEF. However, it also diverts attention from addressing the broader social, environment and development issues that underpin GEF's ability to effectively address global environmental challenges. Environmental issues are intrinsically linked at the community sites; separating one issue from another only offers a partial perspective and often proves to be ineffective.

Project-based evaluation versus programming approach

Most of GEF funding is released to full-sized or medium-sized projects which typically take three to five years to complete. The projects typically have a set of planned activities with budgets set aside to be carried out through a work plan. These project activities have been designed with clearly stated expected outputs and outcomes, which are directly linked to focal area results frameworks. The SGP approach is completely different.

First, SGP's main activities depend on small-scale projects developed and proposed by civil society organizations and communities. SGP itself runs more like a fund, managing its project portfolios and monitoring project progress. Activities are developed and implemented after the Project Documents (the basis of evaluation) are developed and approved.

Second, although SGP is a continuous programme, it is divided into operational phases for funding purposes. In order to aggregate project results it requires certain stability and fixed indicators across all operational phases. To align with GEF's focal area results and strategies which change every operational phase, the SGP Project

Documents also changes its indicators accordingly. The shift and change cannot be implemented as quickly as every three to four years for a global programme covering thousands of projects in more than 120 countries. The constant change in indicators makes it difficult to ensure global coherence and coordination. CPMT staff often find themselves busy communicating the changes in the field, and before they manage to familiarize all NCs with the new indicators and strategies, there are new changes due to a new round of replenishment negotiations. Furthermore, the changing and shifting indicators and targets makes evaluation and aggregation of results more difficult.

Third, the time frames for projects developed under the Project Documents for each operational phase do not necessarily overlap with the time frame of the specific operational phase. Therefore, funding supplied from the previous operational phase may continue to support projects in the next operational phase, with mixed results and impacts that cannot be divided and attributed to the funding of a specific period. The complexities for evaluation far exceed those for a normal GEF project. The fact that SGP is a programme but is requested to fit into a project template not only poses challenges for SGP's replenishment processes, but also makes evaluation devoid of a solid and concrete base document to evaluate against.

Unit of analysis: community project versus country programme

The unit of analysis for SGP's routine monitoring and reporting is on the local project level. There has been a great interest from the GEF Council and Secretariat in reporting direct global environmental benefits through quantifiable indicators at the aggregate level. Quantitative aggregation of outputs from a large number of projects will often be possible only for rather simple common denominator indicators, such as hectares under conservation, tons of carbon emissions avoided or numbers of environmental protection measures enacted. Such indicators are measured and aggregated from individual project results. To meet such requests, ongoing global monitoring of SGP is conducted by CPMT through its global database, which includes all past and ongoing projects. The structure of this database is organized around the focal areas and select quantitative indicators (mainly related to environmental results).

Additionally, qualitative analysis is conducted mainly on individual project level. For instance, SGP National Coordinators, in annual reporting or *ad hoc* knowledge management exercises, select and submit good cases of individual projects for CPMT consideration. Individual community case studies have been developed and disseminated globally to present how 'small' projects can create larger impacts.

The approach to analysing individual projects' results and impacts leaves out some significant changes achieved at the country level, often through non-project activities, such as extensive media coverage, constructive working relationships between the government and civil society, advocacy and upscaling. For instance, NCs and NSC members have in many countries played a key role in developing community capacity, fostering civil society networks, influencing national policies and sharing knowledge and information, but these achievements are outside of the

SGP projects or not directly attributable to them and, consequently, are not routinely recorded and documented.

It has been noted by SGP stakeholders that some of the more critical impacts are generated by SGP's governance approach and presence rather than individual projects. A former UNDP Deputy Country Director in China noted,

> The significance of SGP in China is that it is probably the biggest (if not the only) NGO grant-making mechanism officially recognized by the government of China – yet (unlike other mechanisms) it is not run solely by a ministry. In this case the NSC is unique, with a ministry being just one more voice in a steering committee with [*civil society organizations*] present... In a real sense that SGP represents another milestone in the history of [*non-governmental organizations*] in China...To see an institutional mechanism that brings government and [*non-governmental organizations*] together is indeed progress. (UNDP 2012: 49)

There is a need to shift the level of analysis to place more emphasis on the country programme level. Country case studies should be conducted to look deeply and contextually to upscaling impacts. Country-level aggregation and impact analysis can examine the results achieved by the SGP presence and its portfolio. Mechanical aggregation of individual projects' results (such as summing up the total hectares, tons and numbers) often leaves out the results and impacts achieved outside of physical project sites, which played key roles in environmental conservation and sustainable development.

Non-environmental impacts of SGP

In practice, SGP is an organic web of knowledge, experiences and influence at community, national and global levels, not just an aggregation of many small projects addressing GEF focal area issues. The measurement of SGP successes and achievements should not focus solely on the number of species protected, the tons of CO_2 emissions reduced or prevented or hectares of areas conserved or managed. Rather, measurements of SGP successes should also include changes at the community level, such as community empowerment, enhancement of local livelihoods, achievements in gender equality and knowledge sharing and learning, which over time contribute to enhanced sustainability. Aggregation of biophysical environmental indicators can leave out such non-environmental impacts that foster broader environmental impacts. In the words of the former UNDP Administrator, Mark Malloch Brown,

> Real change comes community by community. It does not come top-down, from the global level or even from national capitals. It takes place at the grassroots, when local communities are empowered to take their future into their own hands: that is the real frontline where the struggle to build a more prosperous and sustainable planet will be won or lost. This where the GEF Small Grants makes a real difference (Qayum 2002: 6).

Furthermore, SGP sites serve as demonstration sites and are often visited by senior government officials from the donors and the governments. These governmental officials then advocate nationally and globally for replication and upscaling of SGP experiences. How to collect and measure the impact of these 'spill-over' activities by senior government officials can be difficult to determine. For example, the president of the Dominican Republic made a televised speech in February 2013 on the occasion of the national Independence Day, citing SGP's micro-hydro project as an example to follow and committing to scaling up the good experiences at the national level. The quantitative aggregation of such 'spill-over' impacts created by the senior government officials, in terms of number of projects, beneficiaries or hectares of land protected as a result of up-scaling, will be difficult to gauge and beyond the abilities of an SGP country team staff.

Baseline and scale of measurement

SGP is a demand-driven grant-making programme. It runs like a fund but with direct implementation and execution activities. When GEF approves the global SGP Project Document, it only contains some global strategic directions and policies towards overall global objectives and targets as they pertain to the global environmental benefits expressed in the focal area results framework. After the Council's approval, CPMT sends grant allocation amount to each country programme. Each country programme then develops a Country Program Strategy that guides the country's priorities in SGP programming. Until then, no project activities were planned. After the approval of the Country Program Strategy, a call for proposals is issued, and communities and non-governmental organizations submit their proposals to SGP country programmes for project selection and approval.

Because SGP covers more than 120 countries working on multiple focal areas of GEF, establishing a global baseline for SGP is akin to undertaking a review and study of global environmental issues and trends. Although it may be possible to establish such baseline information, its meaning would be questionable. Because SGP projects are scattered around the world, while it is possible to trace impact at the country level, attributing global-scale environmental benefits to SGP projects will be difficult.

Decentralized operation of SGP versus global aggregation

SGP is run by country-based staff members, National Coordinators and Programme Assistants, who may not use English as a primary language and have different technical capacities. Any attempt to introduce a methodology can be time-consuming and may generate different data and information as a result of different understanding or interpretation by SGP country teams. A methodology or concept that seems easy or straightforward may turn out to be confusing or complex to field staff members. Hence, monitoring and evaluation of SGP will always remain to be an operational challenge. The SGP global database provides general information and project descriptions, but follow-up to activities and measurement of impacts and results often require technical expertise and capacity that varies among the more than 120 SGP country programmes. In terms of evaluating direct global environmental benefits, a 2007 evaluation team concluded that SGP contributed to direct global environmental benefits and addressed local populations' livelihood needs (GEF 2008: 7). The conclusion was arrived at by aggregating sample projects' and country programmes' results in an individual focal area. Yet, even the extensive Joint Evaluation (costing more than US $1 million, with a team of 25 evaluators) was not able to collect, consolidate and aggregate sufficient data on SGP's direct global environmental benefits, thus demonstrating the operational challenges faced by SGP in monitoring and measuring achievements towards global indicators.

Global quantitative aggregation of project results is inherently incompatible with the concept of demand drivenness,[6] innovation, flexibility and diversity that SGP champions and relies on for success. In order to achieve aggregation, there should be some common and comparative variables across the portfolio. Overemphasizing some common quantitative indicators can send a signal to the global SGP network to focus on short-term approaches, simplify the complexity of development work and limit possible innovation and national ownership. Operationally, SGP is similar to a mini-GEF; hence, aggregation of common indicators globally can prove to be challenging and may not produce meaningful data. That is perhaps the reason why, until today, no efforts have been attempted to calculate the total CO_2 emissions reduced/prevented or hectares of protected areas supported. Strengthening country-level monitoring and evaluation capacity with a focus on country-level impacts can help address the global aggregation challenges.

Standardization versus diversification

Global aggregation of results requires some common standardization or focusing of project activities. Such standardization may not work for SGP, as SGP promotes diverse community-based approaches and innovation. Meaningful aggregation depends on comparable indicators with data and information developed and collected based on similar assumptions. To achieve the necessary comparability and measurability at the global scale, it is often necessary to bring down units and measurement scales to the most elementary and least demanding levels, implying a great loss of information. For example, in order to use an indicator that covers as many projects as possible, a simple indicator (such as hectares, tons and numbers) is selected. Different understanding, definition and applicability of indicators at local contexts further pose challenges to data quality and comparability. Because of the large diversity of small projects and their goals, global-scale quantitative aggregation has its limits. In practice, this means that although it is possible to aggregate the numbers of specific types of activities and outputs, providing aggregate measures of outcomes and impacts are virtually impossible. Relying exclusively on the global-level GEF results framework risks that significant results and impacts of SGP are left out.

As SGP takes on a community-based approach that emphasizes demand drivenness and innovativeness, projects are not tailor-cut to consolidate and aggregate around certain indicators. The diversity of SGP projects poses great challenges to the meaningful global aggregation of results. The global database developed in 2001 provided a list of indicators for SGP. However, no one indicator was applicable to all projects, and most indicators were left unfilled by the majority of projects. Hence, aggregating any one of the indicators may only reflect a small sample of the SGP portfolio, not the entire portfolio results. Therefore, any selection of indicators for aggregation from that set will underestimate real, on-the-ground results.

Even at the project level, for communities, all focal areas are mixed; hence, many projects can be recorded as 'multiple focal area' projects. It may not be possible to separate and report on focal area results. For example, conservation of mangroves can be put under international waters or biodiversity; similarly, reforestation can be counted as land degradation focal area work and as climate mitigation work. Country programmes often report on and account for these activities as considered necessary for their focal area portfolio focus. Consequently, when reporting to GEF, SGP often has to retrofit its results and impacts against the focal area indicators, while leaving out some possibly more fundamental and transformative results and impacts achieved on the ground. A more flexible and adaptive approach to monitoring and evaluation will be perhaps more productive.

Conclusion

In conclusion, it is quite a complex process to implement the idea of 'thinking globally, acting locally', which poses tremendous challenges to global aggregations of local actions' collective impacts. SGP's case demonstrated that the great variations between local complexities and global simplified frameworks make it difficult to comprehensively measure the overall depth and coverage of the impacts achieved by SGP through global lenses. Global environmental complexities are expressed not only in the multiplication of issues, linkages and forms but also in the various manifestations of issues in different localities. As such, although principles and approaches on sustainable environmental management may be generally agreed, specific actions and solutions to environmental issues are largely dependent on locally contextualized conditions. Attempts to 'standardize' for global aggregation should be avoided.

To enhance operation as well as evaluation effectiveness for SGP, an adapted, flexible and inclusive results framework approach that is independent of individual focal area results should be adopted to better monitor and evaluate SGP results and impacts. Such an approach can encompass a comprehensive evaluation framework that incorporates environmental, social, economic and political indicators to be fully evaluated and aggregated at the country programme level for global synthesis. Given the time, effort and high transaction costs needed to translate global policies into local actions, it is recommended a longer time horizon should be considered for such a framework to maintain global consistency and coordination so that country programmes and communities will not constantly shift indicators and their targets.

Notes

1 The modalities include full-sized projects, medium-sized projects, enabling activities, the small grants programme, as well as programmes; see https://www.thegef.org/about/funding.
2 The structure and management of SGP are stipulated in SGP Operational Guidelines as approved by the GEF Council. It regulates all aspects of SGP management and operations.
3 This word is used within the GEF system to describe activities that are not eligible for GEF funding.
4 Yet another joint evaluation by the GEF and UNDP Independent Evaluation Offices has been started while this is being written for presentation to the GEF Council and UNDP Board in 2021.
5 During a global review of SGP ocean and coastal management projects in small island developing states (SIDS) led by CPMT, it was found that although only about 200 projects were coded as 'international waters' projects in SIDS, there are more than 200 projects related to ocean and coastal management coded under the 'biodiversity' and 'land degradation' portfolios. Similarly, it was estimated that among the more than 3,000 projects focusing on forest management, about half were classified under 'biodiversity' and the other half was placed under the 'land degradation' focal area. Such ambiguity reflecting the cross-cutting nature of community projects renders the focal area approach quite ineffective on the ground and becomes meaningless for the purposes of monitoring and evaluation.
6 Demand drivenness refers to the fact that SGP funds project activities demanded by communities and non-governmental organizations (NGOs). Project activities are developed and implemented by communities and NGOs, not by UNDP, GEF or SGP global management team.

References

Auger, P., R. Bravo de la Parr, J.C. Poggiale, E.M. Sánchez Mañes and L. Sanz Lorenzo, 'Aggregation methods in dynamical systems and applications in population and community dynamics', *Physics of Life Reviews*, 5 (2): 79–105, 2008.

Boulanger, P.M., 'Sustainable development indicators: A scientific challenge, a democratic issue', *Surveys and Perspectives Integrating Environment and Society (SAPIENS)*, 1 (1): 45–59, 2008.

Choucri, N., *Global Accord: Environmental Challenges and International Responses*, Cambridge, MA, MIT Press, 1995.

GEF, '*GEF-5 Focal Area Strategies*', Washington, DC, Global Environment Facility, 2010.

GEF EO and UNDP EO, *Joint evaluation of the GEF small grants programme, Evaluation Report No. 39*, Washington DC, GEF Evaluation Office and New York, UNDP Evaluation Office, 2008.

GEF IEO and UNDP IEO, *Joint GEF-UNDP Evaluation of the Small Grants Programme*, Washington, DC, GEF Independent Evaluation Office and New York, UNDP Independent Evaluation Office, 2015.

Ostrom, E., *Governing the Commons: The Evolution of Institutions for Collective Action*, Cambridge, Cambridge University Press, 1990.

Qayum, S., *Hands-on Action for Sustainable Development 1992–2002*, New York, United Nations Development Programme (UNDP), 2002.

UNDP, *20 Years Community Action for the Global Environment*, New York, UNDP, 2012.

Wells, M., D. Ganapin and F. Trempe, '*Second Independent Evaluation of the GEF Small Grants Programme: The Transition to an Operational Phase*', New York, UNDP, 1998.

Wells, M., M. Hosain, B. Ogunseye and J.C. Tresierra, '*Report of the Third Independent Evaluation of the Global Environment Facility Small Grants Programme*', New York, UNDP, 2003.

Yacob, L. and L. Hisas, '*The Reaffirmation of Thinking Globally, Acting Locally: Experiences from NGOs and CBOs Implementing GEF Projects*', New York, UNDP, 2006.

13

GREEN ECONOMY PERFORMANCE OF ENVIRONMENTAL INITIATIVES IN LATIN AMERICA AND THE CARIBBEAN

Ronal Gainza and Simon Lobach

Introduction

A major outcome of the 2012 United Nations Conference on Sustainable Development (Rio+20), is the international community's recognition that a green economy is a tool for achieving sustainable development. Countries attending the conference emphasized that any green economy intervention should simultaneously contribute to the following three goals: sustaining economic growth, enhancing social inclusion and maintaining the healthy functioning of the earth's ecosystems (United Nations Environmental Programme [UNEP] 2011; United Nations 2012). The Green Economy Report produced by UNEP (2011) asserts that the transition towards a green economy contributes to achieving sustainable development. The Sustainable Development Goals (SDGs) that countries adopted in 2015 speak to these same objectives.

As suggested by Strange and Bayley (2008), assessing progress on sustainability has to identify not only the economic, environmental and social impacts but also the synergies and trade-offs across the three pillars of sustainable development. By definition, a green economy has to address the complex connections and interdependence of these three pillars, with the aim of avoiding the trade-offs that traditional sustainable development policies can imply. The key assumption of the green economy approach is the idea that initiatives that help achieve outcomes in one pillar do not need to lead to trade-offs with other pillar objectives. Consistent with this, we argue that any set of indicators for green economy initiatives must measure and give equal weight to economic growth, social equity and ecosystem protection.

UNEP has been at the forefront of promoting a green economy and it is providing policy advice, technical assistance and capacity building to governments around the world. One initial gap was the absence of a measurement approach. Efforts to introduce metrics to evaluate the transition towards a green economy have recently been initiated. Organisation for Economic Co-operation and Development (OECD; 2011) proposes indicators to monitor progress towards green growth; the Global Green Growth Institute launched in 2019 the Green Growth Index, which measures country performance in four green growth dimensions – efficient and sustainable resource use, natural capital protection, green economic opportunities and social inclusion (Acosta et al., 2019), and PAGE (2017) developed the Green Economy Progress Measurement Framework to help countries evaluate their overall progress towards an Inclusive Green Economy. In 2020, UN-Environment has developed the Inclusive Green Economy Policy Review methodology (UNEP, 2020), which assesses the coherence and effectiveness of existing policies in fostering an Inclusive Green Economy transition.

The scope of most existing measurement frameworks is at the country or subnational level[1] and gives little space to comprehensively and simultaneously measure stand-alone initiatives' contributions to green economy and the SDGs. If the green economy is to be viable and successful, then measurement frameworks need to also identify potential trade-offs and win–win–win options between the three pillars of sustainable development.

This chapter proposes a methodology to fill this gap. Acknowledging that indicators traditionally require a lot of system- and measurement-related work, we develop a system of assessment that is quick and helps policy makers and others assess whether so-called green interventions actually meet the objectives of a green economy. We develop criteria built on existing indicator frameworks and a green performance grading system. These criteria help measuring the social, environmental and economic performance of environmental initiatives, and informing about their contribution to the SDGs. We then test this framework by applying it to four environmental initiatives (located in Latin America and the Caribbean).

The remainder of this chapter is organized as follows: we first describe our proposed methodological framework for assessing the green economy performance of environmental initiatives. Then, we present the four environmental initiatives. Finally, we discuss the major results from our analysis, including enabling conditions and financing as well as main challenges and opportunities.

Methodological framework for assessing green economy performance of environmental initiatives in developing countries

A green economy has three pillars of sustainable development: ecosystem protection, economic growth and social equity.

Evidence-based criteria

A checklist that examines initiatives with regard to their green economy performance must address all these criteria. In the following, the three pillars are briefly described.

Ecosystem protection

In a green economy, natural capital must be used efficiently while reducing environmental risk so that resource use is sustainable and ecological scarcities are alleviated.[2] Based on this, this chapter proposes the following proxy indicators to assess the performance of green economy initiatives in developing countries with respect to environmental sustainability in four sectors:

Forest: forest cover stays the same or increases (contributes to SDG 15);
Freshwater: watersheds or water surfaces remain or come under effective protection (contributes to SDG 6);
Renewable energy technologies: cleaner technologies are introduced for improving access to clean energy and energy efficiency as well as reducing GHG (contributes to SDGs 7 and 13); and
Cities: the public transport network stays the same or increases; energy demand is met by green sources; green areas in urban areas increase or remain the same; food is increasingly produced in urban/peri-urban areas; the stock of green buildings and sustainable infrastructure in general increase; and materials are preferably locally sourced and where appropriate they can be composted, recycled and reused in order to reduce waste or avoid its increase (contributes to SDGs 6, 11 and SDG 12).

Economic growth

Green economy initiatives must promote and deliver economic growth over time. Gross domestic product growth is traditionally regarded as the single most important indicator for economic growth and development. Besides assessing the impact of specific green economy initiatives on the local economy, this chapter also proposes that public and private investments that support the initiative can be used as proxy indicators for gross domestic product growth. These indicators contribute to SGDs 8 and 17.

Social equity

Green economy initiatives must improve people's lives and well-being and promote social equity and health benefits. Based on the system of indicators developed by Villatoro and Feres (2007) to monitor social cohesion in Latin America, this chapter proposes the following proxy indicators to assess social equity:

Poverty reduction (contributes to SDG 1)

- People's income increases or at least does not diminish; and
- Additional benefits are received by vulnerable groups in society.

Employment (contributes to SDG 8)

- Jobs are created or at least remain the same.

Social protection (contributes to SDG 1)

- People are incorporated into social protection schemes.

Education (contributes to SDG 1)

- More people are educated or trained through green economy initiatives.

Health (contributes to SDG 3)

- People live in improved environments (i.e. indoor and outdoor pollution is reduced or at least does not increase);
- People have healthier lifestyles.

Consumption and access to basic services (contribute to SDG 1)

- Increased access to basic services including access to safe water and sewerage;
- Increased access to social infrastructure (e.g. supermarkets, hospitals, public transport).

Grade system to assess green performance

Through the assessment of environmental initiatives' performance levels, this chapter provides a framework for determining whether a given initiative can be classified as a green economy initiative (see Table 13.1).[3]

Environmental initiatives in Latin America and the Caribbean

Forest: national forestry financing fund in Costa Rica

Background

Costa Rica has an estimated forest cover of 2.6 million hectares, which represents 51% of its national territory (Food and Agriculture Organization [FAO] 2011). The country suffered extensive deforestation in the beginning of the second half of the 20th century. Vast stretches of rainforest were burned and converted into cattle lands and for agriculture use. Between 1986 and 1991, the country lost 4.2% of its remaining forest cover per year (Daniels et al. 2010), and by 1990 its forest cover was only of 1.6 million hectares (Madrigal, Alpízar and Otárola 2006).

Beginning in the late 1970s, Costa Rica introduced forestry incentives with the aim of enhancing the forest cover. These included favourable credit conditions, tradable tax vouchers and subsidies (Daniels et al. 2010). As a result of a third loan negotiation process with the World Bank, general subsidies (including forestry subsidies) were abolished and the forestry sector started exerting pressure on the government to receive support.

TABLE 13.1 Grading System to Assess the 'Green' level of Performance of Environmental

Performance	*Ecosystem protection*	*Social equity*	*Economic growth*
Good	It has positive externalities on the environment (i.e. reducing environmental risks and ecological scarcities, preserving natural capital).	It significantly contributes to enhancing social equity and reducing poverty, and/or improves the human well-being of all social groups involved.	It has a significant positive spill-over effect on the overall economy at the national or regional level (i.e. it stimulates steady economic growth).
Medium	It is possible to measure a reduction or halt in environmental degradation.	It contributes to reversing/ avoiding social inequalities and/or enables more than one social group to receive direct or indirect benefits.	It has a positive impact on the overall economy.
Poor	Though it is expected to have a positive impact on the environment, there is no reliable evidence that supports it, and/ or the impact on the environment is negligible or neutral.	It benefits/excludes specific social groups or social benefits are minimal, or the impact is neutral.	No impact on local or national economic growth can be observed.
Negative	It has adverse effects on the environment.	It deepens social inequality.	It causes economic losses.

The initiative

In response to this worsening situation, the government of Costa Rica established the National Forestry Financing Fund (FONAFIFO)[4] to complement existing forestry legislation. It is used to compensate the opportunity costs borne by private landholders of forests affected by legislation that prohibits land use change. FONAFIFO collects funds to support the payment for ecosystem services (PES) programme. Small and medium landholders may participate through reforestation, protection of existing forest, natural forest regeneration and agroforestry systems (see Table 13.2 for a list of modalities of compensation).

Functioning

FONAFIFO receives funding from four different sources. First, it receives public funds (the government assigns 3.5% of its fuel tax revenue to the fund). This financing mechanism is based on the 'polluter pays' principle. Second, FONAFIFO makes

TABLE 13.2 Modalities of Compensation in the PES, Costa Rica

Modalities	*Legal status*	*Criteria*	*Current payments ($2011)*	*Contracted (hectares)*[a]
Forest protection	Forest Law 7575 started in 1997, applicable till today	2–300 hectares enrolled, up to 600 hectares within indigenous areas	64/hectares per year for five-year period; renewable	710,095
Reforestation	Forest Law 7575 started in 1997, applicable till today	Between 1 and 300 hectares enrolled	816/hectares over 10-year period	49,039
Natural forest regeneration	2005 to present	Minimum of 2 hectares	41/hectares per year for five-year period; renewable	5,469
Agroforestry systems	2003 to present	350 to 3,500 trees per participant; up to 336,000 trees per joint project, cooperative or indigenous reserve; specific requirements per hectares	1.30 per tree up to 3,500 trees, over three-year period	3,508,873[b]
Forest management	Forest Law 7,575 in 1997, until 2002	Criteria determined by conservation area	About $343 per hectares, over five-year period	28,375

Sources: Compiled from Daniels et al. (2010); Madrigal et al. (2006); FONAFIFO website (2012).
[a] Contracted hectares as of 31 May 2011.
[b] Trees.

voluntary agreements with specific enterprises, which allocate funds for conservation activities in areas of their interest. Third, international organizations provide grants and loans for the provision of global public goods. Fourth, FONAFIFO sells Certificates of Environmental Services to individual investors, private companies and public organizations interested in investing in legally recognized environmental services. Investors can select the forest area of their interest, and the price per hectare will vary depending on the location and features of the area. This is not a trade system, since certificates are not exchangeable among investors. The main motivation for companies to invest is a desire to enhance their corporate image. The government creates an additional incentive, as these investments are tax deductible (see Table 13.3).

TABLE 13.3 Cumulative Contributions to FONAFIFO from 1998 to June 2011

Contributors	*Cumulative contribution (million of $2011)*
Public Financing	
3.5% of collected fuel tax revenues	121.74
Public–private agreements	
Compañía Nacional de Fuerza y Luz	3.77/ to protect 11,900 ha[a]
Florida Ice and Farm and *Empresa Servicios Públicos de Heredia*	0.15/ to protect 1,000 ha[b]
Hydroelectric enterprises	0.42/ to protect 5,711 ha[c]
International financing	
Ecomercados	57.37[d]/ to protect 137,033 hectares of forest/ enhance participation of women and indigenous communities
Kfw	11,606,677.29 (grant)/ to protect 74,000 hectares for seven years
Certificates of Environmental Servicese	0.43
Total	195.49

Source: FONAFIFO (2011); Madrigal et al. (2006).

[a] Compañía Nacional de Fuerza y Luz pays $40/hectares for a period of ten years.

[b] Florida Ice and Farm paid $45/hectares from 2001 to 2007, and Públicos de Heredia has contributed $22/hectares.

[c] Two hydroelectric enterprises have signed agreements with FONAFIFO. Energía Global paid $10/ hectares between 1997 and 2002 and $12/hectares ever since. Hidroelectrica platanar pays $15/ hectares to FONAFIFO for the areas which are already under the PES and $30/hectares directly to landholders who are outside the PES due to a lack of funds and/or because they do not meet the requirements.

[d] Loan of about $32.8 million from the World Bank, a grant of about $8.0 million from the Global Environment Facility (GEF), and $8.6 million from the Costa Rican government.

[e] At the time of writing, around 40 enterprises have acquired Certificates of Environmental Services.

Freshwater: water protection fund, Quito, Ecuador

Background

The availability of water for the Metropolitan District of Quito (approximately 2.3 million inhabitants), depends on the conservation of protected areas upstream. Of the district's water supply, 80% originates in two ecological reserves, the Cayambe–Coca (4,000,000 hectares) and the Antisana (120,000 hectares), both of which are national parks managed by the Ministry of Environment (UNEP 2010). Although these ecological reserves are formally protected for conservation, their ecological balance is menaced by unregulated activities, such as unsustainable agricultural practices. This results in degradation of water quality, which further affects Quito's water supply. Unfortunately, the lack of resources for the operation and protection of the reserves threatens the long-term conservation of these vital ecosystems and the water services they provide (Echavarria and Arroyo 2002).

The initiative

In 1995, the Fundación Antisana carried out a study supported by the United States Agency for International Development (USAID), to design sustainable management plans for the ecological reserves upstream. As a result of this study, the Fund for Water Protection (FONAG) was established in 2000 as an economic instrument to support conservation efforts that were underway. Two other conditions that enabled the creation of FONAG were the political will of local decision makers and the change in the law governing public financing in 1999, which allowed public organizations to assign resources to a private mechanism (Echavarria and Arroyo 2002).

Functioning

FONAG is an economic-financial mechanism that is mandated to operate for eighty years in the form of a private mercantile trust. This trust fund under FONAG collects funding, in principle, from water users who, in turn, can become members of its board and determine FONAG's policies and strategies. Voting power depends on the amount of resources provided to the fund. Furthermore, constituents can appoint the members of the Technical Advisory Committee, which assists in defining and monitoring programmes and projects.

The current constituents of FONAG are the Municipal Water and Sewerage Authority of Quito, the Nature Conservancy, the Electric Utility of Quito, Cervecería Nacional, Swiss Development Cooperation and the Tesalia Springs Company. (FONAG 2013). The initiative also accepts additional funds from other organizations to co-finance specific programmes and projects. However, these additional resources are not allocated in the trust fund and co-financier organizations are not member of FONAG's Board. See Table 13.4 for details about the main contributions to the fund by constituents and other participating organizations as of 2011.

The Technical Secretariat reviews the mechanism's financial performance, ensures project implementation and supervises the distribution of investments. Enlaces Funds, a private bank, is the financial manager of the trust fund (Echavarria and Arroyo 2002). Its main mission is to enhance the fund's profits through stock market investments (Cisneros and Lloret 2008). Only the profits of this trust fund are allocated to co-finance (along with national and international institutions) programmes and projects addressed to undertake upstream watershed protection activities, including reforestation, watershed management, environmental education, waste management and surveillance and monitoring (Echavarria and Arroyo 2002).

By rule, the trust fund under FONAG cannot provide more than a quarter of a project's total funding (Cisneros and Lloret 2008). From 2005 to 2009, for each dollar invested by FONAG in projects and programmes, the counterpart organizations contributed up to $4 (FONAG 2011). Once a year, the fund reports to the government, and this information is made available to the public. Local-level implementing organizations and volunteers from local communities undertake watershed protection activities.

TABLE 13.4 Contributions to FONAG by Constituents and Donors

Contributors	*Contribution/goals*
Constituents	
Municipal Water and Sewerage Authority of Quito	$20,000 as capital seed and 1% drinking water sales per year
The Nature Conservancy	$1,000 as seed capital and $145,000 as technical assistance and support
Electric Utility of Quito	$45,000 per year
Cervecería nacional	$6,000 per year
Swiss Development Cooperation	$30,000 as one-off payment
Tesalia Springs Co.	$7,000
Co-financiers of programmes and projects	
USAID	$3 million (2007–2012), institutional strengthening, environmental education, surveillance, monitoring and communication activities
Dutch Entrepeneurial Development Bank (FMO) - Inter-American Development Bank	$140,000 (2006–2010) development of water management programmes
Deutsche Gesellschaft für Internationale Zusammenarbeit (GIZ)	Capacity building on watersheds management
Environmental Systems Research Institute	In-kind payment (i.e. software, technical books on geographic information systems)
Corporation 'Vida para Quito'*	Reforestation programmes

Sources: FONAG website; USAID website; IDB (2006); Vida para Quito website.

* The Vida para Quito foundation is a non-profit organization subordinate to the Municipality of Quito. Its main goal is to carry out activities to protect and preserve the environment. Natural and legal persons may voluntarily make donations up to 25% of the amount of their income tax.

So far, there has not been any direct monetary compensation to farmers for taking part in protection activities. Nevertheless, FONAG has recently co-financed studies that assess and propose the implementation of PES programmes that might compensate farmers for carrying out reforestation activities.

Renewable energy: solar water heaters in Barbados

Background

Barbados' large potential for solar energy stems from its high solar endowment. Nevertheless, Barbados relies on imported refined fuels to meet nearly all (about 95%) its power and transport needs. In 1999, Barbados imported more than 2 million barrels of petroleum products (Headley 2001). Less than 15% of the refined product comes from domestic oil production. Electricity demand in the domestic and commercial sectors has grown recently at an average annual rate of more the 4%. In 2003, total annual electricity consumption was about 735 gigawatt hours or almost 2,700 kilowatt hours per capita, one of the highest rates in the Caribbean region (Perlack and Hinds 2003). The government of Barbados has been advocating for renewable sources of energy, notably by expanding the use of solar water heaters. This policy has become the best example of the exploitation of a renewable energy technology in the Caribbean.

The initiative

Solar water heater policy in Barbados seeks to reduce energy consumer costs, stimulate the local market (including manufacturers and suppliers), reduce Barbados' dependency on imported fossil fuels and enhance the country's energy security. It has been led mainly through a set of fiscal policies. The first policy, adopted in 1974, suspended import duties on raw materials needed to manufacture the heaters, and introduced a 30% consumption tax on electric water heaters. Perlack and Hinds (2003) estimate that the effect of the duty-free importation of raw materials lowered installed costs by about \$100 per solar water heater. Between 1980 and 1993, homeowners were allowed to deduct the full cost of solar water heater installation, up to a maximum of \$1,750 per year. From 1996, this deduction was reintroduced and extended to repairs, renovations, energy or water saving devices and water storage tanks.

Table 13.5 shows the estimated payback periods for domestic solar water heaters in Barbados. The investment payback periods are short, particularly for households having an income of more than \$12,000.

Cities: sustainable urban planning in Curitiba, Brazil

Background

The processes of urbanization and internal migration in Brazil have caused problems such as pollution, traffic congestion, disappearance of public and green spaces, informal housing settlements and socio-economic ruptures in most of the country's urban

TABLE 13.5 Estimated Payback Periods for Domestic Solar Water Heaters, Barbados

Parameters		*Solar water heater size (gallons)*			
		40	*52*	*66*	*80*
Installed cost (US\$2011)		1,125	1,200	1,425	1,750
Energy savings (kWh)		1,190	1,545	1,965	2,380
Electric price (\$BD/kWh)		0.18	0.18	0.18	0.18
Annual savings (\$BD)		420	546	693	840
Payback period (years)					
- Without fiscal incentives		2.7	2.2	2.1	2.1
- With fiscal incentives:					
Taxable income (US\$2011)	Tax rate				
<12,000	25%	2.0	1.6	1.5	1.6
>12,000	40%	1.6	1.3	1.2	1.2

Source: Slightly modified from Perlack and Hinds (2003).

centres (Rabinovitch and Leitman 2004). The most noteworthy example of an urban policy to counter these developments is the Sustainable Urban Development programme, first implemented in Curitiba in the 1960s. Curitiba, the capital of Paraná state, has 1.8 million inhabitants (the metropolitan region has 3.2 million inhabitants), which makes it the country's eighth largest urban centre in terms of population.

The initiative

The starting point of Sustainable Urban Development stems from the 1965 creation of the Institute for Research and Urban Planning of Curitiba, an independent public authority. The Institute conducted the drafting of the city's 1966 master plan, and in subsequent decades, it coordinated the development of a series of integrated policies to be executed by the municipal authorities (Rabinovitch 1992; Rabinovitch and Leitman 2004), including the following:

- Relocating employment to areas outside the city centre (e.g. through the creation of an 'industrial city' in a concentrated area west of Curitiba, where industries are bound by strict environmental regulations);
- Developing a system of roads with exclusive busways at their centre (Bus Rapid Transit system);
- Rationalizing of the integrated transport system;
- Improving land use legislation, providing clear incentives for commercial developments to be located as closely as possible to the public transport axes and outside the city centre;
- Developing green areas across the city, some of them in former slum areas; and
- Improving, either through relocation or not, of the quality of life in slum areas, from the point of view of public transport access, garbage collection and flood prevention.

Important factors for the success of Sustainable Urban Development in Curitiba included the continuity and consistency of the Institute for Research and Urban Planning's policies; the holistic vision of the institution (which allowed it to design policies accounting for the economic, social and environmental aspects of urban planning); the harmonization between urban development and the legal framework on construction and environment; the availability of specific funding for the project; the fact that the city had been able to easily purchase land for transport, residential and industrial use; and the hydrological features of the area that facilitated the creation of green areas across the city (de Oliveira 2001).

Functioning

The Institute for Research and Urban Planning coordinated various aspects of urban development and ensured continuity and consistency in planning processes amid turnover in city administrations. The Bus Rapid Transit system, which has a construction cost of US $3 million per kilometre, pays for itself. A city agency manages the operation of the system, which is served by private companies. The law stipulates that transportation revenue is exclusively dedicated to paying the Bus Rapid Transit system (World Bank, 2010). All the infrastructure costs of the Bus Rapid Transit system have been financed by the municipality (which still pays for the maintenance of the roads), whereas private bus operators finance the buses and station maintenance themselves, without external funding. The Inter-American Development Bank (IDB) provided more than $262 million in loans to the municipality for additional expansion of the Bus Rapid Transit system (IDB 1995, 2004, 2011).

Policies for spatially reorganizing the city have been financed by a set of taxes and public funds. For example, special property taxes for new neighbourhoods close to green areas partially finance the construction of such green areas and improvements to living conditions in slums. Historical rights to develop certain areas may be exchanged for rights to develop other city areas deemed more propitious for further urban development. In addition, the municipality sells construction and forest exploitation rights, which partially finances slum improvement and historic building preservation. The Institute for Research and Urban Planning regulates and monitors the transfer of development rights among interested parties.

For waste collection, the city implemented the Green Exchange Programme, which compensates people for collecting garbage and litter and handing it in at neighbourhood centres. This programme allows the municipality to save money on waste collection and to create a cleaner living environment while providing additional livelihoods for the poor (World Bank 2010). In addition to these self-financing mechanisms, an Inter-American Development Bank grant of about $850,000 (IDB 2009) and a grant from the Agence Française de Développement (AFD) of more than $50 million (AFD 2011) have supported diverse urban development projects.

Assessment of the initiatives

Major themes: enabling conditions and financing

Enabling conditions

The enabling conditions for the four assessed initiatives have some elements in common. First, the initiatives share the political will and engagement of key local leaders. The Costa Rican Forestry Law that underpins the PES scheme was the result of dedication and particular support from the then Minister for the Environment, who is also the author of a scientific assessment of the feasibility of the scheme. FONAG was supported by the then mayor of Quito, who was interested in fundraising for watershed protection (Pérez et al. 2006). The then prime minister of Barbados personally advocated for the initial fiscal incentives to help stimulate the market for solar water heaters, pointing at their performance and potential energy savings (Perlack and Hinds 2003). In Curitiba, the city's mayor from 1971 to 1992 had previously been president of the Institute of Research and Urban Planning, and drafted the city's 1966 master plan, laying the foundation for today's Sustainable Urban Development initiative (World Bank 2010).

Second, the implementation or modification of the regulatory framework for environment and economy catalysed the conception of the four initiatives. While the local initiatives were only driven by internal issues (e.g. population growth in Curitiba and concerns around water availability and quality in Quito), the national initiatives (FONAFIFO in Costa Rica and solar water heaters in Barbados) were also influenced by international factors. The suppression of forestry subsidies in Costa Rica during the mid-1990s, imposed by the Structural Adjustment Programmes of the World Bank, fostered the pursuit of another way to support forest protection. In Barbados, the first oil peak in 1973–1974 forced the government to find substitutes for imported oil, turning it towards solar energy.

Financing

Table 13.6 highlights the funding sources and the main financing mechanisms employed to finance the four initiatives at their different stages. Following are the important lessons.

Public pre-investment finance was employed to scale up the level of investments in all four cases (UNEP 2011). During the capacity-building and initiation phases, public funds and donors prevailed as the main source of funding for research and development and for creating institutional capacity.

During the initiative's operational phase, the source of funds was diverse and public funding still played a key role. Very well-defined public–private mechanisms were established to support PES in Costa Rica, protect watersheds in Quito, to develop public transport in Curitiba and to boost the national solar water heater industry in Barbados. The private sector is fully engaged in the Barbados and Curitiba initiatives, in which it reacted positively to the financial incentives provided by public funding. Fiscal policies are in place to support PES in Costa Rica and to drive Sustainable Urban Development in Curitiba. In Barbados, the solar water heater initiative is fully funded and driven by fiscal policies.

Multilateral development finance institutions (e.g. IDB and the World Bank), and bilateral development finance institutions (e.g. the French Development Agency, Dutch Entrepreneurial Development Bank FMO, the German Development Fund and USAID) have played a key role in supporting all these initiatives (with the exception of solar water heaters in Barbados). In Curitiba, IDB provided several loans and grants to the local government for developing the transport system and implementing sustainable urban policies. The World Bank is involved in forest protection in Costa Rica through the provision of loans and grants. Bilateral development finance institutions have provided financial assistance through grants.

TABLE 13.6 Type of Funding by Initiative and Phase

Initiatives	*Initiative-specific funding*			*General funding: allocations from other sources*
	Capacity building: research and development, institutional capacity	*Initiation: capital expenditures, set-up costs*	*Maintenance: funding for operating costs*	
National Forestry Financing Fund, Costa Rica	FONAFIFO was established by public funds to set up PES for forest management.	A fiscal policy was started to nourish the fund (3.5% of the fuel tax).	Through a PES scheme nourished by contributions from public funds (3.5% of the fuel tax), public–private partnerships and Certificates of Environmental Services (buyers of these certificates receive an equivalent deduction in their income tax)	Grants from the World Bank and the German Development Fund Loan from the World Bank
Water Protection Fund, Quito, Ecuador	A study supported by a USAID grant recommended the creation of a water protection scheme based on local funding.	Seed capital provided by public enterprises and donors	Semi-PES scheme Public enterprises and minor contributions from institutional and private donors	Grants from USAID, the German Development Fund, Dutch Entrepreneurial Development Bank, Inter-American Development Bank and in-kind payment from the Environmental Systems Research Institute

Solar Water Heater initiative in Barbados	A public grant to the private sector helped spur the development of a marketable solar water heater.	A loan from a public bank helped the private sector to carry out the first project.	Fiscal policies (i.e. tax reductions) aim to encourage the use of solar water heaters. Three private companies dominate the Barbadian solar water heater market.	Minor solar water heater donations to households by the government
Sustainable Urban Development in Curitiba, Brazil	Public funds founded the Institute for Research and Urban Planning of Curitiba and designed the city's sustainable development plan.	Public and private funds	Public–private partnerships for the Bus Rapid Transit system and for the industrial city of Curitiba Fiscal policies to finance slum relocation, park construction and heritage preservation Inter-American Development Bank loans to government of Curitiba for improving public transport	Inter-American Development Bank grant for urban development French Development Agency grant for transport and biodiversity conservation

Green economy performance

When applying the grading system developed in Section 2 to the four environmental initiatives with the aim of assessing their green economy performance, we obtain the following findings (see Table 13.7).

National forestry financing fund, Costa Rica

The PES system to protect forests in Costa Rica shows good performance for the three pillars of sustainable development and can therefore be considered a green economy success story. The PES scheme in Costa Rica contributes to forest expansion, includes special provisions to enhance social inclusiveness, has boosted the forest industry and has fostered private investments to the sector. Sub-national studies show that the PES scheme has lowered deforestation rates and contributed to forest expansion (Daniels et al. 2010). From 2000 to 2010, net forest cover increased by approximately 23,000 hectares per year (FAO 2010). In the initial stage of the initiative, social aspects were not sufficiently taken into account, but some recent measures have enhanced minority access to the programme, including abolishing the requirement of land ownership, introducing PES for agroforestry services and prioritizing cantons with a low social development index (Madrigal et al. 2006). Furthermore, reforestation activities are at least 33% of permanent employment in the forestry sector (Arias 2004).

Forest plantations have become the largest permanent cultivation in the country, contributing more than $141 million to the gross domestic product in 2001. The forest industry has experienced significant growth since the 1997 implementation of PES, reaching an installed capacity of 446 cubic metres of timber per year in 2001. The PES has also fostered private investments in the forestry sector. For example, from 1997 to 2002, private investments were four times the investment made by FONAFIFO (Arias 2004). The initiative shows that a significant growth of the forestry industry can not only be achieved with forest depletion but can also go hand in hand with sustainable forest management and expansion of forest covers, creating a long-term source of revenue.

Water protection fund, Quito, Ecuador

This initiative obtains low evaluations for the three dimensions. In terms of real impact on ecosystem protection, improved watershed management has only been implemented in 65,000 of the potential 520,000 hectares (UNEP 2010). Furthermore, there is no reliable evidence about positive environmental changes that the set of all upstream projects financed by FONAG have produced on the availability and quality of water in Quito. Only a few projects produced observable positive local impacts (Pérez et al. 2006). Concerning social inclusiveness, despite the fact that more than 1,800 farmers upstream are estimated to receive indirect economic benefits (UNEP 2010), there are no specific provisions to ensure social

TABLE 13.7 Green Performance of the Initiatives

Initiatives	*Green performance based on evidence*		
	Ecosystem protection	*Social equity*	*Economic growth*
National Forestry Financing Fund, Costa Rica	Good: PES scheme has lowered deforestation rates and contributed to forest expansion.	Good: Although social aspects were not sufficiently taken into account during the initial stages, some recent measures have readdressed this issue.	Good: Forest plantations and the forest industry have experienced a significant growth and contributed significantly to the gross domestic product. The PES has fostered private investments in the forestry sector.
Water Protection Fund, Quito, Ecuador	Poor: There is no reliable evidence about positive environmental changes that the set of all upstream projects have produced on the availability and quality of water in Quito.	Poor: There are no specific provisions to ensure social inclusiveness.	Poor: There is no reliable evidence that the initiative is contributing to the economic growth of the areas where it is operating.
Solar water heaters in Barbados	Good: This initiative provides global and local environmental benefits.	Medium: Fiscal exceptions have yielded positive results among middle-income households. However, tax incentives do not guarantee the inclusion of the poorest households.	Good: The programme has had a positive spill-over effect on the overall economy.
Sustainable Urban Development in Curitiba, Brazil	Good: This initiative has had very positive impacts on the environment and society.	Good: This initiative has effectively addressed social inclusiveness.	Good: Sustainable development policies have fostered economic development.

inclusiveness. Furthermore, as decisions in FONAG are made by constituents based on their financial contribution, there is a risk of social exclusion (Pérez et al. 2006).

It is not clear whether this initiative is contributing to the project area's economic development. Though some projects are creating the right conditions for developing ecotourism and forestry sector activities, there is no reliable evidence that the initiative is contributing to the economic growth of the areas where it is operating. Since a sound evaluation of the eventual economic, social and environmental benefits of the initiative is absent, the initiative cannot yet be considered a green economy success story, nor can it serve as an example for replication in other areas. A possible explanation might lie in the amount of funding that was made available, which is quite modest, considering the forest area it needs to protect in order to ensure the qualitative and sufficient water supply to the city of Quito. FONAG is the only initiative among the four that is not state-controlled.

Solar water heaters in Barbados

The solar water heater initiative in Barbados obtains good evaluations for environmental sustainability and economic development, and a medium grade in social equity. It provides global and local environmental benefits due to the reduction of fossils fuels. The use of solar water heaters contributes to the reduction of climate change and local air pollution by reducing the consumption of fossil fuels (and consequently greenhouse gas emissions and air pollutants). For example, in 2002 carbon savings amounted to 15,000 metric tons, which represented 4% of the emissions from all Barbadian carbon sources. Fiscal exceptions have yielded positive results among middle-income households. However, tax incentives might not be the most appropriate instrument to achieve the inclusion of the poorest households, which do not have sufficient income to qualify for a tax deduction (Perlack and Hinds 2003).

The programme has had positive spill-over effects on the overall economy. It has fostered the creation and further development of the solar water heater industry in Barbados, which has become the most consolidated in the Caribbean. Sixty percent of the heaters are produced locally (Government of Barbados and IDB 2010). The country has the developing world's highest per capita rate of solar water heater installations. In 2009, 324 heaters were in operation per 1,000 inhabitants (Weiss and Mauthner 2011). Economic benefits have been larger that the tax costs. The cumulative tax cost of solar water heater incentives is estimated at about $10.8 million through 2002, whereas the cumulative value for energy savings is in the order of $134 million (Perlack and Hinds 2003). Furthermore, Barbados benefits from the initiative, as its reduced dependence on fossil fuel imports renders the country less vulnerable to the effects of shocks in the international oil price.

Sustainable urban development in Curitiba, Brazil

The Sustainable Urban Development initiative resulted in very positive impacts on environment and society, enhanced social inclusiveness and fostered economic development in the city.

The initiative has achieved several environmental benefits, including an increase in the green area per person from 1 square metres in 1970 to 50 square metres in 2008. Of all trips in the city, 45% are made in public transport; 32%, on foot or bike using the city's 120-kilometre network of bike lanes. Moreover, the city has low levels of unregulated waste dumping. Around 13% of waste is recycled. Proper tire collection has reduced dengue disease by 99.7%. Furthermore, relocating and improving slum areas and replacing them with green spaces have led to more effective water regulation. Curitiba has one of the lowest rates of ambient air pollution in Brazil due to the strengthening of public transport, the creation of green areas and the good environmental regulation of the industrial city. Greenhouse gas emissions in the area have dropped (World Bank 2010).

Sustainable Urban Development in Curitiba has had a favourable impact on social inclusiveness. It has achieved a positive effect on job creation (estimated at 200,000 jobs). The garbage collection programme has created alternative sources of income for the poorest. Income from the sale of recyclables is being used to support social programmes. Slum areas have decreased and areas for unofficial occupancy have been designed and included in the city planning. The decentralization of city services to areas that are easily reached by public transport has significantly increased the social inclusiveness of the services provided. The flat 'social fare' for public transport has benefitted around 80% of the population, especially the poorest as they tend to commute over longer distances. In addition, the city has provided compensation when relocating slums and promoted the diversity of income groups in new neighbourhoods (World Bank 2010).

Sustainable development policies have fostered economic development. The reorganization of the city and the creation of an industrial city have boosted economic growth. Curitiba's Industrial City produces 20% of Paraná's exports and it accounts for 25% of the state's value added tax revenue on sales and services. After three decades, the industrial city hosts more than 7,000 companies, including the car manufacturer that produces Bus Rapid Transit system buses. By improving infrastructure and traffic plans, the city has saved on construction costs. The Bus Rapid Transit system pays for itself without government subsidies. It has also helped to diminish economic losses that result from traffic congestion. The cost of building parks and relocating slums has been estimated at five times less than the projected cost of building concrete canals to control the significant flood risk. Preservation of culture and heritage maintains a lively cityscape and attracts tourism (World Bank 2010).

Lessons learned and opportunities for improvement

Strengths

The analysis of these initiatives helps to draw some lessons learned and identify their potential for improvement. When determining the main strengths, weaknesses, challenges and opportunities of the initiatives, we arrive at the conclusions that can be found in Table 13.8.

TABLE 13.8 Strengths, Weaknesses, Challenges, Opportunities Matrix

Initiatives	*Strengths*	*Weaknesses*	*Challenges*	*Opportunities*
National Forestry Financing Fund, Costa Rica	• Flexibility on adapting regulations over time for obtaining funding sources • Effective compliance and monitoring mechanisms	• There are not enough incentives for attracting the participation of some kinds of landholders and some modalities	• Available funding covers only a percentage of the requests	• To look for new sources of international funding mechanisms (e.g. REDD+)
Water Protection Fund, Quito, Ecuador	• Political and financial stability	• There are incentives for free-riding • The water price does not reflect watershed protection costs • Scientific basis for benefits is weak • Low monitoring and compliance for watershed protection	• Current funding is insufficient to improve watershed protection activities	• To transit into a well-defined PES scheme
Solar water heaters in Barbados	• Appropriate mix of fiscal and trade incentives	• Fiscal incentives attract mainly middle-income households	• High up-front costs of solar water heaters	• To extend to other Barbadian sectors and Caribbean countries
Sustainable Urban Development in Curitiba, Brazil	• Well-interconnected social, economic and environmental policies • Leadership and continuity • Institutionalized planning	• Lack of regional integration	• Population growth, also due to immigration • Changing consumption patterns	• To launch an initiative beyond the borders of Curitiba that integrates the social, environmental and economic aspects

The strengths of the policies are as diverse as the policies themselves. The high flexibility in obtaining funding, the capacity to adapt over time and the strong compliance mechanisms are strengths of the PES scheme in Costa Rica. The PES scheme is supported by several complementary regulations, some of which can be adapted over time. This initiative includes randomized monitoring visits to farms, undertaken by both independent evaluators and external audits. It also allows for flexibility for obtaining funding sources (Madrigal et al. 2006).

FONAG, in Ecuador, shows both political and financial stability in its operations. The initiative is a local solution, financed by private resources and without direct intervention by the government (Pérez et al. 2006).

In the Barbados initiative, the appropriate mix of fiscal measures and custom incentives for encouraging solar water heater use is the strong point. These have allowed the development of a national solar hot water industry and promoted the introduction of solar water heaters by households.

Sustainable Urban Development's success is based on the implementation of a coherent approach, the leadership of local authorities and the institutionalization of urban planning. It is based on well-interconnected social, economic and environmental policies. There has been significant and consistent political commitment to sustainable urban planning. The Institute for Research and Urban Planning of Curitiba as a public institution of the municipality has provided integrated, cross-sector urban planning and monitoring for several decades (World Bank 2010).

Weaknesses

All policies present weaknesses that will affect long-term sustainability if unaddressed. In the Costa Rican initiative, transaction costs for landholders are still high (15%) and landholders who face high opportunity costs resulting from forest preservation do not have sufficient incentives to participate. Some PES modalities, such as reforestation projects, have been disadvantaged because of specific requirements. For example, landholders who apply for reforestation projects are required to pause their agricultural activities until assessment and procurement processes have ended, which can entail economic losses. Incentives to attract landholders, who face high opportunity costs, have been insufficient (Madrigal et al. 2006).

FONAG has to resolve free-riding problems, internalize watershed protection costs, improve the scientific basis of the scheme and strengthen monitoring and compliance. Concerning free-riding, as financial contributions to the fund are voluntary, there are incentives for small beneficiaries to not contribute to the payment for services provided. Further, the current water fees do not include the full cost of services provided, which include watershed protection. The mechanism's implementation was not based on scientific data about the hydrology of the area. With regard to monitoring and compliance, there is no reliable monitoring of the impacts of sustainable management activities on the improvement of water flows nor are there any penalties for lack of compliance (Pérez et al. 2006).

The solar water heater initiative in Barbados should find ways to include both the higher and lower-income households in the programme because, despite the high rate of solar water heater penetration, fiscal measures do not sufficiently encourage the introduction of solar water heaters in the lower-income households. Further, the measures do sufficiently incentivize higher income households that prefer electric water heaters over rooftop solar panels for aesthetic reasons (Perlack and Hinds 2003).

The achievements of Curitiba's initiative are at stake if a better regional integration is not reached. Integration in the rest of the state could be improved. Polluting industries are being authorized to settle in surrounding municipalities, and Curitiba's water supply depends on reservoirs controlled by other municipalities (Lubow 2007). Additionally, as a result of migration and a lack of innovation of the BRT system since its introduction, Curitiba's achievements are partially offset (e.g. car ownership has risen and use of public transport has decreased). Currently, the policy is by-passed by other cities inspired by Curitiba's example (Giacomini Martínez et al., 2016).

Challenges

A lack of funding presents the main challenge to three of the initiatives. In Costa Rica, funding is available only for 40% of the participation requests that comply with the PES eligibility requirements (Madrigal et al. 2006). FONAG finances only 13% of the 520,000 upstream hectares of watersheds. Financial resources obtained to date are insufficient to include the whole area of the two ecological reserves in sustainable management activities (Pérez et al. 2006). In Barbados, where the funding for the initiative originates from final consumers directly, the lack of financing facilities to overcome the high upfront costs is an economic barrier for the lower-income households to the point that monthly repayment rates equal the installed and electric costs for electric water heaters (Schwerin 2010).

The main challenges to Urban Sustainable Development in Curitiba are shifting consumption patterns and population growth. Successful economic growth has led to increased car ownership. A measure to counter this might be to continuously upgrade the public transport system in order to remain an appealing alternative to private vehicles (Lubow 2007). Migration has become a major challenge for sustaining this policy over time. The city's population has tripled between 1970 and 2008 (World Bank 2011), and although the number of people living in slums is much lower in Curitiba than in other Brazilian cities, slum inhabitants still compose 8% of the city's population (Grostein 2001).

Opportunities

Finally, opportunities for improvement and learning are manifold. For example, in order to increase availability of funding, FONAFIFO needs to be able to integrate new international financial mechanisms that compensate forest protection. An example could be the Reducing Emissions from Deforestation and Degradation (REDD) scheme under the United Nations Framework Convention on Climate Change. FONAFIFO is currently involved in the REDD readiness phase financed by the World Bank/Forest Carbon Partnership Facility. The REDD readiness package also includes the development of a national forest baseline, the creation of a national measurement, reporting and verification system and the development of an environmental and social management framework that includes consultation processes involving all relevant stakeholders (World Bank 2009). These elements could significantly strengthen the PES scheme.

FONAG has the potential to evolve towards a well-defined PES scheme for watershed protection that guarantees water provision to the city of Quito. Once consolidated as a PES scheme, it could be able to take the advantages of a REDD+ mechanism to obtain better access to international funding. However, in order to become a PES scheme, the initiative needs to adopt adequate supportive legislation and regulation, strengthen tenure security in the basins, enhance the scientific basis of the activities with regard to the local hydrology (specifically concerning the link between watershed protection and water supply), include provisions to address leakage issues and provide guarantees that water supply and treatment will remain affordable for the poorest inhabitants of Quito (Pérez et al. 2006).

Barbados faces the same kind of challenges as other Caribbean nations with respect to high fuel costs. For this reason, the Barbados solar water heater initiative has a high potential for replication in the region. The potential solar water heater market in the Caribbean is estimated at 798,000 solar water heater units (based on an envisaged penetration rate of between 10 to 50%, depending on the country (Solar Dynamics 2010). Barbadian solar water heater manufacturers are already creating the conditions that will allow them to meet this market demand. Strengthening current regional frameworks for renewable energy could help to create the enabling environment. This could be achieved, for example, through the Caribbean Renewable Energy Development Programme launched in 1998 by the Caribbean Community and UNDP (Schwerin 2010). Furthermore, solar water heater use could be extended beyond the domestic use, which would scale up the use of solar energy in Barbados.

Similarly, the Sustainable Urban Development initiative in Curitiba could be extended to other cities. The launch of an ambitious initiative beyond the borders of Curitiba that integrates the social, environmental and economic aspects will enable a lasting progress and will prevent development disparities within the region.

Since 2014, all four initiatives have growth, matured and served as a model for other countries. For instance, the Payments for Environmental Services pioneered by Costa Rica has become particularly common in Latin America, embraced by countries like Mexico, Colombia and Chile. More than 20 water protection funds have seen the light in Latin America countries. They are organized under the 'The Latin American Alliance of Water Funds'.[5] The solar water heater experience of Barbados has been expanded to the other Caribbean countries which are providing incentives to promote renewable energy such as Jamaica in building its own wind development and Dominica have all sought to develop geothermal energy projects (The Guardian, 2015). Sustainable Urban Development continues in Curitiba where a new Land Zoning, Use and Occupation Law was adopted late 2019 which will guide the future development of the city for the next 10 years with the support of several public–private programmes.[6]

Conclusion

The main objective of this research is to measure the environmental, social and economic performance of environmental initiatives that have been touted as green economy success stories by diverse international organizations, including UNEP. The chapter assessed in detail four policies that are currently being implemented in Latin America and the Caribbean, covering four sectors (forests, freshwater, renewable technologies and cities). We propose a methodological framework that includes evidence-based criteria and a grading system built on existing indicators. In addition, the study analyses the enabling conditions that favoured the development of the initiatives, the ways in which they are operated and financed and the main challenges and opportunities for further improvement and strengthening. The application of our method to the four case studies revealed the following conclusions.

First, despite the fact that the environmental initiatives assessed are catalysing the transition from a business as usual development pathway to one that is more resource efficient and socially inclusive, not all fulfil the criteria of green economy policies. The PES scheme for forest protection in Costa Rica and the Sustainable Urban Development initiative in Curitiba, Brazil can clearly be considered 'green economy success stories', as they show good performance for the three pillars of sustainable development. These initiatives are closely followed by the solar water heater initiative in Barbados, which obtains good economic and environmental performance. However, the initiative receives a medium grade on social equity, as the programme does not yet guarantee full social inclusion (particularly as it excludes lower-income households from its potential benefits). FONAG, in Ecuador, is far from reaching the criteria of a green economy policy because there is no reliable evidence regarding the positive impact of upstream watershed management on the availability and quality of Quito's water resources. The way that the fund operates does not guarantee that programmes and projects will enhance social inclusion, and it is not clear that this initiative is contributing to the protected area's economic development.

Second, despite the fact that the enabling conditions that promoted the initiatives differed, some key elements for policy-making can be identified: the establishment of sound regulatory frameworks, the full engagement of local leaders and the success of employing public funds to leverage private investments for addressing environmental issues.

Third, the analysis of the strengths, weaknesses, challenges and opportunities of these environmental initiatives shows that the strengths of the policies are as diverse as the policies themselves (e.g. flexibility on both obtaining funding and adapting over time in FONAFIFO, political and finance stability in FONAG, the appropriate mix of fiscal measures in Barbados and the implementation of a coherent approach in Curitiba). All policies present weaknesses that must be addressed in order to improve their effectiveness and likelihood of long-term sustainability (e.g. transaction costs are still high for landholders in the PES scheme in Costa Rica, free-riding problems in FONAG, economic barriers for customers in Barbados and population growth in Curitiba). The main challenge faced by the policies is a lack of funding.

Fourth, despite the progress made since the first edition of this chapter (2014) in the development of measurements frameworks for assessing green economy progress and performance, the approach presented in this chapter remains valid for assessing specific green economy initiatives, in spite of their geographical diversity. Alternative methodologies developed so far have a national or sub-national scope, preventing the evaluation of the impacts of single initiatives and policies. Furthermore, the evidence-based criteria and a grading system are relevant to assess how the green economy initiatives are contributing to the SDGs.

Finally, we recognize that this research has two main caveats. First, for the assessment of the initiatives, we have relied on the accuracy of previous studies, studies that were not all peer-reviewed papers. Furthermore, the sample of policies may not be enough to draw general conclusions. In order to overcome these drawbacks, we recommend enlarging the number of initiative assessments and following a participatory approach with key stakeholders involved in their development and operation.

Notes

1 Some of these methodologies have been adapted to a sub-national level such as the Green Economy Progress Index, which has been used to measure Green Industry Progress in 18 Chinese Provinces (PAGE, 2019).
2 We based our choice on the set of indicators to assess environmental sustainability both in natural capital and in economic sectors proposed by the OECD (2011), which is presently the most complete and practical.
3 An important impact variable that is missing from this listing is governance. However, to the extent that good governance is required to achieve many impacts related to social equity, we assume that presence of good governance is necessary and implicit in the indicators we have laid out. Most indicators are criticized because they ignore enabling conditions and changes in the baseline contextual conditions.
4 FONAFIFO was established under the Payments for Environmental Services programme, by Forestry Law 7575 of 1997.
5 More information about 'The Latin American Alliance of Water Funds' is available at https://www.fondosdeagua.org/es/que-es-la-alianza/, last accessed 20 January 2020.
6 Additional information about recent development of Curitiba's urban planning is available at https://www.curitiba.pr.gov.br/noticias/prefeito-sanciona-a-nova-lei-de-zoneamento-uso-e-ocupacao-do-solo-de-curitiba/53099, last accessed 20 January 2020.

References

Acosta, L.A., P. Maharjan, H. Peyriere, L. Galotto, R.J. Mamiit, C. Ho, B.H. Flores, and O. Anastasia., Green growth index: Concepts, methods and applications, GGGI technical report No. 5, Green Growth Performance Measurement (GGPM) Program, Global Green Growth Institute, Seoul. In: B.H. Flores, A. Sharma, A. Jacob et al., *Green Growth Index: Concept, Methods and Applications*, 2019, available at http://greengrowthindex.gggi.org/wp-content/uploads/2019/12/Green-Growth-Index-Technical-Report_s1213.pdf, accessed January 20 2020.

Agence Française de Développement (AFD), 2011, *Supporting sustainable urban mobility in Curitiba,* available at www.afd.fr/en/carte-des-projets/supporting-sustainable-urban-mobility-curitiba, accessed May 2 2013.

Arias, G., *Análisis del Impacto Económico y Social de las Plantaciones. Forestales en Costa Rica, Fundación para el Desarrollo de la. Cordillera Volcánica Central (FUNDECOR)*, San José, Costa Rica, 2004

Cisneros, J. and P. Loret, El fondo para la protección del agua. mecanismo financiero para la conservación y el cudado del agua en Quito, seminario internacional 'cogestión de cuencas hidrográficas experiencias y desafíos', 2008, available at http://orton.catie.ac.cr/repdoc/A2983e/A2983e11.pdf, accessed May 3 2013.

Daniels, A.E., K. Bagstad, V. Esposito, A. Moulaert and C.M. Rodriguez, 'Understanding the impacts of Costa Rica's PES: Are we asking the right questions?', *Ecological Economics*, 69: 2116–2126, 2010.

de Oliveira, M., "A trajetório do discurso ambiental em Curitiba (1960–2000)", *Revista de Sociologia Política*, 16: 97–106, 2001.

Echavarria, M. and P. Arroyo, *'Financing Watershed Conservation: The FONAG Water Fund in Quito, Ecuador'*, Quito, The Nature Conservancy, 2002.

Food and Agriculture Organization (FAO), 2010, '*Global Forest Resources Assessment 2010*', available at http://www.fao.org/3/i1757e/i1757e00.htm, accessed December 17 2020.

Food and Agriculture Organization (FAO), 2011, '*The Republic of Costa Rica: General Information*', available at http://www.fao.org/countryprofiles/index/en/?iso3=CRI, accessed August 20 2013.

Fund for Water Protection (FONAG), 2012, available at http://www.fonag.org.ec/inicio/english-version.html, accessed August 20 2013.

Giacomini Martínez, J., I. Boas, J. Lenhart and A.P.J. Mol, Revealing Curitiba's flawed sustainability: How discourse can prevent institutional change. *Habitat International*, 53, 2016.

Government of Barbados and Inter-American Development Bank (IDB), '*Sustainable Energy Framework for Barbados*', Barbados 2010.

Grostein, M.D., "*Metrópole e Expansão Urbana: A Persistência de Processos 'Insustentáveis'' São Paulo em Perspetivam* 15 (1): 13, 2001.

Headley O., *'Barbados Renewable Energy Scenario: Current Status and rojections to 2010', Centre for Research Management and Environmental Studies*, Faculty Science and Technology, Barbados, 2001, available at http://www.terryally.com/library/oheadleyrenewable.html, accessed August 20 2013.

Inter-American Development Bank (IDB), '*BR0209: Urban Transport Curitiba*', 1995, available at http://www.iadb.org/en/projects/project,1303.html?id=BR0209, accessed May 5 2013.

Inter-American Development Bank (IDB), '*BR0375 : Urban Transportation Curitiba II*', Washington DC, 2004, available at http://www.iadb.org/en/projects/project,1303.html?id BR0375, accessed May 10 2013.

Inter-American Development Bank (IDB), '*Bienes y servicios ambientales: mercados no tradicionales, mecanismos de financiamiento y buenas prácticas en América Latina y el Caribe*', Washington DC, 2006, available at https://publications.iadb.org/es/publicacion/15361/bienes-y-servicios-ambientales-mercados-no-tradicionales-mecanismos-de, accessed December 17 2020.

Inter-American Development Bank (IDB), '*BR-L1083: PROCIDADES-Curitiba: Curitiba Integrated Social and Urban Development*', Washington DC, 2009, available at http://www.iadb.org/en/projects/project,1303.html?id BR-L1083, accessed May 5 2013.

Inter-American Development Bank (IDB), '*BR-T1165: Support to Improve City Logistics Performance in Curitiba*', Washington, DC, 2011, available at http://www.iadb.org/en/projects/project,1303.html?id BR-T1165, accessed May 10 2013.

International Institute for Environment and Development (IIED), *Watershed markets, Case studies: Costa Rica – national payment for environmental services (PES) programme*, available at http://www.watershedmarkets.org/casestudies/Costa_Rica_National_PES_eng.html, accessed August 20 2013.

Lubow, A., 'Recycle city: The road to Curitiba', *New York Times*, 20 May 2007, available at http://www.nytimes.com/2007/05/20/magazine/20Curitiba-t.html?pagewanted all, accessed August 20 2013.

Madrigal R., and F. Alpízar, 'Fondo Nacional del Agua, Ecuador'. In: F. Alpízar, C.J. Pérez, M. Niklitschek, M. Otárola, and R. Madrigal, eds., *Buenas Prácticas en la Aplicación de Mecanismos de Financiamiento para la obtención de Servicios Ambientales de Prácticas Forestales y Agrícolas Sostenibles en América Latina y El Caribe*, Red de Medio Ambiente, Chapter 4, 1-12, IDB, 2006.

Madrigal, R., F. Alpízar and M. Otárola, 'Fondo Nacional de Financiamiento Forestal, Costa Rica'. In: F. Alpízar, C.J. Pérez, M. Niklitschek, M. Otárola, and R. Madrigal, eds., *Buenas Prácticas en la Aplicación de Mecanismos de Financiamiento para la obtención de Servicios Ambientales de Prácticas Forestales y Agrícolas Sostenibles en América Latina y El Caribe*, Red de Medio Ambiente, Chapter 5 1-18, LOCATION, IDB, National Fund for Forest Financing (FONAFIFO), 2006, available at http://www.fonafifo.go.cr/paginas_espanol/proyectos/e_pr_reforesta.htm, accessed August 20 2013.

Organisation for Economic Co-operation and Development (OECD), '*Towards Green Growth: Monitoring Progress OECD Indicators*', Paris, 2011, available at http://www.oecd.org/dataoecd/37/33/48224574.pdf, accessed May 15 2013.

PAGE, '*The Green Economy Progress Measurement Framework – Methodology*', 2017, Geneva, available at https://www.un-page.org/files/public/gep_methodology.pdf, accessed January 20 2020.

PAGE, '*Green Industry Progress Index for 18 Chinese Provinces*', 2019, Geneva, available at https://www.un-page.org/files/public/green_industry_progress_index_for_18_chinese_provinces.pdf, accessed January 20 2020.

Pérez, C. J., M. Niklitschek, M. Otárola and R. Madrigal, '*Bienes y Servicios Ambientales: Mercados no Tradicionales, Mecanismos de Financiamiento y Buenas Prácticas en América Latina y el Caribe*', Turrialba, Costa Rica, Inter-American Development Bank, 2006.

Perlack, B. and W. Hinds, 'Evaluation of the Barbados solar water heating experience', 2003, available at http://solardynamicsltd.com/wp-content/uploads/2010/07/SWH-report1-2.pdf, accessed April 30 2013.

Rabinovitch, J., 'Curitiba: Towards sustainable urban development', *Environment and Urbanization*, 4(2): 62–73, 1992.

Rabinovitch, J. and J. Leitman, 'Urban planning in Curitiba'. In: S.M. Wheeler and T. Beatley, ed., *The Sustainable Urban Development Reader*, 237–248, London, Routledge, 2004.

Schwerin, A., '*Solar Market Study: Analysis of the Potential Market for Solar Energy in the Caribbean*', Saint Lucia, Caribbean Renewable Energy Development Programme (CREDP), 2010.

Solar Dynamics, '*The financial benefits of solar hot water systems to Barbados', Presentation*, 2010, available at http://solardynamicsltd.com/wp-content/uploads/2010/05/SOLARSEPT12Presentation-Central-BankFinal.pdf, accessed August 20 2013.

Strange, T. and A. Bayley, 'Sustainable development: Linking economy, society, environment', Paris Organisation for Economic Co-Operation and Development (OECD), 2008, available at http://www.oecd-library.org/docserver/download/0108121e.pdf?expires=1377044745&idid&accnameguest&checksum6B802779B854B54F95E142EC02A7CBB4, accessed May 30 2013.

Stuart, F., 'Launch of the government of Barbados-United Nations Environment Programme Partnership for a resource efficient green economy in Barbados and the undertaking of a green economy scoping study by the University of the West Indies, Cave Hill Campus, address', 2011, available at http://www.pnuma.org/documento/DISCURSO%20PRIMER%20MINISTRO%20BARBADOS.pdf, accessed August 20 2013.

The Guardian, 'Is the Caribbean a paradise for renewable energy?', 2015, available at https://www.theguardian.com/global-development-professionals-network/2015/aug/06/caribbean-paradise-for-renewable-energy, accessed January 20 2020.

United Nations, '*The future we want*', Outcome of the United Nations Conference on Sustainable Development. Rio de Jaineiro, Brazil, 20–22 June 2012, available at http://www.uncsd2012.org/content/documents/727The%20Future%20We%20Want%2019%20June%201230pm.pdf, accessed May 10 2013.

United Nations Environment Programme (UNEP) , '*Green Economy: Developing Countries Success Stories*', Nairobi, 2010, available at http://www.unep.org/pdf/GreenEconomy_SuccessStories.pdf, accessed August 10 2013.

UNEP, '*Green Economy Report: Pathways to Sustainable Development and Poverty Eradication*', Nairobi, 2011, available at http://www.unep.org/greeneconomy/Portals/88/documents/ger/ger_final_dec_2011/Green%20EconomyReport_Final_Dec2011.pdf, accessed August 10 2013.

UNEP, '*Measuring Progress Towards a Green Economy*', Nairobi, 2012, available at http://www.unep.org/greeneconomy/Portals/88/documents/research_products/MeasuringProgress.pdf, accessed August 10 2013.

Villatoro, P. and J.C. Feres, '*A System of Indicators for Monitoring Social Cohesion in Latin America*', Santiago, Chile, Economic Commission for Latin America and the Caribbean (ECLAC), 2007, available at http://www.eclac.cl/publicaciones/xml/1/33911/LCG2362i.pdf, accessed August 10 2013.

Weiss, W. and F. Mauthner, '*Solar Heat Worldwide: Markets and Contribution to the Energy supply 2009*', Paris, France, International Energy Agency (IEA), 2011, available at http://www.cansia.ca/sites/default/files/policy_and_research/2009_iea_solarheatworldwide.pdf, accessed August 10 2013.

World Bank, Preparation Grant Agreement for Readiness Plan Readiness Fund of the FCPF Grant No. TF094486, 2009, available at https://forestcarbonpartnership.org/sites/forestcarbonpartnership.org/files/Documents/PDF/Nov2009/Costa_Rica_FCPF_R-PP_Formulation_Grant_Agreement.pdf, accessed August 23 2013.

World Bank, *Eco2 Cities: Ecological Cities as Economic Cities*, Washington, DC, 2010, available at http://siteresources.worldbank.org/INTURBANDEVELOPMENT/Resources/336387-1270074782769/Eco2_Cities_Book.pdf, accessed August 23 2013.

14

EVALUATING INTERNATIONAL SUPPORT FOR TRANSBOUNDARY AQUIFER MANAGEMENT PROGRAMMES

Alan Fox

Introduction

Over the past two decades there has been growing recognition of the transboundary nature of aquifers – systems that cross the borders of at least two countries – and a corresponding increase in international support for managing these complex systems. This chapter considers these shared groundwater resources within the broader, global context of potable water supplies and intensifying water stresses. The chapter notes the legal and development assistance frameworks for international support to developing countries on transboundary aquifer issues and examines a subset of five transboundary aquifer projects implemented with Global Environmental Facility (GEF) support. Evaluative evidence from these projects is used to highlight common issues and lessons for consideration in future transboundary aquifer projects.

Significance of transboundary aquifers

Water scarcity[1] is adding to the difficulties of supplying potable water to poor persons; increasing demand and shifting weather patterns are exacerbating these difficulties. UN-Water notes that

> around 1.2 billion people or almost one-fifth of the world's population, live in areas of physical scarcity, and 500 million people are approaching this situation. Another 1.6 billion people, or almost one quarter of the world's population, face economic water shortage (where countries lack the necessary infrastructure to take water from rivers and aquifers). (United Nations Educational, Scientific and Cultural Organization [UN-Water, FAO 2007: 4)

By 2025, water shortages are forecast to broaden, with as many as 1.8 billion people living in areas with absolute water scarcity and two thirds of the world's population living under water-stressed conditions (UNESCO 2012).

The confluence of poverty and water scarcity exacts a heavy toll. The 'water poor' in water-stressed areas face persistent threats to their livelihoods due to hydrologic extremes. Excess pumping results in greater drawdowns, which increases energy costs to the poor. Persons forced to travel long distances to secure potable water face security risks and lose educational opportunities. There are elevated health risks from living in areas with high levels of water-associated diseases (e.g. bilharzia, cholera, guinea worm, malaria, trachoma, typhoid) (Puri and Aureli 2005).

Facing acute and growing water shortages, societies must consider all potential sources, and groundwater is an obvious choice where available. Aquifers contain almost 96% of the useable freshwater on earth (excepting freshwater locked up as ice; UNESCO 2012). Aquifers account for more than 70% of the water used in the European Union and are often one of the only sources – if not the only source – in arid and semi-arid zones. For example, aquifers account for 100% of water in Malta, 95% in Tunisia and 75% in Morocco (UNESCO 2012). Globally, 67% of groundwater is devoted to irrigation, 22% for domestic purposes and 11% for industry (Margat 2008; Integrated Groundwater Resources Assessment Centre [IGRAC] 2009; Siebert et al. 2010; Aquastat 2011; Eurostat 2013).

Aquifers underlying arid areas are typically (and logically) slow to recharge, and consequently are susceptible to rapid depletion. An analysis of global groundwater use and availability in six major aquifer systems (North Arabian, North China Plain, Persian, Upper Ganges, U.S. High Plains and western Mexico) found that all showed signs of acute overuse, that some recharge rates were inadequate to match withdrawals and that water tables were lowering precipitously (Gleeson et al. 2012). Some aquifers barely recharge at all. 'Fossil' aquifers, such as the Ogallala in the Midwest United States, the Sana'a Basin in Yemen and the vast Nubian aquifer system underlying parts of Chad, Egypt, Libya and Sudan are isolated from the streams that once fed them (Gleeson et al. 2012). In such systems, extraction equals depletion – the resource is non-renewable.

Most large aquifers are transboundary. The UNESCO–International Hydrological Programme has identified 273 transboundary aquifers in the world, which is roughly equal to the number of transboundary river basins: 68 transboundary aquifers are on the American continent, 38 in Africa, 65 in Eastern Europe, 90 in Western Europe and 12 in Asia. One hundred and sixty-six of these transboundary aquifer systems are larger than 5,000 square kilometers (GEF IEO 2018). At least 40% of the world's population resides in areas underlain by transboundary aquifers (IGRAC 2009).

International community engagement

International law and conventions

There are no binding international agreements setting out how governments should cooperate in managing transboundary aquifer systems. This reflects the very limited international legal structures for shared waters as a whole. Efforts to build a stronger legal basis include two UN General Assembly (UNGA) resolutions. The first, passed in July 2010, recognizes 'the right to safe and clean drinking water and sanitation as a human right that is essential for the full enjoyment of life and all human rights' (UNGA 2010: 2) The second, a nonbinding resolution adopted by consensus at the General Assembly in December 2011, seeks to establish a law of Transboundary Aquifers (UNGA 2011). The resolution builds from the International Law Commission Draft Articles on the Law of Transboundary Aquifers (2008), which were formally annexed to the UNGA resolution. The resolution encourages states concerned 'to make appropriate bilateral or regional arrangements for the proper management of their transboundary aquifers', including cooperation among states to prevent, reduce and control pollution of shared aquifers. Under this resolution, states are invited to consider the draft articles as a basis for the elaboration of a convention. The Law of Transboundary Waters has repeatedly come up for discussion in the General Assembly sixth committee; however, it has not progressed further, with some member states contending that bilateral and regional arrangements and agreements are more appropriate for addressing transboundary aquifer management issues.

Regionally, the body of transboundary aquifer legislation, treaties and other obligations is quite limited. This is not just a developing country phenomenon. Organisation for Economic Co-operation and Development (OECD) countries also generally lack formal treaties on aquifer management. For example, 36 aquifers have been identified as straddling the U.S.–Mexico border, many of which provide drinking water to large local populations. The need for a groundwater treaty between the two countries has been discussed and acknowledged as far back as 1973, through the International Boundary and Water Commission (IBWC 1973); yet the U.S. and Mexican governments have never signed an agreement or established guidance on how these systems should be managed (Eckstein 2011).

Official financial flows and international support for water and sanitation

International finance in the water and sanitation sector constitutes one of the largest areas of development assistance. Official financial flows in the water and sanitation sector have averaged 5% annual increases over the last decade, reaching US $14.3 billion in 2014–2015. Official development aid during this period was $8.2 billion, 58% of the total. Other official flows have averaged 13% increase per year since 2006–2007, and amount to $6 billion. In total annual aid commitments for all official donors (OECD), Germany (1.67 $billion) and Japan (1.1 $billion) are the largest donors in the sector. Low-income countries received 22% of total aid in the sector, closely matching the regional breakdown of 21% going to sub-Saharan Africa.

UN and multilateral agency attention to groundwater and aquifer management

In 1997, the International Association of Hydrologists established a Commission on Transboundary Aquifer Resources Management, coincidental to the adoption of the UN Convention on the Law of the Non-Navigational Uses of International Watercourses (UN Watercourses Convention). In 2000, the UNESCO

Intergovernmental Council at its 14th session approved joint activities on transboundary aquifer issues among the International Association of Hydrologists, the UNESCO International Hydrology Programme, the Food and Agriculture Organization and the UN Economic Commission for Europe. This joint effort produced a framework document on Internationally Shared Aquifer Resource Management. Subsequently, the programme has grown to include regional initiatives in the Americas, the Balkans and Europe (Puri & Aureli 2005).

The International Atomic Energy Agency fills an important technical niche in the effort to better manage transboundary aquifers. Agency experts use isotope science to determine the origin, age and renewal rate of groundwater and whether aquifers face contamination risks. Isotope techniques are particularly useful for mapping slow-recharge and non-renewable groundwater resources, which are at risk of rapid depletion if not managed carefully. The Agency has worked to model, characterize and monitor transboundary aquifer systems for a series of projects in Africa, Asia, Europe and Latin America, including the Nubian, North-western Sahara and Iullemeden Aquifer systems of Northern Africa and the Guaraní Aquifer in South America (International Atomic Energy Agency [IAEA] 2013).

The global environment facility

GEF was launched as a pilot effort in 1991 and broadened into a major global programme in 1994 (GEF 2013). The GEF brings 183 countries together with international institutions, civil society organizations and the private sector in order to address global environmental issues and support national sustainable development initiatives. GEF is an independently operating financial organization that provides grants for projects related to biodiversity, climate change, international waters, land degradation, the ozone layer and persistent organic pollutants (GEF 2013). GEF takes a multi-level approach in the international waters sector, providing support for global actions and conventions, regional (catchment) analysis and action planning, and support at national and local levels. By design, GEF is focused on achieving global environmental benefits, and its international waters portfolio covers nearly all large freshwater catchments globally, with 156 GEF recipient countries and 24 non-recipient countries cooperating on transboundary water resource management (GEF 2020).

Transboundary groundwater and aquifers were added to GEF programming during the 2nd fund replenishment (GEF-2), and now include 19 projects. Of these, all but two are focused on specific transboundary aquifers. Eight of the projects have been completed, using $27.83 million in GEF trust fund grants and an estimated $25.58 million in co-finance. The 11 with concepts or projects approved bring the total anticipated GEF trust fund commitment to $83.84 million, with an estimated $1.28 billion in anticipated cofinancing. Eight of the recently approved projects build from previous GEF transboundary aquifer projects (Guarani, Dinaric Karst, Nile Basin, Nubian Sandstone, Iullemeden Aquifer, SADC Groundwater, Nile Basin, Northwest Sahara).

The overriding development objective for most GEF transboundary aquifer projects is to help beneficiary countries jointly elaborate and implement a common institutional and technical framework for the management and preservation of the aquifer. The typical programme of support emulates the two-phase process developed and honed in the GEF International Water surface water programme: a transboundary diagnostic analysis is carried out to determine aquifer pressures and measures (Uitto 2004; Pernetta & Bewers 2012), then a Strategic Action Programme is drafted for partnering countries to agree on concrete actions designed to mitigate threats and protect the shared groundwater resource (Uitto 2004). Support is also provided for enhancing institutional capacities to manage groundwater and reduce pollutant risks. In addition, stakeholder awareness efforts are launched to change local perceptions in order to enable better groundwater management.

Evaluating GEF transboundary aquifer projects

For this analysis, five of the GEF transboundary aquifer projects that have been evaluated at project completion are presented: 1) The Iullemeden Aquifer System (Mali, Niger and Nigeria), 2) Northwest Sahara (Algeria, Libya and Tunisia); (3) Guaraní Aquifer (Argentina, Brazil, Paraguay and Uruguay); (4) Dinaric Karst Aquifer System (Albania, Bosnia-Herzegovina, Croatia and Montenegro); and (5) Southern African Development Community (SADC) Groundwater and Drought Management Project (covering 15 countries in Southern Africa and spanning 14 major transboundary aquifers).

The following is a brief explanation of each project and select evaluation findings.

Iullemeden aquifer system

The Iullemeden Aquifer System underlies Mali, Niger and Nigeria. These countries and the United Nations Environment Programme implemented a GEF-financed project from 2003 to 2007 (GEF provided $1 million of the $1.7 million project budget). The project was designed to establish joint mechanisms to identify risks and uncertainties relating to land use, climate change, extraction and other key drivers that could have an impact on the quality and quantity of water in the aquifer. The project was also expected to develop mechanisms to formulate policies for managing identified risks and uncertainties, and then to establish a legal and institutional cooperative framework among the three countries to address these risks (Hearns 2009).

An evaluation of the project was carried out in January 2009, taking into account the project's achievements beyond its June 2008 termination to include residual achievements through November 2008 (Hearns 2009). The evaluation methodology included interviews, site visits and a desk review of pertinent documents. In keeping with GEF evaluation guidance, the questions focused attention on a range of project design, implementation and outcome aspects (including efficiency, effectiveness and sustainability), the achievement of planned outputs and activities, the catalytic role played by the project, the monitoring and evaluation systems used and the extent of engagement with stakeholders.

The evaluation rated the project satisfactory across most of the evaluation criteria. The evaluator noted in particular that there was good cooperation at the technical level, especially in the transfer of information and data, and good cooperation in the effort to identifying risks to the groundwater resource through a transboundary diagnostic analysis. The project was slow in getting started, requiring 18 months for the project team to get up and running (Hearns 2009). On the positive side, the countries then formed a tripartite steering committee supported by a technical and scientific committee. The evaluator noted a continuing need to provide support to the countries in order to maintain the momentum of the project's outcomes. In particular, the evaluation report highlighted the importance of reaching agreement among the countries to develop and implement measures to minimize the risks of pollution and excessive drawdown of the aquifer and to organize for future close cooperation through a suitable regional institution (either an existing institution or one newly configured for this purpose). Another notable recommendation was to extend the hydrology analysis work to better clarify interactions between surface water and groundwater (Hearns 2009).

A follow on project has been approved, in January 2018, entitled: Improving IWRM, Knowledge-based Management and Governance of the Niger Basin and the Iullemeden-Taoudeni/Tanezrouft Aquifer System (NB-ITTAS). The new project is designed to build on previously separate surface and groundwater projects, integrating their strategic action plan implementation.

Northwest Sahara

The Northwest Sahara Aquifer System underlies Algeria, Libya and Tunisia. It is considered a non-renewable water source, as most of the area has virtually non-existent precipitation and there is no significant surface/ground water mixing. From 2003 to 2006, the three beneficiary countries and the United Nations Environment Programme implemented a GEF project as the second of a two-phase project, using \$600,000 in GEF funding and an additional \$816,000 in co-financing. The project design included expanding the use of a previously developed multi-layer mathematical model for the aquifer system in order to determine the water balance and to identify risks to the aquifer (e.g. excessive water pumping depths, drying up of the Tunisian outlet and salinization). The project also called for developing a water-quality monitoring network, conducting studies to determine water demand and for carrying out water cost analysis (Puyoo 2007).

An evaluation of the project was conducted in March 2007 and included interviews, site visits and a document review (Puyoo 2007). According to the evaluators, there were significant delays in getting the project started and it encountered difficulties in achieving planned outcomes. The planned water-quality monitoring network was not established, and a water-costing analysis was not done. More successfully, a synthesis of environmental impacts connected with exploitation of the aquifer was carried out and an action plan was proposed. Further, the project inventoried wetlands and developed reports on the causes and distribution of salty-soil zones. A permanent consultation mechanism was successfully put in place, signed by the three country ministers of water.

A follow up project was carried out for the North West Sahara Aquifer System, entitled: Reducing Risks to the Sustainable Management of the North West Sahara Aquifer System (NWSAS). The project was approved in 2009 and closed in 2018. It sought to address risks associated with unsustainable exploitation and management of groundwater resources in the NWSAS, to formulate and initially implement a set of actions, focusing on sustainable agricultural practices and environmental management. The project was structured around five linked components: (1) Socio-economic surveys; (2) Pilot demonstration projects; (3) Development of databases and GIS; (4) Support for a regional consultation mechanism; and (5) Project management. A terminal evaluation of the project in 2015, indicating that the planned socioeconomic surveys, databases and pilot demonstration projects were carried out as intended, with one pilot moved from Libya to Tunisia due to political instability. The Regional Consultation Mechanism expectations were less successful, with weaknesses in the set up and support provided to this mechanism. The evaluation notes that the likelihood of long-term impact achievement is not very high, due to the political climate in Algeria, Tunisia and Libya, with water resource management issues not high on the ledger of national priorities.

Guaraní aquifer

The Guaraní Aquifer underlies Argentina, Brazil, Paraguay and Uruguay. One of the world's largest aquifer systems; its current water storage is estimated at 37,000 cubic kilometres, and it has an estimated natural recharge rate of 166 cubic kilometres per year. 24 million persons live within the aquifer boundary area and another 70 million access it through water diversions (Erickson & Rogers 2006).

In 2000, the countries sharing the Guaraní aquifer launched the Environmental Protection and Sustainable Development of the Guaraní Aquifer Systems Project. The overall focus of the project was to support the partnering countries to elaborate and implement a common institutional and technical framework for the management and preservation of the aquifer. GEF contributed $13.4 million and the partner countries equally contributed an additional $12 million, with small contributions from other donors. More than 80 percent of the project's $26.8 million budget was allocated to research, analysis, dissemination and management. The project was implemented by the World Bank; the Organization of American States handled day-to-day management as executing agency (Erickson & Rogers 2006).

An evaluation of the Project was carried out in 2006. The evaluation notes that the participating countries made progress on a number of sub-objectives, yet were far from achieving their overall goals. In particular, the evaluation noted significant delays in developing a transboundary diagnostic analysis and a strategic action plan for the aquifer, serious delays in launching technical studies on the chemical, physical and dynamic aspects of the aquifer system, and delays in establishing a monitoring and information system. The project was extended by 22 months and came in 20% over budget (Erickson & Rogers 2006).

A new GEF project for the Guarani has been approved in concept, entitled: Implementation of the Guarani Aquifer Strategic Action Program: Enabling Regional Actions.

Dinaric Karst aquifer system

The Protection and Sustainable Use of the Dinaric Karst Transboundary Aquifer System Project (DIKTAS) was a cooperative effort by the countries of Albania, Bosnia and Herzegovina, Serbia and Montenegro, executed by UNESCO, with UNDP as the implementing agency, and the International Groundwater Resource Assessment Centre (IGRAC) as another involved partner. The project began in May 2010 and operational closure was in May 2015. The $5.6 million project included a $2.16 million GEF grant, plus $3.4 million in co-financing from the involved governments and other sources. The Dinaric Karst aquifer system is one of the largest karstic geological aquifers in the world, and underlies the Dinaric mountain range.

DIKTAS was designed to help the cooperating countries establish and implement sustainable development models, including harmonized land use policies and physical planning, conceptual frameworks for balancing water resource demand, avoiding over-extraction and coping with strong seasonal variability of water resource usage; and accounting for the impact of wider systemic issues such as population growth and climate change. The project utilized the TDA-SAP process that typifies GEF international waters programming, moving from a transboundary diagnostic analysis to a strategic action plan for addressing risks and pressures to the water body.

The evaluation of DIKTAS indicated an overall moderately satisfactory assessment of project outcomes, noting high relevance, satisfactory efficiency and moderately satisfactory effectiveness and likelihood of sustainability. As can be seen in many of the GEF IW projects, and in particular for transboundary aquifers, the first step of the process – to diagnose the uses and threats to water systems – tends to move slowly yet successfully, but the projects then have serious difficulties in achieving binding agreement across the countries on actions they will take to protect the resource (Komitina 2016).

In the case of DIKTAS, a Strategic Action Plan was not signed by the countries by project end, and the envisioned consultation and information exchange body (CIE) was not created. A follow on study was recommended by the evaluation, in order to continue working towards an approved SAP and CIE. Other recommendations were to establish a joint monitoring programme, improve awareness raising and capacity building and consider enlarging the cooperation to include also Serbia and North Macedonia. This recommendation has led to the approval, in concept, of a $5.145 million GEF grant for a follow on project entitled: Implementation of the SAP of the Dinaric Karst Aquifer System: Improving Groundwater Governance and Sustainability of Related Ecosystems.

Southern African development community groundwater and drought management project

The SADC Groundwater and Drought Management Project covered 15 countries of southern Africa with 14 major transboundary groundwater aquifer systems.[2] The aim of the project was to develop a consensus on a SADC strategic approach to support and enhance the capacity of its member states in defining drought management policies, specifically in relation to the role, availability and supply of potential groundwater resources. The project provided a $7 million grant to SADC for a project implemented by the World Bank and executed by the SADC Secretariat Water Division, with support from United Nations Office for Project Services. The project had four components:

1) Development and testing of a groundwater drought and management plan for the Limpopo River Basin pilot areas;
2) Support for regional groundwater drought management;
3) Establishment of the groundwater institute of Southern Africa; and
4) Project management and administration.

The Implementation Completion and Results Report on the project, dated 31 October 2011 (World Bank 2011), generally noted success in raising awareness on the value of protecting groundwater resources in southern Africa. The Report also noted that the project succeeded in providing 'increased access to groundwater information to facilitate sound technical decisions by policy makers' (World Bank 2011: 27).

The project had a measure of success in strengthening regional coordination through the regional monitoring network, although efforts to more fully engage SADC countries who were not part of the pilot effort would have been useful, as many need assistance to upgrade their data on groundwater resources. Poor data had an impact on the quality of the regional drought and management maps created through the project. The authors of the Completion and Results Report concluded that the project was too ambitious given the complexity of the issue and region and should have had fewer project components. Results were weighed down by the long delay – 18 months – in getting the project started. The project ended prior to achieving discernible impacts in terms of reduced stress on groundwater resources and better capacity of the SADC countries to manage future droughts (World Bank 2011).

A follow-on project, using $8.2 million in GEF grant funding, has been approved, entitled: Sustainable Groundwater Management in SADC Member States. The project was approved for finding in March 2014 and is under implementation by the World Bank.

Future considerations for transboundary aquifer projects

The transboundary aquifer project evaluations discussed here provide evidence of an evolving international support effort spearheaded by the GEF and its implementing agencies. It is not an exhaustive study of the results of international support to transboundary aquifer management, yet the findings from the evaluations of these projects raise important issues and lessons for future effort to protect these critical water resources.

The five transboundary aquifers considered have all demonstrated success building greater awareness of groundwater system boundaries, extraction rates and pollution risks. The projects have also helped raise international awareness of the presence and importance of transboundary aquifers and have helped to enhance governments' capacities to determine risks to groundwater systems. Over an extended period of time, and including follow on projects, the transboundary aquifer projects have also achieved legally binding agreements (Northwest Sahara and Nubian) or are close to achieving agreement (Guarani, Iullemeden) on strategies and action plans aimed at reducing pollution and excessive drawdown risks.

There is a clear progression in the sequencing of these aquifer projects, with medium size projects (under $2 million in grant funding), used to establish the transboundary diagnostic analysis and draft Strategic Action Plan, being followed by a larger SAP-approval and implementation project. This progression has become a hallmark of the GEF International Waters programme, including also for fresh surface waters and coastal marine systems. This recognizes the tendency for the portion of the project focused on transboundary diagnostic analysis to dominate most of the initial project period. Most of the projects have required a year or more extension to complete, and the use of 'no-cost' extensions is common. This suggests the need for more realistic project outcome expectations, longer timeframes for project implementation and a push for greater commitment from participating governments to start earlier on the difficult negotiations to achieve SAP agreements.

GEF transboundary aquifer projects typically call for the creation of joint committees among the countries involved. This mirrors the approach taken in GEF transboundary surface-water projects. The formation of self-standing transboundary aquifer commissions is a slow and difficult process, and those that do form tend to lack the power and capacity to influence national land and water use laws. Many remain viable only so long as international financial support continues.

While technical training in groundwater assessment and awareness-raising initiatives are helpful, many developing countries face significant practical operational difficulties that limit their ability to carry out conservation and protection measures for aquifers at the national and local levels. Many need to improve use and efficiency and reduce pumping in transboundary aquifers through regulatory and fiscal policy changes and through improved water resource management. Although some attention has been paid to resource substitution and augmentation, this area needs increased support. Ultimately, water-scarce nations will need to greatly expand the use of grey water and brackish water for non-potable uses and expand their access to resources through desalination, artificial recharge,[3] conjunctive use of groundwater and surface water and the use of aquifers for surface water storage (Galloway et al. 2003).

These projects have yet to achieve systemic changes in water and land use policies and, ultimately, reductions in environmental stresses and pollution risks. There is an assumption that participating countries will act on policy and management recommendations from the project and agreed to in strategic action programmes. Conflicting use demands among actors within each country often stand in the way of such actions. Results from the aquifer projects highlight the difficulty in forging political agreements on complex resource sharing arrangements, where it may take decades before positive environmental impacts can be discerned.

This review of the results of GEF transboundary aquifer projects also points to the need for greater attention to the equitable use of groundwater resources. It is the poor and disenfranchised who suffer the most when water is scarce, yet few of the transboundary aquifer projects focused attention on access rights and equitable allocations. Of the five evaluated projects, only the SADC Groundwater and Drought Management Project focused specific attention on communities at risk (female-led households, landless labourers, pastoralists and displaced persons; World Bank 2011). Each of the seven pilot drought and groundwater management studies in the SADC project focused on communities at risk as the prime beneficiaries. As water scarcity becomes more acute in many regions, due to increasing consumption coupled with climate change-impacted variability, it will be important for transboundary aquifer projects to pay greater attention to the equity aspects of groundwater access.

Notes

1 'Water scarcity is defined as the point at which the aggregate impact of all users impinges on the supply or quality of water under prevailing institutional arrangements to the extent that the demand by all sectors, including the environment, cannot be satisfied fully' (UN Water and FAO 2007: 4).
2 The SADC countries are Angola, Botswana, Democratic Republic of Congo, Lesotho, Madagascar, Malawi, Mauritius, Mozambique, Namibia, the Seychelles, South Africa, Swaziland, Tanzania, Zambia and Zimbabwe.
3 Artificial recharge involves enhancing natural infiltration into ground-water systems by using spreading basins, recharge wells and induced infiltration of surface water.

References

Aquastat, Online Database, Food and Agriculture Organization of the United Nations, 2011 available at http://www.fao.org/nr/water/aquastat/data/query/index.html, last accessed September 23 2011.

Eckstein, G. E., 'Buried treasure or buried hope? The status of Mexico–US transboundary aquifers under international law', *International Community Law Review*, 13: 273–290, 2011.

Erickson J. and P. Rogers, '*An Independent Evaluation of the World Bank's Support of Regional Programs*', Case study of the Guaraní Aquifer Project, World Bank Independent Evaluation Group, Washington, DC, 2006.

Eurostat, Online Database, Brussels, European Commission, 2013 available at http://epp.eurostat.ec.europa.eu/portal/page/portal/eurostat/home/, last accessed September 26 2013.

Galloway, D. et al. '*Evolving issues and practices in managing ground-water resources: Case studies and the role of science*, US Department of the Interior, US Geological Survey, Circular 1247, 2003.

Gleeson, T., Y. Wada, M. Bierkens, and L. van Beek, 'Water balance of global aquifers revealed by groundwater footprint', *Nature*, 488 (9 August): 197–200, 2012.
Global Environment Facility (GEF), What is the GEF, 2013, http://www.thegef.org/gef/whatisgef, accessed May 8 2013.
GEF, International waters, 2013, http://www.thegef.org/gef/International_Waters, accessed May 8 2013.
GEF, Independent Evaluation Office, International Waters Focal Area Study, October 2018
GEF International Waters, April 2020, https://www.thegef.org/sites/default/files/publications/gef_international_waters_2020_04.pdf
Hearns, G., '*Terminal Evaluation of UNEP/GEF Project GF/1030–03–06 (4728) Managing Hydrogeological Risk in the Iullemeden Aquifer System (IAS)*', Evaluation and Oversight Unit United Nations Environment Programme, Nairobi, January 2009.
Integrated Groundwater Resources Assessment Centre (IGRAC), '*Transboundary aquifers map of the world – update 2009*', 2009, available at http://www.un-igrac.org/publications/320
IAEA, UNDP and Governments of the Arab Republic of Egypt, Libya, Republic of the Sudan and Republic of Chad, '*Regional strategic action programme for the Nubian Aquifer System*', 18 September 2013, available at http://www.iaea.org/newscenter/pressreleases/2013/sap180913.pdf, accessed May 10 2013.
IBWC Minute No. 242, Aug. 30, 1973, Mexico-United States, 24 U.S.T. 1971, T.I.A.S .No. 7708.
Komitina, D., Terminal Evaluation of the GEF/UNDP MSP project 'Protection and Sustainable Use of the Dinaric Karst Aquifer System' (DIKTAS) [PIMS No. 4056, ATLAS 59453] January 2016.
Margat, J., *Les Eaux Souterraines dans le Monde, BRGM Editions*, United Nations Scientific and Cultural Organization, Paris, 2008.
Organisation for Economic Co-operation and Development, Development Assistance Committee (OECD-DAC), '*Financing water and sanitation in developing countries: The contribution of external aid*', June 2010, available at http://www.oecd.org/dac/stats/45902160.pdf, accessed June 2 2013.
Pernetta J. and J.M. Bewers, 'Transboundary diagnostic analysis in international waters interventions funded by the gobal environment facility', *Oceans and Coastal Management*, 55 (January): 1–12, 2012.
Puri, S. and A. Aureli, 'Transboundary aquifers: A global program to assess, evaluate, and develop policy', *Ground Water*, 43 (5): 661–668, 2005.
Puyoo S., '*Terminal evaluation of the UNEP/Swiss/FFEM Project "Protection of the North West Sahara Aquifer System (NWSAS) and Related Humid Zones and Ecosystems, Project Number: GF/2010–03–06"*, Evaluation and Oversight Unit, United Nations Environment Programme, Nairobi, September 2007.
Siebert, S. et al., 'Groundwater use for irrigation – a global inventory', *Hydrology and Earth System Sciences*, 14: 1863–1880, 2010.
Uitto, J. I., 'Multi-country cooperation around shared waters: Role of monitoring and evaluation', *Global Environmental Change*, 14: 5–14, 2004.
United Nations Educational, Scientific and Cultural Organization (UNESCO), *Managing water under uncertainty and risk: The United Nations world water development report*, United Nations World Water Assessment Programme (UN-Water), Paris, March 2012, available at http://www.un.org/waterforlifedecade/scarcity.shtml

UNESCO, '*UN General Assembly adopts resolution on the law of transboundary aquifers*', news article, available at http://www.unesco.org/water/news/transboundary_aquifers.shtml, accessed May 18 2013.

United Nations General Assembly (UNGA), '*Resolution adopted by the General Assembly on 28 July 2010 on The human right to water and sanitation (A/RES/66/104)*, 2010 available at http://www.un.org/en/ga/search/view_doc.asp?symbol=A/RES/64/292

United Nations General Assembly (UNGA), '*Resolution Adopted by the General Assembly on 9 December 2011 [on the report of the Sixth Committee (A/66/477)], 66/104. The Law of Transboundary Aquifers (Agenda Item 85)*', 13 January 2012, available at http://www.un.org/en/ga/search/view_doc.asp?symbol=%20A/RES/66/104.

UNGA, '*Resolution adopted by the General Assembly on 28 July 2010 [without reference to a Main Committee (A/64/L.63/Rev.1 and Add.1)], 64/292. The Human Right to Water and Sanitation*' (Agenda Item 48), 3 August 2010.

United Nations Water (UN Water) and Food and A (FAO) '*Coping with water scarcity. Challenge of the twenty-first century*' 2007 available at http://www.fao.org/nr/water/docs/escarcity.pdf

World Bank, '*Implementation completion and results report (TF-55090) on a grant from the Global Environment Facility (GEF) trust fund in the amount of $7 million to the Southern African Development Community for a Groundwater and Drought Management Project through the World Bank as implementing agency*', 31 October 2011.

15

DISASTER RISK MANAGEMENT IN THE SDG ERA

Vijayalakshmi Vadivelu

Introduction

Frequent natural disasters severely impact poorer sections of the population and exacerbate socio-economic vulnerabilities and reversing development gains. Over the past decade, more than 1.5 billion people have been affected by disasters that have cost at least US$ 1.3 trillion – and disasters have compounded existing problems of poverty and inequality and have reversed development gains. Overall losses from natural disasters in 2019 came to US$ 150 Billion.[1] According to the Sendai Monitor, while there is a marginal decrease in the number of people affected in 2019, there is an increase in the human loss as well as economic cost attributed to disasters in relation to global gross domestic product.[2] These numbers are only the tip of the iceberg, as they are comprised of estimates of the replacement value of the physical infrastructure damaged or lost; the systemic impacts on human development are much larger. Progress towards achieving the Sustainable Development Goals (SDGs) is challenged in many countries by losses from disasters triggered by natural hazards. Even in regions where a comparatively smaller number of disasters have occurred, the economic impact has been significant. Countries with medium to low levels of income and weaker governance have been particularly vulnerable. Reducing disaster risk is therefore critical to poverty reduction and sustainable development. Although government mechanisms and systems to respond to disasters are critical, resilience to disaster risk must be integral to development planning processes.

Drawing on the evaluations of the United Nations Development Programme (UNDP), programme at the global and national level carried out by the Independent Evaluation Office of UNDP, this chapter revisits the disaster risk reduction efforts, progress and challenges since the adoption of the SDGs and Sendai Framework and discusses UNDP's contributions at the national level.[3] This chapter examines integrated approaches to addressing disaster risk and vulnerability reduction in development programming. The chapter draws on the country programme evaluations as well as the conclusions and lessons based on the global "Evaluation of UNDP Support to Poverty Reduction in the Least Developed Countries," "Evaluation of UNDP Contribution to Disaster Prevention and Recovery."[4] These evaluations paid particular attention to the challenges posed by climate change in increasing natural hazards and the need for a more coordinated approach to adaptation. After a brief introduction, this chapter discusses how national governments and the international community have attempted to respond to these challenges. This is followed by the section on the approach and methodology used by the evaluations, followed by a discussion of the UNDP programme. The findings section analyses UNDPs contribution to disaster risk reduction, enabling linkages to poverty reduction and climate change adaptation and addressing multiple crises. The last section presents conclusions and selected recommendations that are relevant to other agencies and governments working in the area.

Poverty, vulnerability and disaster risk

Losses from disasters that are triggered by natural hazards significantly reverse development gains in many countries.[5] The economic cost of disasters on development interventions and human development varies widely. Several studies and assessments have established that disasters heavily affect the poor in developing countries and that disaster risk is fundamentally associated with poverty levels.[6] The adverse effects of disasters on social investments, particularly in health and education, and investments that provide employment and income are considerable. Besides short-term effects such as direct economic losses, disasters affect long-term human development and human security.

The low resilience of the poor is further undermined by weak or absent social-protection measures and the low prevalence of disaster insurance in most countries. While urban and rural areas are equally affected by disasters, poverty translates into disaster risk because of the vulnerability of rural livelihoods.[7] The diversity in the structure of rural societies and economies and their interactions with the environment make livelihoods more susceptible to disasters. Another factor that increases risks from natural disasters in poor rural areas is the lack of safe housing, infrastructure and public services (UNDP 2004; United Nations International Strategy for Disaster Reduction [UNISDR] 2009a; UNDP 2015). The key vulnerability factors that contribute to mortality risk are low GDP per capita and remoteness of location.

Annual exposure to GDP losses is high for cyclones and storms of medium intensity, as is nationally reported disaster loss. Destruction in the housing sector usually accounts for a significant proportion of direct economic loss in disasters. The economic losses and the number of people affected due to natural disasters are increasing at a rapid rate, faster than risk reduction can be achieved (Rodriguez, J, et al. 2009; UNISDR 2009a; UNDRR, 2019). Considerable evidence suggests that the impact on national economies adversely affects social investments, particularly in the areas of health and education and in areas that contribute to employment and income generation. Although disaster risk has been identified as an investment priority for achieving the SDGs, more systematic efforts are required. Though governments often prepare for worst-case disasters, recurrent small- and medium-scale disaster risks are generally insufficiently addressed. Furthermore, well-meaning efforts to increase social and economic development may inadvertently *increase* disaster risk unless disaster risk reduction considerations factored into all development-related investments. Disaster risk reduction as a governance issue is still emerging in both government policy and planning.

There are increasing concerns about the implications of climate change. The consequences of an increase in either slow- or rapid-onset disasters caused by extreme weather events are enormous and threaten agricultural production, food and water security, public health and peace and security. Among many impacts, climate change will increase the frequency and intensity of weather-related hazards, such as floods, cyclones and droughts.[8] Other potential effects of climate change, such as ecosystem degradation, reduced availability of water and food, energy crises and changes in livelihoods will increase communities' vulnerability to natural hazards (Prasad et al. 2009).

Developing countries will be hardest hit by climate change; consequently, they suffer from increased disaster risk. Climate change will have implications for most regions, but some will be more affected than others, such as East Asia and the Pacific and the Caribbean, which are already vulnerable to natural disasters and extreme climatic events.[9] An analysis of the climate risk index and extreme weather events from 1998 to 2007 indicates that the top ten countries hardest hit include Bangladesh, the Dominican Republic, Haiti, Honduras, India, Mozambique, Nicaragua, the Philippines, Venezuela and Viet Nam.

Disasters affect women and men differently. It is widely documented, for example, that women are particularly vulnerable to natural hazards and that mortality from disasters is high among them. Gender inequalities in accessing resources, capabilities and differential opportunities place women at a disadvantage, making them more vulnerable to the impact of disasters (Bhatt 2005; Neumayer and Plümper 2007). Although attention is paid to women as a disadvantaged group, gender perspectives have yet to be systematically integrated into disaster-related interventions.

Lack of attention to gender is a recurring feature in disaster response despite the fact that individually and collectively, governments, international development organizations and donor agencies have made strong commitments to gender equality and women's empowerment. Yet despite such efforts, the operationalization of gender-responsive policies and practices has been *ad hoc* and inconsistent (UNISDR, UNDP and ICUN 2009). Reporting by the Hyogo Framework for Action (HFA) indicates that although an increasing number of governments are recognizing the importance of gender issues in national disaster risk reduction efforts,[10] meaningful progress has yet to be made.

National initiatives

After a decade of concerted effort to achieve the MDGs, and as we approach the mid-point of the ten-year HFA, definite progress can be seen in terms of government action to address disaster-related issues. First, more people are recognizing that disasters can be prevented and disaster impacts can be mitigated. Second, various actors at the national, regional and global levels have acknowledged the added value in coordinating disaster-related interventions. Third, there are positive indications that the perspectives of agencies working on disaster support and those working on long-term development are converging. Fourth, recognition is growing that reducing disaster risk is a development issue – one that requires addressing the underlying risk factors that make people and their livelihoods more vulnerable to both slow- and rapid-onset disasters.

The 2009 *Global Assessment Report on Disaster Risk Reduction* (UNISDR 2009a) appraised the progress made in implementing the HFA. The findings indicate that, globally, national efforts have focused on HFA Priorities 1, 2 and 5: strengthening policy, legislation and institutional frameworks, and on building capacities for disaster preparedness, response, risk assessments and early warning. The effort was found to be less adequate in HFA Priorities 3 and 4: using knowledge, education and outreach programmes to stimulate a culture of disaster resilience and addressing the underlying factors related to social, economic and infrastructure development across rural and urban contexts.

Challenges remain in compiling comprehensive risk assessments in a way that can inform disaster risk reduction and link early warning with disaster preparedness and response planning. Efforts also fell short in using national information to inform local action. One reason why progress in HFA implementation has been limited is that the scale of resources available for disaster risk reduction falls well short of what is needed to ensure the resilience of nations and communities (United Nations General Assembly [UNGA] 2008). Although the HFA pays attention to broader institutional frameworks and policies for risk reduction, the response to major disasters indicates the need for better and more suitable administrative systems and procedures (e.g. the Myanmar earthquake, Gujarat earthquake and the Asian tsunami).

Limitations were also found in the extent to which national development policies and plans included dimensions of disaster risk reduction. An evaluation review of 67 poverty-reduction strategy papers in 2012 indicated that only 20% discussed in detail disaster risk reduction, 25% did not mention disaster risk at all, and 55% mentioned only the relationship between disaster risk and poverty without providing concrete recommendations for addressing it. Countries that have integrated disaster risk reduction into their poverty-reduction strategy papers include Bangladesh (2005), Malawi (2006), Mozambique (2006) and Viet Nam (2006). Since the adoption of Sendai Framework, there is an improvement in incorporating disaster and climate risk factors in national strategies. In terms of the global targets of the Framework, 59 out of 195 countries have initiated efforts to address disaster risk.[11] However such efforts are not sufficient for addressing significant and increasing climate and disaster risks.

Intergovernmental response

Since 2015 the landmark intergovernmental agreements, the Sendai Framework for Disaster Risk Reduction,[12] the Paris Agreement[13] and the Sustainable Development Goals[14] have set the agenda for reducing risks associated with all hazards and unsafe conditions. These agreements are significant as they put risk reduction as central to the development agenda, as integral to sustainable and equitable economic, social and environmental development. The interlinkages between these agreements are equally significant. Effective disaster risk management and reducing vulnerability to natural hazards are key to progress on SDGs. An additional dimension to risk reduction is managing the interrelated vulnerabilities compounded by climate change. The Paris agreement to combat climate change and adapt to its effects is therefore fundamental to the disaster risk reduction agenda. Climate change intensified disaster risks with the increase in the weather and climate hazards and related vulnerabilities, particularly through ecosystem degradation. The three intergovernmental agreements present an opportunity to ensure that risk management became central to development policy and planning and for efforts to reduce disaster losses.

Although most countries are signatories to the Sendai Framework, integrating environment management, climate change adaptation and disaster risk reduction has yet to manifest in practice. Besides, greater regional and global collaboration is a necessity for greater accountability of risk-causing countries, because the countries that will be most affected by climate change have done the least to contribute to it. Greater coordination between disaster risk reduction, development and climate change actors while recognized as critical for responding to the humanitarian challenges of climate change and addressing the root causes of vulnerability concrete actions are evolving but not at a faster pace.

Given the slow progress of the Sendai framework after five years of its adoption, it is important to address the limitations of the previous iterations of the Framework, the HFA. A key issue the intergovernmental efforts should address is the interface of multiple crises and their interlinkages. Disaster risk cannot anymore be seen in isolation from climate-related impacts. Also, climate impact needs new institutional systems and process at the national level that can adapt to new types of risks. The absence accountability mechanism is another issue that is slowing Sendai framework progress.

There has been an international governmental consensus on the importance of gender equality in disaster risk reduction which was reflected in the formulation of the Sendai Framework. In its guiding principles, the Framework emphasizes that disaster risk reduction policies and practices should be informed by gender, age, disability and cultural perspective. Besides, the SDGs provide the necessary thrust on gender quality as a cross-cutting principle for all the goals. Global advocacy on the importance of gender in disaster risk and vulnerability reduction while gained momentum is yet to translate into concrete policies at the national level.

Approach, data and methods

Drawing from an analysis of key concerns in prevention and recovery and UNDP strategic documents on support to countries affected by natural disasters and climate impacts, the evaluation approach acknowledges the multiple dimensions of disaster risk reduction. Reducing disaster risk and vulnerability is a development issue and an important factor in achieving the SDGs. The enormous consequences of disasters for human development, poverty reduction and economic growth necessitate effectively managing disaster risk as an integral part of development planning; an integrated approach during recovery and reconstruction can be a way to reduce future risk. Similarly, links between disaster risk, climate change and environmental management make an integrated national planning and programming approach essential to risk reduction and long-term recovery. Addressing disaster risk reduction and climate change adaptation is critical to minimizing development reversals and reducing poverty and vulnerability, although strategies to accomplish this are still emerging.

Strengthening national capacities, particularly governance and coordination mechanisms, is critical to responding to disasters and reducing risk. Prevention and recovery work provides an opportunity to go beyond restoring things to the way they were – if done strategically, it can enable affected communities to achieve even greater levels of resilience. This also includes systematically integrating gender into development frameworks, which in many instances influences how gender dimensions are addressed in disaster risk reduction and recovery.

The questions of the evaluation of disaster management support related to the standard evaluation criteria of relevance, effectiveness, efficiency and sustainability of UNDP work, including its responses to challenges posed by disasters. The poverty reduction in least developed countries (LDCs) evaluation used a set of criteria, namely UNDP programme positioning, strengthening national capacities, contribution to global policy and advocacy, convening role and enabling partnerships. Areas covered in the evaluation are that of relevance for disaster reduction in the poverty–environment nexus and addressing multiple crises. The evaluations used a variety of methods and data to build evaluative evidence for answering its questions.

The evaluations included case studies of twenty-four countries.[15] Country case studies entailed a comprehensive document review, stakeholder analysis, consultations and interviews. At the country level, a stakeholder analysis was carried out to identify organizations working in the area of disaster management, those involved in development support and those engaged in pertinent aspects of environmental management, climate change adaptation and coastal area management. The consultations involved a wide range of development stakeholders, including government officials, international agencies, UNDP programme donors and international and national non-governmental organizations (NGOs).

Structured and semi-structured interviews and focus group discussions were used to collect primary data. The method took into consideration country-level data limitations, the delineation of different phases of support, the linking of different levels of analysis and varied timeframes and the systematic validation of causality, linking process to results. This evaluation method ensured that different stakeholders' perspectives were captured and that the findings could be triangulated. Other sources of evidence were used to either substantiate findings or further explore the country case studies, thus ensuring that they were credible and robust.

UNDP response

UNDP recognizes the importance of disaster risk management to poverty reduction and sustainable human development and has, over the past four decades, supported interventions in the areas of prevention, response and recovery. The aim of such programmes has been to strengthen national capacities to prevent (reduce risk) as well as to respond to natural disasters. More specifically, UNDP provides assistance to develop government capacity to manage recovery and to ensure renewed progress towards the MDGs and later SDGs while reducing vulnerability to future disasters. Programming in key areas of development, an extensive national presence and partnership with governments and other national stakeholders provides UNDP with a unique opportunity to address disaster risk as a development challenge and to focus recovery on reducing vulnerabilities.

The Strategic Plans of UNDP (for the periods 2008–2011, extended to 2013, 2014–2017 and 2018–2021)[16] strongly emphasizes strengthening the national capacities needed to manage recovery while reducing vulnerability to future disasters. The key areas of UNDP support are as follows: strengthening policies and institutional capacities, legal and regulatory frameworks, assessment and analysis, sectoral strategies for disaster risk reduction, risk-informed development planning and budgeting, disaster recovery governance, community-based rural and urban risk management and gender equality informed disaster management. A keystone of UNDP's approach has been the provision of long-term and sustained support which has been instrumental in accompanying countries through the many ups and downs in their endeavours to strengthen their risk governance capacities and build resilience. UNDP's coverage has grown significantly – from programmes in 34 countries in 2000 to 125 countries in 2020, with over 1500 projects addressing different areas of disaster management. While UNDP has supported large, national-level disaster management programmes over the years (e.g. in Bangladesh, India, Indonesia and Pakistan), other countries have smaller programmes of shorter duration, concentrated at the subnational level.

Resilience approach to disaster risk reduction and climate change adaptation underpins the UNDP approach, for ensuring that development gains are resilient to the impacts of disasters and extreme weather events. UNDP strategic documents highlight the importance of addressing disaster-related issues and their linkages to climate change adaptation and human and economic development. UNDP's support for sustainable development emphasizes the importance of protecting the environmental base and reducing disaster risk as necessary for long-term poverty alleviation.

UNDP sees its role as supporting countries in their efforts to resume public service delivery as early as possible in the post-disaster period. During the humanitarian phase, UNDP aims to assist national governments set up aid coordination mechanisms and strengthen the capacities of local administrations to manage recovery processes. Another objective is to use its global knowledge and experience with disaster risk reduction to engage governments and other partner institutions to develop capacities for recovery and reducing future disaster risks.

Guided by the UN Convention on the Elimination of All Forms of Discrimination against Women,[17] SDGs and other intergovernmental agreements, UNDP corporate strategies place considerable emphasis on promoting gender equality in all of the organization's initiatives and its support to the government. When necessary, this includes specific women's empowerment initiatives.[18] The commitment to achieving the SDGs provided further impetus for a gender equality focus in programme support. The UNDP commitment in this area is reflected in its global gender strategies, the Gender Action Plan (2006–2007), the Gender Equality Strategies (2008–2013; 2014–2017; and 2018–2021)[19] and the Eight-Point Agenda for Women's Empowerment and Gender Equality in Crisis Prevention and Recovery, which provide a framework for all UNDP activities (UNDP 2007b; UNDP 2008a). Gender Equality Strategies acknowledge women's increased vulnerabilities during conflict and disasters. It also recognizes that giving attention to the differing needs of women and men maximizes the potential for full community recovery.

At the country level, areas of thematic engagement include institutional and legislative systems, community-based disaster risk management, support to national governments to establish risk reduction and climate risk management. In recovery efforts, UNDP focused largely on restoring normalcy following a crisis, transitioning effectively from crisis to development, and using recovery work as an opportunity to promote resilience to disasters and climate shocks. Such efforts have focused on strengthening governance structures and policies for better disaster management (e.g. prevention, mitigation and response, and providing post-disaster support in social and economic areas).

In the last decade, several rapid-onset disasters have taken place, both those that are large in scale and annually recurrent events of smaller intensity. UNDP supported responses to all major recent disasters. Support for recovery consisted mainly of post-disaster needs assessments, support to livelihoods and housing, coordination (involving both NGOs and governments) and strengthening government capacities.

Drought-related mitigation and recovery were not included in the UNDP disaster management programme due to the way programmes are categorized in UNDP programme frameworks. Drought and floods are considered as a consequence of climate change, affecting livelihoods and development in general. These are largely addressed as part of poverty reduction and climate change adaptation programmes. UNDP recognizes that climate change is a major threat to sustainable development and has provided support to this area for the past three years. Similar to drought-related mitigation, climate change adaptation is under a different programme unit of UNDP, although the inter-linkages with disaster risk reduction are relevant from the point of achieving programme results.

Findings

The UNDP programme strategy acknowledges disaster risk reduction as an important factor in reducing poverty and vulnerability and achieving the SDGs. In its publications, UNDP advocates giving greater importance to disaster risk reduction in achieving development results. In the last ten years, UNDP has actively participated in debates to further consensus on global policies to strengthen links between climate change adaptation and disaster risk reduction. Sustained commitment is reflected in closer integration of disaster risk reduction with other UNDP priority areas (e.g. poverty reduction, governance and adaptation to climate change). The following sections discuss areas where UNDP contributions, its comparative advantage and programming constraints.

Working with national systems

Governments are making important efforts to fulfil their commitments to the Sendai Framework (and its predecessors) and other conventions, and this has provided the impetus for formulating related legislation and policies. UNDP responded to such needs at the national level and supported governments establish institutional and legal frameworks for disaster management. UNDP support in this area was crucial in creating an enabling environment for policy formulation and in setting up key institutions for disaster risk management. Out of 58 country programme evaluations analysed, UNDP played a key role in policy formulation in 31 countries; in 27 countries, UNDP contributed to creating an enabling environment for disaster risk management.

Contribution to the policy discourse on sustainable livelihoods was evident in UNDP's engagement in the shaping of the SDGs and integration for climate change adaption issues in the Sendai Framework for Disaster Risk Reduction. UNDP remains a leading United Nations provider of environmental protection support at national and local levels and has been a significant provider of technical support to the government during global and regional negotiations on environmental issues such as climate change, biodiversity loss and water pollution. UNDP advocated for environmental budgeting by supporting efforts to engage parliament, creating committees on poverty–environment issues and engaging high-ranking government officials in poverty–environment projects. Most importantly, tracking budgets and expenditures by analysing budget data according to special issues, poverty–environment concerns and climate change adaptation has enabled better advocacy aimed at increasing budget allocations for poverty–environment mainstreaming, as well as to raise awareness on related issues. With a wide-ranging climate change programme in place, UNDP has played a prominent role in regional and global policy debates on global climate change in support of countries preparing for and responding to the 2015 Paris Agreement.

UNDP has been more effective in enabling sector-specific support, particularly when establishing disaster management institutions and policies or pilot interventions in disaster preparedness. Although in many ways this reflects the larger, national-level challenge, UNDP has had limited success in addressing issues related to the integration of disaster risk reduction in development planning and in strengthening government capacities in intergovernmental coordination for disaster risk reduction. UNDP responded to governments' expressions of interest to mainstream disaster risk reduction in Honduras, for example, and at the state level in Mexico. However, this was not often given adequate priority in UNDP programming.[20] In countries such as Colombia, the roles, responsibilities and accountability at different levels of government and among institutions responsible for disaster risk management could be better harmonized.

Increasingly, governments are recognizing the links between disaster risk reduction, poverty reduction and development; efforts are being made to address these links. For example, in Mexico the government is taking measures to include disaster risk reduction in social development programmes. In the Maldives, disaster and climate risk reduction are considered critical issues and are fully integrated into development planning. UNDP's support in Bangladesh provides an example of a typical UNDP programme at the country level in the context of multiple crises. In Bangladesh, as part of the disaster risk reduction, UNDP's Early Recovery Facility initiated a pilot short-term employment project linked to the rehabilitation of community infrastructure and solid waste management. Solid waste management, ecosystem restoration and mapping of social risks are areas of UNDP's support. Each of these initiatives is critical to addressing the vulnerabilities of the host communities as well as the Rohingya refugees in Cox's Bazaar. UNDP played a strategic role in disaster risk reduction in the refugee areas in managing hazards and risks. This support is widely perceived as critical for the local government. Advisory role of UNDP in disaster risk reduction enabled work on resilience in the Rohingya refugee camps and training humanitarian actors on how to manage disasters and extreme weather. UNDP's Early Recovery Facility in the country office facilitated this strategic contribution within the refugee camps, in host communities and preparedness support to the district government. UNDP provided disaster risk reduction technical support to the JRP agencies, a critical requirement in the region with refugees. A series of socio-economic impact assessments and the initiation of a district development planning process have enabled a more structured local response to the crisis. An area that needs further attention is the consolidation of activities by various agencies in the areas of employment and livelihood and local services.

Despite commitments of the countries to international agreements such as Sendai Framework here remain significant challenges in integrating disaster and climate risk reduction into national plans and programmes. The progress remains slow in integrating disaster risk reduction into national development planning in most countries, particularly in the allocation of budget for risk reduction. The same can be said about contributing to implementation in countries where risk reduction is already a development priority.

UNDP strategy acknowledges disaster risk reduction as an important factor in reducing poverty and vulnerability and achieving the SDGs. Although disaster risk reduction is prioritized as a programme area in many countries, UNDP has paid sparse attention to its interface with poverty reduction. Despite the organizational commitment, closer integration of disaster risk reduction with other UNDP priorities, such as poverty reduction, governance and adaptation to climate change, is progressing in some country programmes has not been given sufficient priority in many others. UNDP poverty reduction initiatives are yet to include a risk-reduction dimension, although there are exceptions. A disaster risk reduction or climate change adaptation component in poverty reduction initiatives is seen as an expendable, additional cost. A few exceptions were found, which offer important lessons for strengthening synergies among complementary areas of the UNDP programme, government and other development agencies. In Mexico, for example, integrating disaster risk reduction components into projects significantly contributed to sustaining local-level development investments. Similar results are evident in Bangladesh in a community-based poverty-reduction programme that incorporated disaster preparedness and risk reduction. In Honduras, disaster risk reduction is addressed as a governance issue.

A notable change is the UNDPs resilience approach, introduced in 2008, is enabling a shift towards vulnerability reduction in UNDPs programme support. Resilience approach, with long-term focus, is gathering momentum in UNDPs crisis response. The integrated framework promoted by the 2017 Strategic Plan is enabling a shift in UNDPs programmes, particularly in establishing linkages between its programme response in the areas of poverty reduction, climate change adaptation and disaster risk reduction. Similarly, disaster risk reduction as a governance issue is emphasized in UNDPs support, particularly in enabling policies and governance structures.

In several LDCs, climate impacts have increased the frequency of droughts, floods and cyclones, and the national policy response does not reflect the severity of the issue. Promoting approaches to improve food security and sustainable development linkages through adaptation strategies contributed to livelihoods change processes at the subnational level. Climate-related disaster risk reduction initiatives that have livelihood resilience components were aligned with adaptation efforts, complementing government priorities to reduce poverty and vulnerability to risks and improving food security (e.g. in Mozambique). Cash for work activities supported by UNDP provided income during disaster recovery on a short-term basis (Haiti and Nepal). While debris removal provided employment immediately after disasters, solid waste management in post-disaster situations was critical, with consequences for enhancing community income and living conditions.

Addressing multiple and interlinking crises

While there are conducive organizational policies to promote resilience, intersecting elements of crises and their linkages are yet to be prioritized in implementation. The LDCs, for example, have experienced natural and climate-related disasters (both rapid-onset disasters and droughts), health pandemics and conflict. To better understand the scale of the problem, over half of the LDCs are subject to multiple crises including recurrent disasters, in addition to poverty, the volatility of commodity prices and aid flows, and severe structural challenges. The macroeconomic impact of these episodes of extreme drought and flooding is not only significant by itself but exacerbates the impact on poverty in the context of conflict or early conflict recovery. At any given point in 10–12 LDCs, UNDP programmes are implemented in the context of multiple fragilities.[21] UNDP has programmes in the areas of climate-resilient agriculture and livelihoods, inclusive growth and income-generation initiatives, economic revitalization and peacebuilding; it is also progressively adopting ways to improve resilient development. Despite the range of support provided, opportunities were not used to enable an integrated approach to address intersecting linkages between drought and poverty or drought-conflict and poverty.

Poverty and drought can potentially become drivers of conflict when attention is not paid to nexus issues. In Mali, while each of UNDP's initiatives (in the areas of poverty, crisis and environment) is relevant individually for the development priorities of the country, opportunities were lost in enabling a focus on linkages between multiple fragilities, such as food security, resilience and vulnerability, and conflict. While the humanitarian situation is fragile, the socio-political instability in the northern region of the country, coupled with recurrent floods and pressures due to the events in the Central African Republic and northern Nigeria, have impacted the lives and livelihoods of over 3 million people. UNDP is better positioned to raise the importance of balancing development and crisis support and to advocate for more integrated policies, instead of getting subsumed in the larger conflict-centred development discourse at the country level.

UNDP's resilience approach aims to reduce development risks, prevent crises, avert major development setbacks and promote human security. This approach provided an impetus to closely align climate change adaptation and disaster risk reduction frameworks in livelihood support, and to position policy advice on these intersecting areas with a risk-sensitive approach to poverty reduction. Despite these policies, UNDP's poverty reduction efforts in the context of multiple crises are yet to address the combined effect of multiple crises and resulting vulnerabilities.

Climate change adaptation and disaster risk reduction

Climate change adaptation programmes of UNDP evolved in the past two decades and several interventions that were part of the poverty reduction and environment area had comparable goals. UNDP has aimed to address climate change adaptation as a development issue and as a factor in achieving the MDGs and later SDGs provided the necessary thrust. With increased recognition of the links between environment and climate change adaptation and disaster risk reduction, efforts have been made within UNDP to explore possible synergies in programming. There has been progress in consolidating climate change adaptation and disaster risk reduction teams. There is scope for improving synergies between programmes in these two areas. UNDP is taking measures to strengthen synergies to demonstrate through its programmes the critical urgency of integrating disaster and climate risk reduction.

The countries included in the evaluation have different levels of vulnerability to climate change, ranging from Colombia, India and Mexico (where climate change is one of many challenges), Tanzania (where climate change has had a significant impact on agriculture and livelihood), to the Maldives (where it threatens the very future of the country). In all countries, the anticipated impacts of climate change will likely be superimposed over existing climate-related disasters. This superimposition is particularly true for countries with a large population living in coastal areas and arid regions. Overall, UNDP adaptation projects are designed to decrease vulnerability to climate change impacts, although there is considerable scope for integrating it in poverty-reduction interventions. Some of these constraints of establishing linkages are also due to the funding mechanisms that require specific outcomes.

In the Maldives, the disaster risk reduction and adaptation links are well established by the government through its development plan – but such an example is more of an exception. In most countries, environment, climate change adaptation and disaster risk reduction activities tend to be spread among different government agencies. Besides, national frameworks for implementing the intergovernmental commitments are spread across different ministries, with responsible for each activity.

Coordination between disaster risk reduction and climate change adaptation has been limited in most countries despite intersectoral taskforces. Although governments acknowledge the need for synergies between the two areas, both at the conceptual level as well as in programme implementation, concrete efforts towards this end are rare. UNDP is supporting efforts to addresses the policy, programming and partnership issues that integrated programming would necessitate. Further, the current climate change adaptation and disaster risk reduction frameworks do not lend themselves to an integrated approach.

The severity of recent disasters has pushed the issue of climate change adaptation to centre stage, with direct implications for UNDP programming. Through its assistance to national governments both before and after disasters, coupled with extensive country-support mechanisms covering the environmental protection aspects of climate change, UNDP is well positioned to help countries develop effective adaptation strategies.

UNDP considers its responses to slow-onset disasters (e.g. drought) to be an aspect of poverty reduction and sustainable environment support, and are therefore not under the purview of disaster risk management. The impact of climate change is likely to blur the boundaries between slow- and rapid-onset disasters in the future and measures for better coordination among programme areas are critical. Support to prevent or mitigate slow-onset disasters entails a different approach and alternative strategies. It will require closer coordination with poverty reduction and environment programmes and new partnerships with different government agencies and stakeholders.

UNDP's initiatives in climate change adaptation have been critical for reducing the vulnerability of LDCs to climate change shocks, strengthening their resilience, and mainstreaming sustainable development into national development policies and strategies. Managing over one-third of GEF, GCF and other vertical green funds, UNDP is well situated to enable a national focus on factors that facilitate sustainable livelihoods. Environment and climate change adaptation programmes have consistently incorporated or promoted a sustainable approach to the environment as well as livelihoods by linking community income generation and natural resource management interventions. UNDP has had some success pursuing a greater consideration of poverty and livelihoods within the framework of its support to UN conventions, both climate change and disaster risk reduction in the past five years, which need further consolidation. UNDP should not only further leverage this work for a global policy engagement but also increase the scale of such programmes.

Promoting gender equality

UNDP has taken policy measures to ensure greater attention to gender equality and women's empowerment in programming. The mandatory allocation of 15% of funds for gender-related activities in crisis-related programmes (both conflict and disaster) is a measure unique to UNDP that operationalizes gender policy. At the global and regional levels, UNDP contributed to advocacy and publications to make disaster prevention and recovery more gender sensitive.

A few country programmes (e.g. Mexico) outlined gender equality as a priority area and set up a gender unit to support government efforts and to integrate gender priorities within the UNDP country programme. Important efforts were also made to prepare training modules for creating awareness and integrating gender-related issues into disaster risk reduction. Manuals were produced for regional programmes in South Asia and Mexico. Coordination with other agencies, particularly NGOs, was instrumental in ensuring that a gender perspective was integrated into all aspects of recovery work. In Indonesia, UNDP supported the government to develop strategies for integrating gender in recovery and reconstruction activities. Gender-disaggregated recovery indicators developed by UNDP at the country level were key to including gender and women's empowerment as a cross-cutting dimension in recovery programmes. UNDP contributed to efforts to ensure that women had a say in post-disaster housing and were joint owners of the assets provided as part of recovery programmes in Bangladesh, India, Indonesia and Sri Lanka.

Attention paid to gender-related issues did not reflect UNDP's commitment to accelerating gender equality. Although programmes were targeted at women and efforts were made to ensure their participation in disaster prevention and recovery, gender issues were not addressed systematically in programme planning and implementation. Constraints in addressing gender concerns in disaster risk management persist, including limited progress in dealing with gender priorities in development. While a commitment to gender equality may exist at the national level, practical measures to fulfil commitments were lacking. Reporting on progress of Sendai Framework on integrating gender perspectives in disaster risk reduction and recovery points to similar issues.

An area where there are lessons for synergies with disaster risk reduction is Development Finance Assessments (DFAs). Bangladesh (Climate Fiscal Framework) and Cambodia (Climate Change Financing Framework) have demonstrated leadership in reforming climate financing approaches and institutional arrangements, with indications of improved inter-ministerial coordination and an increasing role for and importance of ministries of finance in climate financing arrangements. In Bangladesh, based on the DFAs, the government has reformed the institutional set-up for managing development cooperation and drafted a National Policy on Development Cooperation; financing needs for the SDGs have also been estimated. Drawing upon lessons learned from Bangladesh and Cambodia on the Climate Fiscal Framework, other countries in the Asia region are developing climate financing frameworks. Such efforts have salience for disaster risk reduction financing arrangements.

Building local-level capacities

An area where UNDP has consolidation its support is strengthening local capacities in disaster management. An area where there were tangible results is the integration of disaster risk reduction in local plans, which were important particularly in the case of recurrent local level disasters. Disaster preparedness and risk reduction initiatives were implemented in more than 45 countries since 2009. Community approaches to sustainable livelihoods, natural resource management and enhancing resilience to disasters and climate change are areas where UNDP engagement has helped generate tangible local-level impacts. Women's economic empowerment received sufficient attention across programmes with contributions at the project level. Urban poverty is an evolving area of UNDP programme support that merits greater attention.

The scale and duration of such programmes varied across countries. Community preparedness initiatives were useful in strengthening local capacities. In several instances, UNDP used community programmes to demonstrate the importance of disaster preparedness and to integrate a disaster risk reduction component into local-level development interventions. In Mexico, for example, UNDP was able to scale up community-based preparedness interventions to the state level. UNDP has also been successful in informing government practices in Bangladesh and India. In India, the programme succeeded in demonstrating the importance of local-level preparedness. Other examples were also found where preparedness programmes contributed to better coping at the community level.[22]

The challenge in programming at the community level was the limited links to related government programmes. The fact that interventions were rarely institutionalized meant that they were one-off successes and failed to inform government programmes and policies. Strengthening local governments' capacities remains a challenge. There is also the risk of community programme mechanisms becoming parallel structures to local governments. With some exceptions, limitations were found in the links established among different levels of government. Excessive focus on contingency planning and preparedness and limited interventions in risk reduction weakened the possible contributions of community-based initiatives.

Conclusion

It is five years since the SDGs and the Sendai Framework have been adopted and commitments were made by countries to sustainable development and reduce the impact of natural and other disasters. Considering its cross-cutting nature, across different sectors of development, there are 25 disaster risk reduction related targets across 10 of the 17 SDGs, reinforcing the importance of addressing this challenge as part of the national development strategy. Besides, SDG 13 underscores the need to strengthen resilience and adaptive capacity to climate change for achieving sustainable development. Compared to the MDGs period, acknowledging the negative implications of disaster risk for development and poverty reduction in the international frameworks is a significant step forward. On both the SDGs and Sendai Framework, while there has been progress, the pace of it has been slow, and there remain significant gaps in achieving the objectives of the Framework. Natural hazards, both slow and rapid onset, are largely foreseeable. They provide governments and international agencies a rationale for taking prevention and preparedness measures to ensure that impacts are minimized. While an increase in the frequency and severity of recent disasters has called attention to the need for disaster risk reduction, challenges persist in taking practical measures to see it realized. Disaster recovery is generally regarded as urgent, but the focus is often limited to recovering what existed before, rather than addressing underlying vulnerabilities and future prevention. Reducing disaster risk is key to achieving objectives in poverty reduction and sustainable development.

The extent to which international agreements resulted in national policies that promote integrated approaches to development, to reduce disaster risk and enable climate change adaptation is evolving. For a resilient development, national poverty reduction efforts, particularly in the area of rural livelihoods need to systematically integrate disaster risk reduction and adaption. The role of international agencies in national disaster risk reduction as part of development support assumes importance in strengthening related policy processes.

In the area of climate-related disasters including slow-onset disasters, disaster risk reduction and climate change adaptation have similar goals, which calls for more coordinated programming at the national level. There has been increasing financing for climate change adaptation through various funding mechanisms further strengthened by Paris Agreement in 2016, while there remain resources challenges for disaster risk reduction efforts, which have similar goals in the area of slow-onset disasters. This highlights the importance of combined efforts in the area of adaptation and climate-related disaster risk reduction efforts, specifically integrating such efforts as part of key development strategies than as stand-alone efforts.

There is a need to strengthen institutional systems and capacities at the local level. Local governments typically lacked the authority and capacity to manage recovery programmes. Even in countries with strong national institutions, local governments were without the financial resources needed to carry out disaster risk reduction activities. Typically, the responsibilities of local governments are ill defined. Agencies such as UNDP that have a long-term presence at the country level have a pivotal position to bring risk-reduction issues into greater focus during recovery and in the development process more generally.

The lack of focus on the interface between poverty reduction, environment and disaster risk management has been compounded by several factors. The compartmentalized nature of programming has often constrained partnerships beyond disaster management agencies. Disaster management agencies in most countries predominantly addressed vulnerability from the perspective of location and physical infrastructure. Engaging only with disaster management institutions narrowed the perspective of disaster risk reduction interventions. If disaster risk management is to focus on vulnerability or poverty reduction, government institutions that have a mandate for poverty reduction, the environment, gender equality and related development issues must be involved.

There are cost implications for considering poverty reduction from the wider perspective of disaster vulnerability reduction and climate change risk, which includes incorporating a disaster risk reduction component. This also applies to recovery programmes in most countries, where integrating long-term risk reduction is not regarded as viable because of the extra costs involved. Although governments in many countries perceived the need for a more integrated approach to development planning, such efforts are at early stages. Most countries lacked a cost–benefit analysis of the advantage of vulnerability and disaster risk reduction in poverty reduction, which could inform government decisions and resource allocation. Advocacy in this area has been minimal. For example, MDG monitoring is not used as a tool to emphasize how disasters, particularly recurrent small-scale natural events, increase poverty levels and reverse development gains.

In recent years, greater attention to climate change adaptation has contributed significantly to raising awareness and understanding of the importance of addressing the interlinkages coherently, including its relationship to work on preventing and recovering from natural disasters. Interrelated policies and legislative frameworks are important from the perspective of disaster risk reduction and climate change adaptation. Aside from poverty reduction strategy papers and national development plans, policies related to climate change, environment, water management, coastal area/resource management, energy management, land use and urban planning are critical to a multidimensional approach to disaster risk reduction. Support for harmonizing overlapping mandates pertaining to disaster risk management and coordination among government agencies furthers policy consolidation.

Notes

1 Munich Re NatCatSERVICE database.
2 UNDRR, 2019, Sendai Monitor. https://sendaimonitor.undrr.org/analytics/global-targets/15.
3 The Independent Evaluation Office (IEO) is charged with conducting evaluations of the relevance and performance of UNDP's work at the country, regional, global and thematic levels. The IEP reports to the UNDP Executive Board, which has requested the office to conduct evaluations of critical aspects of UNDP's work in order to ensure accountability and to achieve organizational learning. In 2018–2019, IEO carried out "Evaluation of UNDP Support to Poverty Reduction in the Least Developed Countries," and 2009–2010, the Evaluation Office carried out the Evaluation of UNDP Contribution to Disaster Prevention and Recovery. See http://web.undp.org/evaluation/evaluations/thematic/poverty-ldc.shtml; http://www.undp.org/evaluation/thematic/par.shtml.
4 IEO, 2019. Evaluation of UNDP Support to Poverty Reduction in the Least Developed Countries. http://web.undp.org/evaluation/evaluations/thematic/poverty-ldc.shtml.
5 See GAR, 2019. https://gar.undrr.org/sites/default/files/reports/2019-05/full_gar_report.pdf.
6 See UNISDR (2009b), Harmeling (2009), Telford and Cosgrave (2006) Benson and Clay (2004), and Wisner et al. (2004).
7 See UNISDR, 2015. Disaster Risk Reduction And Resilience In The 2030 Agenda For Sustainable Development, A reflection Paper; UNISDR (2009), Assessment of Development Results in Tajikistan (EO 2009), Assessment of Development Results in Nicaragua (EO 2007), Telford and Cosgrave (2008), Wisner et al. (2004).
8 Robert Glasser (2020). The Climate Change Imperative to Transform Disaster Risk Management, Int J Disaster Risk Sci (2020) 11:152–154; Sneed, A. 2018. The next climate frontier: Predicting a complex domino effect. Scientific American. https://www.scientificamerican.com/article/the-next-climate-frontier-predicting-a-complex-domino-effect/; Prasad, et al.
9 See Harmeling (2009); UNISDR (2009a); United Nations Development Programme (2007a); IPCC (2007); WFP, IFRCRC & OCHA (2009); and Chibber and Laajaj (2008).
10 There is no significant change in the extent to which national strategies address gender concerns in disaster risk reduction. Sendai Framework has limited information on this.
11 See https://sendaimonitor.undrr.org/.
12 Sendai Framework https://www.undrr.org/implementing-sf.
13 Paris Agreement https://unfccc.int/process-and-meetings/the-paris-agreement/the-paris-agreement.
14 https://www.un.org/sustainabledevelopment/sustainable-development-goals/.
15 For the disaster management evaluation following country case studies were conducted: Colombia, Fiji, India, Indonesia, Madagascar, Maldives, Mexico, Mozambique and Myanmar; and for the Poverty reduction in the LDCs evaluation 15 case studies were conducted in Angola, Comoros, Ethiopia, Madagascar, Malawi, Mali, Senegal, Uganda, Djibouti, Sudan, Yemen, Cambodia, Lao PDR, Samoa, Haiti.

16 UNDP (2008a) Draft Strategic Plan, 2008-2011:Accelerating Global Progress on Human Development (extended to 2013); UNDP (2013), Changing with the World. UNDP Strategic Plan: 2014–17; UNDP,UNDP Strategic Plan 2014–2017', UNDP (2018). UNDP Strategic Plan, 2018-2021.
17 Adopted in 1979 by the United Nations General Assembly.
18 UNDP is bound by several international conventions, including the Beijing Declaration and Platform for Action (1995), Security Council Resolution 1325 on Women, Peace and Security, and the Hyogo Framework for Action (UNGA 2005).
19 UNDP, (2008b). "Gender Equality Strategy; UNDP, 2018." Gender Equality Strategy, 2018–2021; UNDP, 2014. "Gender Equality Strategy, 2018–2021."
20 In Honduras, for example, UNDP is the key agency working on disaster risk reduction. Recent efforts include support to the Ministry of Planning in developing a national strategy for mainstreaming disaster risk reduction. UNDP has focused on linking disaster risk reduction planning at the municipal, regional and national levels.
21 A sizable percentage of major droughts during 2014–2018 globally occurred in Africa, impacting 15 LDCs severely. At least 13 LDCs in Africa are facing two consecutive droughts that will affect the livelihoods of over 30 million people: Angola, Burundi, Djibouti, Eritrea, Ethiopia, Lesotho, Madagascar, Mozambique, Rwanda, Somalia, Sudan, Uganda and the United Republic of Tanzania. In Asia, Cambodia, Myanmar and Timor-Leste have been affected by drought. Some of these countries also face other weather-related challenges, including floods in Mali, Mozambique, South Sudan and Sudan.
22 For example, villages that participated in the programme had fewer casualties during the 2004 Indian Ocean tsunami.

References

Beck, T. et al. *Humanitarian Action: Improving Monitoring to Enhance Accountability and Learning*, London, Active Learning Network on Accountability and Performance in Humanitarian Action, 2003.

Benson, C. and E.J. Clay, *'Understanding the economic and financial impacts of natural disasters, disaster risk management', Series paper # 4*, World Bank, Washington, DC, 2004.

Bhatt, M., *'Gender and Disaster: Perspectives on women as victims of disasters', Discussion paper India*, Disaster Mitigation Institute, Ahmedabad, 2005.

Chibber, A. and R. Laajaj, 'Disasters, climate change and economic development in Sub-Saharan Africa: Lessons and directions', *Journal of African Economies*, 17 (2): 7–49, 2008.

Daniell, J.E., J.E. Daniell, A. Vervaeck, B. Khazai and F. Wenzel, *Worldwide CATDAT Damaging Earthquakes Database in conjunction with Earthquake-report.com – Presenting Past and Present Socio-Economic Earthquake Data*, WCEE, Lisboa, 2012.

Evaluation Office of UNDP (EO), *'Assessment of Development Results: Nicaragua'*, New York, 2007.

EO, '*Assessment of Development Results: Tajikistan*', New York, 2009. EO, UNDP, New York.

EO, '*Evaluation of UNDP Contribution to Environmental Management for Poverty Reduction: The Poverty-Environment Nexus*', New York, 2010a. EO, UNDP, New York.

EO, '*Evaluation of UNDP Contribution to Disaster Prevention and Recovery*', New York, 2010b. EO, UNDP, New York.

Harmeling, S., *Global Climate Risk Index 2009: Weather-Related Loss Events and Their Impact on Countries in 2007 and a Long-Term Comparison, Briefing paper*, German Watch, Berlin, 2009.

Houghton, R. et al., *ALNAP Review of Humanitarian Action in 2003: Field Level Learning*, London, Active Learning Network on Accountability and Performance in Humanitarian Action, 2004.

Inter-Agency Standing Committee, *The Inter-Agency Standing Committee Cluster Approach in Practice Countries and Implementation*, November, New York 2009.

International Federation of Red Cross and Red Crescent Societies, *'World disasters report 2009: Focus on early warning'*, Geneva, 2009.

Intergovernmental Panel on Climate Change (IPCC), Climate change 2007: *Synthesis report contribution of Working Groups I*, II and III to the Fourth Assessment Report of the Intergovernmental Panel on Climate Change, Geneva, 2008.

Neumayer, E. and T. Plümper, 'The gendered nature of natural disasters: The impact of catastrophic events on the gender gap in life expectancy, 1981–2002', *London School of Economics and Political Science and Department of Government*, University of Essex, and Max-Planck Institute of Economics, 2007.

Organization for Economic Co-operation and Development (OECD), *'DAC (Development Assistance Committee) Guiding Principles for Aid Effectiveness, Gender Equality and Women's Empowerment'*, Paris, December 2008.

Prasad, N. et al., *Climate Resilient Cities: A Primer on Reducing Vulnerabilities to Disasters*, Washington, DC, World Bank 2009.

Rodriguez, J., F. Vos, R. Below and D. Guha-Sapir, *'Annual disaster statistical review 2008: The numbers and trends'*, Centre for Research on the Epidemiology of Disasters, Brussels, 2009.

Sachs, J., *Investing in Development: A Practical Plan to Achieve the Millennium Development Goals in 2005*, New York, United Nations Millennium Project, 2005.

Solomon, S. et al., eds., *Climate Change 2007: The Physical Science Basis*. Cambridge, Cambridge University Press, 2007.

Telford, J. and J. Cosgrave, *Joint Evaluation of International Response to Indian Ocean Tsunami*, London, Tsunami Evaluation Coalition, 2006.

Telford, J. and J. Cosgrave, *'Responding to earthquakes 2008: Learning from earthquake relief and recovery operations'*, London, ALNAP and ProVention Consortium, 2008.

United Nations (UN), *The Millennium Development Goals Report 2010*, New York, 2010. UN, New York.

United Nations Development Programme (UNDP), *Reducing Disaster Risk: A Challenge for Development*, New York, 2004.

UNDP, Beyond Scarcity*: Power, Poverty and the Global Water Crisis*, Human Development Report, New York, 2006.

UNDP, Fighting Climate Change*: Human Solidarity in a Divided World*, Human Development Report 2007–2008, New York, 2007.

UNDP, *'The eight-point agenda: Practical, positive outcomes for girls and women in crisis'*, 2007b, available at http://www.undp.org/cpr/we_do/8_pa.shtml.

UNDP, *'Empowered and Equal: Gender Equality Strategy, 2008–2011'*, New York, 2008, available at http://www.undp.org/women/docs/Gender-Equality-Strategy-2008–2011.pdf, accessed January 24 2014.

UNDP Executive Board, *Role of UNDP in Crisis and Post-Conflict Situations, First regular session 2001, UN document DP/2001/4*, New York, UNDP, 2001.

UNDP *Executive Board, 'Multi-Year Funding Framework 2000–2003', Second regular session, UN document DP/1999/30*, New York, 1999.

UNDP Executive Board, *'Second Multi-Year Funding Framework'*, 2004–2007, UN document DP/2003/32, New York, 2003.

UNDP Executive Board, *'Strategic Plan 2008–2011: Accelerating Global Progress on Human Development'*, Second regular session, UN document DP/2007/43, New York, 2007.

UNDP, 2015. *Reducing Disaster Risk, A Challenge for Development*. https://www.undp.org/content/undp/en/home/librarypage/crisis-prevention-and-recovery/reducing-disaster-risk--a-challenge-for-development.html

United Nations International Strategy for Disaster Risk Reduction (UNISDR), 2009 *Global Assessment Report on Disaster Risk Reduction: Risk and Poverty in a Changing World*, Geneva, 2009a.

UNISDR, 'Applying Disaster Risk Reduction for Climate Change Adaptation: Country Practices and Lessons', Geneva, 2009.*Making Disaster Risk Reduction Gender-Sensitive: Policy and Practical Guidelines*, Geneva, 2009.

UNISDR/EM-DAT: *CRED International Disaster Database*, available at http://www.unisdr.org/disaster-statistics/occurren, accessed 4 September 2013.

UNGA, *Implementation of the International Strategy for Disaster Risk Reduction*, Report of the Secretary-General to the UN General Assembly, UN document A/63/351, United Nations, New York, 2008.

UNGA, *Implementation of the international strategy for disaster reduction*, Report of the Secretary-General, UN Document A/63/351, New York, 2012.

United States National Oceanic and Atmospheric Administration, *National Hurricane Center (NOAA/NHC)*, available at http://www.nhc.noaa.gov/aboutsshs.shtml, accessed 11 September 2013.

Wisner, B., B. Piers, T. Cannon and I. Davis, *At Risk: Natural Hazards, People's Vulnerability and Disasters*, London, Routledge, 2004.

World Food Programme (WFP), *International Federation of the Red Cross and Red Crescent Societies (IFRCRC) and the UN Office for the Coordination of Humanitarian Affairs (OCHA), 'Addressing the humanitarian challenges of climate change: Regional and national perspectives', preliminary findings from the IASC regional- and national-level consultations*, 2009.s

16

THE CONSULTATIVE GROUP ON INTERNATIONAL AGRICULTURAL RESEARCH APPROACH TO EVALUATION OF CLIMATE CHANGE, ENVIRONMENT, AND NATURAL RESOURCE MANAGEMENT

Roberto La Rovere

Introduction

The aims of the Consultative Group on International Agricultural Research (CGIAR) are to reduce global poverty and hunger, to improve human health and nutrition, and to enhance ecosystem resilience and the environment through international agricultural research and partnership. CGIAR claims that, had it not existed, world food production would be 4%–5% lower, developing countries would produce 7%–8% less food, world grain prices would be 18%–21% higher (adversely affecting poor consumers in particular), cultivated area in the developing countries would be 11–13 million hectares larger (having expanded into fragile forests that harbour a high biodiversity), and per capita food consumption in developing countries would be 5%–7% lower on the average. In a time of global food and ecological crises and of rapid economic, technology, and climate changes, the role of CGIAR is critical.

These crises impose particularly harsh consequences on the approximately 2.1 billion people who live on less than two US dollars a day – three fourths of whom live in rural areas and depend on agriculture. Although investments in agricultural research had seen a declining trend, the 2008 global food crisis brought agriculture back to the fore of the development agenda, which prompted a global revival of funding for agricultural research. Within this context, the role of impact assessment and evaluation to validate the efficiency of funding and the effectiveness of investment has also been growing. This trend has also been driven by the arrival on the global development stage of new and large donors and foundations demanding clear accountability for returns on their investments.

Agricultural research poses particular challenges for evaluation, distinct from evaluation of technical cooperation, investment, and emergency assistance. Research is often very specialized, so its evaluation also demands specialist skills. Impact assessment in CGIAR is either associated with impact evaluation or serves as an important input to overall evaluation. Furthermore, the impacts of interventions in agriculture and sustainable development cannot generally be assessed until many years after an intervention ends. The time horizon of impact assessment and evaluation in CGIAR means that it cannot usually be utilized for immediate decision-making on current or new programmes.

This chapter outlines the approach to the evaluation of climate change, environment, and natural resource management in the context of the CGIAR. Evaluating the impact of research activities poses specific challenges that differ from evaluating development programmes or normative work. Given the nature of the work of the CGIAR system, it is important to take a systematic and common approach to evaluation that covers the network's various dimensions – including its environmental, social, and economic dimensions. Over the last decade the relative importance, the urgency, and share of CGIAR investments in climate change research in relation to agriculture have also grown dramatically, together with the gearing up of the CGIAR Research Program (CRP) on Climate Change, Agriculture and Food Security (CCAFS) since 2011, and the evaluation of the CCAFS by the CGIAR-IEA (2016), which forms the basis of the discussion of climate change research and evaluation over the last decade, as well as in this chapter.

CGIAR and its role in climate change, environment, and natural resource management

The CGIAR, funded by developing and industrialized country governments, foundations, and international and regional organizations, is a global partnership that unites organizations engaged in research for sustainable development. Its complex and unique architecture of partnerships has no equivalent in other international development organizations. Fifteen international research centres carry out CGIAR work in close collaboration with hundreds of national and regional research partners and institutes, civil society organizations, academia, and the private sector. CGIAR objectives include improving food production (by accelerating sustainable increases in productivity and production of healthy food by and for the poor) and creating a better environment (by conserving, enhancing, and using natural resources and biodiversity to improve livelihoods of the poor in response to climate change and other factors).

CGIAR operates within the context of promoting institutional and policy changes that can stimulate agricultural growth and equity to benefit the world's rural poor. A recent restructuring of the CGIAR system added a new outcome, sustainable management of natural resources, to its three traditional system-level, Millennium Development Goal (MDG)–aligned outcomes (those of reducing rural poverty, increasing food security, and improving nutrition and health). The focus on environmental outcomes is now explicit and environmental impact assessments and evaluations of climate change impacts have become an important element of CGIAR's work.

Environmental, climate change, and natural resource management activities in CGIAR: development and sustainability

The CGIAR research focus has mainly been on natural resource management. Research on environmental aspects is a more recent but growing focus and research on climate change has progressively taken the central stage over the last two decades. Accordingly, impact assessment and evaluation studies on natural resource management, and the focus on climate change in the last decade, have thus far received more attention than environmental impact assessments.

Natural resource management[1] research aims to generate outputs that help maintain or improve the natural resource base for agriculture and to mitigate the often negative environmental side effects of agricultural production. In cases in which benefits from natural resource management research are framed in terms of maintained or improved agricultural productivity, farmers are considered the likely adopters of natural resource management technologies such as improved seed irrigation techniques, pest control, and improved management practices. Often, trade-offs exist between agricultural productivity and conserving natural resources that a society values. In such cases, the incentives for farmers to adopt or not adopt a technology are not always clear. Additional research outputs include influencing policy and creating new institutions to facilitate socially desirable outcomes.

Environment-related work in CGIAR covers different types of agricultural resource use and issues, including land, water, agrochemicals and pesticides, livestock production aspects related to the environment, biodiversity, climate change, forests and deforestation, and greenhouse gas emissions. Environmental impacts in CGIAR refer to public goods associated with ecosystem services that provide inputs into productive processes, such as consumption goods that confer well-being directly (e.g. enjoyment of environmental quality) or indirectly (e.g. drinking water of a given quality), or have non-use values associated with knowing that a particular environmental resource exists (Renkow 2010). Several impact assessments conducted by CGIAR have refrained of measuring environmental impacts due to complexities in assigning monetary values to non-market environmental services.

Natural resource management research impact pathways flow either via adoption of specific outputs by farmers or via institutional innovations and policy influence. In the first case, the outputs (new technologies for managing farm natural resources) are adopted by farmers, leading to either direct (to adopters) or indirect (to non-adopters, labourers, and consumers) impacts that can be either positive or negative and have an economic, social, or environmental nature. In the second case, institutional innovations or policy influence, the outputs consist of engaging with policy makers through dialogue, scientific presentations, briefings, and technical support in creating new institutions for managing natural resources. The resulting outcomes influence policy decision-making, policy changes, and the creation of new institutions contributing to improving natural resource management. Impacts tend to accrue to those ultimately affected by policy changes. CGIAR research on managing soil, fisheries, water, forests, and pests has shown substantial benefits and positive internal rates of return on investment. However, much of the impact reported is on a small scale (although there are some exceptions, such as reduced or no-tillage technology that conserves soil and water and reduces carbon emissions).

The environmental and natural resource management and development sides are closely interlinked within the context of farming systems. The environment-poverty nexus is very strong; people depend on the sustainability of the natural resources and are affected by environmental issues linked to how they manage the natural resource base in their own farming systems. The public goods deriving from CGIAR research are most often technologies and innovations or policy changes that have a direct impact on the farmers' livelihoods and income levels.

Various reviews[2] reveal that assessing the environmental impacts derived from the use of modern technologies has received limited attention from CGIAR centres. Some progress has been achieved, for example, on quantifying the impacts of research on genetic diversity, soil erosion, and pesticide use (though pesticide studies have focused primarily on human health impacts). More environmental impact assessments are being done at the CGIAR centres, but few results have been published.

The methodology for quantifying productivity impacts of research outputs or outcomes is much more advanced than the methodology for quantifying other types of research impacts (e.g. social, health, equity, and environmental impacts; Djurfeldt et al. 2009). Even the assessment of impacts of CGIAR research investments in natural resource management (where environmental aspects would be expected to be prominent) done by the CGIAR Science Council Secretariat (2006)[3] and Waibel and Zilberman (2007) includes little quantification of environmental benefits, and the principal focus of assessing these investments remains on agricultural productivity aspects.

As CGIAR is moving upstream from individual projects to clusters of projects (focusing, for example, on a watershed or an agro-ecological zone), this has bearing on evaluation, which must also move beyond project thinking and consider the context of national sustainable development.

CGIAR research in genetic improvements, natural resource management, and policy research has generated a large set of technology, management, and knowledge products (Renkow 2010). These produced a similarly broad set of economic, social, and environmental impacts. Over the past two decades, ex post assessment of these impacts has become increasingly institutionalized, following the growing demand for evidence that CGIAR research investments have generated benefits and good rates of return (Walker et al. 2008). Various guideline documents for conducting ex post impact assessments have been followed, both at the CGIAR system and individual research centre level, with a growing emphasis on environmental impacts (Maredia and Pingali 2001; Nelson and Maredia 2001; Shiferaw, Freeman and Swinton, 2005; La Rovere and Dixon 2007; Walker et al. 2008). These documents seek, whenever possible, to build on earlier economic impact assessments, resulting in more comprehensive and integrated types of assessments. In addition, the CGIAR Standing Panel on Impact Assessment serves as a repository of such resources, studies, and methodologies on impact assessment and evaluation (https://cas.cgiar.org/spia).

Notable examples of CGIAR studies on natural resource management and environmental impacts

Little has been done to trace the full chain of outputs, outcomes, and impacts of CGIAR research as it pertains to the natural environment. Impact assessment research in CGIAR initially focused on assessing the impacts of germplasm adoption and crop management research (1970s and 1980s), then shifted to rates of return and benefit distribution assessments (1980s), and research on spillovers and inter-sectoral impacts (1980s and 1990s). In the 1990s, the focus broadened to include significant environmental impact assessment studies (Pingali 2001).

The biggest environmental impact from CGIAR research appears to relate to changes in the total area under agricultural production as a result of widespread adoption of productivity-increasing technologies (see Box 16.1). In this regard, there are two competing types of impact. On the positive side, increases in agricultural productivity in areas used for agriculture may provide a disincentive to clear more land (via reduction in the price of outputs). On the negative side, if the technology raises productivity significantly but only dampens output prices a little, there may be incentives for further clearing of land for agriculture. Other environmental impacts relate to externalities to the agricultural production system, for example, whether adopting CGIAR technologies increases net carbon emissions, reduces biodiversity, or increases the rate at which pollutants are emitted from farming systems. Getting good data that can allow evaluating these impacts is difficult and the relative importance of these factors is uncertain. The use of economic valuation methods, such as contingent valuation or choice modelling, is noted as being able to help identify where such impacts are important (Bennett 2009).

BOX 16.1 ENVIRONMENTAL CONSIDERATIONS AROUND THE GREEN REVOLUTION

One of CGIAR's greatest – if not the greatest – success stories is the green revolution in South Asia, catalysed by personalities such as the 1970 Nobel Peace Prize Winner Dr. Norman Borlaug. From 1960 to 2000, international agricultural research centres, together with national research programmes, contributed to developing modern varieties for many crops. These varieties have contributed to large increases in crop production. Productivity gains were, however, uneven across crops and regions. Consumers generally benefitted from declines in food prices. Farmers benefitted only where cost reductions exceeded price reductions (Evenson and Gollin 2003). The green revolution helped to pull the South Asia region back from the edge of an abyss of famine, led to regional food surpluses within two decades, lifted millions of people out of poverty, made crucial contributions to economic growth, and saved large areas of forest, wetlands and other fragile lands from being converted to farmland. The research behind the

(Continued)

green revolution achieved the objectives of the time and yielded high rates of economic return. However, Hazell (2008) points out that new problems and challenges arose that required significant evolution of the research and development system and its research priorities. Poverty and malnutrition were not eliminated and, although poverty shares fell, the number of poor people remained high. The study by Evenson and Gollin (2003) neglected the environmental impacts and the environmental costs (e.g. of pesticide use) that have been largely identified in subsequent studies.

In fact, the green revolution introduced new environmental problems of its own, especially those related to poor management of irrigation water, fertilizers, and pesticides. Doubts have increasingly arisen regarding the sustainability of intensively farmed systems and regarding off-site externalities such as water pollution, siltation of waterways and loss of biodiversity have imposed wider social costs. In this evolving context, research and development priorities have changed from a narrow focus on productivity of food grains to a need to focus on natural resource management and sustainability issues. The results of this changing research agenda are mixed, but considerably more research has focused on South Asia's agriculturally related environmental problems.

In green revolution areas, the best yields and environmental impacts have been obtained from research on more efficient use of fertilizers, water, and integrated pest management practices. For example, the latter appeared to save on pesticide costs, reducing workers' exposure to harmful pesticides and protecting biodiversity. No-tillage and greater incorporation of organic matter into intensively farmed soils have also proven beneficial.

The evidence is less clear about the benefits of organic farming or systems of rice intensification. Research on these topics generated favourable results, but the potential benefits have been constrained by adoption levels that are far too small in relation to the scale of the environmental problems to be solved. Major reasons for poor adoption include the higher labour requirements of many improved management practices, the high levels of knowledge required by farmers, water and fertilizer subsidies in many South Asian countries, and the externality of some environmental issues. These are typical issues emanating from research that need complementary changes in policies and local institutions to be effective.

Following the green revolution model, several examples of research on watershed development and associated soil and water management issues have contributed to successful watershed development programmes in South Asia that integrated environmental impacts. These have been shown to increase agricultural productivity, reduce soil erosion, and improve groundwater levels. In the late 1990s, another CGIAR initiative explored the extent of land savings that were attributable to large productivity increases that followed widespread dissemination of improved varieties (Renkow 2010; Stevenson et al. 2010).

(*Continued*)

Had CGIAR crop genetic improvement work not taken place, an additional 20–25 million hectares of land in developing countries would have been needed at the beginning of the 21st century to produce the same amount of cereal output, with implications for larger carbon emissions, biodiversity loss, and water use. A 2010 review examined the impact on global land-use change of crop germplasm improvements in major mandate crops of CGIAR (e.g. rice, wheat, maize, and several others) between 1965 and 2004 (Stevenson et al. 2010). The study, conducted with the aid of a global multi-commodity, multi-regional computable general equilibrium model linked to a global spatially explicit database on land use, supports Borlaug's hypothesis that increases in cereal yields as a result of widespread adoption of green revolution technologies that have saved natural ecosystems from being converted to agriculture (although the results suggest that this effect is of a much smaller magnitude than hypothesized). The total agricultural area in 2004 would have been between 18 and 27 million hectares larger (of which 12–18 million hectares would have been in developing countries) if the world had not benefitted from crop germplasm improvements since 1965.

CGIAR approaches to evaluation and impact assessment

The CGIAR mandate initially focused on improving crop genetics, but has since expanded to include a range of subjects and activities extending the scope of research and impact assessment to natural resource management and environmental impacts (Djurfeldt et al. 2009) and climate change impacts increasingly more chiefly since the early 2000s. In methodological terms, this broadening of responsibility posed a number of challenges. Although issues in crop genetic improvement may be evaluated with techniques that seem to offer a high level of credibility (e.g. econometrics), social and policy-oriented research often require methods that are less prone to generalization and different from the standards of traditional science (e.g. qualitative approaches). Whereas the CGIAR centres have generally measured poverty by using income and consumption data, current impact evaluations include the concept of sustainable livelihoods. Such assessments seek a broader and more holistic understanding of poverty, taking into account a variety of factors that influence or impinge on people's capacity to address their vulnerability and poverty (e.g. access to land and water, social relationships, physical safety, and personal strategies to achieve context-specific and individual livelihood goals). Given the character of these questions, a combination of qualitative and quantitative methods is the most appropriate. This makes it possible to identify factors such as causal relationships, general trends, and adoption rates while also considering the multidimensional nature of poverty and the indirect consequences of agricultural research.

Problems arise in trying to scale up to larger geographical aggregation levels (particularly at the country level, which, for CGIAR, is not a level of intended impact). Although individual CGIAR centres may have an interest in impact assessment at a lower (farmer or intermediate) scale in order to evaluate specific research products or programmes, there is a clear imperative at the CGIAR system level to demonstrate large-scale impacts. However, the CGIAR level of impact and impact evaluation is either sub-national (e.g. community, watershed, regional) or supranational in multi-centre research programmes designed to address global or regional issues that could solve environment-related problems (e.g. water scarcity and climate change).

In addition to the issue of scale, the choice of appropriate research tools (qualitative and/or quantitative methods), addressing issues such as attribution, the existence of baseline data, the design of counterfactuals, and environmental valuation are considered as critical to adequately and meaningfully conduct an environmental impact assessment. Some of these issues are elaborated on in the following sections.

Qualitative and quantitative methods

The choice between qualitative and survey-based (quantitative) statistical approaches involves trade-offs; combining both is generally recommended. In the assessment of sustainable livelihoods, the combination of qualitative and quantitative methods needs to be comprehensive and carefully planned (La Rovere and Dixon 2007; Walker et al. 2008). Combining approaches makes it possible to estimate the indirect consequences of agricultural research and to establish a detailed and contextual assessment while simultaneously identifying the quantitative patterns of impact. Most recent guidelines recommend CGIAR use combined research impact tools.

Baseline data

A weakness in many studies is the absence of baseline data. This is evident in natural resource management cases, which often rely on the "best" available data and indirect indicators. One explanation for this is that impact assessments were not planned for when projects were designed and launched. To mitigate this, an obvious recommendation is proper planning for evaluation processes in the initial phase of a project. Recently, donors have provided substantial funding to CGIAR, which has enabled the establishment of extensive baseline databases that will permit rigorous tracking of projects or programme impacts over time.

Counterfactuals

In the absence of baseline data, impact assessment is methodologically challenging, not only due to poor benchmarks but also because baseline information is necessary to establish counterfactuals. The history of CGIAR ex post impact assessments at the project and programme levels is significant, but the use of proper before and after counterfactuals (as well as with and without counterfactuals) is less frequent due to the noted scarcity – until recently – of properly designed baselines and comparison groups.

Valuation methods

The majority of impact assessments and evaluations have neglected to incorporate non-market environmental impacts (impacts that do not translate into monetary costs) because estimating research impacts outside market effects is complex (Bennett 2009). With evaluations being established largely within the conceptual rigour of traditional cost–benefit analysis, the inclusion of non-marketed effects requires the estimation of benefits and costs in monetary terms. Hence, for evaluations to include non-market benefits and costs requires not only the already challenging processes of forecasting the impacts of research outputs on various goods and services (marketed and non-marketed) but also the estimation of society's values for all the forecast impacts.

CGIAR's evaluations mostly draw attention to the omission of environmental impacts in their scope. For example, Hazell (2008: XV in a study of agricultural research in South Asia concludes "there are few impact studies from South Asia that estimate a return to a research investment corrected for environmental benefits and costs". He also points to the use of indicators as a means of ranking research investments in terms of both their environmental and poverty impacts. There is also no real consensus as to which indicators should be used. Without a consensus, the use of indicators remains arbitrary and limited. Empirical studies are recommended to link research investments to environmental outcomes in order to assess past investments and design more effective research initiatives.

The 2011 Independent Science and Partnership Council book on CGIAR sheds light on the state-of-the-art methodological progress on valuation methods (choice modelling and contingent valuation) and ongoing work on measurement, modelling, and data collection for environmental impact assessment of agricultural research.

The rise of climate change investments and evaluation

Since 2011, the growing research efforts on climate change impacts on agriculture, until then scattered in individual research activities of the various CGIAR centres and of the Climate Change Challenge Program, converged through the establishment of the Research Program on CCAFS. CCAFS built on the earlier CGIAR Challenge Program on Climate Change to bring together earlier centre-based research efforts on climate-related agricultural matters. CCAFS addresses the challenges that global warming poses on food security and agricultural producers, production systems, policies, and institutions[4] (from the CGIAR-IEA, 2016). One key concept for implementing CCAFS activities, which received increasing attention over the past decade, is climate-smart agriculture (CSA, see Box 16.2).

BOX 16.2 CLIMATE-SMART AGRICULTURE

CSA is a conceptual approach developed to advocate for changes in how agriculture is practised and agricultural development is understood with respect to climate change impacts. CSA involves the optimization of the objectives of: sustainably increasing agricultural productivity to support equitable increases in farm incomes, and better food security; adapting and building resilience of agricultural and food security systems to climate change at multiple levels; and reducing greenhouse gas emissions from agriculture (including crops, livestock, and fisheries). The term CSA was coined by FAO for the 2010 Hague Conference on Food Security, Agriculture and Climate Change,[5] CCAFS being an early partner in developing the CSA. The approach asserts that addressing emerging climate risks while reducing greenhouse gas emissions requires new technologies, policies, institutions, and investment and that context-specific interventions are required. CSA responds to the challenges of climate change to optimize and balance the objectives of productivity, adaptation, and mitigation. CCAFS implements a large proportion of its work on CSA through "climate-smart villages" where CSA interventions are tested with partners, while seeking policy influence and direct engagement with governments.

Since CCAFS started, the CGIAR adopted a new Strategy and Results Framework (SRF) setting common goals for the CGIAR in terms of development impact, strategic objectives and results, and Intermediate Development Outcomes for the CRP portfolio and for individual CRPs. CRPs were instructed to articulate impact pathways and Theories of Change (ToC) and develop targets and achievement indicators. In 2015, CCAFS proposed a second phase for 2017–2022 that included CSA in order to meet the global cross-cutting needs of climate change with comparative advantage for the CGIAR, focusing on the adaptation and mitigation options in agriculture to contribute to resilience to climate shocks. The SRF commits the CGIAR to devote nearly two thirds of its research to such issues. With annual budgets around USD 60–70 million, CCAFS is one of the largest CRPs, with expenditures among the highest in the Research Theme on Adaptation, as well as relatively even among the other Research Themes.

Global context in climate change research and policy

At the 21st Paris Conference of the Parties (COP) in 2015, agreement was reached on Sustainable Development Goals, recognizing that UNFCCC remains paramount regarding climate change issues and setting high level ambitions for adaptation and mitigation. The agreement structures the activities on mitigation around the (voluntary) intended nationally determined contributions (INDCs) and recognizes the need for adaptation. While research on the role of agriculture in mitigating climate change initially concentrated on potential in developed countries, this changed in the past decade. The impacts of climate change on agriculture and food security, especially in developing countries, and the role of agriculture in increasing resilience, became increasingly recognized topics of research. In the Intergovernmental Panel on Climate Change (IPCC) reports, agriculture is treated as a cross-cutting issue related to food security and food production, human health, and adaptation options. With CCAFS, agriculture started being included as a mitigation option for developing countries in the Nationally Appropriate Mitigation Actions (NAMAs), and the CRP aimed at exploring synergies and trade-offs between mitigation and adaptation. These aspects have been gaining relevance and are now recognized as central for addressing climate change and contributing to achieving several Sustainable Development Goals.

Evaluation of climate change and CCAFS in the new setting of the CGIAR

The Independent Evaluation Arrangement (IEA) of the CGIAR evaluated in 2016 the CRP on CCAFS, to improve the CRP's performance and identify ways to maximize the contributions that CCAFS can make to future food security in the context of climate change, by informing decision-making and planning by the CRP management, CRP sponsors, partners, and other stakeholders on aspects of program performance and options for the future of the Program. Performance was evaluated to assess the quality of science by assessing a random sample of journal articles by CCAFS, and the Program's efficiency and organizational performance[6] at global Program, Flagship and Regional Program levels. The evaluation of the research contribution also included bibliometric analysis and H-index analysis of senior researchers, contributing to the CCAFS' comparative advantage and quality of science. CCAFS engages in generating international public goods (IPGs) as global knowledge producer, as a provider of products and services, and as a repository of institutional capacities for international research on climate change related to agriculture and food security. CCAFS outputs with clear applicability across national borders and high IPG potential include weather index-based insurance systems, climate information services (CIS), Web-x Evaluation of the CRP on CCAFS web-based Climate Portal, climate analogues and tools for measuring mitigation benefits in agriculture. With the growing effects of climate change on global development agendas, the CGIAR benefitted from CCAFS integrating research across CGIAR centres and strengthening its presence in policy dialogues. While operating at the global level, CCAFS grounded its research activities in national activities and institutions.

CGIAR-IEA (2016) evaluation examined CCAFS research since its launch, irrespective of funding sources. The evaluation covered investigative activities by CCAFS and partners. The evaluation considered research for development approaches, whereby CCAFS convenes and facilitates investigative action by partners and studies them. The evaluation used both summative and formative dimensions to the case study assessments. Since many projects originated in work started before the CCAFS Challenge Program, some work was assessed in summative ways, and current and proposed future work in formative ways. The governance and financial management of CCAFS was not covered in depth by the IEA as it had been examined by earlier reviews.

Other elements of CGIAR evaluation as well as of planning, monitoring, and learning work of the CGIAR have been subject to studies or assessments. Among these, CCAFS's Monitoring, Learning and Evaluation (ML&E) system[7] provides mechanisms to ensure the quantitative and qualitative monitoring, building on a set of modules in an online ML&E Support Pack. The ML&E strategy was implemented during the second phase of the CCAFS program until 2025 by using a results-based management (RBM) approach and supports an evaluation culture of reflective learning, experimentation, and adaptive management. Also, by integrating ML&E mechanism through CCAFS in projects, it supports outcomes that include changes in practices, skills, and behaviour of researchers, policy makers, extension services, farmers, and other user groups. In terms of planning and monitoring outcomes and learning, Schuetz et al. (2017) provide insights on the approach to theory of change, impact pathways, and results-based management monitoring, evaluation, and learning system. It describes how the CGIAR theory of change[8] can be used to achieve impacts that balance the need to generate knowledge in agricultural research with the priorities of users and beneficiaries of the CGIAR.

Conclusion

CGIAR has a long history of impact assessment and evaluation, which in the last two decades has increasingly covered aspects of natural resource management and, more recently and explicitly, environmental and climate change impacts. However, a scarcity of methods to assess environmental impacts persists. This, rather than capacity, limits the proper assessment of such impacts. The conventional approach of focusing on quantitative tools and on attribution of impacts has evolved, as the use of qualitative approaches and contribution analysis has gained ground. Yet pressure arising from multiple sources (donors and evaluation fora) towards the perceived higher rigour achievable through quantitative approaches and attribution is being reapplied on impact assessment, and evaluation practitioners. This demand is stimulated (or often enforced) by major donors insisting that a quantitative approach is the only credible one.

These influential donors are almost always located in the same places (i.e. countries, cities, intellectual circles) as the academic institutions where such tools are being promoted. It is difficult for evaluation practitioners operating in the field – close to the issues being evaluated but far from the main intellectual and funding hubs – to resist these demands and maintain the otherwise well-accepted practice of a wise, situation-driven choice of mixed methods.

CGIAR covers global-scale issues, although its research outputs and impacts tend to be location specific. It works at two levels of impact, specifically the sub-national and supranational (agro-ecology or watershed), but has recently expanded to operating in more integrated ways with donors and governments at the country level. This is done to facilitate dissemination and uptake of research outputs by a country's public and private sectors.

Scarcity of research resources has only recently been offset by the availability of funds driven by a sense of urgency for CGIAR's work to address food crises worldwide. As a result, ex ante impact assessment studies to inform resource allocation and justify investments have been gaining ground, together with the explicit identification of impact pathways on livelihoods. The CGIAR's impact assessments and evaluations have been typically ex post ones, focusing on impacts beyond the outcomes. This is in line with the nature of CGIAR's mandate on public goods, which refers to achieving both direct and indirect impacts of research outputs with a longer-term timeframe for influencing change in people's lives.

In the future, a more systematic common approach to impact assessment and evaluation that considers jointly the impacts across all dimensions – economic, social, and environmental – is suggested for CGIAR (Renkow 2010). Achieving this is constrained by the fact that, while the economic impacts are more readily measured in quantitative, monetary terms than social or environmental impacts, environmental impacts typically arise to a large degree from changes in flows of goods and services for which there is often no market and are thus less tangible.

The concentration of CGIAR's evaluation policy on principles and on best international evaluation practice is inspired by policies by a number of international organizations' governing bodies as well as by several international financing institutions. The availability of the UN Evaluation Group (UNEG) guidelines for development evaluation can become very useful to the CGIAR towards a more coherent, uniform evaluation practice, and hopefully can halt the proliferation of centre- or issue-specific guidelines. This more unified practice is expected to more systematically include the relevance, effectiveness, impact, and long-term sustainability criteria. For example, CGIAR criteria for deciding on the coverage and frequency of evaluations, including its usefulness for accountability, decision-making, learning, improvement, efficiency, and avoidance of duplication are well in line with those of the United Nations (UN). By heading in a harmonized direction, the evaluation practice in CGIAR can help focus on the main cross-cutting issues and on the big picture, especially at a time when CGIAR centres are converging into a larger consortium that resembles (in terms of modalities and aims) the UN system itself. This new consortium is aimed at coherence, alignment, and a collective strategic effort by the various research centres. This will also respond to the Paris Declaration and Accra Accords through the alignment of financing by international donors for international agricultural research.

The IEA had since 2012 central evaluation functions, with characteristics of independence, and separate lines of responsibility and responsiveness to all parties in the consortium. The IEA evaluation of climate change impacts of the CGIAR (as part of the CCAFS programme) is provided as an example of a comprehensive assessment of the CGIAR increasing research efforts, particularly over the last decade, on climate change matters.

Notes

1 See, for example, https://www.cgiar.org/research/publication/managing-natural-resources-sustainable-production-systems-research-agenda-crossroads/.
2 For example, see Renkow (2010).
3 This assessment reviewed the impacts of past investments in natural resource management research on land, water, and biodiversity resources management in CGIAR. It responded to concerns on the shortage of credible evidence that natural resource management research does contribute to realizing the CGIAR mission on poverty, food security, and the environment. The review covered a set of geographical regions (Asia, North Africa, sub-Saharan Africa, global) including macro- (related to policy and institutions) and micro-oriented (commodities and farm-level technology) research projects. Most research started 20–25 years ago, meaning that there was a good interval between research and evaluation. In the policy cases, it was only possible to identify – not quantify – impacts. Although the returns did not reach levels often achieved for much of the CGIAR's crop breeding research, returns of natural resource management research projects were calculated without estimating the positive spillover environmental benefits, which may outstrip the benefits deriving from crop germplasm improvement research.
4 CCAFS goal is to "promote a food secure world through provision of science-based efforts that support sustainable agriculture, enhance livelihoods, adapt to climate change, conserve natural resources and environmental services". It comprises four Flagship Projects: Climate-smart agricultural practices, climate information services and climate-informed safety nets, low-emissions agricultural development, policies and institutions for climate-resilient food systems.
5 http://www.fao.org/climate-smart-agriculture; https://ccafs.cgiar.org/climate-smart-agriculture-0#.XjVAb2hKjD4.
6 Including aspects relating to resource use; priority setting and planning; reviewing and reporting; learning; internal and external communication and relationships; and stakeholder involvement.
7 https://ccafs.cgiar.org/planning-monitoring-learning-and-evaluation#.XhzljFVKjIV.
8 The Theory of Change of CCAFS emphasizes strategic partnerships, capacity building, open access data, communication, real time monitoring and evaluation, and gender and social inclusion.

References

Bennett, J., 'Advancing ex-post impact assessment of environmental and social impacts of CGIAR', *Independent Science and Partnership Council*, Rome, CGIAR Standing Panel on Impact Assessment, 2009.

CGIAR, Standing Panel on Impact Assessment (SPIA), '*Natural Resources Management Research Impacts: Evidence from the CGIAR*': Rome, Science Council Secretariat, 2006.

CGIAR-IEA (2016), *Evaluation of the CGIAR Research Program on Climate Change, Agriculture and Food Security (CCAFS)*. Rome, Italy, Independent Evaluation Arrangement (IEA) of the CGIAR

Djurfeldt, G., T. Fagerström and A. Fredholm, '*Research Design in Assessing Social and Environmental Impact of Agricultural Research*', Standing Panel on Impact Assessment, Rome, 2009.

Evenson, R. and D. Gollin, 'Assessing the impact of the Green Revolution, 1960 to 2000', *Science* 300: 758, 2003.

Hazell, P.B.R., '*An Assessment of the Impact of Agricultural Research in South Asia Since the Green Revolution*', FAO, Rome, 2008.

Independent Science and Partnership Council, '*Measuring the Environmental Impacts of Agricultural Research: Theory and Applications to CGIAR Research*', CGIAR, Rome, 2011.

La Rovere, R. and J. Dixon, '*Operational Guidelines for Assessing Impact of Agricultural Research on Livelihoods: Good Practices from CIMMYT*', Working document, International Maize and Wheat Improvement Center (CIMMYT), Texcoco, Mexico, 2007.

Maredia, M. and P. Pingali, '*Environmental Impacts of Productivity-Enhancing Crop Research: A Critical Review*', Technical Advisory Committee (TAC), Standing Panel on Impact Assessment (SPIA), Rome, 2001.

Nelson, M. and M. Maredia, *Environmental Impacts of the CGIAR: An Assessment*, TAC SPIA, Rome, 2001.

Pingali, P., *Milestones in Impact Assessment Research in the CGIAR, 1970–1999: With An Annotated Bibliography of Impact Assessment Studies Conducted in the CGIAR, 1970–1999, by Matthew P. Feldmann*, TAC SPIA, Mexico, 2001.

Renkow, M., '*Assessing environmental impacts of CGIAR research: Toward an analytical framework*', Working paper, SPIA, Rome, 2010.

Schuetz T, Förch W, Thornton P, Vasileiou I. 2017. Pathway to impact: Supporting and evaluating enabling environments for research for development. In *Evaluating climate change action for sustainable development*. Uitto JI, Puri J, van den Berg RD (eds.). Chapter 4, pp. 53–79. Springer, Cham, Switzerland.

Shiferaw, B., H. Freeman and S. Swinton, eds., *Natural Resources Management in Agriculture: Methods for Assessing Economic and Environmental Impacts*, CABI Publishing, 2005.

Stevenson, J., D. Byerlee, N. Villoria, T. Kelley and M. Maredia, '*Agricultural Technology, Global Land Use and Deforestation: A Review*', CGIAR, Rome, 2011.

Waibel, H. and D. Zilberman, *International Research on Natural Resource Management: Advances in Impact Assessment, Studies from the CGIAR*, CAB International, Oxfordshire UK, 2007.

Walker, T. et al., '*Strategic guidance for ex-post impact assessment of agricultural research*', Report for the SPIA, CGIAR Science Council Secretariat, Rome, 2008.

INDEX

For Product Safety Concerns and Information please contact our EU
representative GPSR@taylorandfrancis.com
Taylor & Francis Verlag GmbH, Kaufingerstraße 24, 80331 München, Germany

www.ingramcontent.com/pod-product-compliance
Lightning Source LLC
LaVergne TN
LVHW021118300926
849160LV00010B/771
9780367557119